Rethinking Social Justice

Rethinking Social Justice

Edited by

S. Anandhi
Karthick Ram Manoharan
M. Vijayabaskar
A. Kalaiyarasan

With a Foreword by
Partha Chatterjee

Orient BlackSwan

RETHINKING SOCIAL JUSTICE

ORIENT BLACKSWAN PRIVATE LIMITED

Registered Office
3-6-752 Himayatnagar, Hyderabad 500 029, Telangana, India
e-mail: centraloffice@orientblackswan.com

Other Offices
Bengaluru, Bhopal, Chennai, Guwahati, Hyderabad,
Jaipur, Kolkata, Lucknow, Mumbai, New Delhi,
Noida, Patna, Visakhapatnam

First published by Orient Blackswan Private Limited 2020

ISBN 978-93-5287-907-6

Typeset in
Minion Pro 10.5/12.4
by Le Studio Graphique, Gurgaon 122 007

Printed in India at
Akash Press, Delhi

Published by
Orient Blackswan Private Limited
3-6-752, Himayatnagar, Hyderabad 500 029, Telangana, India
e-mail: info@orientblackswan.com

Contents

Part II

Critical Social History

Part III

Nation and the Region

Part IV

Political Economy

Abbreviations

AAY	Antyodaya Anna Yojana
ADB	Asian Development Bank
AIADMK	All-India Anna Dravida Munnetra Kazhagam
AICC	All-India Congress Committee
AIDSO	All-India Democratic Students' Organisation
ANR	A. Nageswara Rao
APL	Above poverty line
BJP	Bharatiya Janata Party
BPL	Below poverty line
CII	Confederation of Indian Industries
CMDA	Chennai Metropolitan Development Authority
COP	Certificate of proficiency
CPI	Communist Party of India
CPI(M)	Communist Party of India (Marxist)
CSSSC	Centre for Studies in Social Sciences, Calcutta
CTH	Critical tiger habitat
DCR	Development Control Rules
DMK	Dravida Munnetra Kazhagam
DVTS	Dravidar Vivasaya Thozilalar Sangam
EVR	E. V. Ramasamy
FLN	Front de Libération Nationale
FSI	Floor space index
IAS	Indian Administrative Services
ICDS	Integrated child development service
IDPAD	Indo-Dutch Programme on Alternatives in Development
IMF	International Monetary Fund

IMR	Infant mortality ratio
INTACH	Indian National Trust for Art and Cultural Heritage
ISO	International Standards Organisation
IT	Information technology
ITEL	IT Express Limited
ITES	IT-enabled services
ITI	Industrial Training Institute
JNU	Jawaharlal Nehru University
LPG	Liquefied petroleum gas
MGR	M. G. Ramachandran
MIDS	Madras Institute of Development Studies
MLA	Members of legislative assembly
MMR	Maternal mortality ratio
MoU	Memorandum of understanding
MP	Member of Parliament
NDA	National Democratic Alliance
NGA	Nilgiri Game Association
NGO	Non-governmental organisation
NIRD & PR	National Institute of Rural Development and Panchayati Raj
NREGA	National Rural Employment Guarantee Act
NSSO	National Sample Survey Organisation
NTCA	National Tiger Conservation Authority
NTR	N. T. Rama Rao
OBC	Other Backward Classes
OMR	Old Mahabalipuram Road
PAC	Public Affairs Centre
PDS	Public distribution system
PHC	Primary health centre
PSP	Praja Socialist Party
RCH	Reproductive and child health
RTR	Record of Tenancy Rights
SC	Scheduled Caste
SFI	Students' Federation of India
SOAS	School of Oriental and African Studies
ST	Scheduled Tribe

TNCSC	Tamil Nadu Civil Supplies Corporation
TNMSC	Tamil Nadu Medical Services Corporation
TNRDC	Tamil Nadu Road Development Corporation
TNSA	Tamil Nadu State Archives
TPDS	Targeted public distribution system
U5MR	Under-5 mortality ratio
WCAR	World Conference against Racism, Racial Discrimination, Xenophobia and Related Intolerance
WPA	Wildlife Protection Act
WPAA	Wildlife Protection Amendment Act
WWF	World Wide Fund for Nature

Tables and Figures

Tables

Figures

Foreword

A Relativist View of the Indian Nation

Partha Chatterjee

M. S. S. Pandian (1958–2014) thought about and wrote on several different themes located in different fields of specialisation—agrarian structure, caste, cinema, urban culture and, most persistently, the history of Tamil modernity. All of these interests are reflected in the articles contributed to this volume by his colleagues and admirers. These articles are testimony to the immensely productive provocation Pandian was capable of supplying in order to unsettle received orthodoxies and generate new arguments and debates.

It is in that spirit that I offer the following outline of an argument about the federal form of the Indian State and the underlying structure of popular consciousness about the Indian nation.[1] The argument, I believe, would have excited Pandian, prompting him to offer reactions of approval as well as disagreement, for it is a theme on which I know he thought about a great deal.

Federalism in India

Broadly speaking, there are two kinds of writing on Indian federalism. One is legal-constitutional, dealing with the federal distribution of powers going back to the Government of India Act 1935, Centre–state political relations, including the role of the governor and Article 365 of the Indian Constitution, inequalities between advanced and backward states, the impact of planning priorities on the economies of different states, financial allocations by the Finance Commissions, alleged discrimination in central policy towards the states, and similar topics.

The other genre of writing concerns the sociocultural foundations of federalism. This includes debates over whether India is a single nation or a federation of nationalities, and if single, then is there a distinct cultural identity of each federal unit? Language becomes a crucial question here, especially the democratic significance of the Congress decision in 1919 to organise its provincial committees according to linguistic regions and the linguistic reorganisation of states after 1956.

In what follows, I will argue that the above distinction corresponds to two different histories—the history of the nation State and the history of the people-nation. The two concepts are seemingly fused in the identity people = nation = state on which the modern State, based on popular sovereignty, is theoretically founded. But if we break up that synthetic idea into its two component parts, namely people = nation and nation = state, we will find that not only in India, but in many other countries of the world, the nation State and the people-nation have rather different histories that do not necessarily move in step with each other. The Indian case is, I think, particularly interesting.

The Nation State and the People-nation

The history of the nation State was a nationalist history discursively produced from the beginning of the twentieth century by tracing, through archaeological and textual evidence, the sequence of state formations in India from ancient times. The high points in this history are the large empires—the Maurya, the Gupta, the Sultanate, the Mughal, the Vijayanagara—all of them endorsing the historical possibility of state formations claiming extensive sovereign jurisdiction over much of the subcontinent. This nationalist history countered the colonial claim that the British were the first to bring about the political unity of India. At the same time, this history also accepted the existent reality of British Indian institutions of law, bureaucracy, army, education and economy as modern State institutions, which would have to be appropriately nationalised into the institutions of a united nation State. The production of this history accompanied the professionalisation of history writing in the twentieth century through learned societies, the universities, the Indian Historical Records Commission, the Indian History Congress, major publishing houses and academic journals. This history was, and continues to be, mainly produced in the English language and claims to be the authoritative version of historical truth.

The history of the people-nation, on the other hand, is a much more fragmented, disparate and contentious field of history writing, carried out in print from the late nineteenth century, mainly in the regional languages. These histories are about caste, sectarian and religious identities, local and regional histories of political conflict and domination, social reform, linguistic identity, etc. One may call this an old social history, quite different from academic social history, in which the achievements, tragedies and aspirations of particular groups or communities are narrated. Academic historians writing in English tended to dismiss these histories as insufficiently rigorous in their methods and unacceptably ideological in their motivations. The allegation was that there is no systematic attempt in these histories to separate historical facts from myths, legends, folk memory and fabulous imagination. But as politics acquired a more democratic mass base from the 1920s, this regional stream of history writing acquired new political significance. The regional languages became the principal medium of mass political communication. The political process by which something called 'the people' was mobilised as a political subject in different parts of India also energised the production of these vernacular histories. It is there, not in the academic histories of professional historians, that 'the people-nation' was imagined as a political community.

Synthesising these two histories of the nation State and the people-nation has remained a persistent, though not generally recognised, problem in independent India. There is an official nationalist history that valorises, as the self-identity of the nation State, the territorial boundaries as inherited from British, French and Portuguese India, minus those that were separated to form Pakistan, plus the princely states integrated into India. There is no necessary cultural logic attached to these boundaries; they are the results of the accidental history of colonial conquests and political negotiation.

On the side of the people-nation, there are two major approaches to the production of a long history of the Indian people. Both rely on a civilisational view, insisting that within the broad geographical mass of India, there has evolved over centuries, beginning from Harappan and Vedic times, a cultural formation that has an integral and unique character. The difference between the two approaches is that whereas one accepts the historicity of large-scale migrations into India from other places and argues that, by including within it the peoples and cultures of all who have come and settled on this land, India has produced a composite culture that enshrines unity in diversity, the other approach insists that the Harappan and Vedic peoples were one and the same—they were Hindus who were subjugated and oppressed by invading Muslims for seven centuries and who reasserted their nationality by winning independence from British rule. The difference between the two approaches was not visible in the late-nineteenth or early-twentieth century, but has become prominent after Independence and Partition of India. One reason for this is the difficulty of reconciling the territorial boundaries of the Indian State with the cultural history of the people. Both approaches face this difficulty and offer different solutions. The chief difficulty, I will argue later, is posed by the real political significance of mass cultural formations of linguistic communities in the different regions of India.

Language and Cultural Formations

The importance of language in the emergence of national consciousness has been explained most influentially by Benedict Anderson (2006). The combination of print technology and capitalism both requires and produces standardised vernaculars as modern print languages. Ernest Gellner (1983) has shown how, through the establishment of universal literacy and secondary education, modern industrial States destroy the earlier hierarchical structure of an elite high culture and many local folk cultures, and create a standard vernacular high culture accessible to all. This history of linguistic nationalism, typical of European countries, is complicated in the Indian case because of the two parallel histories I have described earlier. The history of the nation State has been maintained by the continued use of English as the language of law, the central bureaucracy, corporate business, science and technology, and higher education. The history of the people-nation is being written through the standardised print languages of the provinces which represent the principal medium of secondary education and local bureaucracy.

The Indian case is, therefore, a rather unique example of more than a dozen major linguistic cultural formations collectively imagining a unified nation State. How was this possible? Nationalist histories generally answer this question by denying that the linguistic formations are national at all. They insist that the long history of Indian civilisation produced a national consciousness; the vernaculars merely translated this unified national consciousness into regional versions. But that is not how the histories of the people-nation, as distinct from the history of the nation State, were produced. This becomes clear if we keep the intrinsic connection between the emergence of modern print languages and the formation of a popular consciousness of nationality in mind.

Looking at Indian history from that perspective, it becomes apparent that until the advent of British rule, while there prevailed in the courtly life of Islamic and non-Islamic India a multilingual high culture of the nobility and the literati, combining proficiency in Sanskrit or Persian with the vernaculars, there also developed large linguistic communities among ordinary people in which the regional language was cultivated, often through oral circulation rather than written manuscripts, in verse rather than prose, and strongly promoted by sectarian and devotional movements usually called by the names Bhakti and Sufi. Further, this was also the period that distinct regional caste structures took shape in. The civilisational view, based on Sanskrit Dharmasastra texts, had produced a singular idea of the Indian caste system based on the primacy of the *varna* order (the four-fold theoretical hierarchy of caste). European Orientalists contributed greatly to this idea of a unique and singular hierarchical social order of caste all over India. This idea, based on the overwhelming importance given to Sanskrit Dharmasastra texts, was influential even among Indian nationalist scholars such as P. V. Kane, G. S. Ghurye or Irawati Karve. But from the 1950s, when a discipline of Indian sociology was born based on village ethnography, it became clear that caste practices on the ground were regulated by regional *jati* structures (the actual endogamous caste groups), which often did not conform to the canonical varna order. Moreover, the boundaries of jatis and their hierarchical relation with other jatis were changeable according to regional political forces, as well as the impact of devotional and sectarian movements.

This is the situation when, with the rise of print technology in the nineteenth century, a different historical dynamic of linguistic nationalism was introduced. This phenomenon has been well studied by historians of India since the 1990s, largely inspired by the analytical framework introduced by Anderson. We now have several important studies of the print literatures in the different linguistic regions of India. Based on this research, it is possible to suggest what I will call a relativist rather than singular view of the Indian nation that could reconcile the divergence between the history of the nation State and that of the people-nation.

The Relativist View

My argument is not that there is no such thing as the Indian nation, but that the description of that entity varies according to the language formation in which one is positioned. The nation is imagined and contested in different ways in Tamil, Marathi, Urdu, Hindi or Bengali, and different genres of prose and verse literature, music, art and theatre participate in this project of imagination. But even when the entity may be called the Indian nation, it actually looks different from each regional perspective. My argument, therefore, is that we can only, and necessarily, get a relativist view of the Indian nation—relative to the linguistic region from which one is looking—since there is no available linguistic perspective from which we can obtain an invariant view of the object. Academic histories produced in English by professional historians only give us the history of the nation State. The history of the people-nation and its identity with the State can only be imagined in a vernacular print language: of these there are several in India and each produces a different description of the nation. Consequently, only a relativist view of the nation can reconcile the history of the State with that of the people.

By looking at the Indian nation from a relativist rather than singular point of view, we come upon many interesting, even startling, findings. In the rest of this essay, I will present, from secondary sources, some examples of the differences that result with changes in the linguistic perspective. I bring up the examples of Maharashtra, Tamil Nadu, Punjab, Bengal and Assam, but other examples can be easily added since the literature of most major print languages has now been studied.

Maharashtra

The memory of the Maratha empire as the proximate history of sovereignty that was lost looms large over the nationalist imagination in Maharashtra. By the late-nineteenth century, the dominant nationalist ideology merged the history of the people-nation with that of the state through a construct called Maharashtra Dharma. Based on local historical sources called the *bakhar*, this history claimed that the Marathas were the first nationalists of India who fought to protect Hindu identity against Muslim rule. Maharashtra Dharma as an ideology of righteous rule was different from the ideology of the Mughals because it was Hindu; it was also different from the Hindustani dharma of the Rajputs since the latter was based only on military ethics. According to V. S. Rajwade, Maharashtra Dharma = Hinduism in other parts of India + establishment of righteous rule + protection of cows and Brahmins + freedom, unity and leadership. But the formation of Maharashtra Dharma was internally divided. V. S. Chiplunkar and Rajwade clearly saw it as led and guided by Brahmins. Non-Brahmin intellectuals, while affirming Maharashtra Dharma, rejected Brahmin superiority.[2] Further, in Marathi literature and theatre, the nation was represented as male, with Shivaji as the iconic warrior-hero ruler (Naregal 2001; Deshpande 2007; Guha 2013; Wakankar 2008; Kosambi 2014). Contrast this with Bengal, for instance, where Bankimchandra Chattopadhyay's depiction in his novel *Anandamath* of the nation as the once resplendent but now violated mother became iconic in literature, theatre and art as Bharat Mata, even though Bankim had originally imagined the mother-nation as Bengal, not India. The feminine image of the nation as mother was widely adopted in northern India, and Hindi literature as well as popular posters and prints had a major role to play in that project of imagination (Ramaswamy 2010). In Maharashtra, on the other hand, the founding ideologue of Hindutva, V. D. Savarkar, described the nation as *pitrubhumi*, fatherland.

Tamil Nadu

The attempt to reconcile the history of the people with the history of state takes a very different path in Tamil Nadu. The centrality of language in the imagination of nationhood was sharply posed in the

Tamil region, where the Tamil language itself was deified in the iconic maternal image of *Tamil tai* (Mother Tamil), and the golden age of classical Tamil was identified as the Buddhist period from the fourth century BCE to the first century CE. Tamil thus acquired the status of a classical but living language that rivalled Sanskrit. When the first generation of Brahmin nationalists identified the Indian nation with Aryan Hinduism, they were challenged by the Non-Brahmin Movement in the mid-twentieth century. Maraimalai Adigal, for example, imagined a non-Brahmin Tamil nation that was a Saivite Vellalar idealisation. As a result of the Non-Brahmin Movement, the public register of the Tamil language in the theatre, cinema and political oratory was classicised by replacing Sanskrit with pure Tamil words (Ramaswamy 1997). This was the reverse of what happened with most north Indian languages, which produced a modern vocabulary for public use by adopting or coining neologisms out of Sanskrit words. Further, the historical imagination of the State was stoked in Tamil Nadu by memories of the glory of the Pallava, Chola and Pandyan kingdoms, rivals to the empires of the North.

The development of a national consciousness through the Tamil language is closely tied up with the ethnicised, even racialised, conflict between Dravidianism and Aryanism. The Dravidian movement, launched by the Justice Party which was anti-Congress and pro-British, did not deny the Indian nation, but insisted that there was no normative Indian who was unmarked by ethnicity, language and caste. Consequently, the Indian nation was unequally constituted among its constituent parts. In particular, E. V. Ramasamy (EVR) sustained this critique of mainstream Indian nationalism by pointing to a series of real and imagined overlaps between the Hindu religion, the Brahmin caste, the Sanskrit language, the Aryan race, the valorisation of unproductive status and the patriarchal subordination of women. This reached a critical point in the anti-Hindi agitation of 1937–40 against the language policy of C. Rajagopalachari's Congress ministry when EVR said: 'Tamil Nadu will be made a subject country of the Aryans' (Pandian 2007). The legacy of Dravidianism and the anti-Brahmin movement continues to this day, even though there is no separatist political demand any more. The imagination of the Indian nation in Tamil is thus quite distinctive.

Punjab

To take another example, this time from the north of the country, the official language of bureaucracy and education in Punjab in the colonial period was Urdu. As a result, the modern high-literary culture of the province was built through the medium of Urdu. But the regional and cultural identity signified by Urdu was much larger than Punjab. When the Arya Samaj tried to build a reformed Hindu identity in Punjab, it preferred to use Hindi as its chosen language since Hindi too occupied an equally large cultural space. Ironically, therefore, Punjabi, which was the ordinary spoken language of most Punjabis, did not acquire the full dimensions of a modern print vernacular before the partition of the province in 1947 (Malhotra 2002). Instead of the novel or romantic poetry or drama or newspaper editorials, Punjabi lived on in the older popular narrative forms of the *jhagrra* and *kissa*: the medieval ballads of *Heer Ranjha* and *Sohni Mahiwal* continued to be sung and performed in their unreconstructed shapes (Mir 2010). The imagination of the nation in Punjab, split between three languages—Urdu, Hindi and Punjabi—finally acquired three distinct forms tied to three religious groups—Muslims, Hindus and Sikhs. These divisions were resolved politically not merely by the bloody partition of Punjab between India and Pakistan, but also by the later separation of Haryana from Punjab.

Bengal

The new print literature in Bengal was put together in the nineteenth century by the upper-caste Hindu English-educated *bhadralok* (respectable people). Initially, there was an attempt to classicise the language by relying on Sanskrit and creating an artificial prose form called the Sadhu Bhasha. The political history of Bengal, marked by a series of Muslim-ruling dynasties, was not affirmed, except for the rare occasion during the Swadeshi period when the last ruler, Nawab Siraj-ud-Daulah, who was defeated by the East India Company's troops in the battle of Palashi in 1757, was depicted as a tragic hero. Instead, Hindu Bengali writers turned to the history of Rajasthan, circulated mainly through James Tod's annals, to imagine a valorous political past of the nation. Alongside, there was the attempt to find a popular base of Bengali regional culture in the literature of legends around folk deities (called the *mangalkavya*), ballads of romance and, most prominently, the Vaishnava and Shakta Bhakti literature, and folk musical forms (such as the songs of the *baul*s and *fakir*s). Hence, there was little historical depth to the imagination of the State in Bengal when compared to its cultural identity as a people.

The cultural identity of Bengal was strongly equated for the first time with its political identity by the Hindu elite at the time of the Swadeshi agitations against the partitioning of the province in 1905. This Hindu bias in the imagination of the nation was challenged by a Muslim literati, which asserted the glory of Islamic civilisation and Muslim rule in India as well as the contribution of Muslim poets and folk performers to the shared popular culture of Bengal. An attempt to create a distinct *musalmani bangla* did not succeed. It is important to note that the rise of a mass Muslim politics in Bengal in the twentieth century was caused primarily by agrarian conflicts and not by a cultural divide. That agrarian politics finally led Bengal's Muslim political leaders to identify with the demand for Pakistan. But Pakistan was imagined as a nation almost exclusively in northern India in the Urdu language. The problem was shown up soon after Pakistan was formed when the Bhasha Andolan erupted in East Bengal in 1951 against the imposition of Urdu. This started a process that ultimately led to the formation of Bangladesh 20 years later. The same standardised Bangla language now prevails in both West Bengal and Bangladesh with shared literary, musical and artistic traditions. Thus, the convergence between a history of the people with a history of the State remains fraught in both halves of Bengal.

Assam

There are two alternative classical traditions that have been invoked by intellectuals in Assam. One, associated mainly with the historian Kanaklal Barua, is the tradition of Kamarupa as recorded in the Mahabharata and the Puranas. The other, launched by Suryya Kumar Bhuiyan and based on the *buranji* collections, a Tai-Ahom tradition of chronicle writing that began in the thirteenth century, celebrates the distinct tradition of the kingdom of the Ahom rulers who came from Yunnan and Upper Burma. But the history of the people-nation in Assam is strongly marked by the struggle against the imposition of the Bengali language under British colonial rule and the contentious question of the migration from the early twentieth century of Bengali-speaking people into the agrarian regions of Assam (Baruah 2001; Saikia 2004; Purakayastha 2008). Amalendu Guha (1980) called the imagination of the nation in Assam 'little nationalism', as opposed to the 'great nationalism' of India. Recent politics has sought to exploit the divisive potential of the fact that most Bengali speakers in Assam are also Muslim.

Conclusion

Examples from other linguistic regions will strengthen the argument that the imagination of the nation, and contests over its depiction, vary from region to region. My conclusion is that every view of the Indian nation, even the normative academic view propagated in English, is perspectival. There is no Indian nation that stands on linguistically neutral ground: all views are relative to the linguistic location of the viewer. No view is more or less true than the others.

Therefore, the following propositions become compelling:

1. We cannot say that there is one standard or normative view of the Indian nation with regional variations, since that would establish a hierarchical relation between the normative and the regional. Guha's distinction between great and little nationalism has this implication of a hierarchical relation.
2. We cannot say that the Indian nation could be made more inclusive by adding more regional versions. That would not change the hierarchical relation between the normative view and the added elements.
3. We cannot say that the Indian nation must be seen as plural rather than singular, since the mere multiplicity of elements cannot adequately define the concept.
4. A relativist view provides a more adequate ontological account of the imagined object called the Indian nation as the political identity of the nation State with the people-nation grounded in the material field of linguistic practice.

If we are to adopt this approach to the analysis of federalism in India, we would have to say that the legal-constitutional structure of the State must be made congruent with the formation of the people-nation by recognising the autonomy as well as the equality of the regional cultural formations. The present federal form is premised on the dominance of the institutional structures of the State inherited from British colonial times. Although the linguistic principle was recognised in the territorial reorganisation after 1956 of the former provinces and princely states, it did not lead to a cultural redefinition of the Indian nation State. This is reflected in the superior authority enjoyed by the discourse of the nation State over that of the people-nation, as well as the centralising tendency within the federal structure itself. The relativist approach would require a negotiation of federal relations based on the prior recognition of the equal political legitimacy of each regional formation of the people-nation. That must be the ground from which legal-constitutional questions, such as the administrative and financial relations between the Centre and states, large and small states, developed and backward states, special status of particular states, etc., must be approached.

The Power of the Singular Normative View

While the relativist view provides a critique of the dominant idea of the Indian nation, one must also recognise the ideological power of that singular normative view. As mentioned before, there are two contending normative views of the nation struggling for hegemony at this time—the pluralist view and the Hindutva view—both of which insist that the nation is singular. The pluralist view prioritises the values of the modern liberal-constitutional State, is expressed principally in the English language and seems to be largely confined to an English-speaking urban elite located in corporate business houses, the central organs of the bureaucracy and the higher rungs of the urban professions. The Hindutva view feeds on histories that identify the people with the State in the nationalist imagination propagated through the print literatures of northern and western India. Socially, this view is influential within an alliance of Brahmin, Kshatriya and Baniya castes tied hierarchically to landowning peasant castes through sectarian and devotional communities. In its present phase, the Hindutva view identifies the State with a Hindu nation, superseding divisions of region, language and caste. Both the pluralist and the Hindutva views share the premise that the unity and stability of the existing nation State formation must be given priority over regional claims to autonomy and equality.

It is here that the unique position of Hindi comes to the fore as the language through which the history of the state is sought to be identified with the history of the people. In this respect, the place of Hindi is not equal to that of the other Indian languages. There is, of course, the official promotion of Hindi through various governmental agencies. But far more influential has been the role of Bollywood, television news and entertainment, and commercial advertising. There are indications that the influence of mediatised Hindi has penetrated and even subordinated the autonomy of regional linguistic formations such as Gujarati, Marathi, Bengali and Oriya. The impact of the Hindi media on the recent construction of an imagined people-nation needs to be carefully studied in order to understand the future of federalism and the Indian nation.

Since most of these issues are played out and settled in the field of electoral politics, political parties play the mediating role between the State and the people-nation. Both major national parties—the Bharatiya Janata Party (BJP) and the Congress—are currently highly centralised in their leadership and organisational structure. The ruling BJP is trying its best to align the federal electoral system to a more centralised format, by turning not only parliamentary but even state elections into a US-style federal presidential election, or by insisting that elections to Parliament and the state assemblies be held at the same time. Its strategy is to establish a permanent electoral majority at the Centre and in most of the states in order to facilitate the imposition of its hegemonic vision of the Indian State coinciding perfectly with a Hindu nation. The main obstacle to this strategy is the persistence of local demands, regional grievances, caste conflicts, sectarian claims and all of those other variegated elements that go into the making of the people-nation. They have produced, over the years, distinct party systems in several of the states. These contrary elements will continue to disrupt the hegemonic electoral strategy of the ruling party. The tangled relation between the nation State and the people-nation in India is unlikely to be settled soon.

Notes

[1] An earlier version of this argument was presented as the M. S. S. Pandian Memorial Lecture at the Conference on Dravidianism, Nationalism, Federalism, organised by Ashoka University and Ambedkar University, Delhi, and held at the India International Centre, New Delhi, in January 2018.

[2] References to Chiplunkar's and Rajwade's Marathi writings on the history of Maharashtra are provided in Deshpande (2007).

References

Anderson, Benedict. 2006. *Imagined Communities: Reflections on the Origin and Spread of Nationalism*. London: Verso Books.

Baruah, Sanjib. 2001. *India Against Itself: Assam and the Politics of Nationality*. New Delhi: Oxford University Press.

Deshpande, Prachi. 2007. *Creative Pasts: Historical Memory and Identity in Western India, 1700–1960*. New York: Columbia University Press.

Gellner, Ernest. 1983. *Nations and Nationalism*. Oxford: Blackwell.

Guha, Amalendu. 1980. 'Little Nationalism Turned Chauvinist: Assam's Anti-foreigner Upsurge, 1979–80'. *Economic and Political Weekly* 15(41–43), October: 1699–1720.

Guha, Sumit. 2013. *Beyond Caste: Identity and Power in South Asia, Past and Present*. Ranikhet: Permanent Black.

Kosambi, Meera. 2014. *Gender, Culture, and Performance: Marathi Theatre and Cinema before Independence*. New Delhi: Routledge.

Malhotra, Anshu. 2002. *Gender, Caste, and Religious Identities: Restructuring Class in Colonial Punjab*. New Delhi: Oxford University Press.

Mir, Farina. 2010. *The Social Space of Language: Vernacular Culture in British Colonial Punjab*. Berkeley: University of California Press.

Naregal, Veena. 2001. *Language, Politics, Elites and the Public Sphere: Western India under Colonialism*. New Delhi: Permanent Black.

Pandian, M. S. S. 2007. *Brahmin and Non-Brahmin: Genealogies of the Tamil Political Present*. New Delhi: Permanent Black.

Purakayastha, Sudeshna. 2008. 'Restructuring the Past in Early Twentieth-century Assam: Historiography and the Surya Kumar Bhuyan'. In *History in the Vernacular*, eds Raziuddin Aquil and Partha Chatterjee, 172–208. Ranikhet: Permanent Black.

Ramaswamy, Sumathi. 1997. *Passions of the Tongue: Language Devotion in Tamil India, 1891–1970*. Berkeley: University of California Press.

——— 2010. *The Goddess and the Nation: Mapping Mother India*. Durham, NC: Duke University Press.

Saikia, Yasmin. 2004. *Fragmented Memories: Struggling to be Tai-Ahom in India*. Durham, NC: Duke University Press.

Wakankar, Milind. 2008. 'System and History in Rajwade's "Grammar" for the Dnyaneswari (1909)'. In *History in the Vernacular*, eds Raziuddin Aquil and Partha Chatterjee, 209–49. Ranikhet: Permanent Black.

Publishers' Acknowledgements

For granting permission to reproduce copyrighted material in this volume, the publishers would like to thank the following organisations.

Gender History, for 'The Manifesto and the Modern Self: Reading the Autobiography of Muthulakshmi Reddy'. Originally published under the same title, in *Gender History* 4: 5–16, 2008.

MICA Communications Review, for 'Mastering the Traumatic: *Hey Ram* and its Cultural Narcissism'. Originally published as 'Encountering the Traumatic: *Hey Ram* and its Cultural Narcissism', in *MICA Review* 1(1): 52–73, 2003.

My Society, for 'Lohia's Immanent Critique of Caste and Religion'. Originally published as 'Lohia's Immanent Critique of Caste', in *My Society* 1–4(1–4): 18–32, 2009–10.

The Hindu, for permission to quote excerpts from articles published in the newspaper in Chapter 8.

Acknowledgements

We began discussions on bringing out a volume in honour of M. S. S. Pandian a few months after his untimely demise on 10 November 2014. The aim was to bring together scholars who had worked closely with Pandian as colleagues, co-authors or students to discuss a theme that was a key concern for Pandian—social justice. The essays presented in this book aim to reflect Pandian's critical and passionate engagement on the topic. We would like to thank the contributors for promptly responding to our call for papers and for their patience over the long period it took for this volume to materialise. Partha Chatterjee, a close friend and former colleague of Pandian, provided a befitting Foreword. We thank the Madras Institute of Development Studies and Centre for Studies in Social Sciences, Calcutta, and our colleagues in these institutions, for enabling an intellectual environment to work on this volume. We thank Sukruta Alluri for her assistance in copyediting the initial manuscript. We are much grateful to Nilanjana Majumdar from Orient BlackSwan for helping us throughout the process. We would also like to thank Banita Samantray for handling issues relating to rights and permissions, and Insiya Poonawala for her excellent copyediting of the final manuscript. We thank the anonymous reviewer for their encouraging feedback. The title of the book draws from Yogendra Yadav's lecture on 'Rethinking the Politics of Social Justice' at the M. S. S. Pandian Memorial Lecture, held in Chennai on 1 February 2016.

S. Anandhi
Karthick Ram Manoharan
M. Vijayabaskar
A. Kalaiyarasan

Introduction

The Legacy of a Dravidian Scholar

S. Anandhi, Karthick Ram Manoharan, M. Vijayabaskar and A. Kalaiyarasan

The question of justice has preoccupied philosophers since the dawn of civilisation. For millennia, thinkers, secular and theological, have pondered the intricacies of the concept. The relation of justice to society and the State still provokes considerable debate. John Rawls' massive 1971 work, focusing on the distributive aspects of justice, has greatly informed and augmented the liberal approach to justice. Complementing him, Sen (2009) and Sandel (2010) have expanded the field of inquiry and critique. The Nobel prize winning economist Stiglitz (2002) has also highlighted the importance of prioritising social justice in economic planning. Several other philosophers, political scientists, sociologists, postcolonialists, feminists and culture critics have been intensely questioning the ideas of justice, critiquing it and expanding it. The contributions of thinkers from the last century, like Antonio Gramsci, Frantz Fanon, M. K. Gandhi, B. R. Ambedkar, Paulo Freire and Martin Luther King, Jr, to these debates are well known.

The discourse of social justice has been a much contested terrain in India ever since the time of the Mandal Commission report. Nearly four decades on, debates on culture and identity have not abated; on the contrary, they have sharpened. With Hindu nationalism on the ascendancy, several academic critiques of the Hindu Right have been put forth. While the 'secular–communal' binary seems to dominate mainstream debate, the persisting problem of caste counters this very binary and calls for different perspectivisms towards Indian society and polity. Indeed, intersecting issues of caste, capital, nationalism, gender, region and visual representation must be taken into consideration to rethink the politics of social justice in India.

The work of M. S. S. Pandian (1958–2014) attempted to address these questions. Apart from three books on political economy, film studies and social and intellectual history—*The Political Economy of Agrarian Change: Nanchilnadu 1880–1939* (1990), *The Image Trap: M. G. Ramachandran in Film and Politics* (1992) and *Brahmin and non-Brahmin: Genealogies of the Tamil Political Present* (2007), respectively—Pandian has authored several academic articles and commentaries that addressed the persistent but ever-elusive quest for social justice by several actors in these intersecting spaces. The essays in this volume bring together scholars who have worked with Pandian over the years to build upon his works. Approaching the question of social justice qualitatively and quantitatively, this collection addresses crucial questions in contemporary Indian politics. While quite a few of the essays are focused on South India, they nevertheless open up a view of the panorama of Indian politics.

Pandian's interventions were closely grounded in the unique South Indian experience, particularly the rich legacies of Periyarist intervention that both engaged with and interrogated the caste and cultural elitism of Indian nationalism, as well as the elitism of local regional politics of identity and nationalism. Drawing from this rich experience of contesting the hegemonic aspirations of dominant nationalisms and dominant caste politics, as well as his deep sensitivity towards and engagements with 'minority' voices, oppressed nationalities and caste groupings, Pandian was especially open to the claims of many anti-elite, anti-caste and Dalit movements in South Asia as well as abroad. He was, for example, highly interested in and sympathetic to the struggles taking place in Kashmir and northeastern India, the Tamil Eelam struggle and even the African-American struggle in the United States. His *curriculum vitae* on the website of the Jawaharlal Nehru University (JNU) marks nationalism and Kashmir as his research interests, followed by caste movements, and Tamil cinema and popular culture. Indeed, many of his classes in JNU were dedicated to understanding the violence of nationalist groups towards the marginalised.

Pandian earned his first degree at the Scott Christian College, Nagercoil. Moving to Chennai to pursue a Masters in Economics from the Madras Christian College, he would later enrol for a PhD at Madras University, under the supervision of C. T. Kurien, a political economist. Pandian's first book, *The Political Economy of Agrarian Change*, was based on his PhD thesis. This was an intervention in the prevailing debates on 'mode of production' in the 1980s based on the experiences of the exploited peasantry themselves in Nanchilnadu, an area comprising two taluks, now in the Kanyakumari district of Tamil Nadu. The analysis situated the debate in the lived realities of peasants and Pandian saw the different ways of exploitation and resultant peasant responses. He also brought in fresh ideas, particularly on caste, gender and the environment, into the debate, taking it beyond agriculture and placing it in a critical reading of a wider agrarian social structure.

After a brief stint at the Centre for Studies in Social Sciences, Calcutta (CSSSC), Pandian went to the School of Oriental and African Studies (SOAS) as a Commonwealth postdoctoral fellow. In this period, his interest shifted from political economy to social history, theory and cultural studies. *The Image Trap* offered a novel *political* method of reading cinema. Pandian, who through his Gramscian engagements understood cinema as a medium that subverts the boundaries of 'high' culture and 'low' culture (Pandian 1996a), saw the MGR phenomenon—the political cult of the hugely popular cine-star M. G. Ramachandran—as an instance of 'how dominant ideologies succeed in this terrain of struggle and produce consent among the subaltern masses' (1992: 17). Published a few years after the demise of MGR when the Tamil Nadu government was paranoid about curbing dissent, it was a courageous intervention that exposed the fatal flaws in the carefully cultivated image of MGR.

During his tenure at the Madras Institute of Development Studies (MIDS) which lasted from 1989 to 2001, he contributed several high-caliber research articles to prestigious journals, most notably the *Economic and Political Weekly*. Some of them, like his 'Beyond Colonial Crumbs' (1995) and 'Towards National-popular' (1996b), gave radically new perspectives of looking at Dravidian history, historiography and politics. The culmination of over a decade of a research at MIDS, and short fellowships and teaching abroad, was Pandian's *magnum opus*, *Brahmin and Non-Brahmin*. This work interrogated the modern evolution of the two identities under colonialism, their interactions with the colonial power and with each other, and the negotiations and articulations they engaged in to enter the political sphere and alter it. Indeed, it would be no exaggeration to say that if the publication of the 'Non-Brahmin Manifesto' in 1916 permanently altered the political language of Tamil politics, the publication of *Brahmin and Non-Brahmin* changed the way academics looked at Dravidian politics. From the time Pandian entered JNU as Professor of Modern History to his untimely demise in 2014, he was recognised as the leading authority on Dravidian politics.

Despite being identified as a Dravidian scholar, Pandian never had a fixed constituency. While he was obviously critical of Brahmin hegemony, he was open in acknowledging the tensions in the non-Brahmin project, as the conclusion of his last book indicated. A sharp critic of the excesses of the All-India Anna Dravida Munnetra Kazhagam (AIADMK) both under MGR and J. Jayalalithaa, he was also not averse to criticising Tamil nationalists for their casteist and communalist leanings and also the Dravida Munnetra Kazhagam (DMK) for its failure to take a more proactive stance in condemning the genocide of Tamils in Sri Lanka. An opponent of the Hindu Right, he did not spare the Left for their facile understanding of caste. While supporting the emergence of Dalit politics, he also drew attention to the silencing of Arunthathiyar voices by mainstream Dalit parties in Tamil Nadu. Pandian's leanings, as *Brahmin and Non-Brahmin* indicates, were with the 'politics of the emergent'.

The essays in this volume address this concern, and also engage with other themes and topics that Pandian engaged with in his academic career. While most writings on the theme of social justice tend to be concerned primarily with the political economy of development or with identity without much reference to political economy, the set of essays put together in this volume speak to what Sum and Jessop (2013) refer to as a 'cultural political economy' approach. This transdisciplinary approach recognises the importance of semiotic and discursive practices in constituting material relations and production of hegemony. It, however, continues to emphasise the importance of political economy in structurating power relations. While the individual essays do not necessarily adhere to such an approach, this volume, by combining essays using traditional political economy approaches with ones that deploy discursive and semiotic analyses, allows for conceptualising the politics of social justice as being constituted along such multiple axes. Some essays also point out that the politics of recognition contributes to a politics of distribution. Finally, the volume emphasises the agency of marginal economic and social actors in reconfiguring relations of power without reducing agency to individual choice, but locating it in the terrain of micro-level contestations and sets of contingent political practices. In this, the editors look at this collection as not just a tribute to Pandian, but also a continuation of his work.

***

The book is divided in five broad thematic sections. 'Politics of Culture and Identity' addresses politico-cultural configurations of gender and caste identity. The section on 'Critical Social History' contains a criticism of phenomenological perspectives of caste, an epistemological critique of the ethnography of a tribal community in South India, and an essay on the governmentalisation of forests. Discussions of Tamil nationalism and a counterhegemonic criticism of Indian anti-colonialism occupy the section on 'Nation and the Region', while 'Political Economy' involves essays that address issues of urban geography, agrarian caste-based mobilisations, tenancy reforms and populist development regimes in South India. The final section, 'Cinema and Society', addresses the politics *of* and *in* the cinematic medium.

Part I begins with a critical interrogation of the intersections of caste, gender and modernity. S. Anandhi (Chapter 1) analyses the autobiography of a feminist from colonial Tamil Nadu. Through the work of S. Muthulakshmi Reddy—the first woman medical graduate from the Madras Presidency, the first woman to be elected as a member to the legislative council in British India, an activist and a leader of the women's movement, and an ardent Gandhian nationalist who tirelessly campaigned against the *devadasi* system and child marriage—Anandhi looks at how women's autobiographies, in contrast to those of men, offer a counter-public discourse by imagining an alternate modern selfhood that challenges the elision of masculinity and modernity by reconstituting women's subjectivity as political subject in the modern public sphere. She demonstrates how the gendered discourse of egalitarianism and social justice of the educated middle-class woman like Reddy legitimised the 'moral authority' of the elite woman as a capable rational thinking subject, by denying intersectional experiences of the lower-caste women a place in constituting modern subjectivity for women in colonial India.

Arun Kumar Patnaik (Chapter 2) makes a case for a rereading of Ram Manohar Lohia, a well-known Indian socialist, and his critique of caste. Arguing that the immanence of caste is more important than its external manifestation, Patnaik notes that Lohia's interrogation of caste was to explore how it was sustained for centuries despite resistance from those within and without. Lohia's significant departure from other anti-caste ideologues was his internal critique of caste and the legitimacy that it derived from within. The resolution, thus, lies not just in changing the material base of caste through State policies, but also demands an ideological critique by constructing what Lohia calls 'counter-cultural traditions'. Lohia called for intellectual formation among subalterns. For Lohia, caste is not just a hierarchy of domination, but also a power of legitimation. His critiques of internal strength and of the power of legitimation go together. They offer insights as to why caste has survived as a social system. Lohia's thesis aims to explore appropriate lessons for a socialist movement that must aim at the destruction of caste inequalities. While the manner in which Lohia approaches caste is unexplored by previous thinkers like Gandhi and Ambedkar, in several senses, his assessment of caste complements Ambedkar's theoretical work, *Annihilation of Caste*. Patnaik, through exploring Lohia's critique of caste, hints at the connections between Lohia and his predecessors.

Sundar Kaali (Chapter 3) brings a philosophical approach to social history when he challenges Sundar Sarukkai's phenomenological approach to understanding untouchability. Contesting Sarukkai's view of the human skin as a boundary that cannot be transcended, he argues that boundaries are both impermeable and permeable and, as such, are limits but not barriers. Taking the case of Dalit saints, and considering the phenomenon of untouchability in their lives in the Tamil Saiva and Vaishnava hagiographies, Kaali examines how the embodied self of the Dalit saints, who are boundary transgressors *par excellence*, is marked both by divinity and its denial by the Brahminical elite.

M. Arivalagan (Chapter 4) convincingly argues that if we have to rethink the basis of social justice, we need to critically interrogate the official constructions of caste and tribes, and also the processes of othering that accompanies such meaning-making. In this critical essay on the colonial and postcolonial ethnographies of Kani tribes, he deftly rereads the missionary, colonial and upper-caste ethnographers' accounts of the Kanis as an exercise in objectifying the community, which according to him fed the tribal development discourse and welfare politics of the postcolonial government. Further, he demonstrates how a combination of physical anthropology, environmental determinism and orientalist, evangelist civilisational anxieties performed the tasks of designating the Kanis as 'primitive', 'lazy', 'inefficient' and lacking in civility or modern knowledge, and further taming or 'civilising' them by incorporating them as wage labourers. This, in his view, denied the tribes the right to forest-based livelihood and a sense of entitlement to culture and identity. Importantly, such dominant knowledge practices, as Arivalagan observes, form the basis of postcolonial welfare programmes. From the vantage point of social justice, the author underscores the importance of social memory and oral histories in recovering the subjective experiences of Kani tribes that have hitherto been denied such histories.

Processes generating marginalisation cannot be confined entirely to the sphere of culture or identity politics, or development of capitalism, but they are also enmeshed in processes of State-making that produce a hierarchised segmentation of subjects. The Western Ghats in southern India have emerged as a major site for conservation governmentalities during the postcolonial period. Tracing the genealogy of conservation in the region since the colonial period, Ajit Menon (Chapter 5) points out that such processes, over time, have sought to governmentalise tribal communities in this region by constituting them as encroachers, labourers for generating timber forests and, more recently, as key actors in eco-development tourism projects. Rather than exclusions, marginalisations are, therefore, produced within conservation governmentalities by constituting and incorporating them as such subjects *vis-à-vis* other more powerful actors such as conservation non-governmental organisations (NGOs) and civil-society groups. Pointing out that conservation has historically been tied to resource management essential to State-making, Menon contends, however, that their 'situated politics' is critical to the failure of the project of governmentalising them as aforementioned subjects. State-making is, therefore, also shaped by such situated political practices.

Divisions and binaries emanating from power structures not only enforce these divisions, but also open up discourses of radical critique of such structures. One such terrain is the division of what constitutes the nation and what constitutes the region in Indian polity. The Dravidian movement explicitly challenged assumptions of existing narratives on nationalism and regionalism. The year 2017 was significant, as it marked the centenary of the Non-Brahmin Movement and also the golden jubilee of the Dravidian parties capturing power in Tamil Nadu. Yet, there are increasing questions levelled against the Dravidian ideology, its accomplishments and legacies. Critics have pointed out the allegedly binary cultural politics of Brahmin and non-Brahmin, which supposedly obfuscates other social inequalities and silences, in particular, the interests and voices of Dalits. More recently, there has also been criticism of the Non-Brahmin Movement's continued use of the label 'Dravidian', when in fact through most of its political history the movement had been principally aimed at and found resonance mostly among the Tamil-speaking population. It is in this context that V. Ravi Vaithees (Chapter 6) aims at a retrospective rereading of one of C. N. Annadurai's most important early works, *Arya Mayai*, first published in 1936. Annadurai (1909–68) was perhaps the most pivotal figure in the political ascendancy of Dravidianism as a political and ideological project in the post-Independence era. The author of countless works including novels, dramas and screenplays, he effectively used print and other popular media, especially drama and cinema, as a political tool. While Annadurai wrote on a variety of topics, it is in *Arya Mayai* that he first clearly sets out his social, historical and political vision and ideology. It is also the most scholarly and revealing of his works, and one that, as he acknowledges, was meant to be read as a political manifesto to inform and educate the emerging Dravidian nation. Vaithees provides a close and careful reading of this important work in an effort to both shed light on the nature and genealogy of Annadurai's political and ideological vision as well as correctly assess the Dravidian movement's ideas, particularly in light of the questions and criticisms levelled at it by some of its most recent critics.

The DMK, under the leadership of Annadurai, though willing to work within the constitutional limits of the Indian State, asserted the Tamil/Dravidian identity. Their ideological mentor Periyar E. V. Ramasamy offered a more radical critique of the Indian State and nationalism. Karthick Ram Manoharan (Chapter 7) argues that Periyar professed a political ethic beyond anti-colonialism, and by means of a dialogue between Periyar and anti-colonial theorist Frantz Fanon, brings out Periyar's criticisms of not just Indian anti-colonialism, but of Tamil nationalism as well. Periyar was not just content with dislodging the external oppressor, but keen on disempowering the internal oppressor as well. In this essay, Manoharan explores the pitfalls of anti-colonialism and Fanon's commitment to the same through a Periyarist lens.

Apart from essays on identity, social history and cultural politics, the volume also engages with interactions between collective action, State policies, spatialisations and shifts in political economy. Since the 1990s, Indian cities have been recast as vehicles to attract private investments, generating new symbolic and material economies through the promotion of new infrastructures of production and consumption. A. Srivathsan and Pandian (Chapter 8), in an essay that was in the making prior to the sudden demise of the latter, draw upon distinctions that Timothy Mitchell makes between spaces of 'exhibition' and the 'museum', to spatialise the distinctions between political and civil society in the context of Chennai. They draw attention to the symbolic and the dark side of the violence of the new phase of urban development that seeks to invisibilise the lives and inhabitants of museum spaces such as fishers, cattle herders, rag pickers, slum-dwellers and street hawkers. In the new urban imaginary that is informed by the idea of becoming a 'global' city, such spaces belong to the city's past that cannot be part of its future. The city's future lies in an expansion of the new spaces of 'exhibition' such as world-class infrastructures of living and working for the emerging class of information technology (IT) and elite service professionals. While previous policy imaginations allowed for recognition of the two economies and even flows between them, the recent shifts in State priorities are premised on an erasure and/or inferiorisation of such older spaces, and a clear rupture between the two. They, however, point out that museum spaces do not belong to the past as imagined in the new urban imagination, but constitute backyards that sustain the modern city. In fact, such spaces are home to a set of vibrant and innovative practices that may offer insights for an alternate and spatially just urban future. As a way out of this spatial violence, Srivathsan and Pandian call for a policymaking that privileges the voices of the members of the political society as opposed to those of the members of civil society. In their view, the voices of the latter that seemingly represent the interests of the city on the whole actually undergird their power to homogenise the multiple spaces and voices.

Tamil Nadu is one of the few states that is seen to have combined relatively robust economic growth with considerable achievements in poverty-reduction, healthcare and education. M. Vijayabaskar (Chapter 9) engages with the question of how a vision of social justice rooted in a modernist logic of moving out of traditional caste-based occupations plays out in the context of a bleak urban economy that is increasingly found inadequate to absorb the emerging educated youth from rural Tamil Nadu. Amidst a growing worldwide realisation that such transformations are not easily possible, he uses insights from mobility studies to map the nature and scope of emerging labour mobilities in the state as a result of both economic growth and the range of social welfare measures undertaken by the state. He points to the emergence of translocal livelihoods rooted in a combination of agrarian and non-agrarian work, straddling the urban and the rural that is precarious and highly gendered. The essay importantly asks what such in-between locations and spatial mobilities, without being backed by economic mobility and security, imply for political mobilisation in the state.

A. Kalaiyarasan (Chapter 10) engages with policy processes that led to the development of social sectors in the state of Tamil Nadu by focusing on two domains where the state has witnessed exceptional attainments—the public distribution system (PDS) and the health sector. He argues that despite the prevalence of corruption in the state, political commitment has ensured arguably the most effective PDS in the country. Attributing it to populist measures in response to collective action, he maps the series of policy innovations that plugged leakages and expanded the reach of the PDS during a period when there was a call to roll back such universal welfare programmes at the all-India level. In the domain of health, he contends that the emphasis on public health and on primary care ensured better outcomes despite health expenditure not being particularly high compared to other states or the all-India average. Importantly, he points that such overall outcomes have been accompanied by a high degree of social inclusion, with Schedule Caste (ST) households too experiencing significant improved health status.

A key criticism of the Dravidian movement made by scholars of political economy is that the movement did not adequately engage with material aspects of social justice, land reforms in particular. In Chapter 11, J. Jeyaranjan counters this contention by empirically establishing that despite the inadequacy of explicit state-led land reforms, lands have indeed been transferred from the upper castes to the intermediate classes and, to a lesser extent, to the Dalits. Based on a detailed micro-level study of land transactions over a 30-year period in a village in the Cauvery delta, he argues that it has been made possible through two routes. One, the Dravidian movement had been working among and mobilising tenant farmers and agricultural labourers for a long period of time against the upper-caste landlords in the region. While this paved way for collective action among the lower castes, it was also supplemented by state power. The capture of state power by the DMK was seen by landed families as a threat to their ability to retain control over large tracts of lands. As a result, many of them sought to transfer their lands to the tenant farmers through sale. He argues that *de facto* land relations have transformed much more in favour of lower-caste tenants than what has been said in existing literature.

Since the beginning of 2018, much hype has been generated over the announcements that Rajinikanth and Kamal Haasan, two of the leading celebrities of the Tamil film industry, will be entering politics and contesting elections. Indeed, much has been written on the role that cinema plays in influencing the politics of South India. Venkatesh Chakravarthy (Chapter 12) undertakes a Lacanian reading of the controversial 2000 film *Hey Ram* starring Haasan. Chakravarthy discusses the politics of cultural narcissism in the film, which produces the Hindu Self and the Muslim Other, and feeds into Hindu nationalist imagery, despite its attempts to pass off as a defence of Gandhian secularism.

The historic era of sovereign stars spanning five decades and three south Indian states has just gone into terminal decline. The stars are still there but the people who crown them kings are no longer flocking to the coronation. Enjoying the privileges of fandom and imposing upon their heroes moral and political obligations, these bands of followers used to dominate the theatres on release day. In Chapter 13, M. Madhava Prasad expands upon this observation to argue that what we have witnessed here is nothing short of a restaging of the historic transition from the supremacy of political power to the reign of the economy. Discussing the late careers of the last generation of stars with cine-political potential, including Rajinikanth and Chiranjeevi, Prasad captures the drama of the erosion of political privilege by a rampaging economy. For the demobilised fans, the protective shadow of the sovereign lost forever, the only option left is a fetishistic veneration shorn of the old sense of privilege.

The essays in this volume are not direct deliberations on the philosophy and theories of social justice. What this volume aims at instead is to bring perspectives from across disciplines to rethink the question of social justice in a heterodox manner. Throughout his intellectual career, Pandian attempted to not only critically look at politics and society, but also to bring what passes off in the mainstream as 'critical' to a critical examination. We believe that these essays are not just contributions in the honour of Pandian, but are in conversations with his work even as they continue to foreground his critical perspectives on social justice.

References

Chetty, P. Theagaraya. 2010. 'The Non-Brahmin Manifesto'. In *The Justice Movement 1917*, ed. Varadarajulu Naidu, 1–10. Chennai: Dravidar Kazhagam.

Pandian, M. S. S. 1990. *The Political Economy of Agrarian Change: Nanchilnadu, 1880–1939*. New Delhi: Sage.

——— 1992. *The Image Trap: M. G. Ramachandran in Film and Politics*. New Delhi: Sage.

——— 1995. 'Beyond Colonial Crumbs: Cambridge School, Identity Politics and Dravidian Movement(s)'. *Economic and Political Weekly* 30(7–8), 18–25 February: 385–91.

——— 1996a. 'Tamil Cultural Elites and Cinema: Outlines of an Argument'. *Economic and Political Weekly* 31(15), 13 April: 950–55.

——— 1996b. 'Towards National-Popular: Notes on Self-respecters' Tamil'. *Economic and Political Weekly* 31(51), 21 December: 3323–29.

——— 2007. *Brahmin and Non-Brahmin: Genealogies of the Tamil Political Present*. Ranikhet: Permanent Black.

Rawls, J. 1971. *A Theory of Justice*. Cambridge, Massachusetts: Harvard University Press.

Sandel, M. 2010. *Justice: What's the Right Thing to Do?* London: Penguin.

Sen, A. 2009. *The Idea of Justice*. London: Allen Lane.

Stiglitz, J. 2002. *Globalization and its Discontents*. New Delhi: Penguin.

Sum, L. N., and B. Jessop. 2013. *Towards a Cultural Political Economy: Putting Culture in its Place in Political Economy*. Cheltenham: Edward Elgar.

Part I

Politics of Culture and Identity

1. The Manifesto and the Modern Self

*Reading the Autobiography of Muthulakshmi Reddy**

S. Anandhi

Precisely because it calls into question the subject of a putatively universal, revolutionary "we", the manifesto form is helpful in tracking the vexed efforts of feminist women to enter, occupy and reconstruct the public spheres of modernity by means of manifestoes and related polemical tracts. The use of the manifesto form by women challenges the assumptions about an ideal universal subject.

—Janet Lyon, 1999

Purposeful, bold, contentious, the autobiographical manifesto contests the old inscriptions, the old histories, the old politics, the ancient regime, by working to dislodge the hold of the universal subject through an expressly political collocation of a new "I".

—Sidonie Smith, 1993

Life writing or writing autobiographies by Indian men has been and continues to be an act of fashioning for oneself a modern selfhood. Despite such an openly avowed desire to court the modern,

---

*This chapter is part of my book project on the political biography of Muthulakshmi Reddy. I am grateful to the Graduate School of Development Studies (GSID), Nagoya University, Japan, for the visiting fellowship (August–November 2006) that enabled me to pursue the project. In particular, I would like to acknowledge the help of Professor Atsuko Ohashi and Professor Nakanishi at GSID, Nagoya University, and Padmini Swaminathan, M. S. S. Pandian and the anonymous reviewer for their critical comments on the draft of the chapter. Thanks also to *Gender History* 4: 5–16, 2008, for permission to reproduce this chapter. Usual disclaimers apply.

Indian autobiographies differ distinctly from the Western ones. As Chakrabarty (2000: 95) has argued, if the interiorised 'private self ... pours out incessantly' in Western autobiographies, Indian autobiographies authored by men foreground their 'public' self—as if they narrate a world of 'public without private'. Similarly, Kaviraj (2004) notes that Indian autobiographies are informed by 'a reticence about the private'.

Such singular emphasis placed on the 'public self' by Indian men in their autobiographies needs to be understood as a strategy of defining centres, margins and boundaries of the public and the political, through 'the differential deployments of gendered subjectivity' in the specific context of modernity (Watson and Smith 1992: *xvi*). In presenting a public self as oriented towards enlightened rationality transcending the contingencies of 'desire, affectivity and the body', these autobiographies represent its 'other' as embodied, non-modern and belonging to the affective domain of the private or domestic.[1] In other words, as Felski (1995: 16) has argued, what one finds here is a conflation of the modern with the masculine and an 'equation of modernity with particular public and institutional structures governed by men at the cost of total elision of the lives, concerns and perspectives of women'.

In contrast to men's autobiographies, those by women offer a counter-public discourse by narrating women's experience of modernity as different and by publicly staging such experience to reconstitute women's subjectivities in 'radically new ways' (Sarkar 1993). We have a vast body of literature today by feminist scholars which shows that by imagining an alternative modern selfhood, women's autobiographies differ from the conventional autobiographical form employed by men and challenge the elision of masculinity and modernity.[2]

One such autobiographical form that effectively negotiates a place for the 'modern woman' as a political subject in the modern public sphere is what Smith (1993) has called the 'autobiographical manifesto'. Writing about manifesto as a modern enunciative form of address, Janet Lyon, for instance, argues that it 'narrates in no uncertain terms the incongruous experiences of modernity of those whose needs have been ignored or excluded in a putatively democratic political culture'.[3] According to her, '... the manifesto is the form that exposes the broken promises of modernity ... [they] chronicle the exclusions and deferrals experienced by those outside the "legitimate" bourgeois spheres of public exchange' (Lyon 1999: 2, 3). Similarly, the autobiographical manifestoes of women invoke 'identification around various experiences of oppression and exclusions from the central or centrifugal bourgeois public sphere and its ideology of universal subject' and imagine future possibilities of emancipatory politics. Further, through narrations of the experiences of the self, autobiographical manifestoes of women, as Smith (1993: 159) argues, not only give a call for new political collectivity but also bring about a 'standpoint epistemology' of the experiences of modernity by the hitherto marginalised.

Against this background, this chapter attempts to excavate the possibilities and constraints of the autobiographical manifesto as a self-writing form, by analysing the autobiographical writings of Muthulakshmi Reddy, a middle-class feminist from colonial Tamil Nadu. On a different register, it also engages with the inherent limits of modernity to radical politics.

II

Born to a Brahmin father and a *devadasi* (hereditary temple dancer) mother,[4] Reddy, the first woman medical graduate from Madras Presidency (1912), was the first woman to be nominated as a member of the legislative council in British India (1926–30). She became the first woman ever to become the deputy president of a legislative council world over. As a legislator, she effectively campaigned for and brought in legislations to abolish the devadasi system and child marriage. She also took up a range of welfare issues that favoured women. This included medical inspection in girls' schools, exemption of poor girls from the payment of school fees, maternity and child welfare, and medical aid to women. As a political activist, she lobbied for reservation of seats for women in various governance structures such as municipalities, district and local boards, and the police force. Protesting against the arrest of Gandhi in 1930, Reddy resigned from the Madras legislature but continued her political and public activities within the women's movement and also in the national movement.

Reddy began her political career by joining the women's movement in 1917 and, over time, held various important positions in the Women's India Association and the All India Women's Conference. She became the president of the Women's India Association in 1931 and that of the All India Women's Conference in 1933. She also edited the well-known multilingual women's quarterly *Stridharma*,[5] which promoted Indian nationalism as well as international feminism. Towards her commitment to build solidarity of women internationally, she travelled to Paris in 1926 to participate in the International Congress of Women, and to Chicago in 1929 to deliver lectures on the women's movement and political citizenship. Despite being a committed nationalist, her influence cut across party lines. For instance, in 1937, when the nationalist Congress Party decided to contest election for the legislative councils, she was invited both by the Congress and the Justice Party (which represented the interests of the non-Brahmins and treated the Congress as a party of Brahmins) to contest the election from their platform. However, given her political loyalty to Gandhi, she chose to contest as a Congress candidate only to find that local Congress leaders such as C. Rajagopalachari and S. Satyamurthi denied her a party ticket to contest the election. In 1937, she became the first alderwoman of the Madras Corporation, a position that she resigned from in 1939 due to health reasons. Later, in 1952, she accepted Congress Party's offer of a membership in the Madras legislative council on the condition that the Congress in power would offer her a plot of land for a cancer hospital.

Reddy published her first 246-page autobiographical account, *My Experience as a Legislator*, in 1930. It is a systematic documentation of her speeches and interventions made in the Madras legislative council from December 1926 until her resignation from the council in 1930. It also provides accounts of her experiences and struggles of being the only woman legislator in a council full of men. She published her second autobiographical account, *Autobiography*, in 1964. It also gives us a detailed account of her public activities such as her membership in the British-run Social Service League, her honorary service as medical officer to the Widows' Home run by Sister Subbalakshmi Ammal, her work as the Joint Secretary of the Children's Aid Society, her association with various local women's organisations such as the Sarada Home and Women's Home of Service (Madras Seva Sadan), and her role in founding institutions such as Muslim Ladies Association and the Avvai Home. Interestingly, *Autobiography* is presented as a detailed documentation of her public activities with a series of appendages of public events and personal accolades.[6] Unlike her first autobiographical account, her second one gives details of her early childhood and 'domestic life'.

As she lays out in *My Experience*, her act of self-writing was informed by a definite purpose. She writes,

> In presenting this book to the public, I have two objects [sic] in view. The first one is to show to such of my sisters and others who still hold the view that women are created only for the home and men for the state, how women's activity could be profitably extended from the home to the city and how in the administration of the state as in the management of a household, women could co-operate with their men in promoting the well-being of that large family, the nation. (Reddy 1930: *xi*)

First and foremost, this statement of Reddy's seeks its audience in the community of women and identifies with them in the spirit of wider sisterhood. This is precisely what gives her autobiography the quality of a manifesto. It has a specific addressee and a message.[7] Second, though Chakrabarty (2000) argues that most women's autobiographies are about extended families, in Reddy's statement, extended family becomes a politically enabling metaphor. This is a metaphor which unsettles the division between the private and public, and treats the public domain as an extension of the domestic. In other words, the public is recovered here no longer as the domain of men but of women as well by defining citizenship rights and political subjecthood for women. Finally, the metaphor of nation as a large family opens up the space for affective qualities such as caring and nurturance, instead of the so-called enlightened rationality, as modes of conducting politics.

Within such a framework which foregrounds her role in the colonial public domain, she offers events from her life as an instance of how women could and need to become political subjects. Her appeal to women to take part in the public sphere is based on her understanding that the specific problems and concerns of women would otherwise not be articulated. For instance, while narrating her experience of participating in the International Conference of Women's Suffrage Alliance in Paris in 1926, Reddy insists on the need to recognise that 'women have grievances of some kind or other and suffer persecution, injustice and inequality of treatment', and that women's interests are different from those of men, whose selfishness and claim to superiority 'has inflicted many hardships on women' (Reddy 1964: 42). Men being the source of women's problems, in her view, women's participation in public life alone could serve their interests. As she wrote, 'To see women from 42 countries both near and distant come to Paris to take part in the deliberations of the Congress, not for themselves, not even for the sake of their country, *but for those of their sex* [emphasis mine], whether West or East was an inspiration indeed' (ibid.: 41).

Claiming women's interest as different from that of men, Reddy also argued that women's modes of political response need to be different and autonomous of male response to political events. Yet again this is an invitation for women to occupy the modern public sphere. Her autobiographical accounts are replete with instances of her distinct response to colonialism as a woman activist in the public domain in contrast to male nationalists. Reasoning why she accepted to serve on the Hartog Committee (an auxiliary body of the Simon Commission) even as male nationalists boycotted it, she averred that it was because of her appreciation for the colonial officials, Philip Hartog and R. M. Statham, who 'had great sympathy for the women's cause in India' and that they were 'favourable to women's aspiration for more and better education and equal rights and equal opportunities'. Despite her pronounced anti-colonial politics, in various sections of her autobiography, she acknowledges and appreciates the contributions of the colonial government and missionary women towards women's education and medical services (Reddy 1964: 37, 39, 96).

Reddy gives instances of how her political strategy was not fixed but contingent on the situation. For instance, when it came to male legislators, she kept herself above factions and parties as she needed their favour to get bills enabling women passed:

> Very often I would envy the gentlemen members when I see them sitting together in groups and parties and discussing matters of public importance. As I desired to be above all parties, I could not join any of those political groups and therefore I was left to myself and I had to get on as best as I could except in the cases of bills for which I could not but seek help of one or two, of the senior legislators in the council. (Reddy 1930: 48)

It is precisely such a strategy based on the contingent which offered her the space to be critical of nationalists, even while being an ardent nationalist. For instance, in her autobiography, she readily and openly appreciates the Justice Party leaders, despite her strong loyalty to Congress Party, for their support to her legislation on the abolition of the devadasi system. In contrast, she severely criticises much-respected nationalist leaders such as Rajagopalachari and Satyamurthi.[8] Narrating in detail how Rajagopalachari and Satyamurthi refused to offer a party ticket to her to contest the legislative council election and how the former, without consulting her, amended one of her bills, she writes, 'he [Rajagopalachari] is a reactionary in regard to social reforms, particularly in the emancipation of women' (Reddy 1964: 105).

Significantly for Reddy, it is women's experience in the domestic sphere which can differentiate their politics from that of men. Reddy did treat conjugality and maternal duties as a heavy burden for women. Reflecting on her reluctance to get married even at the considerably late age for that time (she got married in 1914 at the age of 26), she notes, 'I did not want to become saddled with marriage and become subordinate to a man whomsoever he may be. I had seen in my place the ill-treatment accorded to wives by their husbands. So I did not want to be one of such victims of man's superiority and domination' (ibid.: 18).[9] What one notices in her second autobiography is the refusal to narrativise her experiences of conjugality and motherhood as merely personal and makes suggestions for viewing these as collective experiences of women who encounter modernity.[10]

Yet, she privileges women's maternal role and motherhood qualities of caring and nurturing as important qualities that need to be extended to the public life. In both her autobiographical accounts, she invokes the motherhood image to define women's responsibility in the public sphere. For instance, while discussing her efforts to bring about reservation of seats for women in local administration such as the municipalities, Reddy cites her arguments made in the legislative council about extending women's responsibilities as wives and mothers to the public work:

> In regard to the importance of women serving on these municipalities, I contend that the functions of a municipality are in a large measure the functions of a house ... But what are the duties of a woman in the house? Her duty is to keep the house tidy and clean, to prepare food for her husband, to look

> after the children and to see that they get adequate medical relief and proper education ... when the women are recognized as mistresses of the house, why not our City fathers consider them as such as in the administration of municipalities. (Reddy 1930: 157)

Thus, she refuses to treat women's experience of conjugality and motherhood as merely personal or private and treats it as women's collective resource to reinvent a new politics. In other words, maternal duties are a burden *only* if they are tied to the domestic sphere, and women need to bring them to the modern public sphere.

To sum up the argument so far, Reddy's autobiographical writings incite women to become part of the public sphere by giving a series of reasons using own life as example. They include the need to articulate the distinct concerns of women in the public, the need to employ political strategies that are different from those of men, and the distinct women's domestic experience and affective qualities.

While in her autobiographical writings, orientated as a manifesto, Reddy invites women to be part of the public domain, she also shows that it involves a refashioning of the self and sacrifice. Writing about her life as a legislator and a public activist, she says:

> ... I had to read all the dailies both in vernacular and in English to be in touch with the views of all parties in the country ... In addition, I had to participate in many meetings, to enlist public sympathy and support for my bills and resolutions ... Further I had not only to be writing to the press to educate the public but also had to organize large women's meetings in support of my social and moral reform measures. I had to correspond with social and missionary workers in the districts. My correspondence increased to an enormous extent as I had letters from England, Geneva, America, and France in addition to local and provincial correspondence. (Reddy 1930: 85)

Such repositioning of oneself as a political subject required privileging duties to the public over the domestic or private demands. And this necessarily involved sacrifices of different kinds. For example, as Reddy was in the thick of working towards getting the act on the suppression of brothels and immoral traffic passed in the Madras legislature, she was caught in a conflict:

> ... [O]n the 31st Day [the day allotted for the final discussion on the amendment to the bill], a dear and near relation of mine was taken suddenly and seriously ill. I had to tear myself away from his bed-side and with indescribable pain and anguish of heart, I went to the Council that day ... As my father was lying unconscious and did not respond to my prayers, I had the consolation that very soon his spirit would bless me for having discharged my duty to the public! (Ibid.: 201–02)

And the need to combine domestic and public responsibilities (after all, the public is an extension of the domestic in Reddy's argument) can also burden women who choose for themselves a political subjectivity in the public sphere. Talking about the need to balance her domestic demands and her career as a doctor, she writes:

> As a mother I had to look after my delicate baby day and night and as a wife I had to look after my domestic duties and as a medical officer I had to do justice to my profession. I found it a great strain as well as a hardship to go through all these duties ... nobody could imagine the pain and suffering which a woman especially a wife and a mother, nay an educated and economically independent woman, has to go through especially when the husband is not very co-operative in the economy of the family. (Reddy 1964: 22)

Yet, for Reddy, such alienation from the domestic sphere and participating in the public sphere rewards one with a new affective community of women transcending the narrow limits of domesticity. Of her own involvement with international feminism, she wrote thus:

> My stay in England for one year and my delegation to the World's Conference of Women which was held in Paris in June 1926 has brought me in touch with many able women workers and useful women institutions from whom I have been receiving many valuable literature on Health, education and Moral and Social Hygiene for which I cannot but be too grateful to those good and noble women of other climes. (Reddy 1930: 84)

In other words, though repositioning women as a modern political subject in the public sphere involved sacrifices, there was also adequate reason for them to do so.

III

So far we have seen how Reddy has used her autobiographical writings as a means of not only constituting a modern subjectivity to herself but also inviting other similarly placed women to partake in the modern public sphere. While autobiographical manifestoes can open such a space for radical politics, the very form of the manifesto also simultaneously sets limits to such politics. Identity being central to manifestoes, they also function as an act of boundary-making and, hence, of exclusion. Now let me turn to how such limits inform Reddy's autobiographical manifesto.

In her autobiographical writings, Reddy clearly identifies educated women with 'respectable' social standing as ones who could not only become 'cultured and modern citizens' serving modern public institutions such as the legislature, but also speak for the rights of other women (Reddy 1964: 47). One needs to note here that both her autobiographical accounts were written in English, thus demarcating her audience as English-reading women. Reddy's position on which women could make a claim on the modern public sphere could be a result of many different influences. If her own class location as a privileged educated woman accounts for it partly, it could also be an outcome of her association with Gandhian nationalism,[11] which was grounded in so-called notions of women's respectability.[12] Above all, it could be a result of the nature of the colonial public sphere itself that demanded certain competencies such as access to English as a way of gate-keeping the public domain (Pandian 2007). In any case, her manifesto strategy becomes one of what Smith (1993: 17, 157) calls 'mimesis', that is, miming the subjectivity of the universal man in order to proffer 'authority, legitimacy and readability'. This is so despite the fact that she invoked difference as the basis for the need for women to participate in the public sphere.

In contrast to the educated women of respectability, she uses the ideals of 'sexual hygiene' and 'hygienic femininity' as moral categories to produce a discourse of difference to prevent other women from accessing modern public sphere.[13] For instance, while discussing the devadasi problem, Reddy continuously represents devadasis as 'victims of traditions', who are 'ignorant of healthy living' since they have been trained only 'to lead an immoral life, to lead a life of promiscuity, a life leading to the disease of the mind and the body' and that their bodies are oversexed ('set of prostitutes set up by their keepers') (Reddy 1930: 56). She also represents them as lacking in thinking abilities that, according to her, could be achieved only through modern education. She characterises the devadasi counter-discourses,[14] which question the arguments of reform as 'unworthy literature', and claims their associations as 'bogus associations' representing the interest of women standing for backward traditionalism and obstructing the path of progress of all women towards achieving a modern subjectivity. For instance, while narrating her efforts to get the bill on the abolition of the devadasi system passed in the legislative council and how some devadasis resisted it, Reddy remarks: 'The people [devadasis] that had not the courage to oppose me openly in public began to work underhand and set up one or two bogus associations to write petitions to Government and distribute unworthy literature to the public to prevent my bill becoming law' (ibid.: 58).

Most significantly, the devadasis emerge in her discourse as embodied in opposition to being rational, a characterisation men used to exclude women in general from the public sphere. According to her, they were 'propagators of social evil and ... carriers of venereal disease' (Reddy 1964: 44–45). It is important here to take a look at how Reddy consciously sublimates her sexual self in order to emerge as a modern political subject. All through her writings about her experiences of conjugality and motherhood, she makes continuous efforts to dislodge herself from the embodied, the sexualised and the eroticised so as to seek a modern selfhood. First of all, she negates the body as embedded in the aesthetics of the self or in the structure of feelings. Instead, she medicalises it (as in her extensive description of the medical aspects of her deliveries) or de-eroticises it by restoring it to certain pure motherhood devoid of sexual desire (ibid.: 21–35). But, in the context of lower class and uneducated women such as the devadasis, she presents them as embodied, and disenfranchises them from the public domain.[15]

In short, she legitimises the 'moral authority' of the few educated women like her, who are supposed to be capable of rational thinking, to speak on behalf of the entire womenfolk ('Only a few educated women of the land can speak, on behalf of our sex'). Thus, Reddy presents her claim (and that of similarly placed women) to modern selfhood as an 'intellectual and political vanguard at the forefront of history', and thus effectively represents the 'other' women and their varied negotiations with different aspects of the societal life as in need of reform (Reddy 1930: 62, 160; 1964: 47).[16]

What is more, in recovering the educated women as an unsullied category not inflected by other identities, Reddy also denies space for the articulation other subaltern identities. Caste, which was squarely on the political agenda in the Madras Presidency during that time, is a case in point. All through her autobiographical writings, she tries to recover and present her gender identity as if it were independent of her caste identity.[17] For instance, when she mentions her European professor's curiosity about her caste background since she excelled in her medical studies, she evades an engagement with the issue and quickly moves to talk of her experiences of being the only Hindu woman in the medical college.[18] Caste, however, finds its place in her autobiographical accounts as belonging to the unenlightened others. They are either the yet-to-be reformed devadasis or her Yadhava neighbours who were illiterate and had many children. Indeed, she goes on to describe the demand for separate electorates for the 'untouchables' by B. R. Ambedkar and others as a demand of 'narrow minded communals' (Reddy 1964: 66, 78–79, 101).

In short, Reddy's autobiographical writings show us the limits and possibilities of the autobiographical manifesto as a form as well as that of modernity as a political formation. While the manifesto form of autobiography uses life writing to 'represent a group to itself and invite similarly placed others to partake in its identity' (Pandian 2007: 2), the very fact that it is based on a bounded identity necessarily excludes. After all, identities not only forge solidarities but also erect boundaries. This is part of the reason why Reddy's politics, even while being radical in fissuring the male-controlled colonial public sphere, could not help othering lower class/caste women as embodied subjects unfit to be part of the modern public sphere and silencing subaltern identities such as caste. The other part of the reason flows from the very logic of courting modernity. As Felski (1995: 15) argues, '... the idea of the modern is deeply implicated from its beginning with a project of domination over those seen to lack this capacity for reflective reasoning'. These dictates of modernity allow only a limited space for Reddy to recuperate women as political subjects. To participate in the modern public domain, she had to recover women as capable of reflective reasoning. By treating education and social standing as the source of women's capacity to reason, she had to exclude vast sections of women from the modern public sphere. This is so despite her efforts to make qualities such as affect and caring part of the public sphere.

To put it differently, the feminist politics of the early twentieth century represented by Reddy deployed discourses of modernity which, as Joshi (2001: 94, 174) has argued, was 'fractured' and often contradictory. In the fractured modernity coexisted universal claims and particularist assertions, advocacy of liberty and equality and authoritarianism. Even as middle-class feminists like Reddy challenged modernity's gendered politics of exclusion, inescapably they too recuperated a different logic of exclusion in their articulation of a 'new public'. Thus, the feminist modern 'remained trapped within the contrary, fractured, modernity' and its politics of exclusion and power.

Notes

[1] For a detailed discussion on autobiography as gendered construction of selfhood, subjectivity and body, see Smith (1993). I have borrowed this argument mainly from Judith Butler, cited in Smith (1993: 11).

[2] For an interpretation of women's autobiographies and their engagement with gendered identities, collective selves and modernity, see Jelinek (1980), Brodski and Schenck (1988), Benstock (1988), and Watson and Smith (1992).

[3] Lyon's argument about how the manifesto engages with the problems of modernity is important to note here: According to her, it reconceives citizenship and political subjectivity of the marginalised, by recasting the enunciations of modernity such as universal freedom, autonomy, equality and inclusion, etc.

[4] Reddy does not mention her mother's devadasi background. It is only through other sources that one can gather this information. For instance, the recent autobiography of an erstwhile famous Tamil film actor, Gemini Ganesan, makes mention of Reddy's mother, Chandramma, as a devadasi from Pudukottah state whose marriage with a Brahmin man (Reddy's father) led to the excommunication of the family. C. S. Lakshmi mentions an interview with Reddy's distant relative, Siva Brinda Devi, who talked about Reddy's devadasi background. See, *Gemini Ganesanin Vazhkai Varalaru* (Gemini Ganesan's Life History), cited in Sriram (2007) and Lakshmi (1984).

[5] *Stridharma* was started in 1918 as a journal of the Women's India Association. It had at least 550 regular subscribers. Under Reddy's editorship, the journal became a political forum to articulate the feminist/nationalist agenda.

[6] It is important to note here that by attaching verbatim transcripts of her speeches and through various narrative techniques and rhetorical devices, Reddy presents her autobiographies in a mode of 'truth telling' mainly to convey the authentic nature of her arguments and experiences, and also legitimise her speaking position.

[7] Felski (1995: 152) and Lyon (1999: 7) observe how the feminist manifesto constantly invokes the unitary 'we' to offer it as the authentic voice of women and articulate gendered solidarity.
[8] When Congress Party was elected to the Madras legislature, Rajagopalachari became the chief minister and he delayed the introduction of the legislation for the abolition of the devadasi system. While narrating this incident, Reddy remarks: 'Thus Shri C. Rajagopalachari proved to be an opponent of social reforms in our society' (Reddy 1964: 73).
[9] In her second autobiography, there is an extensive narration of the tensions and conflicts in her conjugal life, pointing to how Reddy refuses to consider the new domestic ideals upheld and practised by the reformed household as self-fulfilling for women (Reddy 1964: 19, 20, 24, 27, 28).
[10] Her text here attempts to offer what Nancy Harstock, cited in Smith (1993: 159), calls 'a stand point epistemology' of women's experiences, and suggests possibilities for treating such 'private matters' as public issues that ought to form part of women's struggle.
[11] It is interesting to note how her second autobiography is structured with sequencing of events, etc., to speak for her commitment to Gandhian nationalism, and how she makes a conscious attempt to represent it as an 'emancipatory politics' for women. For instance, the section entitled 'My First Meeting with Gandhiji at Madras' (she mentions this as an 'auspicious moment') is immediately followed with details of the women's meeting with Gandhi with the title, 'The Beginning of Emancipation', though in the previous sections of the book she narrates in detail the wide variety of struggles launched by women's organisations to emancipate women and how she enlightened Gandhi on issues of reform for women. For details of how she constructs Gandhian nationalism and women's rights, see Reddy (1964: 50–53).
[12] The fact that a large number of devadasis participated in the national movement and that they were at the forefront of the struggles created anxiety among the middle-class women political activists who often resorted to the campaign of 'sexual morality' in public participation in order to distinguish themselves from the 'others' and also to invisibilise the latter's public activities. For details on the propagation of the politics of respectability by women nationalists in Tamil Nadu, see Anandhi (1997: 209–10).
[13] While reviewing Mina Loy's *Feminist Manifesto* (1914), Lyon (1999: 6) observes how Loy manipulated the manifesto form to bring in the narrative ideal of republican motherhood, even as it contested the anti-individualist representations of the 'woman'. Similarly, Reddy manipulates her autobiographical manifesto to challenge the nationalist representation of women as representing tradition and ideals of modern domesticity, and at the same time invokes similar images to debar a section of women from participating in public political activities.
[14] It is important to note here that the devadasis and their associations asserted their right to citizenship through the discourse of art and aesthetics, and, thus, vehemently discounted Reddy's discourse of sexual morality as the basis for public participation and citizenship. See Sriram (2007).
[15] Having denied devadasis the right to the modern public sphere, Reddy constantly laments about women of 'education', 'real culture' and 'character' not coming forward to take to the public work. Reddy reflects thus: 'When I look round [sic] for help and sympathy for any of the above national-building and even relief measures, the

educated free women are so few that I have to lament in despair at our sad plight' (Reddy 1930: 63). She also raises concern about wives of government servants being prevented from taking part in active political life through denial of franchise, etc. (ibid.: 98), and this concern needs to be noted in the context of middle-class women's anxiety about the participation of devadasis in the national movement.

[16] Commenting on middle-class women's politics of inclusion and exclusion, Felski (1995: 149) remarks, 'Within this scenario [middle-class women fashioning themselves as political vanguards], women of other races and classes were often depicted as primitive and backward, yet to be awakened to the light of feminist consciousness.'

[17] For a detailed discussion on how the upper-caste male representation of modern self-identity silenced caste and invalidated its presence in the public discourse, see Pandian (2001).

[18] In another instance, she mentions the protest against her admission to the boys college, but does not mention whether the protest was due to her mother's caste background or her gender identity. Throughout the autobiography, Reddy does not bring up her mother's lower-caste identity (the Isai Vellala caste to which most devadasis belonged), but presents her as a 'pious, pure and religious and loyal [wife]'.

References

Anandhi, S. 1997. 'Sexuality and Nation: "Ideal" and "Other" Woman in Nationalist Politics, Tamilnadu, c.1900–1947'. *South Indian Studies* 4: 195–217.

Benstock, Shari (ed.). 1988. *The Private Self: Theory and Practice of Women's Autobiographical Writings*. Chapel Hill and London: University of North Carolina Press.

Brodski, Bella and Celeste Schenck (eds). 1988. *Life/Lines: Theorising Women's Autobiography*. Ithaca: Cornell University Press.

Chakrabarty, Dipesh. 2000. *Provincialising Europe: Postcolonial Thought and Historical Differences*. Princeton and Oxford: Princeton University Press.

Felski, Rita. 1995. *The Gender of Modernity*. Cambridge, Massachusetts, and London: Harvard University Press.

Jelinek, C. Estelle. 1980. *Women's Autobiography: Essays in Criticism*. Bloomington: Indiana University Press.

Joshi, Sanjay. 2001. *Fractured Modernity: Making of a Middle Class in Colonial North India*. New Delhi: Oxford University Press.

Kaviraj, Sudipta. 2004. 'The Invention of Private Life: A Reading of Sibnath Sastri's Autobiography'. In *Telling Lives in India: Biography, Autobiography and Life History*, eds David Arnold and Stuart Blackburn, 83–115. New Delhi: Permanent Black.

Lakshmi, C. S. 1984. *The Face behind the Mask*. Delhi: Vikas Publishing House.

Lyon, Janet. 1999. *Manifestoes: Provocations of the Modern*. Ithaca and London: Cornell University Press.

Pandian, M. S. S. 2001. *One Step Outside Modernity: Caste, Identity Politics and Public Sphere*. SEPHIS-CODESRIA, Amsterdam and Vinlin Press, Dakar.

——— 2007. *Brahmin and Non-Brahmin: Genealogies of the Tamil Political Present*. New Delhi: Permanent Black.

Reddy, Muthulakshmi. 1930. *My Experience as a Legislator*. Madras: Current Thought Press.

_____ 1964. *Autobiography*. Madras: M. L. J. Press.

Sarkar, Tanika. 1993. 'A Book of Her Own. A Life of Her Own: Autobiography of a Nineteenth-century Woman'. *History Workshop Journal* 36(1): 35–65.

Smith, Sidonie. 1993. *Subjectivity, Identity and the Body: Women's Autobiographical Practices in the Twentieth Century*. Bloomington and Indianapolis: Indiana University Press.

Sriram, V. 2007. *The Devadasi and the Saint: The Life and Times of Bangalore Nagarathnamma*. Chennai: East West Books.

Watson, Julia and Sidonie Smith. 1992. 'Introduction: De/colonization and the Politics of Discourse in Women's Autobiographical Practices'. In *De/colonizing the Subject: The Politics of Gender in Women's Autobiography*, eds Sidonie Smith and Julia Watson, *xiii–xxxi*. Minneapolis: University of Minnesota Press.

2. Lohia's Immanent Critique of Caste and Religion*

Arun Kumar Patnaik

This chapter is divided in five sections. The first explores Ram Manohar Lohia's method of immediacy and argues that for Lohia, internal tensions in history or mythologies are very important to develop a critical perspective. The second section tries to look at Lohia's contributions in the light of his predecessors like Gandhi and Ambedkar, two major influences on him in a variety of concerns. The third section examines Lohia's analysis of different aspects of caste and especially its moral order. In the fourth section, I propose to discuss why Lohia focuses on non-historical resources (fables, myths) and their inner contradictions dealing with the caste system. Finally, we come to Lohia's analysis of the three forms of opposition to caste.

Lohia's Method: The Principle of Immediacy

It may be argued that Lohia's immanent criticism is outlined by his principle of immediacy. Recent commentators misunderstand this principle. Yogendra Yadav's lengthy essay on Lohia's intellectual journey underestimates Lohia's method. Where he should notice Lohia's methodological protocols in his principle of immediacy, he argues that Lohia's principle is morally relevant against 'vulgar presentism' (excessively concerned with the present and indifferent to

*A shorter version of this chapter was published in 2009–10 in *My Society* 1–4(1–4): 18–32. Reproduced with permission.

the future), but does not have any analytical significance. Commenting on Lohia's principle of immediacy, Yadav (2010: 94) argues, 'Lohia did not formulate the analytical part of this insight [the principle of immediacy] as clearly as the normative principle.' Kumar (2010) tries to argue for an intersectional understanding of caste, but does not notice that Lohia offers an internal critique of caste and implies that Lohia transcends caste in order to offer his criticism of it. His notion of intersectionality is transcendental based on external limits, rather than immanent based on internal limits of the caste system. Seth (2002: 122) comes very close to acknowledging the internal tensions within the caste system, and argues that 'counter-cultural traditions' of the subaltern castes could be the basis of a new counter-hegemony. Seth argues that Lohia 'does not develop sufficiently to give the symbolism a political content' (ibid.). But Seth fails to notice that Lohia develops new analytical protocols for a new socialist politics to begin with. Lohia intends to develop a new path for a new political programme. Akin to Buddhism, for Lohia, a path (method) may be more important than a destination point (politics). Obsession with a remote destination may destroy our search of a right path which may be waiting for our immediate attention. Let us discuss this issue at length.

While responding to Yadav's position, Hegde (2011: 72), however, suggests that it is possible to argue that in Lohia's principle of immediacy, 'some aspects of this analytical part' may be 'inflecting at once Lohia's ethics and politics.' What are these analytical aspects present in Lohia's principle of immediacy? Though Hegde does not explore methodological protocols present in Lohia's principle, he hints at their presence in his elaborate response to Yadav's thesis. Hegde suggests that Lohia's principle of immediacy is about 'the world imagined (and lived) from the perspective of will (as separate from reason) ... One of the profound weaknesses of this politics on immediacy is that it has no account of the cognitive status of its own history, even though its basic superiority consists in its unique compatibility with prevailing and current historical conditions' (ibid.: 71). Hegde views Lohia's principle as an expression of a perspective of will (non-reason) rather than a perspective of reason. In my view, he thus reduces the analytical import of an immanent criticism of history which is informed by a perspective of reason combined with a perspective of will (non-reason). Do we find a union of reason and will (non-reason) in Lohia's principle of immediacy? Is Lohia's principle of immediacy posited in the unitary sense as claimed by Hegde (ibid.: 70), and thus devoid of a multiplicity of meanings? Let us now answer these questions.

What is Lohia's principle of immediacy? What is it opposed to or different from? How does Lohia discuss it? Lohia is critical of our obsession with 'vulgar presentism' (obsession with the present) on the one hand and 'vulgar futurism' (an excessive concern with a remote future) on the other, and posits the principle of immediacy. In modernist circles, there are two forms of reactions against vulgar presentism. Lohia distinguishes two kinds of tests by modern intellectuals to promote their ideals of progress—the remote test (what may be called 'transcendental principle') and the principle of immediacy (what may be called 'immanent principle').

The Remote Test

Thinkers following a remote test or transcendental principle argue that the modern civilisation is about constant 'progress' in production, democracy and even class struggle. A golden age is expected to come. Right-wing intellectuals may focus on technological progress, whereas Left-wing intellectuals may offer a remote justification of class struggle. Both may portray a golden age in the future. Both have an over-riding faith in remote tests. Thus, Lohia (2011a: 183) argues that the modern world has given rise to dichotomies 'between spirit and matter, individual and social, bread and culture and the like.' As the future appears by suppressing the present, a dichotomy between the present and the future is posited in this remote method. Right-wing intellectuals represent one side of the dichotomy (spirit/individual/culture/technology) and the Left-wing intellectuals represent the exact opposite of it (matter/social/bread/humanity). Lohia argues that this is an unreal opposition. Lohia (2011a: 184) suggests, 'These dichotomies have arisen because immediacy is flouted because history denies fable and fable denies history.' True, Lohia here criticises a rationalist account of history popular in the Left and the Right that suppresses fables/fictions/myths. He seems to be giving up reason. But Lohia does not celebrate fables/myths. He subjects myths to a rational scrutiny and suggests that fables too have moral doctrines that impact history in a linear form or cyclic form. By suppressing fables, a rationalist history presents the partial truth. A typical rationalist account of history is binary and full of dichotomies. Lohia is not giving up history for fables. He is interested in exploring a fruitful dialogue between the two, without sliding into one-sided analytical protocols popular with the philosophers of history (with a moment of flux in history) or moralists (with the moment of eternity in fables). If the moment of flux can be analysed by a perspective of non-reason or will, the moment of eternity can be analysed from a perspective of reason. Reason and will are necessary to analyse both the moments of eternity (fables) and flux (history). That is how Lohia breaks free from the binary of reason and will by combining a critical perspective of history and fables. He is critical of their dichotomy, critical of their gaze over humanity, and proposes a new synthesis. For fables are stories that never take place but moralists assume they are internally real. Historians denounce fables and rightly look for moments of flux/change, thus ignoring what is 'externally real' in fables (Lohia 2011a: 185). Lohia concludes, 'If a man must learn to live in history, he has an equal need to live outside it.'

The Immediacy Test

Lohia proposes, 'We may, in fact, be heading for a golden age if we try to achieve that golden age in the immediate' (ibid.: 186). The principle of immediacy connects the moment of flux (history) with the moment of eternity (fables), the moment of material force with a moment of subjective will, the moment of social with the moment of the individual. The principle of immediacy claims that for each single act, we need not look for transcendental criteria to justify its course of doing. It can be justified with immanent criteria or by a 'here and now' approach to production, governance, culture and class struggle. Lohia argues, 'Compassion and revolution have to interweave and any preferential loyalty to one or the other would heap disaster on the spiritual as well as the material' (ibid.). Lohia clearly is unprepared to give up the reason for a will or *vice versa*. He discards the golden age of the distant future and argues that such an ideal is harmful to Left-wing movements—for they may perform many ignoble acts to fulfil high ideals and think that their acts can be justified by the outcome of a remote future. If I may rephrase him, he implicitly suggests that a perspective of will focuses on compassion or the spiritual realm, whereas a perspective of reason concentrates on material changes in human life. A socialist ideal of progress must concentrate on a combined perspective of will and reason.

Lohia's principle acquires an added analytical significance in the socialist movement to establish classless and casteless society by a here-and-now approach rather than a remote approach. The orthodox notion of progress in socialist circles upholds a rosy future and forgets that subalterns want to gain 'autonomy' here and now rather than in the distant future. Unless socialists identify with the subaltern search for autonomy/solidarity here and now, and would want to identify their struggle with the subaltern search for autonomy, they will lose relevance here and now. Unless socialists identify with the principle of immediacy in production (the will to control production/profits in factory or the agricultural field), in class struggle (democratic participation in pedagogy/action rather than dependence on leadership), and in culture (intellectual formation among subalterns, approximation to other cultures of subalterns and so on), the socialist movement cannot create the golden age it promises to the subaltern strata.

Lohia's thesis is anticipated by Antonio Gramsci's immanent criticism of socialist orthodoxies in Europe. Culturally, Lohia's thesis approximates that of Gramsci's realist immanent critique (as opposed to speculative immanence). Gramsci suggests that a new research is necessary to know how Marxism proposes a new synthesis of the three great currents of German philosophy, English political economy and French socialism. What are the principles from these currents that are affirmed, absorbed and continued by Marxism? Gramsci argues:

> And it seems to me that the unitary "moment" of synthesis is to be identified in the new concept of immanence, which has been translated from the speculative form, as put forward by classical German philosophy, into a historicist form with the aid of French politics and English classical economics. (Gramsci 1971: 400)

Just as Lohia proposes the principle of immediacy to combine materialism and idealism, Gramsci offers an immanent method to offer a new synthesis of the two contrasting positions. Both of them are deeply worried about inheritance from traditions (history/fables). Gramsci (1971: 402) asks questions on his idea of synthesis: 'Is it to be understood as a historical circle already completed ... once for all; or should it be rather understood as a historical process still in motion ...?'. Gramsci discards complacency in a socialist circle and adopts an open approach to synthesis. For him, a new synthesis is part of a historical process in motion. It can never be claimed as a historical circle completed once for all. Probably Lohia would have agreed with Gramsci's realist immanent method.

As in Gramsci, Lohia's analytical protocols also broaden the field of socialist politics. It is not merely concerned with the material transformation through State power, it is equally concerned with spiritual change or intellectual transformation so that the subaltern caste/classes cease to remain subalterns. It is not merely focused on capturing State power but also on the transformation of social power in caste/gender/class/ethnicity/language. Thus, analytically speaking, it is indeed a historic task of the socialist movement to explore forms of immediacy in factory/land, class/caste struggle, governance and culture. It is possible for a new socialist movement to begin by identifying with these multiple forms of immediacy. Thus, new analytical protocols are laid bare in his principle of immediacy required to renew a new socialist movement. His analysis is simultaneously political. His new methodology is at once a new political project. Far from positing a unitary notion of immediacy as claimed by Hegde, Lohia observes a plural notion of immediacy so that socialism can be constructed with multiple trajectories.

Does Lohia apply his own method to understand caste relation? Lohia does it very acutely. He offers a plural notion of immediacy to examine the caste system and identifies caste in relation to gender, language, class and region. He locates its internal strength in providing forms of solidarity and security to members of a particular caste, though in a framework of segregation, and argues that socialism must articulate similar forms of security and solidarity in non-discriminatory mode. Socialism must adopt and universalise solidarity currents practised by caste society, instead of pointing towards a distant future of collective progress. His application of the immanent principle to examine the caste system is very clear. While this could be seen as part of his analysis of 'history', it may be useful to hint at this stage how he analyses fables of the Ram-Vashishtha-Sambhuka story on the one hand, and Vashishtha-Valmiki traditions on the other. He also pays attention to folk legends of fishermen or

Dalit communities that reinforce their subordination, and points to their inner contradictions in these beliefs. In a sense, he offers a subtle criticism of caste-based legends believed by the lower castes. He deftly uses these stories to expose caste contradictions and points a way out. Let us examine these issues next.

Caste as Domination or Legitimation: Gandhi, Ambedkar and Lohia

Since caste is a power structure, it needs to be related to a theory of power. A theory of power is usually caught with a tension between two notions of power—power as a hierarchy of domination on the one hand, and power as a system of legitimation on the other. The former focuses on a hierarchy of elites and subalterns, structural inequalities arising between them and strategies to dominate subaltern strata, and so on. The latter focuses on why subalterns give consent to the domination of elites and its moral and legal paraphernalia.

These notions of power represent two different sides of power, sometimes pushing theorists to take sectarian positions. That is to say, theorists of power may merely echo the one or the other side of power, failing to notice that there are actually two sides in live tension or contradiction with each other. A comprehensive theory of power will have to engage with these two different tendencies of the power structure. Thus, a broad view of caste power may have to take into account the hierarchy of domination and structures of legitimation. It must break with a binary view that treats caste as domination or as a legitimation process.

This chapter primarily focuses on Lohia's accounts that deal with the moral order of caste. He focuses on the legitimising process of the caste system and enquires into why caste has survived as a social system. He throws some light on the resilient strength of the caste system while pleading for the destruction of caste's exclusionary practices. But it would be a terrible mistake to examine Lohia's account of caste in isolation from that of Gandhi and Ambedkar. Moreover, in terms of genealogy, he should be evaluated as a succeeding thinker. If Lohia needs to be examined in relation to his immediate intellectual context, the antecedent tradition of criticism of caste must be placed beforehand, so that we can assess his own contributions fruitfully.

It may not be inaccurate to claim that the earlier thinkers such as Gandhi and Ambedkar describe caste as a hierarchy of domination (untouchability for Gandhi and graded inequalities for Ambedkar). Lohia assumes caste as a hierarchy and proceeds to focus on caste as a legitimising system: How does it draw the support of the people and gain acceptability as a system? In my view, Lohia addresses a question not posed by Gandhi or Ambedkar.

Ambedkar and Lohia on Gandhi's View of Caste

There is one thing common to both Ambedkar and Lohia. Both are dissatisfied with Gandhi's doctrine of least resistance to caste order. Both argue for the rediscovery of Satyagraha against the caste system. If you recall, Gandhi was wary of Satyagraha against caste inequalities, his opposition to British Raj on the grounds of Satyagraha notwithstanding. Gandhi did not think it would be prudent to place Satyagraha against the caste order during the British rule or even after India's independence. Rather, on the caste issues, he proposed the doctrine of least resistance as a matter of principle rather than a time-dependent strategy. Gandhi thinks that caste is an unequal structure between the touchable castes and the untouchable castes.

He argues for changing the upper-caste mentalities by an appeal to their hearts. He argues that if the upper castes can be convinced of the principle of ancestral calling, it would be possible for them to believe in the redundancy of untouchability. According to this principle, we perform different functions as our duties to a village community as ordained by our ancestors. Through an alternative education of the upper castes, it would be possible to convince them that different castes do mere duties to their ancestors. So, there is no low or polluted duty and high or pure duty. All caste functions are duties as per the ancestral calling. Once the upper castes are convinced of a notion of duty in every manual labour, it would be possible for them to remove from their minds that some groups perform menial labour or polluted functions. All functions would be seen as necessary duties to ancestors. Once the upper castes are convinced using this doctrine, they would also undertake street sweeping and so on, as Gandhi himself did. That would bring an end to untouchability. So, Satyagraha against untouchability is not necessary. Ambedkar calls Gandhi's doctrine as one of least resistance.[1]

Both Ambedkar and Lohia remain dissatisfied with Gandhi's doctrine of least resistance. Both argue that Gandhi, as a matter of principle, denies the relevance of Satyagraha against caste inequalities. If you look at India's history, it is full of such Satyagraha resistance movements against the caste system, so argues Ambedkar. By denying Satyagraha against caste, Gandhi denies the relevance of this history to contemporary egalitarians. Ambedkar argues that Gandhi's call for the abolition of untouchability amounts to a case of limited egalitarianism. Lohia too argues that Gandhi's Satyagraha may be extended to caste system and socialism, unlike Gandhi, and may explore the possibility of policy action against caste inequalities, a theme with which Ambedkar is equally concerned. Thus, we find some common threads in their assessment of Gandhism *vis-à-vis* caste order. Both agree that Gandhism reduces caste to the existence of untouchables, and nullifies any concerted policy or political action against the caste system. Both agree that it would be necessary to view caste order as power structure, and offer an all-rounded critique of caste so that it would be entirely abolished.

For both Ambedkar and Lohia, the abolition of caste order is more important than the abolition of untouchability of the Dalits as Gandhism envisages. Both agree that Gandhism is an egalitarian ideology on the caste question but it has limited utilities in a democratic nation determined to abolish caste inequalities. In fact, Ambedkar, unlike his followers, clearly demarcates three egalitarian ideologies against caste—Gandhism, Marxism and Buddhism. For him, as also for Lohia, it would be possible to learn from Gandhism and Marxism while trying to establish an egalitarian ideology, even though lessons from them may have limited applicability in relation to caste order in India. So, I submit, Ambedkar was not anti-Gandhi as made out by his followers today. In dialectical thinking, there are no pro- or anti-Gandhi positions.[2]

Both give credit to Gandhi for discovering Satyagraha as a means of people's struggle against injustice and for popularising Satyagraha at a pan-Indian level. Lohia assumes that it is because of Gandhi that it is now possible to place Satyagraha against the caste system, even though Gandhi might have placed the 'change of heart' doctrine in relation to caste or property disputes (Lohia 1978: 157–58). For, due to Gandhi, Satyagraha is now etched in people's memories on a national level. The people will never forget its relevance in their own social and political struggles. There is no blind anti-Gandhism in Ambedkar as made out by his followers today, even though he is sharply critical of Gandhism.

Ambedkar and Caste as a System of Graded Inequalities

Let us focus on Ambedkar's programme of the annihilation of caste as a prelude to our discussion of Lohia's plea for the destruction of caste order. Ambedkar argues clearly: Gandhism has a weak understanding of caste inequalities and, moreover, has a weaker understanding of solutions to caste order. We have seen the latter aspect and now shall examine the former. Gandhi identifies untouchability of the Dalits as a major problem in the caste order. He is for the abolition of untouchability, even though he prescribes no political action. But, he forgets that untouchability is not simply limited to the Dalit's social experience, it is also the experience of the so-called touchable castes and of all women across caste order. By simply ignoring this simple point, Gandhi misses the essence of the caste system, which consists of grades of untouchability against several human beings, not simply Dalits. Caste is defined by the untouchability practised within the 'touchable' castes and against untouchable castes, rather than by the position of untouchables, as Gandhi imagines. One of the broadest definitions of the caste system as a system of graded inequalities is thus found in Ambedkar. In comparison, the Gandhian conception of caste pales into romantic narrow-mindedness. Let us elaborate this feature of caste as captured by Ambedkar briefly.[3]

Caste is simply not a system of inequalities between castes of purity and pollution. There is no neat division of labour in the caste system. There are grades of pollution, followed by rules of precedence in matters of education, religion, commensalism, marriage, economy and so on. Such rules of precedence exclude not merely Dalits from various sectors of human life, they also exclude Shudras, Vaisyas, non-Vedic Brahmins as well as all women across caste divisions. Caste is thus a hierarchy of grades/ranks of people subdivided by the different rules of precedence in matters governing human life, where the Vedic Brahmin male occupies the top of the hierarchy, with Dalits occupying its bottom. Let us see how rules of precedence occur in education under the caste order. Vedas and Puranas were seen as two different sources of knowledge. Vedic Brahmins occupied superior status over Puranic Brahmins as the Vedic knowledge preceded Puranic knowledge. The Brahmin male occupied a superior status over Brahmin women in matters of knowledge. Women of any caste and all non-Brahmin males were excluded from the education system by caste practices.

Violation of such rules by any group invited proportionate physical punishment. Such punishment rules varied from region to region. If you recall, Ambedkar argues that Gandhi ignores the prevalence of untouchability among the 'touchable' castes. Even non-Vedic Brahmins and Brahmin women are not supposed to know the Vedas. Malas think that they are superior to Madigas in Andhra Pradesh and assume that the latter are untouchables. Such rules of precedence prevail not merely in education, but in all other spheres of life, thus creating a variety of untouchability strata across the caste order. That is why Gandhi's call for the abolition of untouchability of the untouchable castes or Dalits is a weak solution, further weakened by his plea for a change of hearts of the upper castes. Thus, Ambedkar pleads that all-round Satyagraha must be conducted to destroy the essence of caste, which lies in the varieties of untouchability created by the social system. We shall leave Ambedkar here. It should be enough to indicate how Ambedkar examines caste as a hierarchy of power.

Lohia and the Moral Order of Caste

As I said before, Lohia does not explore how caste is organised as a graded hierarchy. I am not aware if Lohia knows Ambedkar's richer analysis. Most probably, unwittingly, he examines what is left out by Ambedkar. Why does the caste order manage to survive in the midst of resistance against caste and foreign conquests? This is a most important question for Lohia (1964: 81): 'Castes have endured over thousands of years.' He goes on to explore how caste creates legitimation processes so that the lower castes feel that they are indeed lower, and so on. He further explores how caste creates insurance or social security for which people do not have to pay a premium. How did castes produce a split personality in average Hindus who were without a stable and sincere voice on anything? How do castes disunite and divide vast masses, which remain passive even on witnessing foreign conquests by tiny armies? No foreign conquests have propelled them to mass action due to caste divisions. Can socialists learn from some positive features by destroying the negative features of the caste system? What strategy ought they to have to do so? What policy actions are possible under socialism?

The Provision for Social Security

To cite Lohia (1964: 80): 'Caste is presumably the world's largest insurance for which one does not pay a formal or regular premium. Solidarity is always there when everything else fails.' Caste provides for social solidarity in matters of child-bearing, marriage, funeral obsequies, feasts and other rituals. Men belonging to the same caste assist each other at these decisive hours of needs. But Lohia does not fail to notice that caste-based security, for which we may not have to pay any premium for insurance protection, does also practise 'excluding men of other castes' who are reduced to the peripheries of such a social security system. This system of insurance without any cost or premium makes it more resilient and durable in the eyes of its members only. It practises segregation in providing social security to needy people from other castes.

I remember one incident from Aska, a small town in Odisha. A Komati (trader) family was not able to arrange their daughter's wedding due to financial difficulties. The Komati Pentha arranged for the money and a boy for her too. Such solidarity is found in caste associations throughout India. Brahmin associations give fellowships to poor Brahmin students in schools. The Kamma Sangam does similar things. Do we ever come across beggars among Komatis or Jat Sikhs? The Langar houses or Penthas take care of them. Such activities provide legitimacy and strength to caste order. Caste continues to survive despite the many crisis points posed by modernisation. This partly explains why caste has survived even foreign conquests. In fact, due to a drive for modernisation, caste has managed to survive in urban areas in form of associations offering many kinds of assistance in times of financial crises. The more a caste group has money, the more it is organised with association offices and schemes for the assistance of the needy members of its own caste. To use a more fashionable term, I would say that caste provides for social capital networks. But such social capital networks are restricted within a particular caste stratum.[4] Can socialism learn from this community network to weaken caste order instead of relying on State power to do so, as at present? I assume Lohia is interested in inferring such a question from his investigation into the caste system, though I must confess I have not been able to see such an explicit query asked by him. Otherwise, why should a socialist leader be interested in telling us about this networking aspect of caste? Lohia does not ask such a sharp question. He purely relies on the State/party model of socialism to overcome barriers of the caste system while offering social security. His model of solution converges with that of the Nehruvian liberals and Communist parties, even though, in the way he examines the caste system frontally, his analysis differs from theirs. However, Lohia does not share their 'wordy opposition' to caste, which will be examined in the last section of this chapter.

A System of Moral Subordination

Another aspect of the caste system is the way it survives with support from the lower castes. The upper castes do not have to dominate them with the rule of the gun. The lower castes justify their own subordination, by discovering their folklore, through a moral discourse innovated by themselves rather than by the upper castes. The lower castes have legends and myths that justify their 'lowly' situation and transform it into a symbol of sacrifice and lustre. Lohia gives an illustration from fisherfolks' life. The Kaivarts (the fisherfolk caste), who presumably number more than one crore in population, tell stories about their mythical ancestors, who were simple, un-greedy, brave and generous, and who lost everything to the ancestors of the Kshatriyas and other higher castes because of the latter groups' greed and deceit. Their current misery is attributed to the unending succession of sacrificial acts for the sake of high principles. This sacrifice is seen not as an active principle that seeks change, but as a passive submission to the caste order. This sort of mythical sacrifice is widespread among the lower castes. They secure their subordination (Lohia 1964: 84).

Weakening of the Nation

Lohia argues that it is widely believed that foreigners were able to invade and conquer India due to our internal quarrels and intrigues.

This is plain misreading of India's history. The single biggest cause is the caste system, which produced imbecility and passivity among the masses who were hardly interested in the nation's tragedies. Caste is the single largest reason why national feeling, national solidarity and action preventing national tragedies could not develop. These forms of national consciousness still do not develop. This is reminiscent of Ambedkar's idea: 'castes are anti-national'.[5] Like Ambedkar, Lohia too argues that unless caste is destroyed, new India cannot revive. India would remain weak, not due to intrigues but because of caste inequalities. If political parties play the caste card in electoral democracy, the nation will remain dormant and docile. India will not be seen as a developed nation. So in Lohia's estimate, caste and the nation have a negative correlation. If one remains strong, the other becomes weak, and the people's languages, their housing and general styles of living remain undeveloped, and their minds continue to be plagued by inferiority complexes instilled in them over a thousand years (Lohia 1964: 83–84). A vibrant India cannot be born in such situations. The destruction of caste is important for nation-building.

A Split Personality among Hindus

Caste induces Hindus to commit the biggest hypocrisies. Hindus like all other religious people tell lies to others. What is, however, unique about Hindus is they lie to themselves. A Hindu lies to himself as well as others and feels most comfortable with its success. A Hindu mind, due to caste, is a bundle of contradictions. Unless caste is destroyed in belief and practice, a Hindu mind will not be able to develop a consistent character and sincere moral personality (Lohia 2011b: 221–22).

There is a very interesting discussion between Lohia and Gandhi. After Lohia returned from Germany, he met Gandhi. Gandhi called him a very brave man. Lohia responded by saying that the tiger is also brave. Gandhi called him a learned man. Lohia laughed it away, saying that a lawyer who enjoys financial benefits as a result of people's growing conflicts is also a learned man. Then, Gandhi concluded that Lohia had *sheel*, which can best be translated as 'continuity in character'. Lohia remained silent.[6]

Lohia assumes that once we believe in caste moralities, our personalities will remain retarded and under-grown. Thus, according to my interpretation of his writings, Lohia thinks that an average Hindu mind (I would extend this idea to the average caste-conscious Muslim and Christian as well) may be brave or may be learned. But in order to have continuity in character, s/he must believe in a caste-free society, must prove that s/he is committed to the destruction of caste in practice. That means s/he must have social networks (friendship, trust) across caste order. Any restriction of this will be hypocritical. Lohia gives two more examples from public life—the cases of a prime minister and a president. Prime Minister Jawaharlal Nehru once, over a week, told the press that he would resign as nobody listened to him, even though the people respected him. The following day, he would continue to hold the post. The day after, again, he would threaten to resign, but change his mind again. Thus, the prime minister indicated that he lacked 'sheel'. President Rajendra Prasad was worse. He was part of the constitutional post which believed in prohibition but he was also the president of the Calcutta Club, founded by the Indian bourgeoisie, where wine flowed every evening. A rich Tanti (a weaver caste) wanted to become a member, but was refused as he was not from the families of 'the Tatas and Birlas' (Lohia 1964: 132–34). The president was still the chief patron of the club, even after a weaver from the upper class was refused its membership. Neither the president nor the prime minister even realised that what they were doing was full of contradictions. Such imbecility of mind (Lohia 2011a: 278) occurs because of the lack of commitment to a caste-free society. Lohia somehow believed that continuity in character can arise only if we the Hindus (or even non-Hindus) are committed to the destruction of the caste order in belief and social practice.

This theme remained dear to his writings and personality throughout his life. Lohia's argument about an average Hindu personality believing in the caste order as a bundle of contradictions was anticipated by D. D. Kosambi, the Marxist historian. Kosambi (1975: 45) argued that 'the complicated Brahminical pantheon' assimilates contradictions, without resolving them. Contradictions between Vedic Brahmins and non-Vedic Brahmins, the contradiction between Brahmin males and Brahmin females, the contradiction between each Shudra caste trying to claim purity against the pollution of other Shudra castes, a contradiction within Dalit castes and the contradiction between Dalits and non-Dalits. If we take the case of Lord Siva's entourage, it will be very clear what Kosambi means. In this entourage, we have different elements that are mutually opposed to each other. We have a bull, a cobra, an elephant god with a rat. We have Parvathi with a lion in her convoy. Quite a few of these characters induce us to believe in a set of contradictions that our caste minds assimilate, without any attempt to resolve them. If we go deeper, we find that caste order evolved by subjugating and assimilating different tribes with the cults—like the snake cult, Basava (bull) cult, elephant cult and so on—producing Siva's entourage. In the process of preserving their cults, the tribes got assimilated into caste-based occupations and a Hindu pantheon was established.[7] Sastras and Puranas began justifying this caste order and prescribed rules of precedence for different people differently, a point already noted by Ambedkar (2014b: 45–47). I do not wish to equate Hinduism with the caste order. But there is a caste core of the Hindu social order which is also a core of the converts from Hinduism to Islam and Christianity in post-Independence India.[8]

Lohia gives some more examples from marriage. For example, a Telugu Brahmin boy may marry a Kannada Brahmin girl, and may claim that their marriage is 'pan-Indian'. According to Lohia, such a marriage is actually a pan-Brahmin marriage. Such hypocrisies are rampant in a caste society. Similarly, an Oriya Khandayata's marriage to an Oriya Chasa is considered an inter-caste marriage. This is a marriage within the 'touchable' castes and can hardly be called inter-caste. We can probably think of contemporary examples too. Politically, a Mala may claim that s/he is a Dalit but does not hesitate to excommunicate the Madigas and deny their assertions of self-identity, thus debunking the Madigas' entire claim for a Dalit identity. Similarly, Madigas may perpetuate discrimination against Erukulas and Erukulas against Chenchus. Such hypocrisy (Lohia 2011c: 15–29)—from social or political life—is plenty in caste order, spreading from top to bottom. These are all cases of a split personality of a person or group owing to the peculiarity of caste contradictions whose resolution is not sought by them.

Classes Oscillate as Caste: Reverse Appropriation?

In a way reminiscent of Gramsci's model of reverse appropriation, Lohia suggests that Western classes also oscillate towards caste order, even though caste order is uniquely Indian. Gramsci argues that the

European ruling classes, after colonial experiences, readopted caste's segregated forms to counter working-class aspirations for equality (Dainotto 2013: 75–86). Gramsci hints that the Western ruling classes reinvented even caste-like language against the class struggle. Caste-like rigidities, privileges, imbecilities and excommunication exist in German, American and Soviet societies (Lohia 1955: 33–34). Similarities exist between castes and classes in certain matters. Faced with class struggle from 1848 till 1890 (the period of 'transformism'), classes shut the door against the lower order and developed rigid and exclusive forms. After 1848, the moment of the spectre of Communism, the ruling classes were afraid of assimilating 'new elements', so argues Gramsci (Dainotto 2013: 84). Gramsci says that the concept of class alone cannot explain this history. Marxists need to use caste in relation to class in those periods of crisis of hegemony when the ruling classes shut the door against the subaltern's upward mobility (ibid.: 85). Lohia suggests that Europe experienced two such moments of appropriation of caste in the class system—the moment of fascism in Germany and the moment of Communism in Russia. Despite huge differences between them, despite their economic antagonism, both these currents are similarly motivated. In these formations, classes oscillate as a caste-like system.

Lohia argues that caste-like response of the class system in Europe is temporary or conjectural. It is essentially a strategy to counter 'the threat of internal disruption' of class struggle. Lohia continues:

> When this struggle amongst classes in Germany became unbearable and the German society was threatened with internal disruption, the national socialist movement essayed to fix up the different classes into castes with their proportionate and fixed incomes and well-defined status. It showed them that their various orders were so co-ordinated as to yield a meaning and purpose of life no matter that this purpose had no enduring or religious quality and was narrowly national. It was essentially a caste movement. (Lohia 2011a: 147)

So also in Russia, Communists tried to abolish classes by creating castes. The groups of toilers were fixed up in their status and incomes. It was not possible for them to struggle for changes. Similarly, untouchability was created in correction or concentration camps in Russia. They nearly constituted India's untouchable population; they were 10 per cent of the Russian population. They rendered cheap labour for economic reconstruction as in the case of India's Shudra and Dalit labour. Caste-like institutions emerged in Russia (ibid.: 149).

Lohia suggests that caste is essentially 'immobile' class. His formulation is akin to what Ambedkar called caste as an 'enclosed' class system. Lohia continues that when Western ruling classes developed enclosures against the initiatives of the subaltern strata for equality in the market, production, language, culture and politics, caste-like structures reappeared in all these spheres. Lohia recounts a form of enclosure (racial) in the marketplace in the United States. For example, like India's untouchable castes, the American black people lived in ghettos and could not visit hotels or 'all-white' cafeteria in Jackson in the Mississippi state in 1964. They were blocked at the entrance by the owner, ably assisted by the police, under 'the rules of privacy'. Merely having purchasing power is not enough in such situations. A culture of segregation on the basis of one's colour or birth exists everywhere.[9] Caste-like barriers are created by people in liberal democratic class societies, even though the people may believe in equality for everybody. In such situations, classes oscillate towards castes. So, a struggle against caste barriers is simultaneously a struggle against class inequalities. There is, however, a subtle difference. In class struggle, socialism is concerned with equality or distribution of resources, whereas socialism is concerned with justice or dignity of each human being in all anti-caste resistance (Lohia 1955: 37). But class struggle must oscillate towards caste struggle as classes veer towards caste system. Otherwise, Lohia argues, we may end up in socialism as it existed in the then Soviet Union, without any concern for justice. Thus, anti-caste movements concerned with justice issues are basically international by nature and are not just India-centred.

If we recall, there was a huge debate on this issue in India in 2001. The World Conference against Racism, Racial Discrimination, Xenophobia and Related Intolerance (WCAR) was being organised by the United Nations in Durban when the National Democratic Alliance (NDA) was in power in India. Both the national government and the *sarkari* (official) intellectuals did not want to internationalise the caste question, and refused to participate in the WCAR in 2001.[10] They claimed that caste is not same as race and tried to argue that caste is uniquely an Indian phenomenon and should, therefore, be delinked from the concerns of the international black people's movements.[11]

Even if the history of caste is not the same as that of race (a point made by Ambedkar against Tamil Dalit intellectuals), Lohia would have argued that the sarkari intellectuals tried to prevent India's anti-caste movements from learning of the concerns for justice raised by black people's movements.

If both these movements have similar concerns of justice—opposing forms of segregation on the grounds of human dignity—then such issues are international rather than national. They have ample scope to learn about moral, political, ideological doctrines of justice from each other. Lohia argues that caste question is concerned with justice, whereas the class question is concerned with equality. So a struggle for equality must be interlinked with a struggle for justice if democratic socialism must avoid the disastrous path of Soviet socialism under the Bolshevik party, which was singularly concerned with 'class'. Incidentally, Ambedkar raises a similar concern against Marxism, for the latter is singularly concerned with equality at the cost of ignoring liberty and justice. Movements for justice must be internationalised along with movements for equality. Internal oscillation must take place in between these two social movements and must provide feedback to each other.

Reconstructing Fables

It goes to the credit of Lohia's method of immediacy to have read internal caste contradiction in fables or myths. After discussing different aspects of 'history' or philosophy of caste, let us now pay attention to Lohia's engagement with fables of Brahminism/*jativaad* (casteism). Once again, his analytical protocols resemble those of Gramsci's analysis of religion, folklore and myths. It cannot be explored here as to how Gramsci examines internal contradiction in myths and religion. Of the many levels of contradiction in religion, two of the most important ones are: the religion of the people *versus* religion of the intellectual and Left-wing Catholic action *versus* Right-wing Catholic action.[12] Lohia identifies similar contradictions internal within the Brahminical order.

As stated earlier, immanent criticism à *la* Gramsci must pay attention to inheritances of a traditional subject for its critical evaluation. Lohia (2011a: 246–69) follows these protocols in his critical evaluation of the fables of Brahminism: the Vashishtha tradition *versus* Valmiki tradition. In my view, Lohia's argument is reminiscent of Gandhi's position in the Gandhi–Ambedkar debate in 1936. In this famous debate, Ambedkar (2014b: 354–55) lampooned all *smriti*s (remembered text of an author) and *shastra*s (rule manual), and also all saints, for reinforcing inequalities in Hinduism. But Gandhi disagreed with Ambedkar's negative thinking about Hinduism. According to him, there were a few progressive saints who spoke up against untouchability and preached equality in Hinduism. In the 1950s, however, Ambedkar revised his thinking. Of the 130-odd smritis, there were two (including Manusmriti) that recognised women's right to ancestral property, immovable and movable. Ambedkar criticised Hindu conservatives for burying these insights in their traditional mindsets. Similarly, Ambedkar argued that the Hindu Upanishads defended social equality, an argument present in his *Annihilation of Caste*, when he was in a debate with Gandhi. But in the debate, Ambedkar dismisses the internal tensions within Hinduism. However, he corrects his transcendental criticism of Hinduism by recognising internal tensions within Hinduism while piloting the Hindu Code Bill.[13] However, like Gandhi, Lohia firmly anchors himself with the immanent criticism of Brahminism/ Hinduism.

Lohia argues that there are two contradictory narratives in the caste system, reflected in the formation of Brahminism. All Brahmins are not pro-caste intellectuals. Look at the fables of Vashishtha and Viswamitra, both Brahmins. While Vashishtha was a pro-caste intellectual, Viswamitra represented the anti-caste spirit. The latter represented the Valmiki tradition of social fraternity across caste barriers. Lohia gives an interesting interpretation of the fable of Shambuka from a Shudra caste. Under an oath to Vashishtha, Ram punished Shambuka for violating the *dvija* (twice-born) monopoly of scriptures at the behest of Vashishtha. On the opposite side, Valmiki, the author of Ramayana, represents a liberal tradition in India. He was the founder and inmate of the heterodox hermitage or *ashram*. Everybody was allowed inside the hermitage irrespective of caste. Viswamitra, the author of the Gayatri Mantra, was highly revolutionary and initiated people irrespective of caste into the chanting of the Gayatri Mantra.

Lohia does not condone Ram's act, but calls him an example of the world's greatest limited personality, always introspective with regrets and obliging the *guru* (teacher) or *praja dharma* (citizen's duty/right). Lohia argues that this is 'one of the four bad acts of Ram, the world's greatest man in the sphere of the limited personality, the other three being, the banishment of Sita, the killing of Bali from a position of concealment, incitement to Lakshman to cut off the nose of Surpanakha, the sister of Ravan' (Lohia 2011a: 269).

On the positive side, the fable of Ram represents introspective reasoning associated with a limited personality. Despite drawbacks, the mythology of Ram epitomises the virtues of introspective reasoning. Lohia offers a complex interpretation of the bad acts of Ram. He discovers multiple narratives of bad and good values in each 'bad act'. While the banishment of Sita was a 'bad act', Ram was also following a praja dharma. Similarly, in the killing of Bali from a position of concealment, he was conducting a 'limited war' with Bali. He avoided open war, which might have killed thousands in Bali's army, saving innocent lives. Thus, there is an introspective reasoning associated with each 'bad' act of Ram, the silent surrender to a higher *dharma* (right/duty) or ideal. Saving innocent lives, obliging a guru tradition and following a praja dharma are Ram's most important ideals. The moral doctrines of even the 'bad acts' of Ram are significant for a modern civilisation to learn and adopt today. Lohia tries to show that Gandhi did adopt these features to some extent.

Extending his discussion of fables, Lohia (2012: 269–88) suggests that the mythologies of Krishna and Siva represent different human values. Krishna represents the spirit of a mass mobiliser, an exuberant personality. But Siva represents the spirit of universal patience or non-dimensional mind. Gandhi represents a synthesis of introspective reasoning, mass-mobilising capacity and universal patience. Lohia implies that mass leaders must represent these three virtues and, as far as possible, synthesise them in their personalities. Only then would it be possible to lead mass movements. Thus, Lohia draws significant lessons from mythologies for a contemporary social and political movement. These three values are properties of the sheel (character) of a mass leader. For Lohia, the character-building of the masses and of leaders is a very important historical task for socialist movements, which must aim at spiritual transformation as well, while transforming society materially. To do so, we must also look at fables or mythologies (not simply history) by following a method of immediacy.

Lohia (2011a: 270–74) was wary of anti-caste movements getting reduced to attacking the Brahmins who failed to notice that there are internal tensions within Brahminism. While praising the Dravidar Kazhagam leader Periyar E. V. Ramasamy for raising an anti-caste movement, he advised him to focus more on the criticism of Brahmin orthodoxies beginning from the Vashishtha tradition, rather than attack individual Brahmins. For him, the criticism of the evil act was more important than criticism of the evil doer. Personal violence of any kind—spiritual or physical—must be abjured from an egalitarian movement. Moreover, a social movement must transform the self rather than the other alone. No self-transformation is possible by criticising the evil doer. For, the evil doer would be seen as outsider of a social movement, and the insiders would gradually acquire a sacred mind like Vashishtha. This is a new orthodoxy which will block spiritual transformation of a social movement. A Vashishtha-like mind is harmful in a social movement that aims to destroy the caste system/Brahminism. The idea of a sacred mind (or Magi mind, as Lohia calls it) in any liberation movement must be resisted at any cost, for it ultimately destroys the critics of the caste order. The Communist mind becomes sacred and is above criticism, whereas the other is subject to rigorous criticism. The Communist Party becomes a Vashishtha or caste leader. So, Lohia concludes that the Vashishtha mindset is extremely harmful in anti-caste movements.

What Is To Be Done: Three Forms of Opposition?

Lohia argues that there are three kinds of opposition to caste order. First, there are those who believe in the wordy opposition to caste, like those put forward by Nehruvian liberals, the Communists and the Praja Socialist Party (PSP). Second, there are those who believe in partial opposition to caste led by the Shudras, like those engaged in the Dravidar Kazhagam politics in the South in the 1950s or Yadav politics of the North during our time. Third, there are those who believe in a wholesale opposition to the caste order. Lohia (2011a: 298) prefers the third alternative, as the first two involve groups that display hypocritical behaviours. True to his sheel, he prefers a broad-based opposition to caste involving Dalits, Shudras, Muslims and women, who are all victims of caste-based hypocritical politics. Here, he disagrees with Ambedkar's strategy of relying on Dalits only for the opposition. Let me elaborate this aspect now.

Wordy Opposition

First, Lohia argues, 'The wordy opposition to caste is the loudest in respect of such generalised condemnation of caste as it leaves the existing structure almost intact' (Lohia 1964: 95). Raise everybody economically, this thesis claims. It also argues that caste denies equality of opportunities. To solve this problem of denial, we must ensure equality of opportunity to everybody irrespective of caste. Communists, the PSP and Nehruvian Congress stand for this thesis. Any other social and political attempt to do away caste inequalities is condemned as 'casteist'. As a result, economic equality for Dalits and Shudras is seen as the most important agenda. But this thesis forgets that the policy of equal opportunity in the economic sphere has helped the upper-caste people entrenched in higher positions. Only the most talented one from among the Shudras and Dalits can be absorbed in the economic sector.

This economic strategy also leaves behind caste traditions in marriage and other aspects of life intact. By condemning anti-caste efforts of all other forces by non-economic means, it fails to see how its economic strategy does not help elevate the lower castes into the economically equal upper castes. It has fostered caste-based inequalities in the job sector. As a result, 90 per cent of the jobs are still cornered by the upper castes who account for 10 per cent of the population in India (Lohia 2011a: 317–18). To quote him, 'when more than 4/5th of nation's vital leadership is traditionally selected from among 1/5th of its population, a state of atrophy is bound to ensue' (Lohia 1964: 97).

Partial Elevation

Second, the wordy war on caste is evenly matched by the second empty struggle against caste, led by select Shudra groups. Among Shudras, certain castes are numerically powerful. The age of adult franchise has placed power in their hands. The Reddys, Mudaliars, Marathas, Yadavas or Ahirs, along with Brahmins and Kshatriyas, comprise nearly 25 per cent of the population (Lohia 2011a: 296). This still leaves three-quarters of the population out. There are three problems in sectional elevation. First, it brings about some changes within the caste system, but leaves the basis of the castes unaltered. Second, still worse, sectional elevation is dangerous because those among the lower castes who rise to high positions tend to assimilate themselves into the existing higher-castes. In the process, they appropriate the baser qualities of the high castes. Third, it generates bitter caste jealousies and intrigues. Caste divisions do not vanish at all. Caste distinctions reappear. Women are segregated and sacred threads reappear among the non-dvijas (Lohia 1964: 101).

Holistic Elevation or Elevation of All

Finally, a true struggle against caste is concerned with an elevation of all rather than one or the other section of the lower castes. This struggle aims to pitchfork the five downgraded groups—women, Shudras, Dalits, backward-caste Muslims and Adivasis—into positions of leadership, irrespective of their merit as it stands today. A doctrine of preferential opportunity in employment must be followed along with a social and political programme against the caste system. Eighty per cent of jobs in the leadership of political parties, national economy and government service should be reserved for three-fourths of our population. However, Lohia thinks that there should be a distinction between equal opportunity in education and preferential opportunity in employment. No child must be preferred or prevented by a policy while pursuing education. Discrimination should be exercised only in the case of government jobs. Educated dvijas should try their luck in other fields. To end caste, social measures like mixed dinners and inter-caste marriages, and economic measures like 'land to the tiller' from among the lower castes must be encouraged. Women's issues involving the need to fetch drinking water from distant areas or lack of lavatories for women in rural areas must be resolved, apart from the distribution of property to further women's rights. Discussions, plays and fairs should be organised (Lohia 1964: 136–37). Even, in government jobs, there should be reservations for those who marry outside their caste. This is a sure way of breaking caste barriers. The socialists must make all efforts towards the destruction of the caste order among Hindus and non-Hindus.

In retrospect, we must distinguish Lohia's critique from those of the followers of Lohia who surrendered his manifold criticism of caste into the sectional politics of the Shudras in North India through the Samajwadi Party of Mulayam Singh Yadav and the Rashtriya Janata Dal of Laloo Prasad Yadav. Lohia's attempts at characterising such partial elevation of Shudras in South India should not be forgotten. He criticises the Shudra politics in the South for being concerned with 'partial elevation' of Shudras, for alienating itself from Dalits, women, backward Muslims and Adivasis, and for not showing interest in carrying out the agenda of destruction of the caste system. While Lohia's critique of caste must be distinguished from that of his followers in the electoral field today, his alternative model merely relies on State action for equality and justice.

There are two major difficulties in accepting Lohia's model of socialism. First, there could be an anomaly in his claim that equal opportunity in education must be followed, while preferential treatment in employment is to be adopted. As Ambedkar argues, caste has denied education to many social groups—women, Shudras, Dalits and Adivasis. If there is no preferential policy protecting education for these groups, it would not be possible to spread education among common people. So, the preferential treatment in education, in view of the long history of caste denying education to many social groups, can lay a strong anti-caste foundation. Thus, Lohia's argument for preferential treatment in employment rather than education is without an anti-caste foundation.

Second, he believes in putting pressure on the State for egalitarian policies through the civil liberties movements. So his model of socialism could be called State socialism. His *chau khamba* (four pillar) model of State—Centre, state, district and village—ultimately becomes one-sided in its emphasis on development. In my view, his model of development begins with the village administration from below, which is synonymous with the village panchayat with specific resources. As Jayaprakash Narayan suggests, even the village panchayat must evolve from the primary communities below it (Prasad 1980: 181–242). Lohia's model tends to neglect the role of the primary communities in resource mobilisation that may also weaken 'occupational' communities (read caste) and help in the emergence of 'territorial' communities at the village level and beyond. In his model of development, the decentralised democratic State is still the motor of social change. Indeed, this is a theme of Narayan's critique of State-centered socialism through his concept of Lokniti, which socialists may have to pay attention to, in order to explore if their contributions may complement each other in the withering away of the caste order in a new India.[14]

Notes

[1] See Ambedkar (2002).
[2] Ambedkar would have possibly agreed with Lohia that he is not anti- or pro-Gandhi. See Lohia (1978: 364).
[3] See the essays, 'Annihilation of Caste' and 'Reply to the Mahatma' in Ambedkar (2002: 263–320).
[4] Blomkvist (2001) has recently applied the concept of 'social capital' to examine caste relations in India.
[5] For Ambedkar's views, see Constitutional Assembly debates, Volumes 10–12, 25 November 1949, 980.
[6] See Wofford, Jr's (2002: *v*) essay, 'About Lohia'.
[7] For a genealogical account of the Hindu pantheon, see Kosambi (1990: 169–71).
[8] Thus, it is possible for all non-Hindus (including atheists) to believe in caste, just as it is possible for a reformist Hindu to reject caste order. For a long time, till 1935, Ambedkar (2014a: 317) thought that as a Hindu it should be possible for him to rejuvenate Hinduism by abolishing the caste order internally. That is the reason why he participated in temple-entry movements before 1935. Gandhi probably did not understand caste order in detail, and yet did not believe in casteism.
[9] Lohia (2011a: 584–85) further clarifies to claim: 'I make it perfectly clear. I am not trying something foul in American life ... Such foul spots exist everywhere—also in India.'
[10] For an elaborated statement on this controversy, see Pinto (2001).
[11] For an orthodox position delinking anti-caste concerns from anti-racial concerns, see Béteille (2001).
[12] For an elaboration of this classification of religion as proposed here, see Fulton (1987).
[13] In fact, Ambedkar's analysis of mythologies in his paper, 'The Riddle of Ram and Krishna', is an exemplar of transcendental criticism of Hinduism. But the text (posthumously published in 1987) was written prior to 1948. By 1950, however, in his dialogue with Hindu women, he shifted his focus from a transcendental to immanent criticism of Hinduism. I have explored Ambedkar's subtle methodological shift in my paper on Ambedkar's theory of democracy (Patnaik 2018). But it is necessary to explore its significance in terms of an epistemology.
[14] I would like to propose an eclectic approach to socialism, rather than choose the side of the State socialism of Lohia/Ambedkar or communitarian socialism of Narayan and others. An alternative construction, however, may need to be worked out.

References

Ambedkar, B. R. 2002, 'An Anti-untouchability Agenda'. In *The Essential Writings of B. R. Ambedkar*, ed. V. Rodrigues, 359–68. New Delhi: Oxford University Press.

——— 2014a. *Annihilation of Caste*, ed. S. Anand. New Delhi: Navayana.

——— 2014b. 'Philosophy of Hinduism'. In *Writings and Speeches*, Volume 3, 3–92. New Delhi: Dr Ambedkar Foundation.

——— 2014c. 'The Riddle of Rama and Krishna'. In *Writings and Speeches*, Volume 4, Appendix 1, 323–43. New Delhi: Dr Ambedkar Foundation.

Béteille, A. 2001. 'Race and Caste'. *The Hindu*, 10 March.

Blomkvist, H. 2001. 'Traditional Communities, Caste and Democracy: The Indian Mystery'. In *Social Capital and Participation in Everyday Life*, eds. Paul Dekker and Eric M. Uslaner, 73–88. London: Routledge.

Dainotto, R. 2013. 'Notes on Q6§32: Gramsci and the Dalits'. In *The Political Philosophies of Antonio Gramsci and B. R. Ambedkar*, ed. Cosimo Zene, 75–86. Oxon and New York: Routledge.

Fulton, J. 1987. 'Religion and Politics in Gramsci: An Introduction'. *Sociological Analysis* 48(3): 197–216.

Gramsci, A. 1971. *Selections from the Prison Notebooks*, ed. and trans. Q. Hoare and G. N. Smith. New York: International Publishers.

Hedge, S. 2011. 'Thinking with and against Lohia: Beyond Discursive Commentary'. *Economic and Political Weekly* 46(36): 66–72.

Kosambi, D. D. 1975. *An Introduction to the Study of Indian History*. Bombay: Popular Prakashan.

——— 1990. *The Culture and Civilisation of Ancient India in Historical Outline*. Delhi: Vikas Publishing House.

Kumar, A. 2010. 'Understanding Lohia's Political Sociology: Intersectionality of Caste, Class, Gender and Language'. *Economic and Political Weekly* 45(40): 64–70.

Lohia, R. M. (n.d.). *Fragments of a World Mind*. Calcutta: Maitrayani.

——— 1955. *Wheel of History*. Delhi: B. R. Publishing.

——— 1964. *The Caste System*. Hyderabad: Rammanohar Lohia Samata Vidyalaya Nyasa.

——— 1978. *Marx, Gandhi and Socialism*. Hyderabad: Rammanohar Lohia Samata Vidyalaya Nyasa.

——— 2011a. *Collected Works of Dr Rammanohar Lohia*, Volume 2, ed. Mastram Kapoor. New Delhi: Anamika.

——— 2011b. *Collected Works of Dr Rammanohar Lohia*, Volume 5, ed. Mastram Kapoor. New Delhi: Anamika.

——— 2011c. 'Hypocrisies and Double'. In *Collected Works of Dr Rammanohar Lohia*, Volume 6, ed. Mastram Kapoor, 15–29. New Delhi: Anamika.

——— 2012. 'The Three Great Myths'. In *Salient Ideas*, eds B. K. Bhattacharya and Mastram Kapoor, 269–88. New Delhi: Anamika.

Patnaik, A. K. 2018. 'Ambedkar on Indian Democracy'. In *Reasoning Indian Politics: Philosopher Politicians to Politicians Seeking Philosophy*, eds. Narendra Pani and Anshuman Behera, 132–54. London: Routledge.

Pinto, A. 2001. 'UN Conference against Racism: Is Caste Race?'. *Economic and Political Weekly* 36(30): 2817–20.

Prasad, Bimal (ed.). 1980. *A Revolutionary's Quest: Selected Writings of Jayaprakash Narayan*. Delhi: Oxford University Press.

Rodrigues, V. (ed.). 2002. *The Essentials Writings of B. R. Ambedkar*. New Delhi: Oxford University Press.

Seth, D. L. 2002. 'Ram Manohar Lohia on Caste in Indian Politics'. In *Caste and Democratic Politics in India*, ed. Ghanasyam Shah, 108–33. Delhi: Permanent Black.

Wofford, Jr, H. 2002. *Lohia and America Meet: 1951 and 1964*. Delhi: B. R. Publishing.

Yadav, Y. 2010. 'What is Living and What is Dead in Rammanohar Lohia?'. *Economic and Political Weekly* 45(40): 92–107.

Part II

Critical Social History

3. Divinity, Denial and the Embodied Self

Changing Perspectives on Untouchability and the Case of the Hagiographies of Dalit Bhaktas[*]

Sundar Kaali

This chapter is an attempt to challenge Sundar Sarukkai's phenomenological approach to understanding untouchability.[1] Contesting Sarukkai's view of the human skin as a boundary that cannot be crossed, this chapter argues that boundaries are both impermeable and permeable, and that they are, above all, limits but not impenetrable barriers. Taking the case of Dalit *bhaktas*, and considering the phenomenon of untouchability in their lives in the Saiva and Vaishnava hagiographies, the chapter examines how the embodied self of the Dalit bhaktas, who are boundary-transgressors *par excellence*, is marked by both divinity and its denial by the Brahminical elite. While the divinisation of the Dalit body is ultimately affirmed in the Brahminical hagiographic discourse, it is also a case where touch is a contested phenomenon and the

*I am grateful to To. Paramasivan and Ma. Pe. Srinivasan for sharing with me their profound knowledge of the Sri Vaishnava texts discussed in this chapter; to N. Muthumohan, Samuel Sudanandha, Su. Venkataraman, S. Ramanujam, Rengaiah Murugan, Cittanai, R. Thirunavukkarasu, V. Selvakumar, S. Kannan, Madurai Babu, Tirumalai Kannan, G. Manikandan, Mohamed Safi, Stalin Rajangam, K. Karthika, P. Raja and Parimalam Sundar for help in other ways. Earlier versions of this chapter were presented at the seminar on 'Elusive Equality: Mapping Social Hegemony in India', organised by the Department of Sociology, University of Hyderabad, 19–20 February 2016; a meeting of the Madurai Research Circle, Madurai; and as the M. S. S. Pandian Memorial Lecture, organised by Tamil Conscience, Jawaharlal Nehru University, 10 November 2016. I thank the participants for their helpful comments.

ascription of sacrality to the Dalit bhaktas' embodied self is a product of protracted negotiation.

Let me begin by summarising Sarukkai's main arguments. For Sarukkai, the moment of touch that establishes a contact with objects does not erase the distance between the subject and the object. He contends: 'This ever-present intervening body constitutes an *untouchable* element in touch, a skin or membrane that separates the skin from things' (Sarukkai 2014: 163). In other words, there exists a 'minute layer' that separates even in the 'moment of touch' (ibid.). This space between the objects of touch, he argues, is 'ever-present' and 'ineradicable' (ibid.: 164). It is 'this ever-present medium that is *untouchable* in the act of touch. Thus, the idea of untouchability is always present, always contiguous to the act of touch' (ibid.).

In this context, Sarukkai puts forth the differences between touch and contact. While contact is a quality that is present in the toucher and the touched, which is a symmetrical relation, the inherent asymmetry of touch is predicated on the fact that the person who touches is not touched by the object (ibid.: 165). For Sarukkai, contact is a quality that belongs to both material and soul substances, whereas touch belongs only to material substances (ibid.: 166). Touch, as a 'limited form of contact', is discernable by the 'tactile organ' alone, whereas contact is 'perceived ... by other organs also' (ibid.). The quality of touch is present in an 'individual substance', while contact 'needs at least two substances' (ibid.). Extending this argument, he observes that touch is a quality that inheres in the object, and argues that the untouchable person betrays a 'sense of *untouch*', irrespective of whether they come in 'contact' with another person (ibid.: 166–67).

According to Sarukkai, the skin is the organ that 'makes possible the differentiation of the interior and the exterior' of the body. 'How we relate to the world is mediated by the gateway of the skin. The skin is literally a boundary ... The practice of untouchability has to do with a boundary that cannot be crossed' (ibid.: 170). The untouchable's skin, he argues, is imbued with the moral quality of a boundary that cannot be traversed. Once untouchability is inscribed on an individual, it is impossible to cross the wall of untouchability (ibid.). However, for Sarukkai, the proscription of touch and the narrative of untouchability are not really about purity and impurity as much as they are about the metaphysics of the body (ibid.: 171). Therefore, touch is not merely a physical sense but a *moral sense* as well (ibid.:

173). 'Those who are morally impure also embody this impurity in their natural body' (ibid.).

Sarukkai then observes that there is a difference between touch and *non-touch*. 'There are different kinds of touch ... but there is only one sense of *not-touching*' (ibid.: 181). The untouchables in the Indian context are objects of the sense of *non-touch* or *un-touch* (ibid.: 182). The creation of the class of untouchables is a creation not of a set of people with some characteristics, but a set of objects of the sense of non-touch (ibid.). According to him, 'It is not that the untouchables cannot be touched but that they ought not to be touched' (ibid.: 185). Differentiating between *not-touchable* and *touch-unable*, Sarukkai says that in the former the object of touch is itself 'inaccessible to the sense of touch', while in the latter, 'the subject is unable to fulfill the act of touching' (ibid.: 186). '[T]he case of the untouchable points to the inability of the toucher rather than any inability of the touched person' (ibid.).

Sarukkai, therefore, contends that the real site of untouchability is the person who refuses to touch the untouchable—that is, the untouchable is *touch-un-able*. 'The impact of not touching is present on both the Brahmin and the Dalit—neither of them can fulfill the act of touching' (ibid.). Therefore, the act of untouchability is symmetrical—the person who does not touch is also not touched. The person who does not like to touch is closing his/her skin. The result is the partial death or decay of the subject. The person is denying himself/herself a part of his/her ability, the capacity to engage with his/her own sense (ibid.: 187). For this person, every act of touching becomes reflective, 'imbued with this sense of doubt' (ibid.). For Sarukkai, one can never practise untouchability only with respect to a defined other, for in so doing one always and necessarily practises untouchability with respect to oneself. '*[I]n the most essential sense, untouchability is actually about the always-present, potential untouchability not of another but of oneself*' (ibid.: 189).

In this connection, Sarukkai points to the class of Brahmins who are permanent untouchables, namely the Acharyas. The Acharyas 'gain their status of absolute untouchability through birth' (ibid.: 192). The untouchability of the Acharyas is hereditary, permanent and part of tradition. '[I]t is not about purity and impurity, but about a *state of being*' (ibid.: 193). In fact, the case of Acharyas suggests that 'to be a Brahmin is to be an untouchable' (ibid.). '[T]he most dominant marker of being a Brahmin ... *lies in the potential of an individual to become an untouchable* ... A Brahmin is one who not only has access to temporal and potential untouchability but also to permanent, hereditary untouchability' (ibid.: 194–95).

Sarukkai then invokes the Derridian notion of supplementation to argue that

> the necessity to construct a group called untouchables arises in large part due to the inherent presence of the notion of untouchablity in the very idea of a Brahmin ... The creation of a supplementary community of untouchables is a necessary consequence of the inability of Brahmins to attain the pure state of untouchable. (Ibid.: 197)

The untouchability inherent in the Brahmins is, therefore, '*outsourced*' to the Dalits, 'who, then, carry that burden' (ibid.: 198–99).

This rather lengthy summary of Sarukkai's arguments should give us a clear picture of the kind of theoretical exercise that he is engaging in. It is an ahistorical and essentialist approach to understanding the phenomenon of untouchability. Significantly, Sarukkai assumes the primacy of Brahmin dominance in the Indian context. That the present-day untouchable communities once enjoyed a high social status and sometimes even ritual supremacy before the ascription of untouchability to them is a point he completely misses out.[2] The emergence of untouchability was a protracted process in which the ritual-social supremacy of the Dalits was gradually devalorised in proportion to the cultural and social capital that accrued to the Brahmins. This chapter will take a different route to understanding untouchability by historicising it.[3]

Sarukkai's main arguments are embedded in a secular discourse, which talks about touch in relation to a profane body. In dismissing the Dumontian purity–pollution opposition in explicating untouchability, he elides the realm of the sacred, which is highly significant when talking about the Dalit bhaktas. In other words, one has to consider the bhaktas' body as a site of divinity, one that belongs to the domain of the sacred. I will, therefore, take up the case of Dalit saints in the Saiva and Vaishnava hagiographies and explore how the embodied self of the Dalit saint is marked by both divinity and its denial. I will show how the Dalit saints are boundary-transgressors *par excellence* and how a politics of *counter-untouchability* is noticeable in their lives.[4] In doing so, I move from principles to practices, practices that evidence a counter-politics of the subalterns within the bounds of elite hegemonies.

According to Sarukkai, the skin is literally a boundary. However, rather than conceiving of limits as impenetrable barriers and, thus, unknowingly subscribing to the views of hegemonic forces that attempt to define them in that fashion, we have to identify the conflicting programmes of setting up and transgressing limits that intersect in any spatiality. In order to do this, we have to consider the potentially porous and permeable character of all boundaries and the attempt of hegemonic forces to preclude the possibility of such porosity and permeability. In fact, the boundaries between the self and the other are always fuzzy. The self is bounded no doubt, but such a boundedness is, nevertheless, uncertain. It is always possible to puncture and make porous the boundaries of the self. As Bachelard (1969: 222) puts it, 'on the surface of being, in that region where being *wants* to be both visible and hidden, the movements of opening and closing are so numerous' and, therefore, 'man is half-open being'. The boundary that divides the self from the other is flexible, constantly developing and invariably shifting.

This leads us to consider the skin, which, according to Sarukkai, is a boundary that cannot be crossed, as a skin-self, or, what Didier Anzieu calls the *skin-ego*. According to Anzieu, 'the body ego is always already a skin ego' (Lafrance 2013: 22). He posits that the skin has three functions—as a sac that retains nourishment, as a barrier that prevents external penetration and as a means of communication with others, an 'inscribing surface' for the marks that they leave (Anzieu 1989: 40).

For Anzieu, therefore, '[t]o acquire a skin-ego is to acquire both a physical and a mental skin of one's own' (Lafrance 2013: 25). The skin-ego is 'both a mental image of the body projected onto the body—of the image of skin onto skin—and, a representation of mental apparatus—a projection of the mind onto skin, onto the body' (Pile 2009: 144). In other words, 'it is a topographic of the self that is simultaneously body and mind' (ibid.: 143).

This psychic skin 'allows the mind to envelope objects beyond itself or, indeed, to withdraw within itself, and abandon the body as being outside itself' (ibid.: 145). As Handcock (2012: 7) puts it, 'objects beyond the bodily boundary can become incorporated into the body-image simply through prolonged placement in the space surrounding the body'. The interaction of the self and the world occurs on the skin boundary, and the self is able 'to incorporate and extend beyond the skin surface' (ibid.: 8). However, in the context of untouchability, the skin-ego retreats into itself and tends to exclude the other. The skin-ego is here a *group ego-skin*.[5] As Anzieu (1999: 320) puts it, 'the group tears away individual psychic skins and sews them on to a *narcissistic group envelope*'. Further, 'the group illusion signifies the joyful belief that the group has a common skin that abolishes differences between its members' (ibid.: 323). This small group then withdraws itself in the face of the large group, that is, the wider society (see ibid.).

The assumption of a *common body* by the Brahminical collective self is, therefore, coterminous with its withdrawal from the 'collective ancestral body of the people' (Bakhtin 1984: 19). The Brahminical skin-ego manages to accomplish this through a strategy of distanciation, which manifests itself as taboos on touching and being touched. What results is a certain thickening and hardening of the ego-skin, something that causes it to become rigid and resistant to change. Ironically, such a solidification of the Brahminical ego-skin does not make it numb or insensitive; it rather turns it hyper-sensitive, something that is constantly vigilant about the potential danger of the pollution caused by the touch of the other. Untouchability is, then, a function of this excessive guarding of the boundaries of the group-self. The cutaneous self, which is fundamentally a group psychic envelope in this case, is rendered essentially pure and kept out of the touch of the impure other.

It is exactly this over-shielding of the boundaries marked by the Brahminical group-skin that the Dalit bhaktas attempt to challenge. By infiltrating the cracks and crevices in the armour of the Brahminical group-skin, the Dalit bhakta lays a claim to the realm of hegemonic elite spatialites (see Anzieu 1999: 322–23). In this attempt, he actually lays a claim to the 'collective ancestral body' of the entire community from which he has been excluded by strategies of distanciation and not-touching. As a result, in some cases, the Brahminical group skin-ego is itself made porous and permeable. As opposed to a logic of solidifying and enclosing, what we see here is a transgressive politics of fluidising and opening up (see Bachelard 1969: 211–31).

Let me now take up the actual cases. I will begin by narrating the story of Nantanar,[6] one of the 63 Tamil Saiva saints known as the Nayanars. Nantanar was born into a community of untouchables known as Pulaiyar/Paraiyar in the village of Atanur. Besides agriculture, he specialised in providing the hides and strings used for musical instruments and *gorocana*, a bezoar taken from the stomach of cows, to be used in worship in Saiva temples. He became an ardent devotee of Lord Siva but could not enter the Agamic temples. For a very long time, he worshipped the Lord from outside the temple premises. Once, he visited Tiruppunkur near his native village, where a famous Siva temple was located. Quite miraculously, here, Lord Siva ordered the Nandi in front of his temple to move aside, thus enabling his devotee to have a clear *darshan* (vision) from outside. Subsequently, he visited many Siva temples in the vicinity and worshipped the Lord by singing and dancing his praise. However, his long-term yearning was to visit Chidambaram, the heart of Saiva faith, and worship Lord Siva there. His low birth prevented him from embarking on this pilgrimage and he kept postponing it. Eventually, one day, he did overcome his hesitation and resolved to go to Chidambaram. However, on reaching the place, he had to wait outside the city for days together before the Lord appeared in the dream of the Brahmin priests of the temple and ordered them to raise a fire on the outskirts of the city that would 'purify' the untouchable saint before he actually entered it.

This famous story from the Tamil Saiva hagiographic epic *Periya Puranam* is a telling example of how a Dalit bhakta is denied entry into the domain of the sacred. Even when the narrative points to a divine intervention to salvage the Dalit bhakta's supreme *bhakti* (devotion), it is ultimately the Brahminical order that prevails. In fact, the Dalit bhakta is punished for his transgressive move and violation of the Brahminical order. The purifying substance that ultimately transforms the bhakta and enables his transportation into the temple is fire and not water, something which Sarukkai thinks has an organic relation with untouchability.

Perran Campan, another Dalit bhakta mentioned in the Saiva hagiographies[7] who also abhorred his birth as an untouchable, like Nantanar, left his native place and reached Chidambaram. There, he regularly provided firewood to the kitchen in the temple of Lord Siva. He would circumambulate the streets around the temple and remain at a safe distance and worship the Lord. One day, Lord Siva appeared as a Brahmin and entreated him to supply firewood to the monastery of Umapati Sivacharya, the well-known fourteenth-century exponent of Saiva Siddhanta at Korravankuti. Perran complied with his wish and started providing firewood to the monastery also. Once, there was a heavy downpour and the whole place was flooded. Unable to find firewood, Perran was distressed. Upon this, his wife suggested that he dismantle a part of his hut and take the bamboo poles therein as firewood to the monastery and temple. Perran readily agreed, but the flood caused by the heavy rain forbade his attempt to reach his destination. Lord Siva now assumed the form of an ascetic and appeared in front of him and asked him why he was late in providing firewood to the temple and the monastery. When Perran explained the circumstances, the ascetic taught him the means by which he could cross the flooded river. He also gave Perran a letter of recommendation addressed to Umapati Sivam, asking him to give *diksha* (initiation) and *mukti* (release) to Perran.

Perran uttered the words of the ascetic and thereupon the floods gave way for him to cross over. When he reached the monastery, Umapati Sivam asked him the reason for his delay. Upon this, Perran presented him the divine letter. Umapati accepted the Lord's entreaty and thereupon performed the diksha. Because he, as a Brahmin, could not touch the untouchable bhakta, he gave him a *nayanadiksha*, a diksha through the gaze. Thereupon, the initiand Perran was burnt to ashes and it is said that he attained mukti instantly.[8] However, Perran's wife, who refused to believe the story of diksha and mukti, complained to the king. When the king asked Umapati for an explanation, he retorted by performing the same diksha again by directing a graceful look at a *mulli* plant[9] that was in the vicinity. The plant was reduced to ashes for everyone to see. The king, Perran's wife and his relatives were all pacified and accepted the greatness of Umapati.[10]

Here again, as in the case of Nantanar, we see a Dalit bhakta being punished for his boundary transgression. Even when a divine intervention in the form of a letter from Lord Siva himself entreats the Brahmin Acharya to give diksha to the Dalit bhakta, the response of the guru is violent, as in the case of Nantanar. In both cases, the Dalit bhaktas are denied the status of saints while still alive. In other words, there is a denial of the divinity of the Dalit bhakta's embodied self. However, the point that untouchability is a contested phenomenon is observable in both cases where there is an eventual ascription of sacrality to the Dalit saint's embodied self.

An interesting parallel to the story of Nantanar is that of Cakkili Svamikal in the Vaishnava hagiographies. A bhakta born into a caste of cobblers, Cakkili Svamikal's untouchable status prevented him from climbing up the Tiruppati hills to have a darshan of Vishnu. Cakkili Svamikal wanted to make slippers to be given to Lord Vishnu at Tiruppati as a votive offering. But he did not know the exact size of the Lord's feet and was distressed. At that, a figure appeared in his dream and entreated him to make slippers of his size which would, in turn, fit the Lord's. Cakkili Svamikal woke up from his dream and made the slippers in the way the dream-figure showed. He then wanted to present them to the Lord and went up to Tiruppati. But he could not climb up the hills to reach the temple as he was an untouchable. Cakkili Svamikal prayed to the Lord to come down and take the slippers. A day passed but the Lord did not listen to his prayers. A highly disturbed Cakkili decided kill himself if the Lord did not oblige him. Then the Lord came down and wore the slippers, went around the hills, and left them in their place the next day. The devotee was filled with joy and continued to make ever-new, ornamental slippers every day. The Lord, on his part, wore them once and left them at their place the following day.

During this time, Lord Vishnu once appeared as a customer before Cakkili asking for slippers and then showed his supernatural, epiphanic form. Cakkili now started making slippers for this epiphanic form. The problem, however, was that the form started growing in his mind every day. Now, Cakkili was caught up in a double crisis: of not finding the money and material to make the extra-large slippers and the pressing need to make them. Eventually, he decided to kill himself. At this, Lord Vishnu appeared before his devotee and showed his life-size form. An overjoyed Cakkili was at last capable of making the slippers that would fit both his Lord and his own means. Later in the story, Cakkili Svamikal merged with the Lord, even now at the foothills, unable to enter the Lord's temple (Arangapprakasa Svamikal 1936: 42–51).

Also interesting is the case of Tiruppanalvar, a bhakta born into a community of untouchables known as Panars, and included in the class of Alvars, the Tamil Vaishnava saint-poets. Panalvar became an ardent devotee of Vishnu and used to sing devotional hymns in praise of the Lord though he could not enter the temple at Srirangam. In fact, hesitant to tread the sacred land of the Lord, he remained well outside the city of Srirangam, on the other side of the river Kaveri. One day, when he was thus singing the Lord's praise, playing on the *veena* in his arms,[11] Lokasaranga Mahamuni, the Brahmin priest of the temple who was on his way to fetch holy water to be used in the Lord's worship, saw him midway and ordered him to move aside. When the Alvar, who was engrossed in ecstatic devotion, failed to notice this, the priest hurled a stone at him. The stone hit the Alvar's face and he started bleeding. Upon this, he realised his mistake and moved aside. However, Lord Vishnu, who was terribly disturbed by the priest's act, appeared in the priest's dream that night and ordered him to bring Panalvar into his temple premises. The priest obliged, approached the low-caste saint, and invited him to the temple. The saint was hesitant to tread the sacred land of the Lord and the priest eventually carried him on his shoulders. While the Vaishnava hagiography *Guruparampara Prabhavam* (1994) by Pinpalakiya Perumal Jiyar notes that he went inside the temple and was united with Lord Vishnu,[12] another hagiographic work titled *Pulavar Puranam* (1931), authored by Vannaccarapam Dandapani Svamikal, extends the story to give it an interesting twist. When Panalvar entered the *garbhagraha* (the innermost chamber with the image of the deity inside), Lord Vishnu engulfed him. While most of Panalvar's body went inside his mouth, a couple of toes were protruding from the Lord's mouth. This was a cause for resentment among the devotees for a very long time. Years went by before the great Vaishnava Acharya Nathamunikal[13] visited the temple and witnessed this scene. The Acharya, obviously distressed, prayed to the Lord and asked for a redressal. And then the Lord swallowed Panalvar's body in its entirety.[14]

The story of Nampatuvan, an outcaste bhakta, mentioned in the Vaishnava hagiographies, is also worth discussing here. Nampatuvan was born into a community of Panars like Panalvar at Tirukkurunkuti, one of the 108 *divyadesas*, sacred centres of Lord Vishnu venerated by Sri Vaishnavas. He was living in a settlement on the outskirts of the village. Every day, Nampatuvan would visit the temple of the Lord late in the night, stand at a distance appropriate to his caste status, and worship him by singing devotional hymns while playing on the veena, and leave before anyone could notice him. One *ekadasi* day, when he was thus venturing out on his nightly visitation, he was intercepted by a *brahmarakshasa*, a Brahmin goblin who had become so due to the incorrect performance of a *yagna*. The goblin was terribly hungry and attempted to consume Nampatuvan. He was only too happy to oblige, but pleaded for some time in order to complete the austerities that were due on that ekadasi day. The *rakshasa* did not budge, saying that the bhakta's words were a mere excuse to escape. Upon this, Nampatuvan made a sincere promise to return.[15] Nampatuvan then reached temple, sang the praise of the Lord to his heart's fill, and then returned to the rakshasa and asked him to consume him. The rakshasa, now knowing the greatness of the bhakta, asked him to part with the strength of his devotional singing to him. When Nampatuvan was hesitant to accept this, the rakshasa fell at his feet and pleaded that he should at least provide the power of one of the songs that he sang that night. On this, Nampatuvan granted him the power of a song set to the *Kaisika Raga*. Receiving the grant, the rakshasa was relieved of his sin and assumed his original state of a Brahmin [*Varaha Puranattin Ullitana Kaisika Puranam* (1987)].

In all the cases mentioned thus far, there is a sense in which the untouchable saint persists in his bhakti against all odds, which ultimately ends up as a boundary transgression. While in the case of Nantanar and Perran Campan, divine intervention enables the untouchable saints to cross the boundary and thus violate the Brahminical order, the final moment of entering sainthood is also a moment of punishment. However, in the case of Panalvar and Cakkili Svamikal, the difficulty of assimilating the Dalit bhakta is couched in quite different terms. The Lord's inability to swallow Panalvar's body in its entirety signifies a much more protracted struggle within a religious faith which, on the one hand, tries to exclude the untouchable and, on the other, co-opt and incorporate him. Note how the Alvar's feet, which he himself considers dirty and polluting, become coded with subversive meanings. When the priest invites him into the temple, he hesitates but eventually ends up riding on his shoulders. And again it is these feet which present a problem to the Lord in his attempt to swallow the devotee. Here, the devotee's feet mark an excess, a part of the subaltern's corporal self that is well beyond wholesome containment.

Such excess is also found in Namputuvan's case, where the brahmarakshasa's attempt to engulf the bhakta is arrested by the latter's mature, overflowing bhakti. It is a bhakti that the Brahmin-goblin lacks, and is saved only by the untouchable saint's grant of a small portion of his own bhakti.[16] The overflowing, excessive bhakti of the untouchable is uncontainable here and his corporeality escapes annihilation in the hands of the Brahmin rakshasa. There is a sense here that the Brahmin is incapable of true bhakti, which is profusely present in the untouchable's self. In fact, Tontaratippoti Alvar, one of the twelve Alvars and himself a Brahmin by birth, succinctly states in a poem that as a Brahmin he is incapable of becoming a true bhakta, and, therefore, relinquishes his Brahminhood[17] (Tontaratippoti Alvar 1982: 290).

In Cakkili Svamikal's case, the Dalit saint's co-option is presented in the trope of fitting and not-fitting. Like Panalvar, Cakkili Svamikal is a bhakta who instantiates a problematic of containment. The bhakta attempts to contain the Lord on the one hand, but the Lord, on the other, tries to tame him. In this contest, the bhakta is ultimately left out as an *untouchable-as-misfit* even after entering sainthood.

Let me now turn to the unseeable in the case of Dalit bhaktas. In Sarukkai's view, although there is an unseeable in untouchability, the force of untouchability lies specifically in the act of touch. Though he notes that seeing is similar to touching, following Merleau-Ponty, he attributes primacy to touch (Sarukkai 2014). However, Dalits were not only considered unseeable, kept out of the sight of Brahmins, but, more particularly, were prevented from having a darshan of divine images. Dalit settlements, known as the *Paraicceri*s and *tintacceri*s, were located on the outskirts of villages.[18] As we saw earlier, Dalit saints like Nantanar, Cakkili Svamikal, Nampatuvan and Tirupanalvar were prevented from entering the temple premises. This is an instance of the forbidden look, something more than the forbidden touch. In Perran's case, the virulent gaze of the Acharya, termed nayanadiksha, substitutes for his touch and ends up punishing the Dalit saint.

We have to understand the dynamics of the visual economy involved in seeing the divine in this context (Kaali 1999). As Eck (1985) points out,

> since, in the Hindu understanding, the deity is present in the image, the visual apprehension of the image is charged with religious meaning. Beholding the image is an act of worship, and through the eyes one gains the blessings of the divine ... The

> prominence of the eyes of Hindu divine images also reminds us that it is not only the worshipper who sees the deity, but the deity sees the worshipper as well. The contact between devotee and deity is exchanged through the eyes. (Ibid.: 3–7)

As Babb (1981: 391) suggests, the mingling of the visions of the deity and the worshipper is aimed at a 'visual consummation'.

Therefore, seeing, in Hindu culture, is a way of touching and not just contact. 'Seeing, according to Indian notions, is a going forth of the sight toward the object. Touch is the ultimate connection by which the visible yields to be grasped. While the eye touches the object, the vitality that pulsates in it is communicated' (Kramrisch, cited in Eck 1985: 9). Or, as Babb (1981: 393) puts it, seeing is an extrusive flow, 'an outward-reaching process that in a sense actually engages ... the objects seen', and brings 'something of those objects back to the seer' (ibid.: 396). Seeing, as a mode of touching, thus, complements and, in some cases, replaces the actual touching of and intimacy with the Lord.

It should also be noted that while most deities worshipped by the subaltern folk are either in the open or housed in simple structures enabling open access and touch to the devotees, those of the elite are installed and worshipped in elaborately structured Agamic temples comprising a series of concentric square spaces with enclosing walls in between. The garbhagraha is considered to be the sanctum sanctorum of the temple. None except the male Brahmin priest is allowed to enter this extremely sacred place.

The nature of gazing at the divine in Hindu culture is, thus, quite ambivalent. Whereas on the one hand, elite practices privilege distance and the gaze, and sanction the upper castes a greater intimacy with the Lord while excluding and marginalising the lower castes, the subalterns themselves, on the other, prefer intimacy and touch in their own sacred spatialities.

But when the untouchable saints cross the barrier of untouchableness, they practise, in spite of the internalisation of the inferiority within the Brahminical order and the untouchability that it entails [what Fanon (1982) calls *epidermalisation* in another context], a politics that is a violation of that very order. In villages, there are practices like chasing away a Brahmin when he happens to enter a Dalit colony and cleansing the space by breaking a pot of cow dung-mixed water to get rid of the pollution caused by his visit.[19] This is exactly a case of *counter-untouchability*, something that is diametrically opposed to what Sarukkai calls the *moral dirt* attached to the untouchables. In fact, Sarukkai talks about classical texts and prescribed norms which contain references to such moral dirt. However, there are other texts which are considered equally authoritative within Sri Vaishnavism that present a picture that is entirely different. It is to these texts that I now turn.

Before taking up the actual cases, let me at the outset clarify two points: While Sarukkai cites the case of the Acharyas to contend that a Brahmin is one who not only has access to temporal and potential untouchability but also to permanent, hereditary untouchability, it should be noted that not all Acharyas are Brahmins. In fact, within the domain of Sri Vaishnavism, any commoner, irrespective of caste, can undergo the *pancasamaskaram*, the initiatory ritual, contrary to Sarukkai's view that such initiation is an exclusive marker of Brahminhood. Sarukkai's contention that the most important marker in becoming a Brahmin has to do essentially with the possibility of being an untouchable is thus overly simplistic as it transposes what he calls the permanent, hereditary untouchability of the Acharyas onto the entire community of Brahmins, including the common householder. Such displacement in Sarukkai's thinking is carried out through the notion of *madi*, a temporary state of ceremonial purity involving restrictions on touching and being touched, which he characterises as a significant form of untouchableness among Brahmins. The common householder-Brahmin observes madi to become an untouchable to others, including members of his own community. This is how a Brahmin is constantly Brahminised, something that is needed for an individual in order to continue to be a member of the Brahmin community (Sarukkai 2014: 194). While this is one of the ways in which the Brahmin distances his corporeal self from others, a feature that is integral to the systemic logic of untouchability, it should be noted that characterising the Acharyas as permanently untouchable is itself highly problematic.

Among the Sri Vaishnava texts that deal with the philosophical sayings of the Alvars and the Acharyas and, thus, present the basic tenets of the faith are the *Acharya Hridayam* (2001) by Alakiya Manavalap Perumal Nayanar (with the commentary by Manavala Mamunikal) and the *Srivacana Bhushanam* (2001) by Pillai

Lokacharyar, two seminal thirteenth-century texts in *manippravala* prose[20] that present instances in the lives of the Acharyas that go explicitly against Sarukkai's characterisation of all Acharyas as Brahmins and permanent untouchables.[21] Periya Nambi, one of the five great teachers of Ramanuja, had a fellow student and friend from the untouchable community by the name Maraneri Nambi. When Maraneri Nambi passed away, Periya Nambi performed the funeral rites according to the last wish of Maraneri Nambi. The orthodox Brahmins deplored the act and Ramanuja himself asked Periya Nambi why he did that. Periya Nambi replied that Maraneri Nambi was also a student of Alavantar like himself, and a cherished one at that, and an exemplary bhakta. He asked, 'Didn't Rama perform the last rites of Jatayu, a bird? Am I greater than Rama and is Maraneri Nambi lesser than the bird? Moreover, can one send a substitute to perform *sandhya vandanam* on his behalf? Are the words of Nammalvar just nonsensical sound like that of the ocean?' (Pillai Lokacharyar 2001: 185–86).

When Sarukkai talks about the *untouchableness* of the Acharyas, he states that the Acharyas will not eat food that is cooked even by their wives and that even Brahmins in a state of madi cannot touch these Acharyas, watch them eat and so on. Contrary to this view, the *Acharya Hridayam* talks about *kaya-*, *anna-* and *sthala-suddhi*s in a different manner.

1. *Kaya-suddhi (purification of the body)*: Ramanuja, while going to bathe in Kaveri every day, used to hold the hand of Mutaliyandan, a Brahmin disciple. However, while returning after his bath, he used to hold the hand of Pillai Urankavillidasar, a Dalit disciple, to demonstrate both the Dalit disciple's immanent state of purity and the kind of purification that it causes on his own person.
2. *Anna-suddhi (purification of food)*: Nampillai, the great Acharya, used to eat the *prasada* from the hands of a Dalit Acharya, Eru Tiruvutaiyardasar, thus proving that the prasada is in a state of absolute purity in the hands of the Dalit.
3. *Sthala-suddhi (purification of the house)*: Once Naduvil Tiruvitippillai Bhattar, a Brahmin Acharya, invited Pillai Vanamamalaidasar, a Dalit Acharya, to his housewarming ceremony at Srirangam. Hesitant to be part of the ceremony, the

> Dalit Acharya visited the place the previous evening. Hearing this, the orthodox Brahmins were agitated and complained about it. Bhattar, however, was happy and said that the house had been cleansed by Pillai Vanamamalaidasar's entry and, therefore, a full-fledged ceremony was no longer needed (Alakiya Manavalap Perumal Nayanar 2001: 199–201).

In fact, *Acharya Hirdayam* explicitly states that the touch of the untouchable bhaktas is highly valuable in nature and touching them and being touched by them elevates the upper castes who are entrenched in evil to a higher spiritual level (ibid.: 200–01). In his commentary to another Sri Vaishnava text, *Vartta Malai* (1982), Krishnaswamy Iyengar remarks that such touch relieves the Brahmin of his caste pride and purifies him. For this reason, Pillai Urankavillidasar was known by the name Ramanuja Sparsavedi, the term *sparsavedi* meaning 'one whose touch performs the magical alchemic act of transmuting iron into gold'[22] (Pinpalakiya Perumal Jiyar 1982: 344).

One could surmise from these instances that a kind of *inverse-outsourcing*, to put it in Sarukkai's own terms, happens here. The absolute untouchability that Sarukkai considers as special to the Brahmin Acharyas is characterised here as a protean phenomenon. The untouchableness of both the Brahmin and the Dalit is seen here to be in a perennial state of contest. As Nagaraj (2010: 154) puts it, 'What is seen as a cause and symbol of degradation is converted into a symbol of protest and transcendence.' The immanent divinity of all bhaktas, irrespective of caste, and the common humanity that it presupposes, are repeatedly emphasised in the life-stories of the Dalit saints mentioned earlier.

Notes

[1] See the chapter, 'Phenomenology of Untouchability', in Guru and Sarukkai (2014: 157–99).

[2] See Paramasivan (1995: 83–91) for an extended discussion of this point; also Rajam (2015) for a persuasive argument that untouchability was markedly absent in ancient Tamil Nadu.

[3] Gopal Guru's incisive critique of Sarukkai's phenomenology rightly argues for an ontological equality of human bodies. By positing an egalitarian value to all human bodies, Guru notes that each body is worthy of respect. In fact, he contends that the

untouchable body is a potential weapon for elevating the upper caste *folded body* and converting it into a *freely-flowing body* (Guru 2014: 200–22).

[4] Sarukkai (2014: 173, 193) does mention the case of saints and bhaktas in a few places. He even notes that untouchable saints are boundary-crossers. However, he fails to discuss the implications of these cases for his 'phenomenology of untouchability', and simply notes that these 'suggest once more the difficulty in understanding caste dynamics in terms of rigid distinctions based on some ideas of purity and impurity' (ibid.: 193).

[5] See Turner (2012) on the *social skin*:

> [T]he surface of the body seems everywhere to be treated not only as the boundary of the individual as a biological and psychological entity but as the frontier of the social self as well ... The surface of the body, as the common frontier of the society, the social self, and the psycho-biological individual becomes the symbolic stage upon which the drama of socialisation is enacted. (Ibid.: 486)

[6] The story of Nantanar is first mentioned by the ninth-century saint-poet Cuntarar in his *Tiruttotattokai,* and later elaborately dealt with in the twelfth-century Saiva hagiography *Tiruttontar Puranam*, also known as *Periya Puranam*. Authored by Cekkilar, this latter work tells the story of the lives of the 63 Tamil Saiva saints in epic form. See Cekkilar (1970: 201–07); also Pattuccami Otuvar (1954) for a prose rendition of the epic. For a nineteenth-century literary-musical treatment of the legend, see Gopalakrishna Bharati (n.d.). Interestingly, Gopalakrishna Bharati introduces the figure of a Brahmin landlord into the story as a counterpoise to Nantanar. This landlord detests Nantanar's intense bhakti to Lord Siva right from the beginning, forces him to work in his fields through verbal abuse and physical torture, and repeatedly prevents him from undertaking his journey to Chidambaram for 10 years. Eventually, it is divine intervention in the form of a miraculous sowing and reaping of the crop overnight that brings about a change of heart in the landlord. This legend has been the most discussed and debated one among the hagiographic legends of Dalit bhaktas. For earlier discussions of various versions of the legend, see Kailasapathy (1970), Uttirapati (2004) and Kaali (2007).

[7] For a brief sketch of the lives of Perran Campan and Umapati Sivam, see *Arulmiku Umapati Sivacharya Svami Avarkalin Varalaru* (2015). For an elaborate literary-musical narration of the story of Perran Campan in the *kirttanam* (a particular kind of musical genre) mode, see Tyagaraja Desikar (n.d.). Also, see Ilattu Atikal (2013: 107–08) for a different reading of the legend of Perran Campan. On the philosophical treatises and literary works authored by Umapati Sivam, see Arunachalam (2005) and Smith (1998).

[8] Oddly enough, Smith (1998: 115) takes this 'conferring of enlightenment' quite literally as the 'descent of Siva's grace' and argues that it is likely 'that the account of the incident was inspired by an uninformed view of the fiery nature of extreme *Saktinipata*' and that '[a]ssuming the event had a historical basis ... it might readily be supposed that the shock of the initiation was so great that the outcaste died of a heart attack, a *cause célèbre* that yet ended favourably for Umapati'.

[9] This mulli plant was, according to the Acharya, the only living being in the vicinity which had acquired the state of maturity needed for undergoing the diksha. The plant had acquired this status owing to the fact that it was fed by the holy water which the Acharya had used to anoint the idol of Siva that he worshipped every day.

[10] Besides these two nayanadikshas, Umapati Sivam gave dikshas to three others—his disciple Kutauluntalanta Muni, a Garuda that habitually flew over his monastery while he was distributing the prasada after the *puja*, and his own wife. While the first two were reduced to ashes like Perran by the Acharya's nayanadiksha, the case of the wife's initiation is quite different. Though it was not a nayanadiksha and did not burn her down, it was equally traumatic:

> The *Parthavana Mahatmya* ... describes Umapati's giving of enlightenment to his wife, Parvati. When he became an ascetic, his wife went with him to the penance grove. He taught the *Pauskara Agama* to devotees there for a month, then she asked for release from rebirth for herself, a wife not being dependent on a man who is a *yogin*. Umapati, after other preliminaries, fed her *pancagavya*, the five products of the cow, to remove her sins, blindfolded her, and entered her body through her vagina (*bhogamargya*), took out the particle (*kala*) that is support of life and coming out again through the vagina placed [her life force] in the supreme space of *atman*. He burned her lifeless body, bathed, and regained his purity. (Smith 1998: 115)

[11] Sporting the veena denotes the hereditary status of Panalvar, he being a member of the community of Panars, a community of bards and musicians whose early history could be traced back to the Sangam classics (BCE 300–300 CE). For a historical and ethnographic account of the Panars, see Bhaktavatsala Bharati (2012).
[12] See Pinpalakiya Perumal Jiyar (1994: 62–68) for a detailed account of this life-story.
[13] Nathamunikal is the Acharya who compiled the *Nalayira Divya Prabandham*, the 4,000 devotional hymns of the Alvars, during the latter half of the ninth century or the earlier half of the tenth century. See Pinpalakiya Perumal Jiyar (1994: 114–26) for a detailed account of his life; also *Arayirappati Pannirayirappati Mutaliya Guruparampara Prabhavam* (1909) for a more elaborate account.
[14] See Vannaccarapam Dandapani Svamikal (1931) for a detailed account of this part of the story; also, Venkataraman (2004).
[15] He made altogether 18 pledges. The rakshasa, who was not moved by the first 17, let him go only when Nampatuvan uttered the eighteenth one.
[16] It is for this reason that Nampatuvan is known in Sri Vaishnavism by the name Brahmana Velvikkurai Mutitta Bhagavatan, meaning 'the *bhagavata* who corrected the improper performance of a Brahmin's yagna'.
[17] See Paramasivan (2013: 77–81) for a discussion of this point.
[18] On the social position of untouchables in medieval Tamil Nadu, see Karashima (1997: 21–30). Mark (2001: 291), in his excellent study of the Aruntatiyar community in Tamil Nadu, observes that the settlements of the community are usually located in the eastern side of the villages. This, he notes, is to avoid the pollution caused by the wind that would touch the living quarters of the untouchables, as it is commonly believed that the east is the direction from which very little or no wind blows.
[19] Pandit Iyotheethasar (1854–1914), a towering Dalit intellectual, notes the prevalence of this practice at several places in his writings. See, for instance, Iyotheethasar (1999a: 36, 46, 74, 128, 139, 308, 592, 616, 639, 687; 1999b: 23).
[20] A particular kind of Tamil prose, mostly employed by Jains and Vaishnavas in their works, in which there is a high admixture of Sanskrit words.
[21] Caste status has been a contested phenomenon within Sri Vaishnavism throughout the medieval period in the Tamil country. In fact, differences in this and other matters led to sectarian schism in the post-Ramanuja period and the formation of two distinct

communities, the Vatakalai and the Tenkalai. Theologians belonging to these two groups continued to debate the issue in the subsequent period. See Paramasivan (1995: 56–70) and Jagadeesan (1977: 169–208) for a discussion of this theme; also Clooney (2002: 399–419) for the terms of the debate.

[22] See also Nampillai's commentary to Nammalvar's *Tiruvaymoli* (2012: 328–31), where the term is mentioned in connection with the story of Nampatuvan.

References

Alakiya Manavalap Perumal Nayanar. 2001. *Acharya Hridayam*, with commentary by Manavala Mamunikal, trans. B. R. Purushothama Naidu. Chennai: University of Madras.

Anzieu, Didier. 1989. *The Skin Ego*, trans. Chris Turner. New Haven and London: Yale University Press.

——— 1999. 'The Group Ego-Skin', trans. Brenda Dean. *Group Analysis* 32(3): 319–29.

Arangapprakasa Svamikal. 1936. *Sri Venkatesvara Bhakta Vijayam*. Tiruppati: Sri Padmavati Press.

Arayirappati Pannirayirappati Mutaliya Guruparampara Prabhavam. 1909. Chennai: Cenci Arangasamy Mudaliar Publication.

Arulmiku Umapati Sivacharya Svami Avarkalin Varalaru. 2015. Tirumutukunram: Kumaratevar Matam.

Arunachalam, M. 2005. *Tamil Ilakkiya Varalaru: Patinankam Nurrantu*, Volume 8. Chennai: The Parker.

Babb, Lawrence A. 1981. 'Glancing: Visual Interaction in Hinduism'. *Journal of Anthropological Research* 37(4): 387–401.

Bachelard, Gaston. 1969. *The Poetics of Space*, trans. Maria Jolas. Boston: Beacon Press.

Bakhtin, Mikhail. 1984. *Rabelais and his World*, trans. Helene Iswolsky. Bloomington: Indiana University Press.

Bhaktavatsala Bharati. 2012. *Panar Inavaraiviyal*. Chennai: International Institute of Tamil Studies.

Cekkilar. 1970. *Tiruttontar Makkatai*. Tirunelveli: The South India Saiva Siddhanta Works Publishing Society.

Clooney, Francis X. 2002. 'Fierce Words: Repositioning of Caste and Devotion in Traditional Ethics'. *The Journal of Religious Ethics* 30(3): 399–419.

Eck, Diana L. 1985. *Darsan: Seeing the Divine in India*. Chambersburg, PA: Anima Books.

Fanon, Frantz. 1982. *Black Skin, White Masks*. New York: Grove Press.

Gopalakrishna Bharati (n.d.). *Nantanar Carittirak Kirttanai*. Chennai: B. Rathina Nayakar Sons.

Guru, Gopal. 2014. 'Archaeology of Untouchability'. In *The Cracked Mirror: An Indian Debate on Experience and Theory*, Gopal Guru and Sundar Sarukkai, 200–22. New Delhi: Oxford University Press.

Guru, Gopal and Sundar Sarukkai. 2014. *The Cracked Mirror: An Indian Debate on Experience and Theory*. New Delhi: Oxford University Press.

Handcock, T. 2012. 'Transgressing Boundaries: Skin in the Construction of Bodily Interior'. In *The Proceedings of the 2012 IDEA Symposium*, ed. S. Attiwill, 1–8. Perth: Curtin University.

Ilattu Atikal, Karuvur. 2013. *Periya Purana Araycci*. Chennai: Periyar Self-respect Propaganda Institution.
Iyotheethasar, Pandit. 1999a and 1999b. *Iyotheethasar Cintanaikal*, 2 volumes, ed. Gnana Aloysius. Palayamkottai: Folklore Resources and Research Centre, St Xavier's College.
Jagadeesan, N. 1977. *History of Sri Vaishnavism in the Tamil Country (Post-Ramanuja)*. Madurai: Koodal Publishers.
Kaali, Sundar. 1999. 'Spatialising History: Subaltern Carnivalisations of Space in Tiruppuvanam, Tamil Nadu'. In *Subaltern Studies X: Writings on South Asian History and Society*, eds Gautam Bhadra, Gyan Prakash and Susie Tharu, 126–69. New Delhi: Oxford University Press.
____ 2007. 'Aracan Mutal Atimai Varai: Vettiyan Pattai Munvaittuc Cila Kurippukal'. *Vallinam* 15, June–August: 51–55.
Kailasapathy, K. 1970. 'Pulaippatiyum Kopuravacalum'. In *Atiyum Mutiyum*. Chennai: Pari Nilaiyam.
Karashima, Noboru. 1997. 'The Untouchables in Tamil Inscriptions and Other Historical Sources in Tamil Nadu'. In *Caste System, Untouchability and the Depressed*, ed. H. Kotani, 21–30. New Delhi: Manohar.
Lafrance, Marc. 2013. 'From the Skin Ego to the Psychic Envelope: An Introduction to the Work of Didier Anzieu'. In *Skin, Culture and Psychoanalysis*, eds Sheila L. Cavanagh, Angela Failler and Rachel Alpha Johnston Hurst. Basingstoke: Palgrave Macmillan.
Mark. 2001. *Aruntatiyar Valum Varalaru*. Palayamkottai: Folklore Resources and Research Centre, St Xavier's College.
Nagaraj, D. R. 2010. *The Flaming Feet and Other Essays: The Dalit Movement in India*, eds Prithvi Datta and Chandra Shobi. Ranikhet: Permanent Black.
Nammalvar. 2012. *Tiruvaymoli*, with commentary *Itu* by Nampillai, trans. B. R. Purushothama Naidu. Chennai: University of Madras.
Paramasivan, To. 1995. *Teyvankalum Camuka Marapukalum*. Chennai: New Century Book House.
____ 2013. *Vitupukkal*. Chennai: Kayal Kavin Books.
Pattuccami Otuvar. 1954. *Periya Puranam Enapperum Tiruttontar Puranam*. Tiruppanantal: Sri Kasimatam.
Pile, Steel. 2009. 'Topographies of the Body-and-mind: Skin Ego, Body Ego and the Film *Memento*'. *Subjectivity* 27(1): 134–54.
Pillai Lokacharyar. 2001. *Srivacana Bhushanam*. Tiruchirappalli: Srisudarsanar Trust.
Pinpalakiya Perumal Jiyar. 1982. *Vartta Malai*. Tiruchirappalli: Srisudarsanar Trust.
____ 1994. *Arayirappati Guruparampara Prabhavam*. Tiruchirappalli: Srisudarsanar Trust.
Rajam, V. S. 2015. *Cankap Patalkalil Cati, Tintamai Innapira* ... Chennai: Manarkeni Patippakam.
Sarukkai, Sundar. 2014. 'Phenomenology of Untouchability'. In *The Cracked Mirror: An Indian Debate on Experience and Theory*, Gopal Guru and Sundar Sarukkai, 157–99. New Delhi: Oxford University Press.
Smith, David. 1998. *The Dance of Siva: Religion, Art and Poetry in South India*. New Delhi: Foundation Books.

Tontaratippoti Alvar. 1982. *Tirumalai*, with commentary by Periyavaccan Pillai. Tiruchirappalli: Srisudarsanar Trust.

Turner, Terence S. 2012. 'The Social Skin'. *Journal of Ethnographic Theory* 2(2): 486–504.

Tyagaraja Desikar (n.d.). *Perran Campanar Carittirak Kirttanam*. Chidambaram: C. G. Ramanujam Chettiar and Son.

Uttirapati, M. 2004. *Kalantorum Nantan Katai*. Chennai: Alaikal Veliyittakam.

Vannaccarapam Dandapani Svamikal. 1931. *Pulavar Puranam*. Chennai: Ti. Mu. Centinayakam Pillai Publication.

Varaha Puranattin Ullitana Kaisika Puranam. 1987. Tiruchirappalli: Srisudarsanar Trust.

Venkataraman, S. 2004. *Ariyappatata Tamil Ilakkiya Varalaru*. Madurai: Meenakshi Bookhouse.

4. 'Self' Rather than the 'Other'

Towards a Subjective Ethnography of the Kani Community[*]

M. Arivalagan

Kanikkaran communities live in the southern parts of the Western Ghats, particularly in the Tirunelveli, Kanyakumari, Thiruvananthapuram and Kollam districts. They inhabit the states of Tamil Nadu and Kerala. My friend, M. Thirunavukkarasu, and I conducted fieldwork in the Papanasam forest area in the Tirunelveli district of Tamil Nadu. It was for a period of five months, from October 1997 to March 1998, for the project 'Ethnographic Study of the Kanis in the Kalakad-Mundunthurai Tiger Reserve Forest'. During our stay with the Kanis, two researchers came to the area where we were working, to study the ethno-botany of the Kanis. They approached Pillayar Kani (one of the Kani community's leaders) to approve their stay in the village. I quote the conversation as it happened between the researchers, who were from Manonmanium Sundaranar University, Tirunelveli, and Pillayar Kani at Agasthiyar Nagar Kanikkudiruppu, Papanasam.

---

*I express sincere thanks to Professor A. R. Venkatachalapathy for his constant support and encouragement. I owe thanks to Dr Manjula Rajan, who corrected the draft at an earlier stage. I am extremely grateful to (Late) Professor M. S. S. Pandian, JNU, who edited this draft meticulously; whatever gratitude I express to him is inadequate. This paper benefited a lot from discussions with MIDS faculty members Ajit Menon, S. Anandhi and M. Vijayabaskar, and fellow research scholars Jayashree, Ann George, R. Manivasagan and Preetha. I also thank my friends Karmegam and Rengaiya Murugan for providing ethnographic materials. I am thankful to MIDS, Chennai, for publishing this article in the working paper series.

Researchers: *Aiyya vanakkam. Nanga Manonmanium Sundaranar Palkalaikkazhagatthzha irunthu varrome.* [Sir, *vanakkam.* We come from M. S. University.]

Pillayar Kani: *Vanakkam. Vaanga. Romba nallathu. Inga, neenga ethappatthi padikka poringa?* [Welcome, very good. What are you going to study?]

R: *Nanga vungaludaiya mooliga marutthuvattha pattri padikka vanthuirukkom.* [We have come here to study your herbal medicinal system.]

PK: *Sari. Aana nanga muttalgal. Engalukku mooligayappathi onnum theriyathu. Neega* Mundanthorai forest office-*kku ethutthapla pathikanna mooliga pannai vacchurukkanga. Anga pona neraya mooliga kedaikkumeengalukku mooligaya patthi yuthuvumey theriyathu. Nanga adivasinga.* [Okay. But we are fools. We do not know anything about herbs. A herbal farm has been set up just opposite the forest department office of Mundanthorai. If you go there, you can collect lots of herbs. We do not know anything about herbs. We are Adivasis.]

In the conversation, Pillayar Kani makes an ironic statement about his own community: 'We are fools. We do not know anything about herbs ... We are Adivasis (tribals).' Here, Henry Louis Gates, Jr's 1988 concept of 'the narrator's "signifyin[g]"[1] tactic of employing dual surface and latent layers of meaning' is helpful to understand the 'mock critique' of the narrator (cited in Vargas 2008: 56). To figure out the meanings of the self-derogatory statement made by Pillayar Kani, we need to begin with an analysis of the wide range of ethnographic notes produced from the colonial period to the present on the concept of the tribe.

I begin with a critical review of the ethnographies produced by the colonial and postcolonial ethnographers that objectified the Kanis. Then, I move on to propose an alternative methodology based on social memory, life experiences and oral history as a means to recover the voices of the community. Recovering the voices of the community is essential, as I will show, to write the Kanis as subjects of their own narrative.

Narratives of Static Portrayal

Since the early phase of the colonial period, the Kani community has been variously named Malai Arasars, Malai Arayars (*arachan* means 'chief', more distantly from *raja* or 'king'), Vellanmar (spearmen), Kanikaran (Kani, 'hereditary proprietor of land'), Natives, pre-Dravidians, Primitive Tribe, Aborigines, Tribals, Adivasi and Scheduled Tribes. The earlier ethnography of the community was conducted by European missionaries, administrators, traders and ethnographers. The first wave of ethnographic description, which adopted a 'fourteen-point format'[2] to report their lives, was a product of Orientalism. The narratives give an overall picture of a community. It treated the community as 'frozen', 'relics of the past' and 'static'. This was done by means of physical anthropology. The second wave of literature, once again produced by the colonial State, by and large, depicted the community as 'static', even though its descriptive intensity and methods varied. In general, the colonial ethnography depicted the Kanis as 'uncivilised', on the basis of moral value judgement, location of habitation, agricultural practices, religion, etc. Let me now turn to the details of these colonial constructions of the Kani community.

'Devil Gods'—Christianity—Othering

One of the strategies used by the colonial ethnographers to Other the natives was through specific readings of their 'beliefs' and 'rituals'. Such colonialist readings presented the native beliefs and practices as 'animistic' and 'strange'. In doing so, they claimed them to be pre-religious. As Ram (2007) rightly notes:

> We have scarcely begun to explore the smaller and seemingly innocuous categories through which castes and tribes were investigated and which have shaped the "beliefs" and "rituals" ... The centrality assigned to "beliefs", for example, in defining and investigating the "religion" of other cultures rests on a thoroughly Christian theology of religion. (Ibid.: 77)

Thus, Christianity was assigned the status of religion proper, and native faiths were treated as inadequately religious.

As an illustration, let me begin with a missionary-ethnographer's account of the healing ritual practice of the Kanis called *chattruppattu*. Samuel Mateer (1991: 68), the missionary-ethnographer in question, writes, 'When any one takes ill the headman is at once consulted; he visits the sick and orders two drumming and singing ceremonies to be performed. A whole night is spent in dancing, singing, drumming, and prayer for the recovery of the patient.' The ritual reflects the cosmology of the community that is however not focused on this description. Chattruppattu has played, and continues to play, a vital role in contacting deities for Kanis' wellness. But, the extract of the 1901 Census report constructs this as a sign of the Kanis' lack of faith in medicine: 'The Kanis have no faith in medicine. It is their Chattu and Pattu (hymns and songs) that cure them and not medicine' (Census of India 1961: 114). The gods of the Kanis were also not assigned the status of gods. They were described as 'devil-gods' and spirits. For instance, Pate (1993: 8) notes that the spirits and 'devil-gods' live in 'the lonely parts of the jungle [that] are inhabited by vaguely conceived but powerful spirits, and for sixteen days after a relative's death a man who wishes to avoid them should either stop at home or keep to the frequent paths'. The Christian cosmology, which works with the binary of devil as opposed to god, is modified here to devalue the Kanis' worship.

These ethnographic accounts are suffused with references to the relative superiority of Christianity. For instance, Mateer (1991) writes:

> The Kanikars have not much idea of the soul or immortality. When asked, they say, "Who can tell?" Some with whom we conversed said they knew nothing of a hell, or of the wicked going there. Some of their superstitions are connected with the serpent; for example, a vein in a certain granite rock is said to have been caused by a snake creeping over it before it hardened. (Ibid.: 69)

The reference to the soul, immortality and hell are obvious references from Christianity which are employed here to mark as inferior the Kani religious practices.

In carrying forward such a representation of the Kani religion, the missionary ethnographers, presented their beliefs and practices as based on irrational fear and their gods as powerless. According to Mateer:

> When the Christian religion is recommended to them, they reply that if they embraced it, the jungle-demons would be offended, and send elephants and other wild beasts to kill them, and destroy their cultivations. "Why then," it was asked, "do not the Europeans suffer, who cut down the forests?" to which they answered, "As the white men worship a mighty God, the

> demons take their flight from their presence." Jungle fever also is attributed to the agency of these deities, and they move from a place where it prevails. Some altogether refused to hear our exhortations. When they see books in the hands of the Christian teachers, they will say, "Do you come to destroy us by bringing the wrath of the demons upon us?" One woman said, "I have only two children; do not kill them by teaching them your Vedam." (Ibid.: 70)

As Bhukya (2008: 106) notes, the 'implication [of such ethnographic representations] was that such communities could be saved and civilised through conversion to Christianity'. This was evident in the case of the Kanikars as well. According to Mateer (1991), the Christian missionaries started coffee plantations in the mountainside to 'civilise' the people:

> Coffee planting in this country seems as if largely intended, in the Providence of God, for the good of this hill tribe. In the plantations Kanikars and Christians meet and work together, and some of the latter are not backward in showing what the Lord has done for them in spiritual as well as in temporal things ... In these plantations, too, catechists, and occasionally missionaries can speak with as many *Kanikars* as take employment there; and staying there at night, can spend the day in preaching in the unhealthy valleys below. (Ibid.: 70–71)

According to Mateer, the encounters between the Christians and the Kanis led to the latter losing faith in the power of their gods and accepting the superiority of Christianity. He notes that the Kani community had learnt

> ... two valuable lessons. One is, that the spirits they worship have no power over Christians from Europe and the plains. When Europeans and native Christians began planting on the hills, some of the Kanikars went to their priests, and in the most solemn and religious manner got awful curses pronounced on their new neighbours. All were to be utterly destroyed unless they went away. This was done repeatedly, but nothing happened. Some of the priests now declare that it is in vain to curse Christians, or, as they call them, "the people that have books". Another lesson they have learnt is that Christianity is a

> civilizing and an elevating religion, and a good religion for this life generally. (Ibid.: 71)

In producing an overlap between Christianity and civilisation, the missionary ethnography could not but produce the Kani religious practices as less than proper religion.

Significantly, the Indian elite too represented the Kanis in the same manner as the colonial ethnographers. For instance, the Indian elite-cum-colonial State ethnographer, Aiya (1989: 411), mentioned in his account, 'The Kanikkar is thus still, if not in the fetish, in the primitive stage of worship—probably the first stage in the religious evolution of all races. Ethically he is much an undefiled being so far—however unclean he may be from a physical point of view'. The politics of such adoption of the ethnographic representations of the colonisers by the local elite has been well captured by Guha (1999). He rightly notes, 'Racial ethnography was ... being appropriated by the indigenous elites to justify indigenous hierarchy on the one hand, and to assert parity with the European upper classes, on the other' (ibid.: 16).

Occupation: Food Gathering—Unsettled Cultivation

As much as Kani religious practices, their mode of cultivation and their unwillingness to assimilate themselves into new jobs were treated in colonial ethnography as signs of their primitiveness, Kanis' traditional farming was usually criticised as destructive of forest resources. For instance, a description of agrarian practices runs as follows:

> These wandering husbandmen cut down a patch of forest, burn and clear it, and sow a crop, with little or no tillage ... This mode of cultivation yields a larger return for the same amount of labour than permanent plough husbandry, but is highly destructive of valuable forest lands. Their migrant habits arise partly from laziness: it is easier to cut down and burn new forest than to rear cattle, plant trees, manure land, and build houses. (Mateer 1991: 64)

Shifting cultivation was, in the colonial accounts, not only destructive of forest resources, but also symbolised the so-called laziness of the native. The solution offered to the problem was settled cultivation, which was claimed to usher in civilisation among the Kanis: 'They ... should be encouraged to settle if possible: only by such means can they be reclaimed to civilization and education, as has been done farther north' (ibid.: 64–65).

Similarly, Aiya (1989) too wrote:

> These untrained people unable to apply advanced methods of rejuvenating the lands, mercilessly extract every iota of vitality out of it; thus the land sapped gradually of its richness by ignorance and avarice, refuses to yield after a certain time. The margin of cultivation being thus reduced to the lowest point, the cultivator has no other option but to quit the land upon which he has squatted. (Ibid.: 409)

If Mateer attributed the Kanis' laziness as the reason for them practising shifting cultivation, in the account of Iyer and Pillai (1933), it was their ignorance of working within an environment-deterministic model. Often, the ethnographic accounts, Indian and colonial, attribute the Kanis' so-called indolence to the hot climate: 'Excessive heat in the summer burns out the energy of the *Kanikar* ... and others who live in forests of low elevation, and makes them slothful. In fact, the debilitating effect of heat and humidity, aided by diseases, has reduced them to the dead level of economic inefficiency' (Hutton 1986: 236).

What is more, the Kani community did not show much willingness to participate in the colonial civilising mission of weaning them away from shifting cultivation. It was only those who joined the mission by becoming wage labourers who were given a positive evaluation in the colonial accounts. As Mateer (1991: 66) writes, 'Their [Kanikars'] circumstances have greatly improved of late wherever coffee estates have been opened and worked; but those who are unwilling to take work are driven farther into the hills in search of fresh lands'. Supporting his claim, Mateer quotes Honiss, a colonial ethnographer:

> The fate of the hill-kings, says Mr. Honiss, is rather sad. For ages past they have boasted of being the undisputed lords of the primeval forests. The elephant and tiger were their only foes; but with snares and traps they could hold their own against these enemies. But they could not resist the onward march of a superior race. The planter approaches them in a peaceful way, offering wages for their hire, but demanding as his right the

> land he has purchased. The proud men of the woods decline to herd with coolies, and work like common people. As soon as the planter's axe is heard, the hill kings pack their traps and desert their homes to establish themselves in another valley. In this way they have been driven from hill to hill and from valley to valley, until some have found now a safe resting place in the dense jungles of the low lands of Travancore. If the planter wishes to penetrate some unexplored jungle, or cut a path in some out-of-the-way place, the hill men are ready to assist, and it is the universal testimony that they are more faithful to their engagements than their more civilized brethren from the plains. (Ibid.: 66–67)

In this account, the profit-seeking deforestation does not get written as destructive of forests, but as the march of civilisation. In contrast, the Kanis' attempt to preserve his autonomy by not participating in wage slavery gets ceded as a mark of their primitiveness.

The forest department trained the Kanis as watchers. Those who took up this vocation, like those who joined the plantations as labourers, were given a positive evaluation: 'Though their physique is poor and fever seems to be almost general amongst them, they make excellent forest guides and show wonderful powers of endurance' (Pate 1993: 7).

'Good' Qualities

Most of the missionaries, ethnographers and officials alluded to some of the 'good' qualities of the local communities. Mateer (1991: 69) noted, 'These wild men [Kanis] are usually ranked above the more civilized Hindus of the plains in point of morals. Though rude, hardy, and courageous, they are inoffensive, and are regarded as somewhat truthful, honest, chaste, and hospitable'. The community was also portrayed as 'quiet, simple and inoffensive folks', and 'straight-forward, honest and truthful to a fault' (Census of India 1961: 113, 115). The Census of India (1911: 115) wrote of the Kanis thus: 'high standard of domestic honour and social helpfulness and, in their unsophisticated purity, they are truthful to a fault'. Likewise, Aiya (1989: 412) noted, 'These hill tribes inhabiting the inaccessible wilds keep to their pristine purity in thought, word and deed. They in some respects surpass the civilised townsmen in the practice of cardinal virtues that regulate human life—truth, honesty, simplicity, credulity, modesty, law-abiding quality and above all hospitality'. Thurston's (1975) assessment was no different. He wrote of them as of 'a high standard of honour, and straightforward, honest and truthful' (ibid.: 163).

Such descriptions, which attribute certain positive qualities to the Kanis, simultaneously infantalise them as childlike. As Bhukya (2008: 107) notes, the colonial officials 'equated the egalitarian values (honesty, frankness, communal life) of the tribals with Rousseau's state of nature, seeing them as innocent and childlike. They depicted them as noble, honest, loyal and ruggedly independent'. In other words, they are yet to reach the adulthood of civilisation. Once again, they are marked as primitive.

Body Description

In the later part of colonialism, physical anthropology was used by the colonial ethnographers to represent the colonised communities as primitive. The politics of physical anthropology has been analysed by several scholars. For example, Uberoi, Deshpande and Sundar (2007) note:

> Many of the early anthropologists maintained an active interest in physical anthropology, pre-history, or linguistics, even as they focused primarily on society and culture. Most of them had prior training as natural scientists, and they accordingly sought to employ the tools, methodologies, and protocols of the natural sciences as they understood them. In this model, society was conceived as a "laboratory" in which specimens of primitive humanity could be measured, and their social and cultural characteristics recorded and classified according to received scales and protocols. (Ibid.: 33–34)

On a different count, as Dirks (1992: 70) notes, the physical anthropology works within the binary of body and mind and reduces the colonised to their bodies: 'The individual for colonial anthropology thus became the body—the body that had been in precolonial times subjected by tradition, now the body as caste that could be measured by science, significantly always a body that could be described without any reference to mind, will, or agency.'

In South India, Thurston (1975) is the first ethnographer to describe the physical features of any particular community. He portrayed the Kani community thus: 'the primitive short, dark-skinned and platyrhine type, though surviving, has become changed as the result of contact metamorphosis, and many leptorhine or mesorhine individuals above middle height are to be met with' (ibid.: 162).

Following Thurston, Iyer and Pillai (1933) prepared notes on the so-called primitive tribes of Travancore, in which the Kanikar community was described from the perspective of a social evolutionary model. It was a model which represented the 'primitive tribes' as savages and that to become civilised, they had to come in contact with the civilised. Before moving on to the accounts of Iyer and Pillai on the Kanis, we need to bear in mind that the Indian ethnographers' intentions might be different from those of the colonial ethnographers.[3] As Uberoi, Deshpande and Sundar (2007) note:

> Their purpose was not, however, merely to serve the empire – to open India and its peoples to scientific scrutiny and thereby enable its efficient administration and control. On the contrary, they believed that mastery of the science of that coloniser was the essential first step to qualify for self-rule and establish India as a modern-state within the world community of nations' (Ibid.: 32).

Whatever the intentions of Iyer and Pillai, their accounts of Kanis, as we shall see later, were not much different from those of the colonial ethnographers.

Following colonial anthropology, Iyer and Pillai identified 'short stature, low forehead, flat face and nose, and dark complexion' (Census of India 1933: 220) as the characteristic feature of the primitive people. Of the Kanikkars, for instance, Iyer (1968: 46) wrote, 'average broad nostril of the *Kanikkars* is a primitive feature', and also claimed a racial affinity between the Kanikkar community and the Negrito based on studies of physical anthropology and serology (the study of blood grouping) which were conducted by Ruggles Gates, pointing out that 'the *Kanikkars* have short stature and kinky hair indicating Negrito relationship' (ibid.: 35).

Here again, an environmental deterministic approach model is evoked to explain the physical features of the 'primitive tribes'. The explanation offered for the dark skin tone of the Kanikkars by Iyer and Pillai is a case in point:

> The pigment of the skin is found in the epidermis, and the influence of light favours its formation. In a cold climate, where the thermal action is weak, a discoloration of pigment in the skin and others parts of the body produces a kind of albinism. The *Kanikar*, the Ulladan ... who live on the plains and at low elevations are darker than the Muduvan, the Mannan ... of the High-Ranges. (Hutton 1986: 219)

Moreover, whenever so-called positive physical features are identified in Kanikkars or others they are often attributed to their coming in touch with superior communities and admixture of blood. As an illustration, let me cite Iyer and Pillai (1933):

> The other tribes [included the *Kanikar* community] have been subjected to extraneous influences and have, therefore, received an infusion of fresh blood and new ideas from the more civilized people with whom they have come in contact. This is seen clearly in ... the Kanikar. Owing to the admixture of foreign blood these tribes are now approaching the composite type of civilized humanity. (Ibid.: 219)

Postcolonial Ethnographies

Only those who respect the law and assist the Forest department are eligible to live and obtain rights in the forest.[4]

—Nitin Sethi, 2008

The ethnographies that appeared in the postcolonial period followed more or less exclusively the same modalities of the colonial ethnographers. However, their intentions were different. These ethnographies carried out by Indian scholars were meant for the 'efficient administration and control' to be exercised by the postcolonial Indian State.

In his preface to the Census of India 1961, P. K. Nambiar, a postcolonial ethnographer, noted that Thurston's ethnographic survey on castes and tribes was totally 'outdated', even though it contained useful material on the different communities. He stated that the main objective of Census 1961 was to capture the 'present conditions with the impact of the post-colonial period on tribal communities those who were living in the remote areas and not yet dealt with any ethnographic study' (Census of India 1961). In the Census, the Kani community was described by and large within the framework of colonial anthropology. Like the colonial anthropology, the postcolonial ethnographies too presented them as primitive and unchanging. For example, Iyer (1968) notes:

> No doubt a lot of effort has been put in to educate the *Kani*, provide him with alternate employment and alter his manner of living, but the *Kani* has not undergone any fundamental change in his nature and still appears to be as simple and as primitive as Mr. Pate found him in 1917. (Ibid.: 87)

Let us now turn to some accounts of the Kanis made by Indian ethnographers in the post-Independence period. Like the colonial ethnographies, Census 1961 represented the Kani community as dirty and unhygienic: '... the flowers were the only pleasant things we noticed ... The exterior of the house was clean but the interior presented a picture of squalor and filth' (Census of India 1961: 89). Moreover, their personal cleanliness was also presented as not meeting the standards of the civilised. The Census of 1961 noted:

> The average *Kani* is short, not more than 5'5" in height apparently with a lot of fussy hair. On a closer scrutiny we found that the hair was not fussy, but was matted due to the constant accumulation of dust mixed with grease, as the *Kanis* shirk from anything resembling a bath. Personal cleanliness is set at a low premium. We know it, not only from our observation, but also from their own statements that they do not even brush their teeth or wash their mouths. The colour of their loin cloth, which is the only thing most *Kanis* like to wear, provides a dull grayish black in contrast to the surrounding vivid green and blue. This cloth, they seldom like to wash. This lack of personal cleanliness and hygiene was uniform whether the *Kanis* live in pucca houses built for them by the Government, or in their crude huts set amidst the forest. (Ibid.)

Additionally, the ethnographers lamented, 'the *Kanis* live amidst the dirt'. In a similar vein, a study by Agesthiyalingom (1976: *vii–viii*), a well-known Tamil linguist, done in the 1970s notes: 'They do not keep their huts clean and tidy though the surroundings are very picturesque and beautiful. The healthy and hilly surroundings are marked by the unhealthy and filthy upkeep of the huts'. These descriptions of the Kanis are no different from those of colonial ethnographers such as Mateer.

The colonial stereotype of the lazy native also finds its rearticulation in the postcolonial ethnographies carried out by Indian scholars. Agesthiyalingom, for instance, writes in his study, 'They are generally lazy and they grow all these [vegetables, plantains, jack fruit, pepper] not in a systematic and scientific way' (ibid.: *vii*). Similarly, Census 1961 noted that their agricultural practice is quite different from the people in the plains: 'If we take them overnight from the forest and give them fertile lands and ask them to cultivate the lands, they will be helpless. Forest is to them just as water is to the fish' (Census of India 1961: 101). Based on this observation, it suggested that 'they need proper guidance' to avoid soil erosion on the terrace slope, and noted that 'they cannot be called steady hardworking cultivators'. Likewise, the same stereotypical description was once again reproduced with slight modification by the postcolonial ethnographers (Parthasarathy 1997; Singh 1998, 2001; *Dravidian Encyclopaedia* 1990).

The colonial-type physical anthropology was also employed by these scholars to present the Kanis as primitive. Let me once again quote Agesthiyalingom (1976):

> The Kanis are generally very short and dark skinned as most of the tribes of Tamil Nadu ... They have round face and stout and flat noses. They used to grow their hair and knot it at the back of the head which was found to be not uncommon among the rural people of the plains. Their hair looks more curly than that of the people in the plains and it would not be very difficult for the people like the present author to distinguish them even from their hair. (Ibid.: *vii*)

Similar to the Christian missionaries, the postcolonial State treats the Kanis' religious practices as unworthy. The Kanis' access to forest is intimately associated with their religious system which has god, Thambiran and Vadai. These all reside in 'trees, rock crevices, caves and hill tops' inside the forest. The denial of access to the forests by the forest department came in the way of the Kanis performing their annual rituals to their Vadais and Thambiran. The Kani comment,

'*Vadai vathi pochu padai thavari pochu*' [Spirit has withered away, we have lost the way], reflects the desolation of the community (Jayapathy 1981). According to Jayapathy, the community is increasingly borrowing the religious practices of the plains folk such as the Sabarimala pilgrimage to cope with its present problems.

As noted earlier, the colonial ethnographies infantalised the Kanis by presenting them as childlike. Similar representations continued to be part of the postcolonial ethnographers. The Census of India (1961), for example, noted:

> The Kanis are a peace loving tribe. They love the jungle and its life. Forest is their home ... There is no timidity associated with any Kani ... The code of conduct of the Kani clan as practiced by them is simple and not elaborate ... The Kanis have simple and practical laws regulating their social conduct. They can be changed from time to time. The changes are made by the slow processes of evolution and by acculturation. (Ibid.: 99)

If the civilising mission of the colonisers saw the salvation of the Kanis in embracing Christianity and becoming wage labourers in plantations, the same agenda took the shape of welfare programmes in the postcolonial period. The government set up a Tribal Welfare School and provided 'free food' to the school-going children. The deadly disease of small-pox claimed around 100 lives in 1962. When health officials visited the area, the Kani people allowed them to administer the vaccination. Earlier, as we saw, the Kanis had fully depended upon the traditional healing performance of chattruppattu, performed by their shaman, Pilathi, to cure such diseases. A housing scheme was also initiated for the Kani community to improve their quality of life. However, the government-built houses did not afford any privacy to the Kanis compared to what their traditional houses provided.

Towards 'Subjectification'

> *... the story has remained like a knot in my stomach. It is my memory.*
>
> —Radkibai[5]

It is evident from the accounts presented here of the ethnographers' forays into the Kanis' lives that they have failed to capture the subjectivity of the community. They are objectified and treated as the 'other' of the analysis. This has been done both by the colonial and indigenous ethnographers.

In developing an alternative methodology, which would return subjectivity to the Kanis, let me begin with a cue from Diouf (2003) who, in the context of Africa, critiques the existing historical methods for not accommodating existing narratives of 'plural consciousness of history' in terms of 'the memories of communities and individuals'. According to him, the available method borrowed from the Western historiography

> ... established in the Enlightenment vouches for a linear history that associates reason, progress and civilization. This history, which spread as universal history and was imposed as a chief modality of producing the frameworks for understanding the past, organizing the present and preparing for the future, is on every continent in a deep crisis and/or a phase of continual recomposition. Although it has accompanied and strongly supported the construction of nations and their juridical formulas such as the state (or perhaps it is the other way around, when the state becomes a historian), the challenging of the paradigms of Western modernity, of the postcolonial promises, has opened up new directions and new orientations. (Ibid.: 5)

To challenge the Western historiographic paradigm, Diouf (2003: 4) recommends Archie Mafeje's statements that abandoning the fixed categories of 'tribe', 'ethnic group/ethnicity', 'nation-state' and 'racial groups' is very important to 'comprehend the developments and transformations of social formations instead of fragments' and to 'conceive social history as an enterprise of coding and decoding the people's ethnographic texts in historic time'. Diouf's proposition is quite helpful here, to move beyond the existing 'objectification' history of the Kanis to write a new history of subjectification. To write such a history what sort of genres need to be taken up for analysis?

In the studies of ethnography, as we have already seen, the 'other' has uniformly been portrayed as an object. Hence, it cannot 'address the basic issue of human self-constructing the other' because it considers 'the non-western people as living fossils who drew support from the historical and biological theories of the times' (Sarukkai 1997: 1406). The rational epistemology denies any 'ethical relation between the self and object'. However, there are other epistemological systems which play important roles in terms of capturing the subjectivity of people and communities. From an ethical ground,[6] the objectification has been questioned by Sarukkai. To go beyond the objectification, fiction—auto-ethnography—of the community has been identified as a legitimate tool. Pandian (2008) proposes that the creative genre and life stories are 'a compensation for the deficiencies of dominant modes of theory-making in social sciences'. Here, Pandian underscores the importance of life stories and fictions which are: 'Not bound by the evidentiary rules of social science, the privileged notion of teleological time, and claims to objectivity, and authorial neutrality, these narrative forms can produce enabling re-descriptions of life-worlds and facilitate the re-imagination of the political' (ibid.: 35). In the context of literary studies, Vargas (2008) places his emphasis on the importance of the locals' episteme. When the creative writings employ oral testimonies, it opens up the possibilities of alternative readings from the perspective of the subaltern, against the established State histories. In this context, he notes '... the valorisation of subalternised archives of knowledge and manners of expression such as gossip and exaggeration that are traditionally not granted much epistemic importance' (ibid.: 56). This is precisely where the importance of Pillayar Kani's ironic comment, with which I began this chapter, lies.

To change the misconception about the tribal communities—conceptualised as primitive, static, simple and uncivilised—Sunepsungla (2006) prescribes a tribal epistemology[7] which stands in diametric opposition to Western knowledge—'modern scientific thinking—rational, logical, conceptual and abstract thinking—as cognitive part of man cannot decrease the space of the unknown, the finite, for man's faculty is limited and regressive' (ibid.: 108). 'To bring to life the tribal epistemology, one needs to take into account the "cultural insiders" ways of theorization which is based on legends, myths, symbols, folklore, poetry, etc., that are ... vital constituents of a tribal culture' (ibid.). In general, the tribal epistemology of a particular community can contribute towards pluralising the reason, truth and knowledge in opposition to the singularity of the Westernised knowledge system. In addition, Uberoi, Deshpande and Sundar (2007: 14–15) recommend 'methodological innovations proposed to address the asymmetries and biases inherent in the production of anthropological knowledge, including "dialogical" or "experimental" ethnography, a greater emphasis on life histories and oral histories, and an anthropology of the "self" rather than the other'.

Let me allude to a piece of fiction based on the real life of a Kani person. *Anandha Vikatan*, a popular Tamil weekly, published a 36-episode thriller, 'Krishnaveni'. The story plot was set against the backdrop of the place, characters, dialect and incidents related to the Kani community. The story is about Vikraman Kani, a dead-body rescuer from the waterfalls in Vanatheertham, situated in the Kalakad-Mundanthurai Tiger Reserve. The rescuing activity was considered risky and his wife Valliammal asked him to give it up and go to the neighbouring state of Kerala to find another job there. He answered: '*Vura vittu na yeam yena povanum. Intha-k-kadu, intha yedattha vitta vera vazhiyum yenakku theriyathu. Vellath-larnthu thani-c-cha meenu pola chetthu-p-povum*' [If I leave this place, where will I go? I do not have any place other than this forest. I will die like a fish out of water] (Rajanarayanan 2009). On another occasion, he replied to his wife in a voice of sorrow that: '*Enthru yena parai-nathu. E kat-t-tina vittu po-vuthu nadakkuna kariyama? E kadu, mala, aruviya vittu na yengoottu povum*?' [What do you say? Is it feasible to leave the forest? After leaving this forest, mountain, falls—where will I go?] (Ibid.). The answer expresses the kind of intense feeling and attachment he has with the forest which goes beyond the reason of sustenance. Without life stories, capturing these shades of feelings and yearnings is impossible. And without capturing them, the ethnography of subjectification is not possible.

Likewise, here, I propose the use of 'social memory' and 'individual memory' as one more methodological tool to capture the subjectivity of the Kanis. At this juncture, we have to take a detour to figure out the importance of these memories in the field of anthropological history.

Connerton (1989), in general, classifies memory into three types: personal memory, cognitive memory and habit-memory. Personal memory offers meaning of 'a personal past'. The past is narrated and expressed by a particular subject itself. It remembers its own past histories, which are quite helpful in bringing forth the different voices of the community, even though it 'cannot have the histories and identities of other persons and things'. As Connerton precisely notes, personal memory is, to a certain extent, not adequate to capture the subjectivity of a community because of its own principle—'own conception' of its 'own character and potentialities'. Now, move on to cognitive memory, which is closely associated with 'remembering'. The remembering of things—'the meaning of words, or lines of verse, or jokes, or stories ... or mathematical equations, or truths of logic, or facts about the future ... must have met, experienced or learned of it in the past' (ibid.: 22). Both memories are very closely associated with the individuals' capability of remembering—a mental act. On the contrary, 'habit-memory' has proficiency 'to reproduce a certain performance' through body, for instance, how to respect elders in a society or to participate in a ritual or to follow traffic rules—this kind of memory is sedimented in the body. Connerton rightly clarifies the uniqueness of this memory that

> ... it has all the remarks of a habit, and the better we remember this class of memories, the less likely it is what we will recall some previous occasion on which we did the thing in question; it is only when we find ourselves in difficulties that we may turn to our recollections as a guide. (Ibid.: 23)

Here, again, 'habit-memory' has been classified into two types—individual habit and social habit. As compared to individual habit-memory, social habit-memory is socially constructed. This social construction of memory 'works within kinship groups, within religious groups, and within classes' (ibid.: 37). So, social-habit memory was identified as an appropriate methodological tool for this study.

Social-habit memory has rarely been used in historical studies to recover the subjectivity of community. Now, one question arises: How is the social memory recollected by communities? To answer the question, I take a cue from Connerton (1989), who correctly explains that the social recollection activity is at work in two different areas. One is in '*commemorative ceremonies*' and another is in '*bodily practices*'. In the social activity, bodily social memory is extremely important, even though it has been completely ignored. Once again, here, Madison (2005) underscores the importance of bodily expression against the written expression in the Western tradition of social science research, and notes: 'Writing is valued within the higher realms of knowledge, cosmopolitanism, and civility' (ibid.: 166). Madison was inspired by Dwight Conquergood's proposition of the body—he 'dignifies the body by recognizing embodied practices as constituting knowledge, emotion, and creation' (ibid.). Moreover, he says that it has a mind and soul beyond physical appearances. How does this category of knowledge become insignificant? The act of insignificance of the bodily expression happens when the writing becomes the centre of attention, which wipes out 'the everyday expressions of orality and symbolic embodiment that pervade in cultural spaces often hidden and cast out from the center of writing' (ibid.). Here, Connerton cautiously writes that the insight of 'reading' ritual or bodily practices should not be taken in literal terms. If it is taken in too literal a sense then one misses 'a literary political tract'. Further, he argues for the importance of habitual performances in terms of its characteristic feature of ambiguity and the 'significance of the second term of its meaning'. As a whole, both the memories—social-habit memory and personal memory—were applied in our ethnographic study of the Kanis, to bring out the different voices of the community.

Let me conclude with a reference to the bodily social memory, particularly a healing ritual, of the Kani community. The music instrument, *kokkarai*, and healing songs, *chattru pattu*, are both identified as symbols of the community by Kani society—identified from preliminary fieldwork—and by outsiders too. This is the prime cause for choosing this ritual for our study. The performance of chattruppattu starts at night and ends the next day, early morning. Its principal intention is to cure an ailing person from any sort of severe suffering, but this is the last resort after the failure of medication. If the chattruppattu fails to cure the ailing person from the diseases, the Kani community does not try to save the life of the sick person again, because the sick person would then become a 'wrong doer' in the eyes of nature and the deities and spirits. The ritual has been empirically described[8] in the post-Independence period. Here, I quote notes of Hardiman (2007) on the chattruppattu ritual and its importance in Kani lives: 'Despite the advent of modern medical facilities, the ritual continues to be popular, as it satisfies a demand for a community based healing over and above the more individualistic forms of healing provided by allopathy' (ibid.: 1405). Community-based healing needs to be understood from the subjective experience of the Kanis. Otherwise, capturing their subjectivity would be impossible.

Notes

[1] Gates defines *signifyin'* as the linguistic technique of repeating, imitating, revising, parodying and critiquing the nature of meaning and representation. When used as

a rhetorical technique, signifyin[g] 'is the figurative difference between the literal and the metaphorical, between surface and latent meaning', and it 'presupposes an "encoded" intention to say one thing but to mean quite another' (Gates 1988: 82, cited in Vargas 2008: 56).

[2] It 'consisted of the following sorts of categories: origin and tradition of caste or tribe; habitation; marriage customs; pregnancy and childbirth; inheritance and tribal organisation; religion, magic, and sorcery; funeral ceremonies; occupation; physical and mental characteristics; food; and social status' (Ram 2007: 77).

[3] Iyer (1968) and Iyer and Ratnam (1961) used the same description once again to establish the Kani community as 'primitive tribe' in the later works, which appeared in the postcolonial period.

[4] Quoted in a notice, which was served by the deputy director of Kalakad Mundunthurai Tiger Reserve Forest to the Kanis, who did not give the information to the forest department when the fire broke out in the forest.

[5] Quoted in Munshi (2007: 100).

[6] The ethical ground 'demands responsibility of the observing self towards the native other' (Sarukkai 1997: 1407).

[7] Sunepsungla (2006: 122) means that the 'tribal epistemology focuses on the process through which knowledge is constructed and validated by a cultural group, and the role of that process in shaping, thinking and behavior'.

[8] See Jayapathy (1981), Stephen (1997), Arivalagan (2002), Dharmaraj (2005), Rajashree (2006) and Karmegam (2008).

References

'Kanikkar'. 1990. In *Dravidian Encyclopaedia*, ed. V. I. Subramoniam, 379–80. Thiruvananthapuram: The International School of Dravidian Linguistics.

Agesthiyalingom, S. 1976. *Kanikkara Dialect*. Annamalainagar: Annamalai University.

Aiya, Nagam, V. 1989. *The Travancore State Manual*, Volume 2 (reprint). New Delhi and Madras: Asian Educational Services.

Arivalagan, M. 2002. 'Isaitthal Kattamai-k-kum Pal-verupadugal'. *Exil* 4(12): 52–65.

Bhukya, Bhangya. 2008. 'The Mapping of the Adivasi Social: Colonial Anthropology and Adivasis'. *Economic and Political Weekly* 43(39): 103–09.

Census of India. 1901. Extract from the Census of India 1901, Travancore—I.

——— 1911. Extract from the Census of India 1911.

——— 1933. 'Tour Notes of the Census Commissioner for India, 1930–31'. In *Census of India 1931: With Complete Survey of Tribal Life and System*, Volume 3, Part B, ed. J. H. Hutton.

——— 1961. IX, Madras, V–B—(1), Ethnographic Notes on Scheduled Tribes.

Connerton, Paul. 1989. *How Societies Remember*. Cambridge, New York, Port Chester, Melbourne Sydney: Cambridge University Press.

Dharmaraj, Yo. 2005. *Kani-p-pazhankudi Makkalin Padalgalum Vazha-k-karugalum*. Chennai: Thirukkural Pathipagam.

Diouf, Mamadou. 2003. *Historians and Histories: What For? African Historiography between the State and the Communities*. The Netherlands: SEPHIS–CSSSC.

Dirks, Nicholas B. 1992. 'Castes of Mind'. *Representations* 37: 56–78.

Guha, Sumit. 1999. *Environment and Ethnicity in India, 1200–1991*. Cambridge: Cambridge University Press.

Hardiman, David. 2007. 'Healing, Medical Power and the Poor: Contests in Tribal India' (commentary). *Economic and Political Weekly* 42(16): 1404–08.

Hutton, J. H. 1986. 'Tour Notes of the Census Commissioner for India, 1930–31'. In *Ethnographic Notes by Various Hands* (reprint), ed. J. H. Hutton, 245–62. Delhi: Gian Publishing House.

Iyer, L. A. Krishna. 1968. *Social History of Kerala: The Pre-Dravidians*, Volume 1. Madras: Book Centre Publications.

Iyer, L. A. Krishna and L. K. Bala Ratnam. 1961. *Anthropology in India*. Bombay: Bharatiya Vidya Bhavan.

Iyer, L. A. Krishna and N. Kunjan Pillai. 1933. 'The Primitive Tribes of Travancore'. In *Ethnographic Notes by Various Hands* (reprint 1986), ed. J. H. Hutton, 217–43. Delhi: Gian Publishing House.

Jayapathy, F. 1981. 'The Kanikkar Religion'. M.Phil dissertation, University of Delhi, Delhi.

Karmegam, S. 2008. 'Healing, Ritual and Theatre: Understanding Chattruppattu Performance of Kanikkarar of South India'. M.Phil dissertation, Jawaharlal Nehru University, New Delhi.

Madison, D. Soyini. 2005. *Critical Anthropology*. Thousand Oaks, London, New Delhi: Sage.

Maruthakutti. R. 1998. 'Ethnographic Study of Kanis in Kalakad Mundanthurai Tiger Reserve'. Report, Manonmanium Sundaranar University, Tirunelveli.

Mateer, Samuel. 1991. *Native Life in Travancore* (reprint). New Delhi and Madras: Asian Educational Services.

Munshi, Indra. 2007. *Adivasi Life Stories: Context, Constraints, Choices*. Jaipur, New Delhi, Bangalore, Mumbai, Hyderabad and Guwahati: Rawat Publications.

Nambiar, P. K. 1964. 'Preface'. In *Census of India 1961, IX, Madras, Part V–B—(1), Ethnographic Notes On Scheduled Tribes*.

Pandian, M. S. S. 2008. 'Writing Ordinary Lives'. *Economic and Political Weekly* 43(38): 34–40.

Parthasarathy, Jakka. 1997. 'Kanikaran'. In *People of India: Tamilnadu XL, Part-II*, ed. K. S. Singh, 816–21. Madras: Affiliated East–West Press Pvt. Ltd.

Pate, H. R. 1993. *Tinnevelly District Gazetteer* (reprint). Tirunelveli: Manonmanium Sundaranar University.

Pillayar Kani. 1997. Interviewed by M. Arivalagan, Agasthiyar Nagar Kanikudiyiruppu, Papanasam, October.

Rajanarayanan, Pa. 2009. 'Krishnaveni: Nija Thikil Thodar'. *Anandha Vikatan*, series 36, 23 July 2008–25 March 2009.

Rajashree, R. S. 2006. 'Kanyakumari Mavatta Kanikkararkalin Pini-chattru Padalgal: Oru Aivu'. Ph.D dissertation, University of Kerala, Thiruvananthapuram.

Ram, Kalpana. 2007. 'Anthropology as "Ananthropology": L. K. Ananthakrishna Iyer (1861–1937), Colonial Anthropology, and the "Native Anthropologist" as Pioneer'. In *Anthropology in the East: Founders of Indian Sociology and Anthropology*, eds Particia Uberoi, Nandini Sundar and Satish Deshpande, 64–105. Ranikhet: Permanent Black.

Sarukkai, Sundar. 1997. 'The "Other" in Anthropology and Philosophy'. *Economic and Political Weekly* 32(24): 1406–09.

Sethi, Nitin. 2008. 'Tribe Feels the Heat as Forest Fire Rages'. *Times of India*, 7 July.

Singh, K. S. 2001. 'Kanikkar'. In *The Scheduled Tribes*, National Series 3, 460–64. New Delhi: Oxford University Press.

——— 1998. 'Kanikkar'. In *India's Communities H–M: People of India*, National Series 5, 1533–34. Delhi, Calcutta, Chennai and Mumbai: Oxford University Press.

Srivastava, Vinay Kumar. 2008. 'Concept of "Tribe" in the Draft National Tribal Policy'. *Economic and Political Weekly* 43(50): 29–35.

Stephen, I. 1997. *Kokkarai: Kanikkarar Vazhivum Panpadum*. Nagercoil: Thinai Veliyeetagam.

Sunepsungla. 2006. 'An Understanding of Tribal Epistemology'. *Journal of Indian Council of Philosophical Research* 23(1): 105–25.

Thurston, Edgar. 1975. 'Kanikar'. In *Castes and Tribes of Southern India* III-K (reprint), 162–77. Delhi: Cosmo Publications.

Uberoi, Patricia, Satish Deshpande and Nandini Sundar. 2007. 'Introduction—The Professionalisation of Indian Anthropology and Sociology: People, Places and Institutions'. In *Anthropology in the East: Founders of Indian Sociology and Anthropology*, eds Uberoi, Sundar and Deshpande, 1–64. Ranikhet: Permanent Black.

Vargas, Jennifer Harford. 2008. 'A Tale of Two Novels from the Global South'. *Economic and Political Weekly* 43(50): 52–61.

5. Mudumalai's Logics

*Governmentalising 'Forests' and Conservation Subjects**

Ajit Menon

In the mid-1950s E. A. Lasrado, the Conservator of Forests for the Nilgiris, in a series of internal forest department letters, recommended that the government move the Mudumalai Wildlife Sanctuary and National Park to the Sigur region east of Mudumalai because of the presence of paddy cultivation in Mudumalai.[1] Lasrado felt that Mudumalai was an important site of much-needed wetland cultivation and should not be interfered with unnecessarily. The Nilgiri Game Association (NGA), an organisation of colonial hunters, whose members were often also honorary forest guards, argued against Lasrado's recommendation because British hunters depended on the Sigur area for small-game hunting. Mudumalai remained where it was while the debates around it were buried in archival record rooms. More than 50 years later in 2007, with increasing emphasis on tiger conservation nationally and globally, the National Tiger Conservation Authority (NTCA) in India declared Mudumalai a tiger reserve, resulting once again in conflicts regarding boundaries. Local people protested against Mudumalai being declared an inviolate tiger reserve

*M. S. S. Pandian was a friend and mentor. He always found time to discuss ideas and encouraged me not to be timid while conceptualising my research. I am sure I am a long way away from heeding his advice, but I take his words seriously. This chapter is about conservation and its politics, an issue Pandian touched upon in his writing about colonial game-hunting in the Nilgiris. I would like to thank Nitin Rai and Manasi Karthik for comments on an earlier version of this chapter.

and its area being extended to include a buffer zone. Disputes raged about whether people should be allowed to stay on inside Mudumalai and how and to whom forest rights should be distributed under the newly enacted Scheduled Tribes and Other Traditional Forest Dwellers (Recognition of Forest Rights) Act 2006 (Taghioff and Menon 2010).

What both the discussions in the forest department in the 1950s and conflicts over the tiger reserve on the ground more recently highlight is that conservation is political, that is, it is contested, and situated within wider political and cultural economies. Initiatives such as the Save Our Tiger campaign, a flagship campaign aimed at creating awareness about tiger conservation, jointly sponsored by NDTV and Aircel, ignore these political and cultural economies. Tiger conservation is seen to be 'natural' both in terms of it being the natural thing to do and in its pursuit of preserving an authentic nature. Conservation is depoliticised and rendered 'technical' and 'managerial', and the complex factors that shape its social ecology are ignored.

This chapter, by analysing the genealogy of conservation in Mudumalai, attempts to unpack the multiple priorities that have shaped the broad discursive and material boundaries of conservation over time.[2] The State's privileging of hunting and the creation of a tiger reserve were but two priorities that helped configure conservation in Mudumalai. Other priorities included the colonial and postcolonial States' demand for timber and the promotion of ecotourism in a big way from the 1990s. I argue that these priorities are often implicitly threaded together in 'official' accounts of the making of Mudumalai to suggest that a 'universal' conservation has always been part of colonial and postcolonial statemaking. I question this through a retelling of the history of Mudumalai so as to emphasise that political concerns have often trumped ecological ones in the shaping of conservation. I further argue that Mudumalai's conservation history must be situated within wider regional processes of statemaking in Gudalur. Colonialism and the promotion of a capitalist estate economy initially drove forest conservation (Menon, Hinnewinkel and Guillerme 2013). While the expansion of colonial rule in the upper plateau of the Nilgiris resulted in huge demand for timber, the promotion of an estate economy meant that timber could only be procured locally from areas such as Mudumalai that remained forested. Although the capitalist estate economy continued to expand in Gudalur and other neighbouring areas of the Western Ghats (Ravi Raman 2010) in the postcolonial period, the postcolonial State had other concerns too in which Gudalur was implicated—foremost the production of food and the repatriation of Indian Tamils from erstwhile Ceylon. Gudalur became home to large numbers of small-scale farmers (Menon, Hinnewinkel and Guillerme 2013). I argue that these developments too shaped the politics around conservation in Gudalur as a whole and in Mudumalai in particular.

By telling the story of Mudumalai's making, I not only hope to highlight the diverse political and cultural economies that shape conservation priorities within statemaking, but also the manner in which multiple types of governmentalities aim to create the 'right' conservation subjects. Finally, I suggest that people's capacity for situated politics (Li 2008) often prevent the 'success' of these governmentalised projects of protected-area conservation in the ways intended. There are, in other words, ruptures in the conservation project when either conservation subjects or those excluded from governmentalised conservation take issue with the form and substance of the latter. These ruptures potentially provide a different lens through which to imagine conservation in the future.

Understanding Protected-area Conservation

Much of the recent literature on protected-area conservation has focused on capitalism and conservation, most prominently in its neoliberal avatar (Brockington and Duffy 2010; Dressler and Büscher 2008; Duffy 2008). As Brockington and Duffy (2010) argue, capitalism has at many historical junctures shaped the nature of conservation. In the Western world, capitalist philanthropists advocated the setting up of the first protected areas in the United States and elsewhere. And today, neoliberal conservation appears to be a new avenue for capital accumulation (Münster and Münster 2012).

I suggest that while capitalism has had a significant impact in shaping protected-area conservation in India as well, it alone cannot explain the manner in which protected areas such as Mudumalai have been constructed over time. My conceptual starting point, therefore, in understanding the political ecology of conservation in Mudumalai is that of statemaking. Sivaramakrishnan (1999: 4) defines statemaking as the mutual constitution of State and society. He emphasises that statemaking is a fluid concept where neither the State nor society should be taken for granted, but rather situated historically. In other words, characterising the State is an empirical question. As a point of departure, I believe this to be useful as it allows me to deconstruct internal segmentations within the State and also understand how different social groups have shaped the State over time. It is worth pointing out, however, that the idea of statemaking still privileges the State (that is, we are not talking about society-making). It is also worth pointing out that not taking the State for granted does not mean that the State cannot represent particular class interests, but rather that interests other than that of class might be shaping conservation as well.

How then should one go about problematising this institutional fixity (or the lack thereof) of the State? I start with the question of the State's reach because I am primarily concerned with the State's conservation project. The vast literature on environmental history debates the extent of the colonial State's territorial reach (Guha 1989; Rangarajan 1996; Scott 1999, 2009; Sivaramakrishnan 1999; Agrawal 2005; Vandergeest and Peluso 1995). Suffice it to say that more recently some scholars (Sivaramakrishnan 1999; Scott 2009) have illustrated that large swathes of British India remained beyond the direct control of the British. Mudumalai, prior to being declared reserved land and then a wildlife sanctuary, was one such region. That part of Mudumalai's conservation history, therefore, must be understood keeping in mind the limited purview of the colonial State. Equally important to the reach question is the micro-politics of the everyday (Scott 1987). Even when protected areas such as Mudumalai come under the legal control of the State, this does not necessarily mean that the State's legal writ is obeyed. As Chhatre and Saberwal (2006) argue in the case of the Great Himalayan National Park, the State's imposition of legal restrictions on forest-adjacent communities collecting forest produce are often bypassed when villagers negotiate with local State functionaries. At times, local communities do not negotiate but just resist by 'illegally' entering protected areas. These negotiations and resistances must also be part of the telling of Mudumalai's conservation history (Scott 1987).

Another important dimension of statemaking is the question of substantive unity within the State. Is the State unitary with singular interests? This question is important to keep in mind given the Marxian political economy accounts of capitalism and conservation that see conservation primarily either as a product of capitalism or, more recently, as a green form of capital accumulation (Fairhead, Leach and Scoones 2012). This is, no doubt, partly true; the history of conservation is linked at various stages to the growth of the capitalist economy. But while capitalism might well be a substantive part of Mudumalai's history, it might not be the only part. Capitalism does not necessarily explain why the colonial State promoted a particular type of wildlife conservation that aimed at addressing the leisure needs of British hunters. Nor does capitalism fully explain why postcolonial conservation became a nationalist project. As Baviskar (2003) argues, cultural politics might help explain this better than political economy. More importantly, cultural politics do not necessarily overlap with class politics. The State, in other words, might have interests that go beyond the promotion of capital accumulation.

This brings me back to the idea that statemaking is about the mutual constitution of State and society. The reason that the State might not be institutionally or substantively fixed across time is because different societal actors might shape decisions made by the State at particular historical junctures (Sivaramakrishnan 1999). I illustrated this at the outset when delineating the broad contours of Mudumalai's conservation project and detail it further in what follows. There are three dimensions to the State–society dynamic: the relationship between different actors within the State, the relationship between different societal actors, and the nature of interaction between the State and societal actors. All of these need to be explored in the telling of regional histories such as this.

Sivaramakrishnan (1999: 5) also argues that 'statemaking is fundamentally about defining the forms and legitimations of government and governmentality'. Governmentality speaks to the manner in which the government invokes the compliance and commitment of society through the constitution of new subjects. Bose, Arts and van Dijk (2012), building on Michel Foucault's notion of governmentality, argue that (forest) governmentalities have three dimensions: (i) categorisation of groups of the population, (ii) a politics of social identity tied to categorisations and (iii) technologies of power. These three, seen together, help understand how disciplining 'defined' populations shape the conduct of subjects. Mudumalai's conservation history is very much about the act of governing and the attempt to create particularised conservation subjects. At different points of time, different social identities have been central to the conservation story and to the making of these environmental subjects.

The nature of these governmentalities is of equal importance. Fletcher (2010) makes the case for categorising environmental governmentalities (or environmentalities) into different categories that capture the means through which governing takes place. He speaks of sovereign environmentalities that allude to creating environmental subjects who are excluded from environmental spaces through fines and fences; disciplinary environmentalities that refer to attempts to govern by changing the ethics or values of environmental subjects; and neoliberal environmentalities that use the market and commodification to change behaviour. All of these, I believe, are disciplinary in different ways. People are either disciplined to follow rules, disciplined to become more concerned about the environment or disciplined as market subjects. I am less concerned, therefore, with categorising different governmentalities and more interested in their disciplinary character.

Li (2008) reminds us that governmental power has limits. I have already alluded to that while discussing the everyday negotiations with and resistances to the State. This must be understood, however, also in the context of governmentalities and subject formation. Li (2008) talks about the capacity for situated politics in highlighting that the State does not always meet with success. Agrawal (2005) also talks about this when trying to analyse who did and who did not become environmental subjects when the British introduced new decentralised governmentalities for forest management in Kumaon. In historical analyses of conservation, such as the one undertaken in this chapter, I can at best refer to how sub-populations resist being made environmental subjects as opposed to speak about individual subjects. There are also cases of people claiming particular environmental subjectivities that the government has not attributed to them.

Looking at statemaking and the governmentalisation of conservation allows me to problematise the State's priorities of conservation at given points of time. Much has been written about how the colonial government deemed 'unproductive' land as wasteland and tried to civilise nature (Philip 2003). The British often cut down large tracts of forests in favour of plantation crops or tree plantations. In such contexts, tree plantations were forest conservation in practice. But equally important is seeing how game-hunters, despite their targeting of game, were seen to be ideal wildlife conservationists and how the essentialised Adivasi (tribal) has become synonymous with present-day conservation. In other words, the battle over nature is as much about conservation for whom and/or what as it is about conservation *versus* development. Again, regional histories are of importance here—regional histories that unpack the changing conservation priorities of the State as opposed to suggesting that they are static or singular.

Conservation as Sustainable Timber Supply

In the mid-nineteenth century, Mudumalai, like much of Gudalur, was under the control of the Nilambur Kovilakam *jenmi* (landed aristocracy or landlord). Although the British had acquired Gudalur when they defeated Tipu Sultan at the end of the eighteenth century, they chose to recognise the Kovilakam's proprietorship of land. The Nilambur Kovilakam and other smaller jenmis leased out large areas of land primarily to British capitalists, who invested first in coffee and later in tea. Jenmis charged a *janmabhogam* or land tax and shared the produce equally with farmers. The British were content as they collected taxes on the produce without having the supervisory burden of monitoring farmers (Menon, Hinnewinkel and Guillerme 2013: 455–56; Menon 2015: 39).

The promotion of the plantation economy was central to the priorities of colonial statemaking (Krishnan 2009). The colonial State wanted to civilise nature as a way to raise revenue (Philip 2003). The revenue wing of the colonial administration ensured that land policies facilitated the expansion of plantations so that the 'opening up of the Nilgiris' was 'not indefinitely retarded'.[3] They were only interested that forests situated 50 yards on either side of ridges and within a 30 yard radius of the heads of streams should be preserved.[4] Not surprisingly, therefore, the latter part of the nineteenth century witnessed the growth of the plantation economy in the Gudalur region and also increased revenue to the British.[5]

Mudumalai's conservation history must be seen within the purview of this colonial statemaking. As the colonial State facilitated the conversion of forests into plantations across Gudalur, Mudumalai, as a wooded landscape, remained paramount for timber, both for the railways and the building of Ootacamund and the cantonment areas on the upper plateau. The Nilambur Kovilakam, however, had leased out Mudumalai to a timber merchant, Muddanah, who paid a stump fee to fell the accessible areas of Mudumalai. This was to change, however, when the Madras Railway contractor Williams, in search of sleepers, first expressed concern to the collector of Malabar in 1855 about the excessive felling of Mudumalai. The Madras Presidency government asked the collector, a Mr Robinson, to report on this felling and suggest ways to best work these forests (Sekar 2004: 30).

On the ground in the Nilgiris, Mudumalai was important primarily for its timber. In 1858, the forest department finally leased Mudumalai from the Nilambur Kovilakam for Rs 2,300 per annum. Mudumalai was a well-stocked forest with important timber species such as teak (*Tectona grandis*), black wood (*Dalbergia latifolia*), venteak (*Lagerstroemia lanceolate*), marudu (*Terminalia glabra*) and vengai (*Pterocarpus marsopium*) (ibid.: 30–31). The forest department leased Mudumalai so as to reduce its dependence on timber from other areas such as the Annamalai Hills and Burma.

The department took a 99-year lease from the Kovilakam in 1863 at the rate of Rs 3,500 per year. The prime reason it took a long lease for Mudumalai was the continued availability of the timber species mentioned earlier. Teak, the most important timber species for the British, existed in plenty although periodically different officers expressed chagrin at its fast rate of depletion (ibid.: 33). When teak supplies declined to crisis levels, the forest department promoted teak plantations; however, they stopped them by 1878 because of their poor growth.

In the latter decades of the nineteenth century, the forest department 'sustainably' worked the forests for timber. The Nilambur Kovilakam, while leasing timber rights to private actors and then the forest department, had retained the right to collect minor forest produce and lease the right to collect the same to others. In 1875, the commissioner of the Nilgiris expressed concern about such an arrangement because minor forest produce collectors, he argued, might encourage forest fires that would be detrimental to the collection of timber.[6] He also expressed concern that the smuggling of timber might become rampant. The colonial administration, and the forest department in particular, were all the more concerned because areas outside Mudumalai had already been converted into private estates and consequently large areas of teak and black wood felled.[7]

The forest department, at the end of the nineteenth century, exerted increasing control over Mudumalai. In 1885, it inspected the forests of southeast Wayanad and the Moyar Valley, and as a result of poor stocks, called for institutionalising a system of working timber. In 1889, Mudumalai was declared reserved land under the Madras Forest Act 1878. Doing so served the twin purpose of restricting others from collecting minor forest produce from Mudumalai, while also making it possible for the forest department to direct timber operations. The Kumbarakolli block of forests was added to Mudumalai in 1892 (Sekar 2004: 27). Over the next 50 years or so, the forest department experimented with different types of felling operations: improvement felling, selective felling and clear felling.

The forest department also institutionalised new forest governmentalities as part of its timber project. Forest governmentalities refer to technologies of power through which new subjects are created for governing the forest. As Bose, Arts and van Dijk (2012) detail in the case of the Bhils, the State created 'tribal' subjects in the nineteenth century by restricting their historical access to forests, and giving them certain concessions to forest produce instead. In Mudumalai, a similar situation prevailed. The forest department employed the Kurumbas for timber-planting operations by subjecting them to coercive and economic measures (Prabhakar 1994: 91). The department allowed the Kurumbas to undertake their traditional *kumri* or *taungya* cultivation (shifting cultivation), in the midst of teak trees, as an incentive of sorts. But they were primarily drafted in as a source of labour for teak-planting. Taungya cultivation was first permitted in the Benne forests adjacent to Mudumalai in 1896; dry crops were planted in the clearing between teak, rosewood and vengai trees (Sekar 2004: 35).

The colonial State went further. The forest department, in the Inspection Notes of a Reconnaisance Report it penned in 1926, made an earnest plea to settle labour in forests and give taungya rights to the Kurumbas.[8] In that same report, it recommended that swamps (or wet lands) be given to the Chettis and Paniyans on lease, and that the latter should be encouraged to cultivate their own land as opposed to serving the Chettis. R. S Browne, the district forest officer of the Nilgiris, in 1936, argued that the department should support lease applications, because giving leases would attract labourers who then as part of the terms of their contract would have to supply labour to the forest department whenever necessary.[9] The Reconnaisance Report also mentioned that the depressed classes (Paniyans) would be 'performing a national duty and assisting the Forest Department'.[10]

Wildlife, Hunting and the NGA

According to Sekar (2004: 91), as he mentions in his *Forest History of the Nilgiris*, a group of concerned hunters formed the NGA in 1877 because of their common concern that wildlife was rapidly dwindling. From the 1830s onwards, Sekar argues, the landed gentry took to hunting. However, according to the colonial administration, the 'race of local shikaries', who also took to hunting and were involved in the meat trade, caused the indiscriminate killing of wildlife, especially sambhars. The NGA was a voluntary game association that also had as one of its aims the preservation of wildlife in the Nilgiris. It formulated rules for a closed season and restrictions on the slaying of calves, hinds and cow bison. A number of other rules were scripted regarding the registration of *shikaris* (hunters) and payments for licenses. In 1879, the government passed the Nilgiri Fish and Game Preservation Act in support of the NGA's initiatives.[11] Wildlife conservation and hunting were, in other words, from the outset inextricably linked. As in the case of timber, the British cared mostly about managing the resource.

As Pandian (1995) highlights, British hunters distinguished themselves from native hunters. British hunters claimed that game hunting was a sport that provided an arena in which their masculine prowess could be showcased. They viewed native hunters as effeminate, targeting game at close quarters either to protect their crops or to market the meat but not as a sportive challenge. British hunters also claimed that hunting for sport was not a threat to wildlife. The distinction between colonial and native hunting, Pandian goes on to argue, was that hunting was also one way in which the colonial State claimed superiority over the native other in its project of statemaking.

The role of the NGA can also be unpacked through the lens of colonial governmentality. At one level, the colonial State saw the NGA as critical to the colonial State's wildlife conservation agenda in much the same way the tribals were instrumental to the colonial State's timber project. What was different was that no disciplinary or coercive tactics were necessary to bring on board the NGA. Rather, the government treated the NGA as resourceful hunters who efficiently hunted game within the biological limits of the resource. The native hunters were the indiscriminate ones.

Wildlife conservation, to a great extent, became important because of colonial hunting and the NGA. The employment of NGA members as honorary forest guards is illustrative of the increasing importance the association played in wildlife conservation. It is important to point out that NGA members became honorary guards at their own request. Even fines levied by these honorary forest guards went into the coffers of the NGA despite intermittent protest by members of the forest department.[12]

The NGA's role became more significant in the early-twentieth century when the government directed that fisheries management should also be transferred to the NGA. The NGA regulated fishing in accordance with the rules and regulations of the 1879 Act. The NGA, in return for ensuring 'efficient' fishing, was allowed to appropriate receipts generated through licences.[13] A main reason the colonial government handed over fisheries management to the NGA was to deal with the native threat. The colonial government primarily held the Kurumbas responsible for poaching fish and overfishing, and felt the NGA had their ears closer to the ground to ensure that poaching was prevented.[14]

NGA's willingness to work with the colonial State was also its way of ensuring that hunting spaces remained intact. In 1929, the secretary of the NGA wrote a letter to the government highlighting that schemes to grow more tea and tanning bark had resulted in the decline of sporting facilities.[15] The forest department too echoed similar concerns. A. Wimbush, the chief conservator of forests, urged the department to address NGA's worries so as to ensure future cooperation of the organisation to help protect wildlife. When the colonial government sought to declare Mudumalai a wildlife sanctuary in the late 1930s, due to increasing concerns that both wildlife and timber were in decline, the NGA argued that a similar, equally productive hunting area should be given to them in another locality.[16] If a letter written by the honorary secretary of the NGA is anything to go by, the government passed orders for the formation of the sanctuary after the NGA gave its consent and the government transferred the Muthanga block in Wayanad to the NGA for hunting purposes.[17]

The NGA continued to voice its concern about the boundaries of Mudumalai after its declaration as a sanctuary in 1940. They did so because the forest department became increasingly vociferous about the decline of wildlife. Many forest officers argued that the Mudumalai sanctuary be extended. The call for doing so became even stronger once India had become an independent country. The department put forward proposals in the early 1950s to extend the sanctuary west to include parts of the Sultan Bathery range, in present-day Kerala, and east to include parts of the Moyar and Sigur range.[18] The Central Board of Wildlife, at about the same time, in line with the general objectives of the International Union for the Protection of Nature, also spoke about the creation of national parks.[19] The NGA, which continued to exist in independent India, opposed the extension of the Mudumalai sanctuary to Sigur. It did so because it considered Sigur to be the only small-game hunting area in the district, an excellent area in which to hunt bison and spotted deer, and also a first-class tiger-shooting area. It also believed that only it could stop poachers from Mysore from indiscriminately killing wildlife. Finally, it argued that the Sigur area encompassed a number of smallholder farmers who would be adversely affected, and that the NGA as an organisation would be crippled financially.[20]

Moving towards Inviolate Areas for Wildlife Conservation

What is apparent from the discussion thus far is that Mudumalai was not an untouched, pristine wildlife zone. It underwent many transformations as a result, I argue, of the fact that the different actors and priorities shaped its socioecological making. This is in line with wider historical evidence of the significant changes that the Nilgiri region had experienced for hundreds of years (Morrison and Lycett 2014). It is also in line with wider conceptual arguments about the social construction of nature (Jeffery 1998). This, of course, is not to say that Mudumalai in its transformed form cannot be imagined as a wildlife sanctuary or even a tiger reserve, but rather that the physical form it takes is the product of politics and power as much as it might be of ecology.

It was with the passing of the Wildlife Protection Act (WPA) in 1972 that the State governmentalised areas such as Mudumalai primarily keeping wildlife conservation in mind. Of course, the idea of sanctuaries pre-dated this by a few decades. The colonial government had declared an area of approximately 54 square km as Mudumalai Sanctuary in 1940. In 1958, Mudumalai Sanctuary was enlarged to an area of 318 square km. Although discussions took place within the forest department and the State Wildlife Board about banning shooting licences for hunting and crop protection, this did not occur for some time to come.[21] According to Sekar (2004: 102–03), the forest department continued to heavily exploit timber in Mudumalai until the 1960s and engaged in selective felling up to 1985. In 1977, the Wildlife Warden assumed control over Mudumalai Sanctuary. This signalled the beginning of the end of timber exploitation, though hunting appears to have continued for a longer time.[22] John Joseph's Working Plan for 1977–87 highlighted the need to resettle people still located in Mudumalai to areas outside. In 2005, 103.24 square km of Mudumalai were declared a national park.

Rangarajan (2001: 100–01) argues that wildlife conservation was symbolically important to save India's national emblem, the tiger. Project Tiger was launched in 1973, targeting nine sanctuaries not including Mudumalai. Though the government focused on checking the dwindling number of tigers, wildlife conservationists argued that the measures needed to undertake that, for example, restricting forestry activities in the core areas of reserves, resulted in the overall improved health of the ecosystem. This further resulted in the protection of other birds, animals and plants too. What is certain is that activities that had been fairly common within sanctuaries in the past were now deemed harmful. In the most recent Working Plan for Mudumalai, the major threats identified are headloading (by both residents and non-residents), cattle, felling, poaching, pilgrims, tourists and traffic (Dogra 2007: 131–40).

In 2007, the central government notified Mudumalai as a tiger reserve and a critical tiger habitat.[23] All 321 square km of Mudumalai Sanctuary and National Park became inviolate area under Section 38V(4) of the Wildlife Protection Amendment Act (WPAA) 2006. Although under Section 38V(5) of the Act forest dwellers cannot be relocated without consent of their Gram Sabhas, a 2017 notification of the NTCA stipulates that forest rights will be not be recognised in critical tiger habitats. In effect, therefore, what has happened in tiger reserves is that people living inside the reserve have lost their rights to claim title to lands they use. In the case of Mudumalai, this implies that the approximately 500 families that lived in Mudumalai, comprising Kattunayakans, Kurumbas, Paniyans and Moundaden Chettis, have become encroachers. In practice, of course, the story is far more nuanced. A number of households continue to live in Mudumalai either because of a very slow relocation and rehabilitation process, or because they are reluctant to leave (Taghioff and Menon 2010). For those who do not want to leave, the fact that Mudumalai is now legally inviolate means that the human costs of remaining are considerably higher than they were before. In the buffer areas of Mudumalai around Masinagudi, which have been designated as elephant corridors, local households too complain about the difficulties they face *vis-à-vis* grazing cattle, etc. Moreover, as Karthik and Menon (2016: 45) illustrate, conservationists filed a court case in 2008 aimed at evicting many local residents, and in 2010 the government passed an order aimed at acquiring land in the Sigur plateau.

The intent of the forest department is that Mudumalai becomes part of a larger wildlife corridor from Wayanad to Sathyamangalam. Many conservationists continue to argue that protected areas occupy a miniscule per cent of total land area in India and hence expanding them, while critical to wildlife survival, will not have significant social costs (Menon and Karthik 2017: 21). Even more recently, the discussion about ecologically sensitive areas has emerged on the agenda once more with a number of prominent conservationists calling for such areas to be declared (WWF 2016).

To a large extent, the idea of inviolate tiger reserves adopts what Fletcher (2010) calls a sovereign form of governmentality. People are fenced out. But this type of sovereign governmentality, at least partly, goes hand in hand with what he calls disciplinary governmentalities aimed at creating new ethically grounded environmental subjects. In order to ensure the sanctity of inviolate areas, the wildlife wing of the forest department promotes eco-development activities aimed at weaning forest-dwelling communities away from their dependence on forests. The logic of eco-development is that by providing alternative livelihoods outside the forests, communities have less need to go to forests for fuelwood and other non-timber forest produce. Examples of eco-development near Mudumalai include the Chembakolli village in Gudalur and Anaikatty in the Bokapuram area.

Mudumalai and Neoliberal Conservation

A lot has been written about how conservation has increasingly been neoliberalised. In other words, instead of seeing the environment as a possible second contradiction of capitalism, one can see it as a possible site in which accumulation is greened. The State, by facilitating investment by private capital, is very much part of this neoliberal project (Fletcher 2010; Parenti 2014). Much of the literature on neoliberal conservation, however, is Africa-specific. Examples exist of privatised national parks. Of more importance is the role of private security firms patrolling and even militarising national parks (Dressler and Büscher 2008; Duffy 2008). Büscher highlights how NGOs engaged in conservation often solicit donations from private individuals for which, in return, these individuals can make suggestions as to how to improve wildlife conservation, making them feel as if they are part of the solution as well.

What is the evidence with regard to India? Similar NGOs exist in India too such as the Wildlife Trust of India, which employs similar fund-raising tactics. More recently, media houses and cellphone companies have become part of wildlife conservation. NDTV and Aircel, for example, have put tiger conservation on the top of their agendas through the Save Our Tiger Campaign.[24] Celebrities such as Amitabh Bachchan have been their star campaigners. The use of star celebrities is, as Brockington and Duffy (2010: 73) argue, to create a spectacle that people want to be part of in some way. Given that the tiger is a national emblem makes it even more important for people to help in whatever way possible to save it. In the Mudumalai context, this private capital must be channelled through the Mudumalai Tiger Conservation Foundation, a foundation under the auspices of the forest department.

Ecotourism is the other possible site where neoliberalising conservation takes place. Despite the declaration of Mudumalai as an inviolate tiger reserve, tourism continues to be promoted. The reason for this is that from the outset, in the 1970s, tourism has been the means by which the State has tried to create environmentally sensitive subjects who care about wildlife. In John Joseph's Working Plan, it was stated that 'publicity should be designed to remove false notions about wild animals and birds and their exaggerated harmful effects to man and his crops. General public should be convinced about the need to conserve wildlife for their various uses and values' (John Joseph 1977: 67). This goal remained important, perhaps became even more important, after the declaration of the tiger reserve. What is 'new' about ecotourism in its neoliberal form is the much more active role played by private tourist operators (Münster and Münster 2012).

Private tourism has picked up in Mudumalai too. In the latest Working Plan for Mudumalai, it is stated that, in 2005–06, approximately 120,000 tourists visited Mudumalai. Expectations were that this number would rise to 150,000 (Dogra 2007: 142). Revenue in 2005–06 was estimated to be around Rs 50 lakhs. A report by the World Wide Fund for Nature (WWF) on tourism in the Sigur plateau highlighted that it was during this time that the number of private resorts burgeoned in the Masinagudi area (Nathan 2008). Münster and Münster (2012), in the context of Wayanad, Kerala (an area bordering Gudalur), argue that nature tourism has increasingly become a site for accumulation in a post-agrarian economy. Whether Gudalur can be called a post-agrarian economy is debatable; however, private tourism has certainly burgeoned.

Questions also remain to be answered with regard to the nature of accumulation. As pointed out earlier, it is the Mudumalai Tiger Conservation Foundation, under the auspices of the forest department, that regulates wildlife tourism. Over the last few years, there have been a number of incidents in which private tourism operators have engaged in 'illegal' tourism, resulting, on a couple of occasions, in the death of foreign tourists (Radhakrishnan 2013). As a result, the forest department has become stricter, preventing private tourist operators from conducting their own wildlife sightseeing tours.

This apart, the neoliberalisation of conservation has certainly resulted in the creation of neoliberal conservation subjects at many levels. First, there are the tourist operators, NGOs and private individuals (celebrities and common people), who are increasingly investing in the green economy. Second and equally important are local subjects. On the website of the Mudumalai Tiger Conservation Foundation,[25] one of the stated objectives is to 'create opportunities for the local people to compensate for their sacrifices for conservation'.

I mentioned earlier how disciplinary governmentalities were often aimed at weaning people away from their dependence on the natural-resource base. Eco-development was one way to reward them. Showcasing culture is another way. Safari Land Resort, on the Foundation website, offer guests the chance to witness the Bokapuram tribal dance at an additional cost, a dance advertised as performed in moments of happiness and during festivals. These tribal dances, though advertised as being very much part of the tribals' caring for nature, happen outside natural spaces such as Mudumalai.

Critical to the neoliberal project is the act of depoliticisation. As Dempsey and Suarez (2016) argue, nature tourism while aimed at conserving wildlife has depoliticised important debates about the human–animal conflict around protected areas. Wildlife conservation is seen to require inviolate zones for wildlife. What is not adequately considered is the possibility of people living with wildlife, or the fact that human impacts could vary significantly between different human actors. Somewhat ironically, local people with perhaps very small ecological footprints are perceived as threats, while tourists can continue to visit in large numbers despite their potential adverse impacts.

Governmentalities and Subject Formation

A. Agrawal's *Environmentality: Technologies of Government and the Making of Subjects* (2005), though heavily criticised by some for not being historically accurate, remains important because of its conceptualisation of how State policies try to shape the making of particular environmental subjects. As I have illustrated, colonial forest policy in Mudumalai from the outset targeted select groups of people to push the colonial government's conservation agendas. The colonial State targeted the Kurumbas as their main source of labour for tree-felling and the movement of timber to the upper plateau. Similarly, it saw in British hunters honorary foresters capable of protecting wildlife. And, increasingly in the postcolonial period, the forest department staff with, it must be said, the continued help of the Kurumbas, who reside in colonies just outside the tiger reserve, took over the role of protecting wildlife and the non-human world more generally. Their efforts were to be facilitated by the types of eco-development and ecotourism schemes referred to earlier that aimed at creating conservation subjects who cared for the forests but did not depend on them any longer.

At the outset, I argued that conservation governmentalities must be located within wider processes of statemaking. Mudumalai became important as a conservation landscape at the end of the nineteenth century to supply sustainable timber because much of the rest of Gudalur had been transformed into a tea-estate economy. In the early–twenty first century, the history of Mudumalai has been increasingly shaped by the agrarian question and forest rights. After a long struggle and extensive deliberations within and outside Parliament, the Scheduled Tribes and Other Traditional Forest Dwellers (Recognition of Forest Rights) Act was passed in 2006. The Act, in summary, permitted both the Scheduled Tribes (STs) and other forest dwellers to stake claim to both private and community lands if they could establish that they had historically used these lands. In what the WPA designated as critical wildlife habitats, the legal requirement was that the rights settlement process be completed before areas could be declared as inviolate.

Elsewhere, Karthik and Menon (2016) analyse the politics of claim-making around the Forest Rights Act. Claim-making assumes importance in the context of these new conservation governmentalities aimed at creating inviolate spaces for wildlife, and the making of new conservation subjects. Agrawal (2005) alerts us to the fact that not all 'subjects' would necessarily buy into the logic of the State's environmentalities. Li (2008), in the context of the hill communities of Indonesia, speaks about the 'capacity for politics' and how hill communities often challenge who the State believes them to be. This capacity for politics has been evident from the moment Mudumalai came under the legal control of the forest department. Kurumbas often did not heed to the colonial government's directive to engage in taungya cultivation and tend timber species. The NGA often challenged the diktat of the forest department when the latter sought to impose restrictions on their hunting activities. Even native hunters who were not part of the governmentalised logics continued to hunt beyond the watchful eyes of the forest department and the NGA. More recently, communities bordering Mudumalai have challenged the declaration of a buffer zone and an elephant corridor. And as the WWF report (Nathan 2008: 15) on wildlife tourism highlights, tribal cultural performances often do not go to plan according to tourism proprietors who often lament that tribals do not show up with their authentic tribal dress.

Communities around Mudumalai have recently also used other tactics to stake their claims. Agrawal (2005: 165) points out that subjects need not be seen either fully in opposition to citizens or as objects. I have illustrated in the course of this chapter that the State has imagined subjects in very different ways in the making of Mudumalai. It imagined the Kurumba subject as an object, whereas it saw the NGA much more as a civic group of citizens, though this perhaps changed over time. Krithivisan (2011) suggests that in the buffer areas of Mudumalai, non-tribals have often claimed to be *padivasi*s (half-tribal) in their quest to access government schemes such as eco-development or rights to graze their cattle in Mudumalai as tribals do. In other parts of Gudalur, including in some of the border areas of Mudumalai, communities question the very idea of being a conservation citizen that the State appears to be promoting. They point to their tree-growing practices and ask why they are treated as encroachers (Menon, Hinnewinkel and Guillerme 2013).

All of this suggests that the State's project of governmentalising conservation has faced its challenges. Governmentalities, in other words, have not always created conservation subjects in the ways intended because of people's situated capacity for politics. It is this capacity for politics that continues to raise questions about the fortress approach to conservation embedded in protected-area management. History tells us that select 'local' actors have always been part of the protected-area story in some way or the other. What situated politics highlights is how different actors speak to the protected-area project either by way of their inclusion or exclusion. It also alerts us to possible critiques of existing governmentalities for protected-area management.

Conclusion

My main aim in this chapter has been to shed light on the actors and factors that have shaped the parameters of conservation in Mudumalai. In doing so, I wanted to highlight how protected-area conservation is as much about politics as ecology, that is, about power as it is about conserving natural forest landscapes. Why this is important is because protected-area conservation has increasingly become depoliticised through its neoliberalisation. Celebrity actors speak on behalf of the tiger, and the general public is encouraged to contribute to saving the national animal. A historical reflection of conservation in one tiger reserve, Mudumalai, will help understand how we got here.

Much has been written about capitalism and conservation. And capitalism is clearly part of the story of Mudumalai's making. However, I have chosen to examine conservation in Mudumalai within the conceptual boundaries of statemaking or the process by which State priorities come about in the mutual constitution of State and society. Statemaking allows me to examine the impact of capital on the making of conservation, but it does not foreclose the possibility of other important influences. I argue that Mudumalai was also shaped by seemingly peripheral concerns such as the identity of game-hunters and nationalist pride as it was by the compulsions of capital.

Central to statemaking and conservation has been the making of conservation subjects. The nature of these subjects has been shaped by the conservation priorities of statemaking, itself the product of the dynamics of State–society relations. From tribal subjects employed to grow timber to hunters made honorary forest guards to conservation NGOs commodifying nature, each in different ways has promoted something generically called 'conservation', and set the boundaries of what this conservation might be. These governmentalities have employed different disciplinary techniques and both have included and excluded various actors.

Protected-area conservation has been a contested domain. I illustrated that conservation in Mudumalai has always been challenged in different ways by conservation subjects and those excluded. These challenges are situated politics posing challenges to both the social and ecological project of conservation. With increasing emphasis being put on inviolate protected areas, this situated politics raises fresh questions about the manner in which conservation in protected areas is being imagined, and raises questions as to whether there are other ways of doing it.

Notes

[1] See Tamil Nadu State Archives (TNSA), Proceedings of the Chief Conservator of Forests, G. O. miscellaneous 234/61, dated 30 September 1961.

[2] I do not go into a detailed discussion of the ecological meanings of conservation *per se*, rather focus on how particular social priorities shaped what I call the 'boundary conditions' of conservation.

[3] See TNSA, Proceedings of the Board of Revenue, forest no. 162, board no. 2,210, dated 7 August 1875, letter from J. R. Cockerell, Commissioner of the Nilgiris to H. E. Stokes, Acting Secretary to Board of Revenue, dated 6 July 1875, no. 66, Ootacamund.

[4] Ibid.

[5] See Menon, Hinnewinkel and Guillerme (2013) for a more elaborate discussion.

[6] See TNSA, Proceedings of the Board of Revenue, no. 1725, forest no. 114, dated 22 June 1875, letter from J. R. Cockerell, Commissioner of the Nilgiris to H. E. Stokes, Acting Secretary to the Board of Revenue.

[7] See TNSA, Proceedings of the Board of Revenue, March 1878, no. 709, dated 16 March 1878, letter from R. H. Beddome, Conservator of Forests to C. A. Galton, Honorary Acting Secretary, Board of Revenue, dated 28 February 1878.

[8] See TNSA, Chief Conservator of Forests, press no. 311, dated 27 September 1927.

[9] See TNSA, Chief Conservator of Forests, G. O. 179 (miscellaneous), dated 16 April 1937.

[10] See TNSA, Chief Conservator of Forests, press no. 97, dated 4 May 1926.

[11] See TNSA, Board of Revenue, forest no. 545, 11 October 1886.

[12] See TNSA, Chief Conservator of Forests, miscellaneous 327, dated 28 May 1919.

[13] See TNSA, Chief Conservator of Forests, G. O. no. 1289 press.

[14] See TNSA, Chief Conservator of Forests, G. O. miscellaneous 168/39, dated 1 April 1939.

[15] See TNSA, Chief Conservator of Forests, G. O. miscellaneous 64, dated 14 February 1929.

[16] See TNSA, Chief Conservator of Forests, G. O. no. 103 (miscellaneous), dated 23 March 1942, letter from Honourable Secretary, NGA, to Chief Conservator of Forests, dated 25 February 1940, G. O.

[17] See TNSA, Food and Agriculture Department, G. O. no. 1047, dated 5 April 1956, letter from the Honorary Secretary, NGA to Chief Conservator of Forests, dated 22 September 1953.

[18] See ibid., letter from V. V. Subramanian, Conservator of Forests to Secretary Government, Development Department, reference no. 14824/48, dated 7 April 1953.

[19] See ibid., copy of letter no. 23-2(5)/53-F, dated 2 March 1953.

[20] See ibid., letter from Honorary Secretary, NGA, to the Chief Conservator of Forests, dated 22 September 1953.

[21] See TNSA, Chief Conservator of Forests, G. O. 71/59 (miscellaneous), dated 28 February 1959.

[22] Prior to 1977, Mudumalai had come under Nilgiris North Division. From 1977, it came under a separate wildlife division (Dogra 2007: 114). With the passing of the WPA, sanctuaries and national parks were now under the jurisdiction of the central government.

[23] The tiger reserve was notified under G. O. miscellaneous no. 50, dated 2 April 2007, and the critical tiger habitat (CTH) under G. O. miscellaneous no. 145, dated 28 December 2007. The former was notified under Project Tiger, while the latter under Section 38V of the WPAA of 2006. See Taghioff and Menon (2010) for a more elaborate discussion.

[24] See http://tiger.ndtv.com/aboutourcampaign.aspx (accessed 27 March 2017).
[25] See http://www.mudumalaitigerfoundation.in/tiger-conservation-foundation (accessed 27 March 2017).

References

Agrawal, A. 2005. *Environmentality: Technologies of Government and the Making of Subjects*. Durham: Duke University Press.

Baviskar, A. 2003. 'For a Cultural Politics of Natural Resources'. *Economic and Political Weekly* 38(48): 5051–55.

Bose, P., B. Arts and H. van Dijk. 2012. '"Forest Governmentality": A Genealogy of Subject-making of Forest-dependent "Scheduled Tribes" in India'. *Land Use Policy* 29(3): 664–73.

Brockington, D., and R. Duffy. 2010. 'Capitalism and Conservation: The Production and Reproduction of Biodiversity Conservation'. *Antipode* 42(3): 469–84.

Chhatre, A., and V. Saberwal. 2006. *Democratizing Nature: Politics, Conservation, and Development in India*. New Delhi: Oxford University Press.

Dempsey, J., and D. C. Suarez. 2016. 'Arrested Development: The Promises and Paradoxes of "Selling Nature to Save It"'. *Annals of the American Association of Geographers* 106(3): 653–71.

Dogra, R. K. 2007. 'Management Plan for Mudumalai Wildlife Sanctuary and National Park'. Tamil Nadu Forest Department, Udhagamandalam.

Dressler, W., and B. Büscher. 2008. 'Market Triumphalism and the CBNRM "Crises" at the South African Section of the Great Limpopo Transfrontier Park'. *Geoforum* 39(1): 452–65.

Duffy, R. 2008. 'Neoliberalising Nature: Global Networks and Ecotourism Development in Madagascar'. *Journal of Sustainable Tourism* 16(3): 327–44.

Fairhead, J., M. Leach and I. Scoones. 2012. 'Green Grabbing: A New Appropriation of Nature?'. *Journal of Peasant Studies* 39(2): 237–61.

Fletcher, R. 2010. 'Neoliberal Environmentality: Towards a Poststructuralist Political Ecology of the Conservation Debate'. *Conservation and Society* 8(3): 171–81.

Gnanavelu, T. 1987. 'Working Plan for Gudalur Forest Division 1.4.1987 to 31.3.1997'. Tamil Nadu Forest Department, Coimbatore.

Guha, R. 1989. *The Unquiet Woods: Ecological Change and Peasant Resistance in the Himalaya*. New Delhi: Oxford University Press.

Jeffery, R. 1998. *The Social Construction of Indian Forests*. New Delhi: Manohar Publishers.

John Joseph, S. 1977. 'Management Plan for Mudumalai Wildlife Sanctuary, 1977–1987'. Tamil Nadu Forest Department, Udhagamandalam.

Karthik, M., and A. Menon. 2016. 'Blurred Boundaries: Identity and Rights in the Forested Landscapes of Gudalur, Tamil Nadu'. *Economic and Political Weekly* 51(10): 43–50.

Krishnan, S. 2009. 'Of Land, Legislation and Litigation: Forest Leases, Agrarian Reform, Legal Ambiguity and Landscape Anomaly in the Nilgiris, 1969–2007'. *Conservation and Society* 7(4): 283–98.

Krithivasan, R. 2011. 'Tiger Conservation, Forest Rights and Tribal Identity: Narratives of the Defenders and the Dependents of Mudumalai Wildlife Sanctuary, India'. Masters of Environment Science dissertation, Yale School of Forestry and Environmental Studies, Yale University, New Haven, Connecticut.

Li, Tania Murray. 2008. 'Social Reproduction, Situated Politics, and the Will to Improve'. *Focaal Journal of Global and Historical Anthropology* 52: 111–18.

Menon, A. 2015. 'The Godavarman Judgment: Erasing the Plurality of Land Use in Gudalur, Nilgiris'. In *Conflict, Negotiations and Natural Resource Management: A Legal Pluralism Perspective from India*, eds. M. Bavinck and A. Jyothishi, 33–50. Abingdon, UK: Routledge Publications.

Menon, A., and M. Karthik. 2017. 'Sedentarising Conservation: The Politics of Belonging and Rootedness in Gudalur, Nilgiris'. MIDS working paper no. 225, Madras Institute of Development Studies, Chennai.

Menon, A., C. Hinnewinkel and S. Guillerme. 2013. 'Denuded Forests, Wooded Landscapes: Statemaking in a Janmam Area of Gudalur, Nilgiris'. *Indian Economic Social History Review* 50(4): 449–71.

Morrison, K. D., and M. T. Lycett. 2014. 'Constructing Nature: Socio-natural Histories of an Indian Forest'. In *The Social Lives of Forests: Past, Present and Future of Woodland Resurgence*, eds S. B. Hecht, K. D. Morrison and C. Padoch, 148–60. Chicago: University of Chicago Press.

Münster, D., and U. Münster. 2012. 'Consuming the Forest in an Environment of Crisis: Nature Tourism, Forest Conservation and Neoliberal Agriculture in South India'. *Development and Change* 43(1): 205–27.

Nathan, I. A. 2008. 'Status Assessment of Tourism on the Sigur Plateau, Tamil Nadu: Impacts and Recommendations'. Report compiled for the Nilgiri and Eastern Ghats Landscape Office, WWF India.

Pandian, M. S. S. 1995. 'Gendered Negotiations: Hunting and Colonialism in the Late 19th Century Nilgiris'. *Contributions to Indian Sociology* 29(1–2): 239–63.

Parenti, C. 2014. 'The Environment Making State: Territory, Nature, and Value'. *Antipode* 47(4): 829–48.

Philip, K. 2003. *Civilizing Natures: Race, Resources, and Modernity in Colonial South India*. New Delhi: Oxford University Press.

Prabhakar, R. 1994. 'Resource Use, Culture, and Ecological Change: A Case Study of the Nilgiri Hills of Southern India'. Ph.D. dissertation, Centre for Ecological Studies, Indian Institute of Science, Bangalore.

Radhakrishnan, D. 2013. 'Mishap to British Tourist Triggers Demand for Regulating Wildlife Tourism'. *The Hindu*, 22 September. Available at https://www.thehindu.com/news/national/tamil-nadu/mishap-to-british-tourist-triggers-demand-for-regulating-wildlife-tourism/article5154548.ece (accessed 28 March 2017).

Rangarajan, M. 1996. *Fencing the Forest: Conservation and Ecological Change in India's Central Provinces 1860–1914*. New Delhi: Oxford University Press.

——— 2001. *India's Wildlife History: An Introduction*. New Delhi: Permanent Black.

Ravi Raman, K. 2010. *Global Capital, Peripheral Labour: The History and Political Economy of Plantation Workers in India*. London: Routledge.

Scott, J. 1987. *Weapons of the Weak: Everyday Forms of Peasant Resistance*. New Haven: Yale University Press.

Scott. 1999. *Seeing Like a State: How Certain Schemes to Improve the Human Condition Have Failed*. New Haven: Yale University Press.

——— 2009. *The Art of Not Being Governed: An Anarchist History of Upland Southeast Asia*. New Haven: Yale University Press.

Sekar, T. 2004. *Forest History of the Nilgiris*. Chennai: Tamil Nadu Forest Department.

Sivaramakrishnan, K. 1999. *Modern Forests, Statemaking and Environmental Change in Colonial Eastern India*. New Delhi: Oxford University Press.

Taghioff, D., and A. Menon. 2010. 'Can a Tiger Change its Stripes: The Politics of Conservation as Translated in Mudumalai'. *Economic and Political Weekly* 45(28): 69–76.

Vandergeest, P., and N. L. Peluso. 1995. 'Territorialization and State Power in Thailand'. *Theory and Society* 24(3): 385–426.

WWF. 2016. 'Legal Spaces for Wildlife Corridors: Exploring Legal Spaces for Corridor Protection as ESZs, Community Reserves, Conservation Reserves, Community Forest Resources, and Biodiversity Heritage Sites'. CEL legal brief 1, WWF India, New Delhi.

Part III

Nation and the Region

6. Rereading Anna's *Arya Mayai*

Reflections on C. N. Annadurai and the Cultural Politics of the Dravidian Movement

V. Ravi Vaithees

Arya Mayai[1] by C. N. Annadurai (1909–69), or 'Anna' as he is popularly known, was first published in 1943 and has, over the years, acquired some sort of status as a minor modern Tamil classic. Written and published while Anna was still the chief lieutenant of Periyar—well before their bitter split in 1949 with Periyar and the Dravidar Kazhagam—it can be regarded as young Anna's own rendition of the manifesto of the Dravidian movement. He was barely 30 years old at the time of writing. Written with great passion and a clear pedagogic intent, it was regarded at the time as a work that clearly articulated and explicated the core ideas and objectives of the Dravidian movement. The book became highly popular during its time, enjoying over 10 reprints, and was read aloud in various corners of the Tamil region (Kannan 2011: 251). The banning of the book soon after Independence in 1950 by the then Congress government served only to increase the visibility of both Anna and the book. Anna was also sent to jail on the charge of promoting communal divisions.

Anna was perhaps the most pivotal figure in the political ascendancy of 'Dravidianism' as a political and ideological project in the post-Independence era. He began his political career as a staunch follower of the Justice Party that was soon to come under the leadership of the radical and iconoclastic figure of E. V. Ramasamy, otherwise known as 'Periyar' (great man). Annadurai's dramatic breakaway in 1944, and his brilliant leadership and subtle reconfiguration and redeployment of the radical message of the Dravidar Kazhagam under Periyar, is considered central to the electoral popularity of the Dravidian movement and ultimately its political ascendancy from the year 1967. Scholars and commentators alike have attributed this remarkable political ascendancy to Anna's exceptional abilities as a leader and his remarkable oratorical and literary skills in the Tamil language. The author of countless works including novels, short stories, dramas, political essays and screenplays, he effectively used print and other popular media, particularly essays, drama and cinema, for his political campaigns—an aspect of his political persona that earned him the popular title 'Aringar Anna' (philosopher/scholar Anna). His popularity and lasting legacy is attested not only by the numerous statues of him in every nook and cranny of Tamil Nadu today, but also by the fact that no mainstream Dravidian party to date has dared to ignore his contributions. While Anna wrote on a variety of topics, it is in *Arya Mayai*, loosely translated as 'Aryan Illusion', that he first sets out clearly his social, historical and political vision and, therefore, it can be regarded as a key manifesto and 'call to arms'. It is also the most scholarly and revealing of his works and one that, as he acknowledged himself, was meant to be read as a political manifesto to inform and educate the emerging 'Dravidian nation'.

As we mark 100 years of the founding of the non-Brahmin Dravidian movement, a movement that went on to successfully capture state power in 1967 and remained the dominant ideology in Tamil Nadu ever since, there still remain lingering questions regarding the movement's ideology, the political and ideological transition and transformation that led up to its rather sudden and remarkable capture of state power in 1967, including the distinct roles played by its prominent leaders in this transition and march to power. The scholarship on this transition and its results has been particularly murky. Anna's role and ideology in this transition and march to power have been particularly understudied. Part of the problem is that despite the long history of the Dravidian movement and the profound impact it and its many permutations has had on the region, the movement has received relatively little critical scholarly attention. The extant scholarship on the movement is marked by at least two major lacunae. First, the predominant trend has been towards chronicling the movement's formal political history to the relative neglect of its cultural, linguistic or religious aspects and achievements. Thus, the early scholarship, for the most part, stayed clear of language, religion, culture and ideology, and tended to adopt a strictly empiricist orientation, attempting to trace the origin and causes of the Dravidian movement to a narrowly circumscribed view of what counted as politics—in this case, the intense competition for civil service jobs between Brahmins and the dominant non-Brahmin castes in the early decades of the twentieth century, a conflict that apparently was the main impetus behind the formation of the Justice Party, which was the earliest precursor to the Dravidian political parties.[2] This has led not only to the neglect of the early intellectual and cultural roots of the movement, but also to a failure to adequately examine and understand the social, intellectual and cultural dimensions and reach of the movement. Second, given the movement's long and complex history, involving significant transitions in leadership and ideology, the predominant trend has been to treat the movement as consisting of distinct and discrete phases, and to focus narrowly on one or another of these 'distinct' phases.[3]

Nevertheless, a general scholarly consensus appears to have emerged on the origins and trajectory of the different phases of the movement. It is this broad consensus on the different phases of the movement that Pandian, one of the most distinguished scholars of the movement, works with and sharpens in his own work with its principal focus on Periyar and the self-respect phase of the Dravidian movement (Pandian 2007). While Pandian locates the formal political articulation of the Dravidian movement beginning with the Justice Party, much like his predecessors, as a response to Brahmin social, political and ideological ascendancy in government and the professions in the context of the gathering Indian nationalist movement in Madras Presidency in the early decades of the twentieth century, he traces its ideological roots to the writings of colonial and Christian missionary orientalists, as well as to the pioneer indigenisers of this ideology, such as the neo-Saivite Maraimalai Adigal and the radical neo–Buddhist revivalist Ayothee Thass. While conceding that the ideology can be traced to these early indigenisers, he nevertheless speaks of a radical break with this rather elitist and limited ideology, and with the old Justice Party elites, with the entry of Periyar and the Self-respect Movement by the late 1920s. Thus, for Pandian, the Dravidian movement from this period on was radically transformed and its social base significantly widened with the entry of Periyar. As he argues, the anti-Brahmin discourses of pioneer Dravidian ideologues such as Ayothee Thass and the Maraimalai Adigal were essentially limited and ineffective responses to the new configurations of Brahmin power under colonialism, and were thus merely attempts at refashioning 'a new selfhood for their respective communities by centralizing the figure of the Brahmin in their intellectual and interlocutive writings' (ibid.: 103). Confined principally to the domain of the religious and spiritual, and failing to engage with the 'material consequences of Brahmin power', such efforts by figures such as Maraimalai Adigal, he argues, 'could not carry ... beyond the narrow public constituted by the Vellalar elite' (ibid.: 136–45).

Pandian's work here is significant in that it attempts to explain how the Dravidian movement and its ideology were radically transformed by the entry of Periyar and the Self-respect Movement from its earlier apparently 'limited' and 'elitist' beginnings in the late 1920s. He also suggests that the Dravidian ideology, so far trapped and limited by its colonial heritage with its 'binary' thinking, was 'exceeded' by the work of Periyar and the Self-respect Movement. Periyar, for example, did not fall into the trap of valorising Tamil or Dravidian culture as a counter to Aryan/Brahmin hegemony but called for radical reforms that went beyond such nationalist binaries. While Pandian does not focus on developments subsequent to Periyar and the Self-respect Movement, particularly the trajectory of the Dravidian movement after the split with Periyar and the founding of the Dravida Munnetra Kazhagam (DMK) in 1944 by prominent second-generation leaders,[4] it certainly points to the serious lacunae in critical scholarship on subsequent developments in the movement. It points to the relative neglect of the more mature phase of the movement, especially how the movement under second-generation leaders such as Anna was able to capture state power, and the political and ideological transitions and transformations these changes entailed.

One of the few detailed scholarly works that focuses on this period and on the role of second-generation Dravidian leaders such as Anna, and their role in the march of the Dravidian movement to state power, is that by the American scholar Marguerite Ross Barnett. Barnett (1976) attributes the split between Periyar and Anna, and the founding of the breakaway DMK, as arising not from any fundamental ideological differences between Anna and Periyar, but due to the differences in temperament, leadership styles and, most importantly, differing political and temporal conditions prevailing during their years of leadership.[5] Thus, for Barnett, Anna's different political and ideological trajectory could be explained by the fact that he was faced with a different set of conditions in the 1940s and 1950s, when he was thrust into a leadership position. If the principal contradictions in the 1920s and 1930s had been between the Brahmins and the 'forward' non-Brahmins, with the introduction of universal adult franchise in the 1940s, the centre of political gravity gradually shifted towards the aspirations of the rising backward non-Brahmin castes for whom anti-Brahminism was no longer the principal issue.[6] Anna's apparent 'deradicalisation' and shift towards a form of Tamil cultural nationalism starting in the 1950s was thus instigated by the need to appeal to this new vast electoral base comprising the backward classes or, as Barnett put it, to the 'common man'.[7] Thus, for Barnett the 'late 50s and early 60s mark the emergence of the politics of (Tamil) cultural nationalism and the mass internalization of the Tamil identity' (Barnett 1976: 89). As the party of the 'common man', in DMK, the 'concept of social reform was redefined from meaning attacks on religion and Hinduism to the uplift of backward non-Brahmins' (ibid.: 114–15). Thus 'radical ideas of social reform were transformed to promoting rationality ... by the 60s films were theistic, one god and one caste rather than atheistic' (ibid.: 89). However, this stress on the 'pragmatic' and temporally limited explanation for Anna's alleged deradicalisation and Tamil nationalism in the 1950s and 1960s coexist rather uncomfortably with Barnett's own description of the very basis of Anna's politics and mass appeal—his appeal to Tamil nationalism.

It is in this regard that Barnett's stress on Anna's appeal to Tamil nationalism, including his engagement with the Tamil literary and cultural renaissance, is noteworthy. Thus, she concedes that the party attracted many Tamil scholars and that the party's top leaders themselves were Tamil scholars. The party's major leaders made a point of speaking in scholastic Tamil. This, she asserts, helped renew interest in Tamil literature and linguistics, and contributed to the renaissance of Tamil literature. 'The party increasingly combined political, literary conferences and films ... films, oratory and pamphlets were used to develop new forms of political and social consciousness' (ibid.: 84). Thus, she signals Anna's foregrounding of the importance of intellectuals as an important indicator of the Anna and DMK method of penetrating the mass media through intellectuals (ibid.: 82). What was emphasised upon, she observes, were not radical ideas but the cultural definition of what it means to be a Dravidian—an identity linked to the past. Writing specifically of Anna's *Arya Mayai*—written well before this apparent shift—she notes that, Anna 'undertakes thorough explication of the cultural foundation of the movement ... and the book eventually became the key text stating the ideology of the movement', without, however, explaining what this 'cultural foundation' of the movement for Anna was (ibid.: 72).[8]

With faint echoes of Barnett, but without as much of the detailed accounting of the changing sociopolitical realities behind the rise of the DMK movement, Arunan, in his 2008 work aptly titled *Anna: Aatchiyai Pidtha Varalaru* (The Story of How Anna Captured State Power), offers a detailed chronological narrative of how Anna moved away from Periyar and Dravidar Kazhagam to found the DMK, and went on to capture state power. Again, what Arunan emphasises is not any major ideological difference between Periyar and Anna, but their different approaches to politics from the very start of their political careers. Anna is described here as one oriented towards electoral politics, if not populist politics, from the very beginning of his career, in contrast to Periyar who is described as more principled and not as politically shrewd.[9] Arunan argues that right from the beginning of his career, Anna's public speeches and political strategy were geared towards electoral politics (Arunan 2008: 66). Like Barnett, Arunan also suggests that Anna, despite his Dravidianist rhetoric, clearly presented and appealed to a nascent Tamil nationalism that, for example, never failed to protect Tamil interests when given a stark choice between Tamil and pan-Dravidian interests.[10] Much as in Barnett, there is an attempt to portray Anna as steeped in Tamil literary, creative and the dramatic arts, those which enabled him to utilise his formidable literary, oratorical and dramatic skills for his political project. For example, when Anna started the magazine *Thiravida Nadu* in 1942, he also started the Thiravida Nadigar Sangam at the same time (ibid.: 51). In fact, Arunan points out that one of Anna's earliest films, *Velaikari* (1949)—originally a play that was first performed in 1947 (ibid.: 67)—for which he wrote the screenplay, not only begins with a popular Tamil/Hindu devotional scene, but ends with the words of a Saivite/Siddha mystic Tirumular, '*onre kulam, oruvane thevan*' (one caste, one god), rather than with the Periyarist homily of atheism (ibid.: 69). In other words, Arunan suggests that

Anna had a great sense of the way religio-cultural hegemony worked in Tamil/Indic society, and used his formidable knowledge and skills in Tamil to craft a counter-hegemonic Dravidianist project.

While the two works by Barnett and Arunan seek to delineate Anna's unique 'populist' role in the Dravidian movement and especially how he was able to capture state power,[11] the first highly detailed biography of Anna in English, *Anna: The Life and Times of C. N. Annadurai* (2011) by Ira Kannan, offers a broad exploration of the life and career of Anna. The work, richly detailed and documented, and integrating the views of many of Anna's important contemporaries including critics, provides important insights into Anna's formative years, life and motivations, rather than answer specific questions about his role in the Dravidian movement.[12] Kannan provides a vivid account of the life of Anna, especially his formative years including his early schooling, his early encounter with the Tamil literary renaissance and Justice Party propaganda through his teachers. Kannan notes, for example, that Anna's English teacher and early mentor at the time, Mr Varadarajan, was a member of the youth wing of the Justice Party. It was through Varadarajan that Anna began to first engage with Justice Party politics. His Tamil teacher Mani Thirunavukarasu Mudaliar, who incidentally was one of the most promising students of the Tamil-purist, Maraimalai Adigal, imbibed in Anna a great love for Tamil literature. It was teachers such as these who ensured, according to Kannan, not only Anna's lifelong devotion to Tamil, but the significant role that Tamil language and culture played in his political writings and speeches (Kannan 2011: 25–26).

However, such things as Anna's greater immersion in the Tamil literary renaissance or want of radicalism were not reasons for Anna's parting of the ways with Periyar and his foundation of the DMK, but were, according to Kannan (2011: 213–26), much like Barnett and Arunan, the result of their different sensibilities, leadership styles and approach to politics. For example, differences arose over Periyar's order to senior party cadre to compulsorily wear black shirts, or even over how to respond to India's formal independence from Britain. Kannan ultimately portrays Anna as a rather reluctant leader and founder of the DMK who would have preferred to focus on being a playwright rather than founder-leader of a breakaway party. It was, he argues, Periyar's own nephew and fellow Dravidar Kazhagam leader, E. V. K. Sampath, who persuaded Anna to found the DMK.

Like many of the other accounts, Kannan's too highlights Anna's deep engagement with the Tamil literary and creative worlds, though without elaborating on how exactly it affected his unique role in the movement. What ensured Anna's great success then, for Kannan, were his extraordinary qualities as a truly democratic leader, his great intelligence and his impressive oratorical skills.

If these three works on Anna concede Anna's utilisation of Tamil literary and cultural material as important elements of his political project (though there is a tendency to depict this as his turn towards populism and as a sign of his deradicalisation in contrast to Periyar), it is in Thamizhavan's 2014 work *Thiravidam, Thamil Thesam, Kathaiyadal: Oru Nootrandu Thamil Sinthanai Varalaru* (Dravidianism, Tamil Nation, a Dialogue: Hundred Years of Tamil Intellectual History) that Anna's engagement with the Tamil literary and cultural world takes centre-stage as the key feature of his politics. Describing Anna's role as decisive in the modern political history of Tamil Nadu, Thamizhavan argues that Anna was the first to introduce what he calls the *aathi Thamil marabou*, loosely translated as 'ancient Tamil heritage', into modern political discourse which was first reintroduced into the Tamil literary world by the modern Tamil poet Bharathidasan (Thamizhavan 2014: 23, 25–26). Bharathidasan, for Thamizhavan, was the first to reconnect contemporary Tamil poetry to its ancient Sangam roots after a lapse of over 1,000 years, when it was increasingly swallowed by Sanskrit and the northern influence. It was Anna's appeal to reconnect with this 'ancient Tamil heritage' in his political discourse that, according to Thamizhavan, enabled him to reach out to the Tamil masses so rapidly, and explains the extraordinary strength of the political discourse introduced by him (ibid.: 23, 41, 44). Highlighting the politics of language and its imbrications with politics, Thamizhavan argues that it is more than a coincidence that Bharathidasan returns to 'Dravidian poetry' in the 1930s, from his earlier engagement with the tradition of poetry-writing inaugurated by the Indian nationalist poet Bharathy, and Anna joins the Justice Party in 1932. For Thamizhavan, this near-temporal coincidence reveals just how thought and language are complexly intertwined and inseparable (ibid.: 47). Speaking more broadly of the trajectory and impact of the Dravidian movement, Thamizhavan notes that the Tamil language and culture, which had become thoroughly Sanskritised, and increasingly conceived as having a Sanskrit heritage, at least since the twelfth century, were returned to its Tamil roots and heritage by the Dravidian movement. If Maraimalai Adigal sought to do this in one way, the role of Bharathidasan was to do it in another way—to reintroduce the spirit of ancient Sangam poetry into the world of modern Tamil poetry (ibid.: 16–23). Citing Anna's own words at a function celebrating Bharathidasan, he writes that Bharathidasan helped radically transform the quality of Tamil poetry from its earlier 'other-worldly focus' to one more centered on 'this-world', one with a much more materialist focus. Thamizhavan argues that it was this very aspect of Bharathidasan's poetry that Anna sought to celebrate and encourage (ibid.: 58–59). Speaking of the different roles of Periyar and Anna, Thamizhavan notes that if Periyar's political discourse is a continuation of the Western enlightenment tradition, one that gained popularity with the emergence of urbanisation and urban culture in Tamil Nadu, there was another more rural Tamil Nadu that was happily unaware of Periyar, continuing its age-old practice of sacrificing goats and chicken to minor gods, holding fire-walking rituals, and singing folk ballads. It was only after Anna began leading the Dravidian movement that these two separate cultural worlds of Tamil Nadu were bridged (ibid.: 45). Speaking of the profound and powerful nature of Anna's impact, Thamizhavan noted: 'the great missionary Robert Caldwell could not have even dreamt that someone like Anna would come along' (ibid.: 76).

This brief review of the extant scholarship on the Dravidian movement is certainly instructive and worth keeping in mind as we engage with Anna's *Arya Mayai*. It certainly helps us get a sense of how scholars have sought to understand the Dravidian movement, particularly the developments that followed Anna's split with Periyar and the Dravidar Kazhagam, the founding of the DMK and the cultural politics of DMK under Anna's leadership. It points to one of the most glaring questions that remain unanswered, which is the nature of the transition that was effected as a result of the splintering of the Dravidar Kazhagam and the founding of the DMK. What kind of changes did this development entail? That is a question that raises the spectre of the precise nature of the difference between Periyar and Anna, including their political and ideological differences and orientations. What does *Arya Mayai*, for example, reveal about Anna's own rendition of the Dravidian ideology and mandate, particularly during his years of close collaboration with Periyar? What are the principal elements in that ideology and what is the level of radicalism or lack thereof? Does the ideology propounded by Anna in *Arya Mayai* constitute a radical break from the earlier, allegedly more 'elitist' and binary vision advanced by his predecessors, namely figures such as Sundaram Pillai or Maraimalai Adigal, who were the first to indigenise the Dravidian ideology? Are there portends of the kind of deradicalisation and espousal of a form of Tamil nationalism evident in the work, attributed by scholars to be his later, more pragmatic approach to populist electoral politics? These would be some of the principal questions to keep in mind as we re-engage with this half century–old modern Tamil classic.[13]

Arya Mayai[14] is an extraordinary collection of essays written with great passion and fervour by the young Anna. A variety of sources, ranging from the writings of European missionary and orientalist scholars to contemporary Tamil/Indian scholars, notably historians, both Brahmin and non-Brahmin, are brought together to offer a compelling narrative advocating the liberation of the Tamils/Dravidians from their alleged Aryan yoke. Anna had himself revealed this pedagogic intent when he wrote in the brief preface, 'It is my belief that this book will be an inspiration for those who desire the liberation of the Dravidian nation from Aryan Oppression. In this regard I implore my Dravidian comrades to utilize this work effectively and appropriately' (Annadurai 1948: 3). He added:

> This work which is culled from a series of essays written over the years,[15] has utilized the scholarship of researchers who support the emancipation of a racial group. Many useful sources therefore have been included. It is not just meant for private reading but is intended as a source book to explain our cause to others and to clear doubts and provide effective counter responses to our critics. It is also intended as a source book for public speakers. (Ibid.: 2)

What is striking here is not as much the fact that Anna was able to bring together these diverse sources of scholarship and historical information, as the ways in which he brilliantly weaves them together in a highly personalised, Tamil popular idiom. While Anna makes extended use of these sources in the form of direct quotes of long passages, they are often selected to seamlessly fit in with his wider narrative and message, so as to make it difficult to separate the authorial voice and message from that of the sources he cites, with the implicit suggestion that the author's beliefs and the views expressed in the quotes are one and the same.

There are five or six core concerns and themes that animate the discussion in the entire work. First, the nature of the problems or challenges facing the Tamils/Dravidians are outlined, which essentially, for Anna, is centred on Aryans/Brahmins and their domination and cultural hegemony over the Tamils/Dravidians. It is along these lines that the second major theme is presented: the question of how the Aryans/Brahmins allegedly came to conquer and hold such power over the Tamils/Dravidians. This is where the historical writings of European missionaries, orientalists and their Indian counterparts are brought into play to provide a narrative history of the alleged Aryan conquest, written, however, from the vantage point of the once 'great' Tamil/Dravidian civilisation. While conventional practices of historical writings are interrogated, especially the writings of early orientalists like Max Müller, 'true' archeological/historical writings revealing the ancient glories of the Tamil/Dravidian civilisation are marshalled and extolled (Annadurai 1948: 10). These include the works of figures such as John Marshall, the reverend Robert Caldwell, the Russian author Viacheslav Ragozin and other European writers such as E. P. Havell and John Slater. Thus, a substantial section of the work is devoted to providing a historical account of the development of the Indo-Aryan theory of Indian civilisation, and the more recent scholarship that had begun to discredit this narrative and present in its stead the 'glory' and 'grandeur' of the ancient Tamil/Dravidian civilisation.

A third core, though again related, element of the work is explicating the precise mechanism and nature of how Aryan conquest/hegemony over the Dravidians was achieved. Here, the principal argument advanced is that the oppression or hegemony was not gained through physical strength or military valour (since for Anna, the Tamil/Dravidians were known for their brave and fearless nature), but through duplicity and cunning, utilising the weapons of religion and culture.[16] In other words, he declares that the oppression is, first and foremost, cultural, involving religion, language and everyday cultural practices. This is where Anna is at his most eloquent and his best. Fourth, there is an attempt to engage and address the challenges posed by the discourse of Indian nationalism in the region to allegedly upstage this growing Dravidian awareness. Fifth, there is an attempt to illuminate and explicate what the author considers to be the fundamental and irreconcilable differences between Aryans and Dravidians in every aspect of life and culture, including religion, language, family, law and values. Finally, there is a call to arms, not one that privileges physical rebellion, rather a call to awaken the Tamils/ Dravidians through the dissemination of this new knowledge and education, a call for students and educators to actively work towards this goal of educating and awakening the Tamils/Dravidians.

Anna's opening salvo is in the form of a praise-poem in the style and form of a Saivite bhakti hymn familiar to many Tamilians. However, in this case, the praise-poem is not in praise of Siva or any other Hindu god, but has been cleverly replaced with praise for a series of negative adjectives used to describe the Aryans/Brahmins. Some of these adjectives are: avaricious, wily, double-tongued, fraudulent, oppressive, servile, etc. (ibid.: 4). The first two lines, loosely translated, read: 'O Praise to the Greedy and the very embodiment of Greed! O Praise to the one who is Double-tongued!' (ibid.: 5). These words, used to describe the nature of the Aryans/Brahmins, he asserts, 'are not the words written today or yesterday or inspired by the words of Dr. Nair [a prominent member of the Non-Brahmin Justice Party] or any communal minded speech', but what have been used by an 'impartial observer', who had lived among the South Indians for over 20 years and who had recorded his observations faithfully in a book published 135 years ago, to describe the 'Brahmins' (ibid.: 6). The author in question was none other than the eighteenth-century French Catholic missionary, Abbe Dubois. For Anna, the fact that he was a *parangi* (European) who lived among the South Indians and recorded his observations over a century ago made his findings seem all the more 'impartial' and authoritative. That an Englishmen, Henry Beachamp, translated it and C. V. Munusamy Iyer, no less a Brahmin, went through its proofs, made it, Anna asserted, all the more authoritative and unbiased.

Having, thus, neatly identified and established the 'enemy' and its alleged 'duplicitous' and 'cunning' nature, he proceeds to utilise Dubois's observations to describe how the Aryan/Brahmin was able to acquire such high status and wield such enormous power, power to profoundly influence, reorganise and reorder society through the system of caste. Here again the emphasis is on the fact that this acquisition of power was not through military might or physical valour, but through cunning, deceit and duplicity, traits which had helped them seduce and fool the martial Tamil kings and become their advisors and legitimisers. The means through which they achieved this hegemony included the creation and utilisation of magical rites and rituals, and the creations of fabulous and fantastic Puranic legends (Annadurai 1948: 7). In another passage, Anna refers to the principal weapons of the Aryans/Brahmins as sacrificial rituals, gods, magical rites and *yagam* (a Brahminical religious/magical ritual involving fire) under the principle guise of religion (ibid.: 13–15). Their greed for power and wealth, he points out, is in sharp contrast to their much-extolled 'Vedantic spirit' of detachment. Here, Anna provides as illustration the powerful then-contemporary head of the all-India Vedantic *mutt* (monastic institution), the Sankarachariar 'who while strutting the same "Mayavada" (Vedanta), still manages to travel in a Gold palanquin' (ibid.: 7).

Tamil kings had also acceded and been seduced by the power of Brahmins and Brahminism, since they not only profited from the legitimisation they derived from the Brahmins, but also as Brahmanism provided the necessary ideological tools in the form of the *varna* system (system of caste hierarchy) through which the kings could control and exploit the masses. The water-tight system of castes brought disunity and prevented any chance of unity or rebellion by the oppressed. The practice of 'double-speak' and deceit to gain the trust of rulers and acquire power, Anna notes, is not confined to ancient history, but is very much evident to this day, as can be seen in the British-controlled kingdoms of Travancore, Baroda or Mewar, where Brahmins served as the principal ministers or *diwans* to the royalty. They can even be seen in the British Indian bureaucracy, where it is the Brahmins who serve as chief secretaries, chief ministers or advocate generals. He concludes the chapter by noting 'that these truths we can see today with our very own eyes have been faithfully observed and recorded so long ago by Abbe Dubois' (ibid.: 8–9).

The utilisation of history and historiography then forms an essential ingredient in Anna's discourse. It is in the same vein that he proceeds to question the history and historiography of India, to argue how the conventional accounts of the Indian past had been Aryan-centric, thanks to the efforts of early German orientalists such as Max Müller. This, he states, helped lay the foundation for the view that civilisation and high culture in India began only with the arrival of the Indo-Aryans, writing cynically that this 'had made the local Agraharams (Brahmin settlements) jump for joy' (Annadurai 1948: 10). It took some time, he argues, before scholars realised that there was already a much anterior civilisation, and that it was the mingling with the Aryans that had brought destitution and destruction to the Tamils, their civilisation and culture. Here, as in many other instances, Anna often interchanges the term 'Dravidian' and 'Tamil', implicitly suggesting to the reader that both are one and the same. 'Until the work of John Marshall the world saw Indian civilization as an Aryan Civilization and India as "Aryavarta"' (ibid.: 11). It was after Marshall's work, Anna notes, that scholars began to realise the extent to which Dravidian civilisation had been undermined and damaged by mingling with the Aryans. This, he asserts, inspired researchers to explore how and to what extent the Aryans had damaged the Dravidian civilisation. Much like the early pioneer Dravidian ideologues as Sundaram Pillai and Maraimalai Adigal, Anna then proceeds to offer the following narrative: The Aryans/Brahmins by feeding the Dravidians with their fabulous Puranic tales and culture had emaciated and made cowards of the once great and proud Dravidians. The Dravidians had once lived a life that was not only close to and in harmony with nature, but they were outstanding warriors who were guided by the highest ethical ideals (ibid.). The gradual penetration of Aryan culture full of fabulous and fantastic Puranic tales began to gradually penetrate and destroy the culture of the Dravidians. Again, just as his predecessors, Anna underlines the 'rationality' and 'this-worldly' spirit of the Dravidians in contrast to the Aryans. Thus, the Dravidians were prone to learning and wisdom and were not 'interested or immersed as the Aryans in things that were not visible to the naked eye, things that were beyond ideas, proof or logic' (ibid.: 12).

However, such findings on the destructive impact of the Aryans were offered by scholars as a kind of postmortem report rather than to awaken a fallen race or as a call to arms. In today's Tamil/Dravidian society, where even ordinary education or common knowledge has hardly penetrated, there is little chance, Anna argues, of this knowledge being spread or disseminated.

> If educated people or people with knowledge come forward to make efforts in this field and help disseminate these fresh new

> ideas, there is a chance to save the Dravidian race. Otherwise, just as many other races had fallen and become extinct over the centuries, the once glorious Dravidian race is surely destined towards extinction. (Annadurai 1948: 11)

Anna added ominously that just as his missionary and neo-Saivite predecessors had warned, 'which-ever race that loses its culture, its ancient glory and takes refuge in the hands of the enemy, that race is surely headed towards extinction' (ibid.: 11).

Anna is, however, at his most eloquent and literary when he turns to explicating the precise nature and mechanism of this alleged 'insidious' Aryan domination and cultural hegemony. While the force and eloquence of his language are largely lost in translation, an attempt is made here to loosely translate his words. For example, describing the mechanism of conquest as 'mental' or 'psychological' rather than physical, he observes that the way Aryan hegemony gained traction was by

> loading intoxicants in the ideas and thoughts of the Dravidians and when they were fully drunk ... rolled them over ... Thus, Dravidians were not defeated by Aryan bravery. Rather, Dravidians came to carry and bear the brunt of Aryan ideas ... Reminiescent of Sundaram Pillai's sad refrain about the plight of the Tamils, he writes, "Those who do not know this 'truth' do not know Tamilian history!" (Annadurai 1948: 14)[17]

In another passage, he emphatically notes, 'The Tamils who see themselves as matchless warriors, if they fall into this Aryan pit, will lose their knowledge, their abilities, their manliness, their dignity and their values' (ibid.: 15). He then goes on to pose the following questions: 'Does not their Vedanta preach, that which exists, to not exist? Is not their idealized patron-lord Narayana (the lord of deception)? The rule of Aryans is the rule of tricksters ... Aryan history is the history of how they (Aryans) oppressed and tortured the innocent hearted people (Tamils) ...' (ibid.: 14–15).

There is also a persistent tendency in Anna to draw parallels between and make allusions to Aryan hegemony or 'Aryan Mayai' and the dangerous power of the female—to utilise the language and cultural politics of the dangerous female, the female seductress. Thus, he writes of a man who had been 'darkened/blackened' and shrunk by ceaseless wandering and whose mind had therefore only found relief in the desire for a fair and lovely form, with long and beautiful black hair. But he warns that this apparition is, in fact, merely a false appearance, that it is actually grey hair that has been cleverly dyed. Continuing in this vein, he reproaches the Dravidian who may have fallen for such temptations by noting:

> Your own lust along with her white-washing skills are making you swoon ... While you sing of beholding the beautiful moon or the flowering rose, if only you could control yourself and look a little more closely ... notice her bloodless pale-white face, full of wrinkles made by the ravages of time ... by the lusty embrace of her myriad suitors ... (Annadurai 1948: 16)

Developing on such allusions, Anna notes:

> [Y]ou will be besotted by her bewitching smile, the smile however, is the language of a spider. It is a ploy to win you over ... Your life has now come under her control and you have become her slave. In the veritable embrace that destroys your knowledge you find joy! ... Destroying your very values, her shining skin is just a shallow powdered exterior ... Her smiling face hides the torment of a fiery volcano. She is simply a walking evil, a seductress. You really do not need this kind of love! ... You who describe a breaker of families, as a "slim-waisted damsel", you who make fun of your trusted friends when they try to prevent you from falling into such a trap ... This is the nature of Aryanism/Brahmanism. It hides its evil design by dressing it in a blanket of religion ... and feeds its poison to our race with a smiling face. To the Self Respecters who are warning you not to ingest this poison, you hurl abuses ... (Ibid.: 17)

In his narrative, Anna powerfully underscores the close imbrications of literature with religion in the service of perpetuating Aryan hegemony. Taking recourse again to the use of flowery, literary language, he writes:

> In the name of Arts and literature, Tamils have been bewitched and entrapped by the web spun by Aryans ... the beauty of a painting ... the composition of a poem ... the epics *Kambaramayanam* and *Periyapuranam*, in the name of literature feed religion to the people ... works that promote slavery towards the Aryans. They

> have been cast upon the Tamils, as works that are priceless and paid for in cash ... for the Tamils to imbibe this poison. (Ibid.: 64)

Even more eloquently, he remarks, 'In a flesh-hook called religion, dangles literature in the form of food. Without knowing this an innocent man ingests it thinking it is food only to be caught in the Aryan hook and forfeits his life. This is the fate of the Tamilian!' (Annadurai 1948). This idea of being defeated not by arms but by 'mental' cunning and malice is one of the most persistent and enduring themes in Anna's writings. It also, for example, appears famously in a verse in the screenplay to the film *Velaikari* (servant maid), the drama sequel (1943) of which Anna wrote and acted in. Here, the principal protagonist, when tricked by the wealthy and pious landlord (incidentally named Vedachalam, loosely translated as 'mountain of Vedas'), is driven to dejection and contemplates murdering the landlord by sharpening his knife. His mentor and advisor, however, intercedes and advises famously: '*Kathiyai theetahe undhan puthiyai theetu!*' (Instead of sharpening your knife, you should sharpen your mind!). The suggestion here is that true deliverance from 'Aryan Mayai' can only be achieved through mental agility rather than physical strength.

Another section of *Arya Mayai* is devoted to a chronological narrative outline of Indian history, divided in different temporal periods, a sort of historical palimpsest to chart the Aryans and the Dravidians, both in relation to each other, to highlight their differences and to illuminate the slow erosion of Dravidian civilisation and culture due to this Aryan impact. Anna felt the need to do so, he explains, as:

> I am providing below the much needed historical information that should be recorded in the hearts of all Tamil students ... Tamil teachers with a race/ethnic consciousness should provide these evidences and other pertinent information to all students. Since Aryans are presently dominating educational institutions, the truth has remained hidden. To spread this new awakening and to increase mobilization there is a need to make students understand what terrible deeds Aryanism has done from the ancient times to the present ... (Annadurai 1948: 17–19)[18]

Here, Anna restates many of the arguments favourable to the Dravidians advanced by orientalist scholarship. For example, he states that in the earliest epoch, the period before 5000 BCE, before the spread of the Aryans, there were no caste or four-varna divisions; the Aryan rite of marriage centered on fire was absent; the language spoken all over India was the language that you find in parts of South India today. It was between 3000 and 1500 BCE that you get the elaboration of a new form of worship centered on fire. Those who accepted this mode of worship, Anna asserts, were called Aryans, and those who did not, the Dasyus. The four-fold division of caste-society was created to serve the needs of these Aryan forms of worship. Aryan influence on the South had to wait till around the beginning of the Christian era. Curiously, he concludes this segment by making the rather tall claim that despite Aryan influence, the society and culture in the Tamil region from 5000 BCE to 400 CE remained fundamentally intact (ibid.: 18–20).

One of the underlying themes in this narrative is to both demonstrate the evil of Aryan influence, as well as the Aryan–Dravidian separateness, a subject that Anna elaborates a great deal on when he responds to the challenge posed by the Indian nationalists and, more specifically, to an agitation that was sparked in South India at the time by a speaker from the Hindu Mahasabha. The speaker had allegedly claimed that Hindustan was for Hindus (ibid.: 22–23), defining Hindus as persons born in India and who consider India as their sacred land. Anna's rather combative response takes the form of a challenge: 'What business does a Hindu have in the Dravidian country?'. He retorted, 'To really answer such questions, "What is Hindustan? Who are the Dravidians? What is the Dravidian Country?" one does not have to go very far than a decent library or an international encyclopedia/dictionary or even good historical writings' (ibid.: 22). Citing a sample of such historical literature, including the Cambridge Ancient History series (1924–39), H. G. Wells and Vincent Smith's *Oxford History of India* (1919) (ibid.: 22–25), Anna asserts that all these sources would not deny the simple fact that 'Hindustan' was restricted to the states of Gujarat, Rajasthan and the United Provinces (upper Indian states), what had traditionally been referred to as 'Aryavarta', and that all of these 'standard' sources clearly delineated the existence of a separate Dravidian territory to the South. That separateness had been marked not only by geography but by history, since all the major north Indian historical dynasties had been confined to the North, never penetrating south of the Vindhya mountains—'That between us (Dravidians) and the Aryans, the river Narmada has flown steadily without interruption' (ibid.). All the valiant kings of the northern dynasties, even the great warrior Chandragupta Maurya, could not display his valour in Dravidian country (ibid.: 25).

Responding to another statement by the Mahasabha speaker—that 'Hindus are generous hearted and are an exemplary people' (Annadurai 1948: 31)—he responds with equal outrage:

> Would anyone who had even once visited a *Cheri* (Indian slum) agree with such pronouncements? Are there any better example of a spiritual "Guru" who is the very embodiment of the exploitation of man by man; for treating humans like animals, than the Hindu seer, Manu? Can we not see the generosity of the Hindus here? Do we have to look any further? (Ibid.)

His principal argument here is, as he notes:

> Between Hindu, Hindustan and Hinduism and Dravidian Nation ... there are fundamental differences ... From the land to the people ... there are differences. It is pointless to hide them ... Even the intelligent strategy of the Aryans to rope in the Congress, or even the Hindu Mahasabha, or the aid of the British, any attempt to stop the Dravidian revival will only lead to delay not a halt to the revival. The inescapable conclusion is separation. (Ibid.: 27)

Staying on the theme of Hinduism and specifically the criticism that the Hindu Mahasabha speaker directed at the non-Brahmin claim, 'that they are not Hindus' (ibid.: 36), he goes on to explain:

> the Hindus worship ... four-headed gods, three-eyed gods ... elephant-headed gods ... gods who fly on a crow ... If we call ourselves Hindus, he asks, should we not accept and worship such Gods ... If civilized people hear that we worship such gods, would they not think we are more disgraceful than the Negroes and make fun of us? (Ibid.: 38)

Continuing on this note, he writes, 'We don't need four, six or even forty-eight eyed gods, one god will do! A formless God, a god who does not eat flesh, a god who does not transform the people's hard earned cash into ashes ...'. Speaking of the many worlds described in Hindu texts, he writes that 'we don't need a world for humans, another for ghosts, seven worlds above and seven below and all together fourteen worlds. We don't need all these. The country/nation in which we dwell, if we can have that it will be quite enough for us!' (Annadurai 1948: 37–38).

Anna then moves on to underlining what he believes to be the fundamental difference between the Aryans and the Dravidians in every aspect of life and culture, including family, law, marriage and values, including everyday rituals and practices. For example, he states, citing the authorial voice of another 'impartial' scholar, S. Somasundara Bharathy, that the Aryan view of family is determined by their presence in India as aliens, hence the Aryan stress on the male, the patriarchy, the joint family system and the division of property along male lines of descent. This arose, he argues, as a defensive strategy to deal with an alien environment, whereas the Tamils, who were neither invaders nor were invaded by others, believed in being free and living independently without depending on the wealth of their parents. Similarly, love and companionship were the basis of marriage for the Dravidians, unlike the Aryans where marriage formed the functional basis of begetting male progeny for defence and property rights (ibid.: 72–73).

Arya Mayai concludes with one of the most common refrains found in the work—the goal and means of liberation from this 'Arya Mayai' that for him had come to inform and permeate every aspect of Tamil/Dravidian life and culture. Thus, Anna concludes with a warning and a plea:

> If we keep following the rites, rituals, religion and festivals of the alien Aryans; by accepting them as high caste and as our gurus and by helping them to live comfortable and luxurious lives; by giving them material goods and falling at their feet and without common sense; doling out huge amounts of hard earned money to temples under the hegemony of Aryans we have allowed the Aryans to gain power and allowed ourselves to become enfeebled. (Annadurai 1948: 57)

Reminding the reader here of his own position and that of his party, the DMK, he adds:

> It is due to the hard work of Dravidian nation's greatest leader, E. Ve Ra (Periyar) that the evils hoisted upon the Tamils by the Aryans are daily being eliminated one by one. In this opportune

> time, the great Tamil people should once again make every attempt to revive and bring back into the practice of everyday life, the glorious ancient Tamil culture that had been covered up by Aryan cunning and duplicity. It is the revival of Dravidian-Tamil culture that will lead to the uplift of the Dravidians and the liberation of the Dravidian nation. (Ibid.: 59)

Concluding Remarks

This rereading and review of Anna's *Arya Mayai* brings out some of the central elements of the Dravidian ideology as seen through the eyes of Anna while he was the principal lieutenant of Periyar and the Self-respect Movement. One can clearly see in the work not only a clear 'racial' as well as cultural demarcation between the Aryan and the Dravidian, but a call for a retrieval and revival of the Tamil/Dravidian civilisation from the clutches of the Aryan/Brahmin hegemony as the central goal of the Dravidian ideology. That the Aryan/Brahmin conquest or hegemony was not through military valour, but through 'mental' and cultural process that had affected every aspect of culture and language and, thus, required a profound critical reflection, re-evaluation and retrieval of culture of the Tamil/Dravidians, is one of the central messages in the work. Far from exceeding the binary vision characteristic of the ideology of the earlier, apparently more 'limited' and 'elitist' phase of the movement, namely the earlier neo-Saivite phase, there is remarkable similarity between the ideology/discourse that Anna is presenting here and the ideology/discourse put forward by his Christian missionary and neo-Saivite predecessors. Though some of the sources utilised, the examples given and the mandate put forward has been made more contemporary in Anna's rendition, the overall content and thrust of the message conveyed is remarkably similar.[19]

Both discourses (those of the neo-Saivite and Anna's) focus on the Aryan/Brahmin as the enemy, and make a clear racial, linguistic and cultural divide between the Aryan and the Dravidian. Both link the decline of this 'Dravidian culture' and civilisation with the arrival and encounter with the Aryans. Both speak of the fundamental and irreconcilable differences in the nature and culture of the Aryans and Dravidians. Both speak of the main mechanism of Aryan/Brahmin conquest and control not as a physical conquest but as mental and cultural phenomena, as taking place not through military valour but through religion, culture and language. More specifically, both speak of the Aryan/Brahmin conquest and control through Aryan religious rituals and rites, culture and language. Both speak of ancient Tamil/ Dravidian culture in positive terms as close to nature, given to 'true' learning and wisdom, egalitarian and rational. Both equate radical social and cultural reform with a return to this lost golden age of Tamil society, language and culture. While both point to the insidious nature of Aryan/Brahmin religion and cultural hegemony in terms of religious rituals and rites, language and culture, it can be argued that Anna more clearly and powerfully brings this out than do his missionary and neo-Saivite predecessors. In other words, Anna's great gift appears to be his ability to probe every aspect of contemporary Tamil/Dravidian society, be it in the realm of religion, language, culture, or indeed in everyday practices of the Tamil/Dravidians, and bring to light or deconstruct the nature of this alleged Aryan/ Brahmin hegemony.

One can also observe some differences between Anna's views in *Arya Mayai* and those of his missionary and neo-Saivite predecessors. The most obvious difference is the inclusion of Saivism, more specifically the important Saivite text *Periyapuranam*, in the overarching attack on Aryan/Brahmin religion, although even here it is somewhat modulated by a statement in another passage to the effect that Saiva Siddhanta is the real religion/philosophy of the Tamils and that Saivite bhakti hymns are frowned upon by the Aryan/ Brahmins as a lower form of hymnal worship compared to their Sanskrit counterparts in temple worship. Here, the attack on Saivism, specifically, the Saivite text *Periyapuranam*, is only in the context that it too had become the handmaiden of Aryan/Brahmin hegemony in the Tamil region. The other difference between Anna and his predecessors, as noted earlier, is in Anna's greater sensitivity and more overtly political response to the contemporary political context of the time, namely the context of the gathering Indian nationalist struggle on the eve of Independence. Thus, Anna much more than his predecessors directly engages with the claims of Indian nationalism and Hindu nationalism articulated by the Indian National Congress and Hindu Mahasabha.

If this is Anna's rendition of the Dravidian ideology before the major split with Periyar and the founding of the DMK, then at the very least we must concede that right from his early engagement with the Justice Party and Self-respect Movement, Anna's rendition of the Dravidian ideology appears quite different from that of Periyar, and embodies much of the binary elements of his missionary and neo-Saivite predecessors, including its strong Tamil/Dravidian nationalist element. It confirms that from at least his days as the chief lieutenant of Periyar Anna had a deep engagement with Tamil revival and nationalism, a fact which contradicts the argument that Anna's Tamil nationalism or 'populism' was only a matter of pragmatic reaction to the exigencies of changing electoral politics of the 1950s and 1960s and especially the rise of backward-caste politics, essentially a type of pragmatic 'populism'. What does this mean for our understanding of the Dravidian movement and particularly for our understanding of the crucial transition from Periyar's Dravidar Kazhagam to Anna's DMK? For a start, it means that even before their fateful split, Anna's 'Dravidianism' differed from that of Periyar in fundamental ways.[20] It is important to recall here that many of the explanations given so far for the difference between Periyar, the Dravidar Kazhagam, Anna and the DMK surmise that they differed not so much on fundamentals, but that the difference and subsequent splintering of the Dravidar Kazhagam was caused by the populist streak in Anna and the DMK. While Anna and other senior leaders in the DMK may have adopted some pragmatic and strategic actions to contest electoral politics during their long march to power from 1949 to 1967, it would be unwise to brand all this under the banner or theoretical explanation of 'populism', without taking into account the fundamental differences in their ideology and outlook from the start. What we may want to consider here is that with Anna's break away and the founding of the DMK, what was finally fully released for popular mobilisation was a form of Tamil/Dravidian nationalism that harked back to the Tamil/Dravidian nationalist thought of his neo-Saivite predecessors such as Sundaram Pillai and Maraimalai Adigal.

This brings us to the point that both Arunan and Thamizhavan, each in their own way, have attempted to make regarding Anna and the type of political discourse/culture he introduced, one that explains for them how Anna was able to win over the masses so rapidly and the reason for the dramatic political ascendancy of Anna and the DMK. While Arunan speaks of Anna's deep engagement with Tamil revival in combination with an instinctive/organic sense of the Tamil masses and his unusual flair for mounting a successful counter-hegemonic cultural discourse, Thamizhavan speaks of Anna's success in terms of his ability to reintroduce a radical new political discourse that drew from the 'ancient Tamil heritage'. This close reading of *Arya Mayai* certainly confirms both these aspects, since it points to how Anna was able to introduce a new critical discourse into Tamil political and literary culture that drew upon colonial and modern, 'rationalist' critique of Aryan/Brahmin cultural hegemony in every aspect of Tamil/Dravidian culture and civilisation, one that, given Anna's and the DMK's extensive use of print culture and media, had a powerful impact not only on Tamil political culture for decades to come but also on Tamil popular culture and, ultimately, the shape of Tamil modernity in the second half of the twentieth century.

Notes

[1] See Annadurai (1948).

[2] The tendency then was to portray the Dravidian movement as the unfortunate result of elite competition and their cynical manipulation of existing social cleavages, contradictions and ethnic symbols to gain political power. The most powerful advocates of such a view belong to that school of Indian historiography often referred to as the Cambridge school, which, in characteristic fashion, depicted the movement as a battle by regional elites for a greater share of the 'loaves and fishes' of the colonial State (Hardgrave 1965; Irschik 1969; Washbrook 1976, 1989; Baker 1976). The more limited Marxist and neo-Marxist writings on the Dravidian movement were no less critical of the Dravidian project. Revealing the unusual alliance and imbrication of Marxism and 'official' Indian nationalism at that time, the predominant trend here was to adopt an anti-imperialist, Indian-nationalist stance and present 'minority' Tamil nationalism and the Dravidian movement as emerging out of the spaces opened up by British efforts to counter the rising Indian nationalist movement—a version of the divide and rule–argument (Ramamoorthy 1983; Kailasapathy 1979).

[3] See, for example, Pandian (1994) and Venkatachalapathy (1994).

[4] The exception to this is a work Pandian co-authored on cartoons (Pandian, Subagunarajan and Trotsky 2009) that appeared during Anna's time, which explores both Anna's use of cartoons as a form of political tool as well as the cartoons that appeared at the time that were critical of Anna and the DMK.

[5] Pandian (1992) also wrote on the Tamil matinee idol-turned-politician, M. G. Ramachandran. However, this brilliant critical work, following earlier works on cinema as a form of political tool in Dravidian cultural politics, focuses mostly on Ramachandran's filmic message, and how he was able to build up a mass personal

following while still within the DMK party. Thus, Pandian's work on Ramachandran is centred principally on explicating the nexus between the Dravidian movement and mass media messages broadly, and Ramachandran more specifically, rather than attempting to locate them in the longer history of the Dravidian movement. These works by Pandian certainly underlined the need for more critical work on understanding the political and ideological transition and transformations that enabled such political actors and political developments in the more mature phase of the Dravidian movement.

[6] These castes did not identify with the interests of the forward non-Brahmin castes as the earlier struggles had only helped serve their narrow interests and left the vast majority of the population still in the cold.

[7] 'More specifically, they were the rising urban lower middle classes, educated unemployed and middling farmers from backward castes' (Barnett 1976: 98–100).

[8] Barnett's views on the nature of Tamil nationalism are also interesting. She, for example, noted: 'In contemporary Tamil Nadu, we find caste ethnic-like ... The symbols of caste society are taken over and their meaning transformed in an ethnic-like and cultural nationalist context' (ibid.: 165). And also, 'Tamilians see themselves not as an ethnic group within a nationwide system of ethnic groups—but as a nation with an intrinsic legitimacy of its own' (ibid.: 164). Her views on the trajectory of the Dravidian movement are also important to note: 'the malleability of political identity has been shown in Tamil Nadu. It has been defined as non-Brahmin, Dravidian and Tamilian at various historical points' (ibid.: 315). This suggests that if it had first started out as 'non-Brahmin' under the multi-ethnic context of the Madras Presidency, it was spurred by the loss of status of both the urban impact and British administration in changing the status of Brahmins and elite non-Brahmins—and tied to the negative symbol of 'Shudra' and confined mainly to elite non-Brahmins. It is this that was slowly transformed into Dravidian and, ultimately, a form of Dravidian/Tamil nationalism over the years by a variety of factors and actors, including the compulsory introduction of Hindi, introduction of universal adult franchise, linguistic reorganisation and, of course, the work of principal actors such as Periyar and Anna.

[9] Anna had from the start of his political life been schooled in the electoral politics of the Justice Party and was anti-Congress, while Periyar had been an ardent Congressite before joining the Justice Party and was averse to electoral politics. There were also big differences in their educational attainments, with Anna having acquired higher–post secondary qualifications including a Masters in Tamil literature, which had given him mastery of Tamil literature and the English language, compared to Periyar's rather limited formal educational attainments. Their ultimate split was not so much over Periyar's second marriage to a woman much younger than him, but due to their underlying different approach to politics (Arunan 2008: 46).

[10] Arunan points this out by giving the example of Anna confronted with questions of retaining Tamil-speaking areas for Tamil Nadu during the struggles for linguistic reorganisation of the former Madras state that included various Dravidian-language speakers (ibid.: 37).

[11] If these two works, which directly engage with the question of Anna's role in the Dravidian movement, point to the turn towards 'populism' as the principal explanatory/theoretical term to delineate and explain the success of Anna and the DMK, other works with a much wider focus, such as V. Horoz's *Valarmuga Nadugalil*

Populism: Netrum Indrum (1986) and Narendra Subramaniam's *Ethicity and Populist Mobilization* (1997), also tend to confirm such a reading, although offering a much more complex understanding of this drift towards 'populism' with the advent of Anna as leader and the founding father of the DMK.

[12] One of the other strengths of the work is its liberal utilisation of the notes and perspective of many of Anna's contemporaries and critics including Sampath, the well-known songwriter Kavingar Kannadasan, the Communist leader P. Ramamurthy and the Leftist novelist Jeyakanthan (Kannan 2011: 229–30). His description of Kannadasan's initial encounter with Anna's oratory leaving Kannadasan spellbound and his later disillusionment with the DMK are particularly interesting in this regard (ibid.). So is the critique offered of Anna's *Arya Mayai* by the Ramamurthy (ibid.: 253). It would have been more instructive if Kannan were to have integrated such observations and critique in his overall analysis of Anna and his role in the Dravidian movement. The book is also available in the Tamil translation. I have used the Tamil translation in this chapter.

[13] Political articulation of the Dravidian movement began in 1916 with the formation of the South Indian Liberal Federation, later known as the Justice Party.

[14] The citations from *Arya Mayai* that follow are from Annadurai's 1948 work.

[15] The essays were originally published in Anna's *Dravida Nadu* magazine in 1942. See Arunan (2008: 131).

[16] More specifically, through various modes as religious rituals and rites, language and culture.

[17] He goes on to note, 'Will they ever stop feeding this poisonous intoxicants?', he asks rhetorically. 'Can you ask a peddler of heroin to stop peddling?' (Annadurai 1948: 13–14).

[18] He goes on to note, 'What was the state of India before the Aryans? What calamities arose as a result of the Aryan ways to the Dravidians? How did the Dravidians resist and what was their status during ancient times? I have provided below the findings from ancient historical research ... which have been culled from the work of the historian and comrade, Srinivasa Iyengar's work, entitled the *History of India* published in 1923' (ibid.: 18).

[19] From this essentially postcolonial reading, we can then view Anna's rendition of the Dravidian ideology as an integral legacy of European orientalist interventions and their pioneering indigenous advocates.

[20] This reading posits that there was a fundamental difference between Periyar and Anna, at least from the time *Arya Mayai* was penned, and that Anna's ideology drew deeply from the legacy of his Christian missionary and neo-Saivite predecessors, and the ideology he articulated was essentially similar to the form of Tamil nationalism that they articulated. One must concede, however, that they shared some views that enabled them to identify with each other and work together.

References

Anbalagan, Ka. 2009. *Mamanithan Anna* (Anna, The Great Man). Chennai: Poombuhar Veliyeedu.

Annadurai, C. N. (n.d.). *Aryan Illusion*. Guindy, Chennai: Sinthanai Pathipakam.

—— 1948. *Arya Mayai*, 3rd edition. Tiruchirappalli: Tiravitap Pannai.

Arunan. 2008. *Anna: Aatchiyai Pidtha Varalaru* (The History of How Anna Captured State Power). Madurai: Vasantham Veliyeetakam.

Baker, Christopher John. 1976. *The Politics of South India 1920–1937*. Cambridge: Cambridge University Press.

Barnett, Marguerite Ross. 1976. *The Politics of Cultural Nationalism in South India*. Princeton: Princeton University Press.

Citibabu, Sai. Ve. 2000. *Valterum Annavum* (Voltaire and Anna). Madurai: Madurai Kamraj Palkalaikazham.

Hardgrave, Robert L. 1965. *The Dravidian Movement*. Bombay: Popular Prakashan.

Horoz, V. 1986. *Valarmuga Nadugalil Populism: Netrum Indrum* (Populism in the Developing World: Yesterday and Today), trans. Ira Bhaskaran. Chennai: New Century Book House.

Irschik, Eugene F. 1969. *Politics and Social Conflict in South India: The Non-Brahmin Movement and Tamil Separatism*. Berkeley: University of California Press.

Jeyakanthan. 2010. *Or Ilakiyavadiyin Arasiyal Anubavankal* (A Literary Writer's Political Experience), first published 1974. Madurai: Meenakshi Puthaka Nilayam.

Kailasapathy, K. 1979. 'The Tamil Purist Movement: A Re-evaluation'. *Social Scientist* 7(10): 23–51.

Kannan, Ira. 2011. *Anna: Oru Sathara Manithanin Asatharana Valkai* (Anna: The Life and Times of C. N. Annadurai). Chennai: Vikatan Piracuran.

Nedunchelian, Ka. (ed.). 2016. *Peraarignan Annavum Perung Kavignar Kumaran Asanum* (Great Thinker Anna and Great Poet Kumaran Asan). Tiruchirappalli: Manitham Publishers.

Pandian, M. S. S. 1992. *The Image Trap: M. G. Ramachandran in Film and Politics*. New Delhi: Sage Publications.

——— 1994. 'Notes on the Transformation of "Dravidian" Ideology: Tamilnadu, c. 1900–1940'. *Social Scientist* 22(5–6), May–June: 84–104.

——— 2007. *Brahmin and Non-Brahmin: Genealogies of the Tamil Political Present*. New Delhi: Permanent Black.

Pandian, M. S. S., V. M. S. Subagunarajan and Maruthu Trotsky (eds). 2009. *Kartooniyam: Peraringnar Annavaipatria Kelisithirangalum Sithirathokupukalum*. Chennai: Kayalvin.

Parimalam, Anna (ed.). 2009. *Arignar Annavin Pakutharivu Kalangiyam* (Great Thinker Anna's Collection of Rationalist Writings). Chennai: Tiravida Kalazham.

Pavendan, Ira (ed.). 2009. *Karuppu Sikappu Ithaliyal* (Black and Red Literary Magazines). Chennai: Kayalvin.

Ramamoorthy, P. 1983. *The Freedom Struggle and Dravidian Movement*. Madras: Orient Longman.

Sanmugasundaram, Su. 2015. *Arignar Anna, Indiya Ilakiya Sirpikal* (Great Thinker Anna, Series on Indian Literary Greats). New Delhi: Sahitya Akademi.

Subramaniam, Narendra. 1997. *Ethicity and Populist Mobilization: Political Parties, Citizens and Democracy in South India*. Delhi: Oxford University Press.

Thamizhavan. 2014. *Thiravidam, Thamil Thesam, Kathaiyadal: Oru Nootrandu Thamil Sinthanai Varalaru* (Dravidianism, Tamil Nation, a Dialogue: Hundred Years of Tamil Intellectual History). Tiruchirappalli: Adayalam.

Venkatachalapathy, A. R. 1994. *Thiravida Iyakkamum Vellalarum*. Chennai: South Vision Books.

Viswanathan, G. 2015. *Anna, Arumai Anna* (Anna, the Wonderful Anna). Chennai: Kannadasan Pathipakkam.

Washbrook, D. A. 1976. *The Emergence of Provincial Politics: The Madras Presidency 1870–1920*. Cambridge: Cambridge University Press.

—— 1989. 'Caste, Class, and Dominance in Modern Tamil Nadu: Non-Brahminism, Dravidianism and Tamil Nationalism'. In *Dominance and State Power in Modern India: Decline of a Social Order*, Volume 1, eds Francine R. Frankel and M. S. A. Rao, 204–64. Delhi: Oxford University Press.

7. An Ethic beyond Anti-colonialism

*A Periyarist Engagement with Fanonism**

Karthick Ram Manoharan

In this chapter, through a dialogue between Periyar and Frantz Fanon, I shall use Periyar's critiques of Indian nationalism to point out the limitations in Fanon's support for anti-colonialism, and probe how the logic of anti-colonialism need not be viewed in a positive fashion by all political groups in a colony, that is, it need not be the single most important empty signifier that creates *identification* of groups against the colonising Other. I start with a discussion about Indian history, more specifically about how it was received and constructed by Indian nationalist historiographers, and how it was interpreted by Periyar. Periyar rejected the idea of an Indian nation existing in history and considered it a construct of the British Empire. However, Fanon had very romanticised and non-problematised notions about Third World nations. While he was apprehensive about their future, he did not question their legitimacy. While to Fanon, anti-colonial nationalism was the manifestation of one socio-politico unit, Periyar deconstructed the idea of nation and nationalism from within. Likewise, this chapter also contrasts the respective positions of Fanon and Periyar on the question of women. In the Fanonian corpus, women merely appear as sexual objects or political instruments, rarely getting mention as autonomous agents of political and social change. To Periyar, on the other hand, respecting the agency and

---

*An earlier version of this chapter was discussed in my PhD thesis at the Department of Government, University of Essex. Feedback from Aletta Norval, David Howarth, M. S. S. Pandian and Ravi Vaithees helped shape this chapter as it is today.

autonomy of women's struggle was key to his Self-respect Movement. We can see that Fanon's sensitivity to the external oppressor does not extend much to the internal one, that is, he never assumes that the native's anti-colonial discourse might itself be a process of privileging certain identities over others. Periyar was keen on challenging the internal and native forms of oppression as he considered them far more insidious and persistent than colonialism, which he identified as a passing phase. The chapter concludes that a democratic identity politics, which I consider, taking from Mouffe (1999: 52), a 'political process of hegemonic articulation', needs to lay a claim to universalism by finding a commonality, while simultaneously recognising the particular claims of discrete social groups and pluralisms that exist in a society.

A Short Note from and about 'Indian History'

It is interesting how after over seven decades of Indian Independence, Indian scholars who problematise European conception of Indian pasts are reluctant to problematise how Indians conceptualised their own past and who were excluded in these conceptualisations. Considered to be a seminal work of secular Indian nationalism, *The Discovery of India* (1969) by Congress leader and the first Indian prime minister, Jawaharlal Nehru, is an unproblematic teleology, which moves from antiquity to modernity. Nehru did not have an intellectual problem in conceiving the people in the Indian territory, a subcontinent whose people are as diverse in languages and cultures as the people of Africa, Europe and the Middle East taken together, as constituting one nation, with one common culture and with one civilisational continuity. In his words:

> Some kind of dream of unity has occupied the mind of India since the dawn of civilization. That unity was not conceived as something imposed from outside, a standardization of externals or even of beliefs. It was something deeper and, within its fold, the widest tolerance of belief and custom was practised and every variety acknowledged and even encouraged. (Nehru 1969: 65)

In Nehru's view, 'we see in the past some inner urge towards synthesis' that this was 'the dominant feature of Indian cultural, and even racial development', and this was brought about by the philosophical referent of the Sanskrit texts, mainly the Vedas (ibid.: 76). Interestingly, his ideological nemesis, the Hindu nationalist demagogue V. D. Savarkar, also based his claims for the Hindus being a nation on more or less the same premises (Savarkar 2007: 90).

Mainstream Indian nationalist historiography and debates about Indian history, whether secular in nature or not, have uncritically accepted the idea of India as a single sociocultural entity. In a perceptive note, Anderson (2012: 9) remarks that such intellectuals share the rhetoric of the Indian State and uphold four central tropes from the official imaginary of India, namely 'antiquity-continuity; diversity-unity; massivity-democracy; multi-confessionality-secularity'. Further noting that there was never a singular politico-cultural entity called India prior to the arrival of colonialism, he argues:

> The "idea of India" was essentially a European, not a local invention, as the name itself makes clear. No such term, or equivalent, as India existed in any indigenous language. A Greek coinage, taken from the Indus river, it was so exogenous to the subcontinent that as late as the 16th century, Europeans could define Indians simply as "all natives of an unknown country", and so call the inhabitants of the Americas. (Ibid.: 11)

In direct contrast to the Indian nationalists, Periyar disputes the existence of an Indian nation in history: 'Can anyone say that the formation of the Indian union and the formation of the Indian law happened in an organic fashion without a great fraud? Can anyone say that India is not an artificial creation, and since when has a country called India existed?' (*Viduthalai*, 14 December 1967).

To Periyar, India, the idea of the Indian nation, Indian nationalism and its symbols were part of a Brahminical ideological device to rule over the Dravidians. Questioning the concept of an 'Indian nation', he argues that it was only under the period of colonialism that the Tamil region was brought together under an Indian entity, and calls for the rejection of all Indian nationalist symbols (*Viduthalai*, 20 July 1955). In a controversial move in the mid-1950s to oppose the central government's imposition of Hindi as a pan-Indian language, he called for the burning of Indian flags. His logic:

> We want our rule in our country. In our country, a language which is not our own should not be a language of the state,

> nation and education. To show the rulers that our country does not want a rule that forces Hindi upon us – we had to do this as an agitation strategy. (Ramasamy 2009: 2893)

In Periyar's perspective, colonialism and anti-colonialism were phases of history. His greater concern was with social institutions which have greater endurance in history. As early as 1925, he makes his priorities clear. Arguing that self-respect is more important than self-rule, he further emphasised that the demand for self-rule must be postponed till a self-respecting society was achieved (*Kudiarasu*, 24 January 1925). Further, at a speech delivered at Triuchirappalli in 1943, he called on the youth to demand the separation of 'Dravidanadu'.

> We are today Shudras. We are degraded. We have no right to enter the temple or eating houses. We are considered low untouchables. In the government we are given menial jobs. Those who betray us are cared by the government and Congress. We remain as downtrodden for ever. We are being exploited by the Brahmins and the bureaucracy. (Ramasamy 1998: 4)

It is worthy to compare Periyar's views with those of other anti-caste activists in his time. For instance, according to the Dalit leader, Ambedkar (2006: 6), Indian nationalism was dominated by the upper castes and further 'it is beyond question that the Congress is a body of middle class Hindus supported by the Hindu capitalists whose object is not to make Indians free but to be independent of British control and to occupy places of power now occupied by the British'.

This is a crucial point that differentiated Periyar from other anti-caste activists like Ambedkar. This contrast is worth briefly considering here. Ambedkar also agreed that eradication of casteism should precede self-rule and independence. In his opinion, 'only when the Hindu society becomes a casteless society that it can hope to have strength enough to defend itself. Without such internal strength, Swaraj for Hindus may turn out to be only a step towards slavery' (Ambedkar 2007: 50). However, while Ambedkar was critical of Indian nationalism, the domination of upper-castes in framing the nationalist imaginary, and the frequent exaltation of the Hindu way of life by the Indian nationalists, he nevertheless saw a modern Indian State and constitutional reforms as a possible means for pushing for social justice for the Dalits and the lower castes. To Periyar on the other hand, the very political entity called India represented the domination of Brahmins over the lower castes, especially the Dravidians, and nothing short of separation would be a step towards the annihilation of caste.

What could be Fanon's perspective on this?

Notions of Nations

In a passage in *The Wretched of the Earth* (1963), Fanon writes:

> By its very structure, colonialism is separatist and regionalist. Colonialism does not simply state the existence of tribes; it also reinforces it and separates them. The colonial system encourages chieftaincies and keeps alive the old Marabout confraternities. Violence is in action all-inclusive and national. It follows that it is closely involved in the liquidation of regionalism and of tribalism. Thus the national parties show no pity at all toward the caids and the customary chiefs. Their destruction is the preliminary to the unification of the people. (Ibid.: 94)

In his works, Fanon problematised the notion of an essentialised black identity. However, with regard to decolonisation, while Fanon was acutely aware of the problems that an elitist leadership might cause in a postcolonial society, he nevertheless took anti-colonial nationalism to be positive in general and did not venture into critiquing the discourse of the group that presents itself as the national group. To Fanon, the sovereignty of the decolonised nation was sacrosanct and 'separatist' and 'regionalist' demands were just colonial manoeuvres to destabilise the process of decolonisation. The postcolonial society might have problems with various social groups, but still, anti-colonial nationalism was a virtue to be defended. The very core of Fanon's (1988: 44) politics of identity, recognition of particularities and universality depended on it: '... [U]niversality resides in this decision to recognize and accept the reciprocal relativism of different cultures once the colonial status is irreversibly reduced.'

In the essay, 'First Truths on the Colonial Problem', while placing Nehru, Gamal Abdel Nasser and Sukarno together as anti-imperialists, Fanon (1988: 125) comments on India, saying, 'What no one sees is that the 350 million Hindus, who have known the hunger of British imperialism, are now demanding bread, peace, and well-being.' What Fanon did not see was that at the very time this essay was being composed, there were voices in India problematising the idea of 'Hindus' as a community and 'India' as a nation.[1]

Decolonisation was the precondition to the acceptance of the relativism of different cultures for Fanon, whereas for Periyar, the recognition of the existence of fundamentally different cultures was the precondition to the acceptance of decolonisation. Periyar was extremely critical of essentialised notions of an Indian nation, and instead proposed a Dravidian identity based on reason, argument and shared solidarity against the native oppressive caste. Fanon, on the other hand, never critically examines the idea of 'nation' that opposes the colonial power, but is more opposed to 'separatist' and 'regionalist' tendencies within a broader anti-colonialism.

Fanon seems to be subscribing to 'strategic use of essentialism in a scrupulously visible political interest' (Spivak 1987: 205), in this case, decolonisation. The argument in favour of such a strategy would be that a critical situation, like that of colonialism, demands certain essentialised notions of 'we' if at all 'they' have to be countered. Fanon's conception of identity is shaped largely by a violent encounter with colonialism. Though he makes a claim for an eventual transcendence into a larger humanism, the settling of the colonial encounter is a precondition to it. Fanon's perspective on colonialism is sharply Manichean—one is either for colonialism, which is 'evil', or one is against it, which is 'good'. The real political dilemma, as Sartre (2008: 34) discovered in the late 1960s, 'of being "for, but" or "against, but"' is never acutely addressed by Fanon in the context of colonialism.

Given the wake of the brutalities of French colonialism in Algeria, and Fanon's own role as a partisan of the Front de Libération Nationale (FLN), it might have been strategically necessary for him to invoke certain types of essentialism. However, when Fanonism is taken as a theory, this type of essentialism can be quite dangerous when taken in different contexts. As Spivak (1993: 4) who has a cautious support for the concept notes, 'a strategy suits a situation; a strategy is not a theory'. When Fanonism is uncritically applied in a context like that of India, where the 'nation' as a project was itself a product of the colonial intervention, it can but have disastrous consequences for those social groups at the margins of the newly constructed nation. Of course, while Fanon himself can be excused for being ignorant of the specificities of the Indian or, more particularly, the Tamil condition,

Fanonism needs to critiqued and critically expanded to include the plurality of political interests that existed in the colonial period.

Fanon's emphasis is more on political unity against the enemy of colonialism. Here, he is most Schmittian in his understanding that: 'Political unity can contain and comprehend different contents. But it always designates the most intensive degree of a unity, from which, consequently, the most intensive distinction—the grouping of friend and enemy—is determined' (Schmitt 1999: 203). To Fanon, anti-colonialism as an empty signifier serves as 'means of representation that enable the building of alliances between different groups and identities by pointing an enemy to be opposed and proposing solutions to the problem facing groups' (Howarth 2013: 251). Fanon believes that anti-colonial nationalism, or national consciousness, would create a sense of solidarity among different social groups in the colonised territory against the ultimate adversary, the colonial apparatus. Fanon is most influenced by Sartre's arguments about the 'dialectic of the group' from *Critique of Dialectical Reason* of how in a critical situation of violence or insurrection, 'separate individuals overcome their seriality and combine under threat to form a fused group' (Aronson 1980: 251). Fanon also takes the practico-inert concept to heart that says, 'We become dominated by the unintended features of our product, or by our own tools', especially when he discusses how the structural limitations of the newly decolonised society allows a comprador elite to take over. However, his complete non-consideration of precolonial history as a critical factor causes him to not explore why a fused group could be legitimately formed against a dominant social group within the colonised territory rather than against the coloniser.

Periyar, on the other hand, shared the Schmittian scepticism that 'it is a dangerous deception when one single group pursues its special interests in the name of the whole, and unjustifiably identifies itself with the state' (Schmitt 1999: 205). Periyar, who unlike Fanon, was acutely aware of the distinctiveness of the precolonial history of his region, was convinced that the Indian nation-building project was designed to protect the interests of the Brahmin castes. Periyar understood that as far as Tamil Nadu was concerned,

> [t]he colonial public sphere was restricted in its scope and substance not merely because of the dynamics of colonialism,

> but also by the very character of the indigenous elite who participated in it. Without being informed by notions of substantive citizenship, it was an elite who were, by and large, unwilling to relinquish their traditional modes of semi-feudal authority, and hence failed to speak for a broader public. (Pandian 1995: 388)

Hence, the central thrust of Periyar's political discourse was to create an alternative public sphere, which would exclude the native elites and provide spaces for voices silenced by the Indian nationalist discourse. The Dravidian identity he espoused was a 'resistance identity' as opposed to the 'legitimising identity' of Indian nationalism. Given the threat he perceived from unmediated Brahmin hegemony in a postcolonial India, he argued that 'regionalism'—even if it had to be carried out to the extreme of separating from the Indian Union—would be the only permanent safeguard against the domination of the native elite.

In a critique of two influential Cambridge School historians of South India—David Washbrook and Christopher Baker—who restricted their discussion of caste to purely the confines of the colonialism/anti-colonialism binary, Pandian (1995) wrote:

> In short, the disavowal of caste identity as part of the political is complete in the writings of the Cambridge school. If fragmentation of different castes denies caste the status of caste-in-itself, the way in which caste identity was supposed to have been invoked in colonial Tamil Nadu denies it the status of caste-for-itself. Caste identity is thus out in the cold with no political past or future. (Ibid.: 386)

The meta-narrative of Indian anti-colonialism in general displayed a gross insensitivity to historical and sociopolitical questions of caste and region. Motifs similar to Fanon's perspective on regionalism and separatism keep recurring in not just Indian nationalist discourse, but in Indian historiography and sociology as well. For instance, Ghurye (1950: 290), a well-known Indian sociologist, wrote, 'Where it is a question of engendering a feeling of unity the people must be made to cooperate irrespective of caste.' To those like Ghurye, the British were responsible for introducing caste divisions in Indian society as a 'divide-and-rule' strategy and that the nationalist discourse led by the elite castes was justified in projecting a homogenous Indian nation.

Periyar's opinion stands in direct contrast to Ghurye's in that he accuses the Brahmins of being the initiators of the divide-and-rule strategy, and further accuses the colonial powers of collaborating with the native elites for the smooth functioning of the administrative apparatus. For instance, in a speech in 1957 in the wake of the Mudukulathur riots between Dalits and the intermediate castes where there were casualties on both sides, while placing his stand firmly on the side of the Dalits, Periyar also stated, 'The Brahmin rejoices when clashes break within our people', alleging that the Brahmin benefits from divisions within the non-Brahmins (Ramasamy 2011a: 291). Following this up in another speech, he accused the political legacy of the Indian nationalists, Gandhi and the Congress party of benefiting only the Brahmins. To Periyar:

> We need a revolution to change this state of affairs. Revolutionary words are not enough. We may need to resort to the sword. Jinnah struggled in front of our eyes. He raised the sword! Why we (Muslims) should be trapped under the Hindus, he asked; after rivers of blood flowed, they gave him Pakistan. Today, it is a powerful country. Nehru is frightened of it.[2] (Ibid.: 302)

Periyar's discourse understood that the meta-narrative of anti-colonialism was a garb in which the interests of the Tamil region would be compromised and that in postcolonial India, the Brahmin secured his domination in administrative posts by virtue of an agreement with the erstwhile coloniser (*Viduthalai*, 4 November 1960). Further, according to him, in postcolonial India,

> [o]nly those who betray our nation, only those who betray our society, can prosper in this state. Those who prioritize the Dravidian people or Tamil Nadu cannot. Either one lives under open slavery or, if one wants a respectful position in the administration, one has to live as a slave under the Brahmin. (Ibid.)

To Periyar, there never was an Indian nation in history, and it was only owing to colonialism that the Tamil region was brought under the Indian entity (*Viduthalai*, 20 July 1955).

Periyar's discourse repeated the idea that the Brahmin was an Aryan, an alien Other who was divorced from the community of Dravidians, often in terms that frequently overlapped race with caste. It is instructive to consider the persistence of this image in the Dravidian political imaginary in Tamil Nadu, where, according to Dirks (2004):

> ... the post-colonial picture is complicated by the double presence of the displaced colonial other, figured most directly and conspicuously in the Brahman (and by implication or association the north Indian and Aryan). In a history that begins with the language of Caldwell in casting the Aryan as a colonial figure, we confront a post-colonial condition with a difference. And thus both colonialism and post-colonialism move offstage, to be replaced by a colonial theatre of double mimesis, in which the Brahman plays the role – not quite, but well enough – of the British colonial ruler, and in which colonialism might be said to have ended not in 1947, but only in 1967, with the ascension to political power of the DMK. (Ibid.: 293)

Thus, in the popular Dravidian political imaginary as articulated by Periyar, more than the colonial encounter, it was the precolonial encounter with the Aryan-Brahmin-alien-Other that determined the contours of the political discourse. A Fanonist understanding, which considers anti-colonialism as the primary contradiction in a colonised society as a *universal* given, is bound to be problematic in a society like India, largely because it is ignorant of the precolonial history which might have similar or greater influence in shaping *particular* political discourses like those which emerged in colonial Tamil Nadu.

This tension between the abstract universality of Fanon and the concrete particularity of Periyar can also be observed in the approach of both to the language of the coloniser and the colonised. To Fanon, even though he wrote only in French, the colonial language was by itself an act of aggression in the colony. He laments that under the colonial situation, 'We witness the destruction of cultural values, of ways of life. Language, dress, techniques, are devalorized' (Fanon 1988: 33). The oppressed, when confronted by the colonial power, develop a complex about their culture and language, and begin to shy away from them and mimic the coloniser. 'Having judged, condemned, abandoned his cultural forms, his language, his food habits, his sexual behavior, his way of sitting down, of resting, of laughing, of enjoying himself, the oppressed flings himself upon the imposed culture with the desperation of a drowning man' (ibid.: 39). To Fanon, language was yet another tool used by colonialism's ideology to enslave a nation and inferiorise the native's sense of self-respect.

Periyar too had strong opinions on how imposition of alien languages inferiorised a native's sense of self-respect—but to him the native was the Tamil and the alien languages were Hindi and Sanskrit. In 1938, at a time when the local chapter of Congress Party was pushing for the propagation of Hindi as a national language, Periyar called on the youth and women to oppose the imposition of the same, as it would benefit the Aryans at the cost of the Dravidians. In polemic fashion, he writes, 'What is happening now is not British rule. It is the rule of the priests of the *varna* system. Its each living breath intends to enslave the Tamil people' (*Kudiarasu*, 8 May 1938). Following up with another essay titled 'The Brahmin Rule Takes its Revenge', he argues that the Brahminical castes were seeking to dominate the South through Hinduism and Hindi, and that anti-colonialism was a garb through which 'the Brahmins are trying to retrieve their rule, their religion, their language' (*Kudiarasu*, 5 June 1938). Therefore, if the social integrity of the Tamil people had to be preserved, Hindi as a language had to be opposed. Periyar and his organisation were at the forefront of several anti-Hindi agitations from the 1930s continuing to the mid-1960s, when his protégé Annadurai was elected as the Tamil Nadu chief minister, riding on the wave of the massive anti-Hindi imposition struggles that rocked the state in the 1960s.

However, while Tamil nationalists countered the imposition of Hindi with claims of antiquity and superiority of the Tamil language, Periyar had no such romantic notions about the native language. Calling Tamil a 'barbaric language', he laments that there is no Tamil version of Kemal Atatürk who would substitute the classical Tamil script with the Latin alphabet (Ramasamy 2011b: 8). Periyar indicated a marked preference for English in that he considered English to be a universal language, a language of modernity and enlightenment. To Periyar, the Shudra Tamils needed to 'rise above a state of barbarism', and for that, 'it is not enough that one hates god, religion, the Vedas, the traditional puranas, temples, festivals and religious processions. One also must detest the Tamil language which upholds the puranas and religious epics. This is so because the Tamil language is structured so as to degrade the Tamil' (ibid.: 138). Further, provocatively, he calls on the Tamils to ignore the Tamil language and emulate English modernity (ibid.: 140). According to Periyar, 'English governance,

English education, English customs and English civilization have over time have dented to some extent the caste system and caste hierarchies' (*Kudiarasu*, 13 March 1938).

Besides, to Periyar, the Tamil language was also structurally sexist in the way in it described women. This brings us to another crucial point of divergence between the two thinkers.

White Men, Coloured Women

In 1927, American writer Katherine Mayo published *Mother India*, a controversial book on colonial India that justified the prolonging of British rule over the territory citing, among other things, the poor condition of the lower castes and women which, according to her, the Indians were incapable of justly handling by themselves. In the introduction to the abridged version, the Indian scholar Sinha (2000: 1) writes that the book 'was celebrated and reviled by die-hard imperialists and outraged nationalists'. However, there was also a third opinion. Periyar welcomed the book (*Kudiarasu*, 29 December 1929), and one of his disciples, Kovai A. Ayyamuthu, wrote a set of essays in *Kudiarasu*, the party paper of the Self-respect Movement, in the late 1920s defending Mayo against her critics. While recognising that Mayo's motivations were not exactly benign, the writer nevertheless conceded to her that her charges against India were accurate and that peoples in the subcontinent could not achieve true freedom without social reform.[3]

In her most celebrated essay, 'Can the Subaltern Speak?', Spivak (1988: 299) writes, 'Imperialism's image as the establisher of the good society is marked by the espousal of the woman as object of protection from her own kind.' Spivak gives the example of Sati, or the Hindu practice of burning widows on the pyre of their dead husbands, and explains how the colonial intervention into the banning of this practice was done with the intention of legitimising the colonial rule and also silence the voice of the 'victim' they were saving. The Fanonian influence here is impossible to miss. Periyar, however, thanked the 'White man' without whom, 'in the name of religion and tradition, women would have been burnt along with their dead husbands. It was only the White man's law that changed this' (*Viduthalai*, 17 July 1970). Periyar had no faith in the Indian anti-colonialist project to secure liberation for women. If anything, he viewed it as a politics that reinforced patriarchy and misogyny, which he argued, were inherent to Hindu society. Let us consider Fanon's perspectives on women *vis-à-vis* colonialism and anti-colonialism briefly.

In *Black Skin, White Masks*, women to Fanon are mere sexual objects.[4] His black women are filled with an inferiority complex and desire to move up the social ladder by virtue of sexual relationships with the white coloniser. In his assessment of Martinican writer Mayotte Capécia, his argument is that women like her *desire* lactification: 'the race must be whitened; every woman in Martinique knows this, says it, repeats it' (Fanon 2008: 33). His white woman *fantasises* about being raped by black men.

> If we go farther into the labyrinth, we discover that when a woman lives the fantasy of rape by a Negro, it is in some way the fulfilment of a private dream, of an inner wish. Accomplishing the phenomenon of turning against self, it is the woman who rapes herself. (Ibid.: 138)

In his critically acclaimed book about race and racism, a woman gets a place only by virtue of association with a man of this or that race, and that too only as an object of desire.

A similar approach can be noted in the essay, 'Algeria Unveiled'. Here, Fanon defends a traditional cultural device like the veil with the argument that it served as a symbolic as well as a practical resistance to colonialism. His perspective of promotion of French liberal values to women in Algeria was wholly negative, as he considered it an integral part of the colonial strategy to separate the Algerian woman from the Algerian man, and making both feel ashamed of their national culture. 'Convening the woman, winning her over to the foreign values, wrenching her free from her status, was at the same time achieving a real power over the man and attaining a practical, effective means of destructuring Algerian culture' (Fanon 1965: 39). The colonial sought to unveil the Algerian woman, and the authentic act of resistance against this was for the woman to be veiled. Though he asserts, 'The Algerian woman is at the heart of the combat. Arrested, tortured, raped, shot down, she testifies to the violence of the occupier and to his inhumanity. As a nurse, a liaison agent, a fighter, she bears witness to the depth and the density of the struggle' (ibid.: 66), it is only the woman as an instrument of the anti-colonial resistance struggle that is of interest to Fanon. The woman who confronts the internal oppressor, the home-grown patriarch, is totally absent.

One could credit Fanon's comments on the veil and his utopian belief that its significance would fade away post decolonisation to his naivety with regard to the role of Islam in the Arab world.[5] In fact, Fanon maintains ambivalence with respect to his position on religion. While he was himself born in a practising Christian family, he does not seem to have much regard for Christianity as such. While it is likely that, at a personal level, Fanon was an atheist inspired by Sartrean existentialism, his writings on the Algerian decolonisation movement saw a tolerance for Islamism. To Fanon, this upheaval, which had religious undertones, was a legitimate reaction to colonialism and any regressive social practices that may come up in its wake would and should be resolved once, and only once, the coloniser exited the land. Colonial interventions to set right any regressive native practices were done only with the intention of maintaining the colonial system and they were to be rejected outright.

Periyar, on the other hand, welcomed the liberating effect some aspects of colonialism had on women in the Tamil society. In a comment on the role of the native national culture and its effects on women, he writes, 'To state it frankly, we are still living according to values established in barbaric times' (*Viduthalai*, 31 August 1963). Arguing that the spread of English education contributed to the spread of modern egalitarian values with respect to the women's question, he asserts that the 'White man' banning Sati and providing women access to modern education was one of the reasons of the anti-colonial movement, which wanted to preserve traditional, reactionary values. In Periyar's perspective, the Brahminical culture, the influence of religion, and Tamil patriarchy all contributed to the oppression of women and women were better off Westernised than relying on native cultural-social values for liberation. Where Fanon considered native dress codes an act of resistance against the coloniser, Periyar condemned them as regressive, and asked women to adopt Western attire to attain greater mobility. The practical effects of Periyar's discourse could be seen in that the 'women members of the Self Respect Movement not only participated in the non-agitational programmes of the movement like conferences, but also quite actively in mass agitations' (Bharadwaj 1991: 32). Not just that, women from the most marginalised sections, like that of the devadasis or the 'temple prostitute' communities, also became active participants in social reform movements in the state. These women took part in anti-caste struggles, the anti-Hindi agitations and protests demanding greater social and economic rights for women.

However, it is to be noted, Periyar's radicalism with regard to women's question was not taken up in good faith by many of those who claimed to be his followers. Many of the leaders of the Dravidian movement were not averse to using sexist and objectifying terms in political discourse. Terms like 'chastity' and projecting the Tamil language as a 'virgin goddess' were employed as rhetorical devices by many who participated in the anti-Hindi agitations, especially the leaders of the DMK under Annadurai. These led Periyar to be sceptical and critical of the uses and abuses of the Tamil language in imagining a Tamil national community which objectified the body of women.

Periyar's discourse also involved a critique of the terms that he considered patriarchal in the Tamil language. For instance, he launched a devastating attack on the dominant notions of 'chastity' that existed in that period that placed several social restrictions on women. To Periyar, these notions of community that sought to exercise sexual control over the bodies of women were remnants of barbaric times (Ramasamy 2011c: 195). He further lampooned Tamil scholars and poets for expecting women to be chaste, while placing no such demands on men (*Viduthalai*, 18 June 1970). Periyar was also not averse to attacking ancient Tamil poetry and classics—exalted by Tamil nationalists—for their sexism and misogyny. He was convinced that any ideology that places the past, any past, on a high pedestal was likely to be sexist.

Periyar starkly differed from Fanon in that neither did he define women in pure sexual relation to men, nor did he consider them as instruments of social struggle. Instead of speaking *for* them and limiting the spaces for women, he spoke *with* them and acted as an ally of the women's struggle. Echoing contemporary proponents of standpoint theory, he argued that the pain of the 'lived experience' of being a woman in a patriarchal society was unique (*Viduthalai*, 11 August 1963) and more spaces should be opened up for their voices to be heard. While with Fanon, the woman who transgressed the boundaries of the family was praised only when she was part of the anti-colonial struggle, Periyar encouraged women to break traditional family norms for their own good as autonomous individuals exercising control over their sexual choices, irrespective of whether they sought to contribute to the Dravidian movement or not. Ironically, while Fanon was well acquainted with the works of feminist giants like Simone de Beauvoir, the idea of the woman existing as an autonomous political subject never appeared in his works. The iconoclastic social reformer who never had a formal education had more perceptiveness when it came to this subject.

Towards a Constitutive, but Conditional, Pluralism

Fanon's conception of identity politics was informed by a commitment to anti-racism and anti-colonialism, a consideration of identity as a passing stage in the dialectic, leading to a universal humanism that is based on an ethical reciprocal recognition of the Other. In this chapter, we explored the gaps in Fanon's insistence on anti-colonialism being the precondition for political engagement and its limitations by drawing a parallel with the manner in which Periyar encountered the colonial condition. We can see that Fanon's naïvety with respect to the internal contradictions within the countries of the so-called 'Third World' led him to make sweeping generalisations, most of which could have dangerous implications. Fanon's generalising approach towards colonialism and anti-colonialism, which makes political sense in the context of Algeria, sounds both lazy and ahistorical if transposed to India. His views on women leave much to be desired, and in comparison to Periyar, he appears an apologist for misogyny, where he expects women to sacrifice their interests for the sake of a revolution led and dominated by men.

Periyar, on the other hand, was acutely aware of the specificities of the Indian situation. He saw region, religion, caste, gender and language as deep faultlines within the Indian country, contradictions that existed before and would exist after colonialism. While Periyar created his political discourse on identity by critiquing the axis of caste and religion and by challenging the idea of the Indian nation and anti-colonial nationalism, he was also uncompromising on his commitment to the emancipation of women and provided unconditional endorsement for the creation of political and social spaces for women, supporting women as autonomous political agents.

I think we are at a stage to agree that, despite their differences, Fanon and Periyar were organic intellectuals by the virtue of them being individuals 'engaged in the practice of articulation as the essential component in the construction of the hegemony of a group' (Laclau 2000: 287). Both were partisans of what Castells (2010: 8) would call a 'resistance identity', and while Fanon had a 'project identity' of a universal humanism, it was left ambiguous in Periyar's discourse.

We can understand identities as 'contingent constructs, the products of social and political *identifications* with the roles and subject positions made available by historically produced discourses' (Howarth 2013: 250). Identity politics requires not just an *identification* of the Self, but also an *identification* of the Other, and the relation of the Self to the Other. We saw in this chapter how very problematic Fanon's notion of Self was. Is it possible to work out a democratic and pluralist politics of identity from this dialogue? If we can arrive at a normative politics of identity from this chapter, it would have to be one that is cautiously sensitive to pluralism without encouraging sectarianism, or without imposing conditions for universalism that are not actually universally applicable. I have discussed in an earlier paper (Manoharan 2017) how Periyar's fixed perceptions of the identity of the Brahmin Other, his stress on the inferiorised status of the non-Brahmin identity and his encouragement of Dalit particularity failed to create an identity that would be accommodative of all these identities while transforming these identities into something common and larger. Likewise, with Fanon, we saw in this chapter how his insistence on *identification* with anti-colonialism as being a compulsory requirement for a politics of the future need not be universally applicable. While Periyar could be accused of failing to create a discourse centred on universality, Fanon could be accused of not being sensitive to particularities of groups within the colonised.

However, despite its limitations, Fanon's humanism nevertheless offers a framework for assessment of identity politics. It can be complemented in this case by Periyar's sensitivities towards addressing the particular issues of caste, region and gender so as to arrive at a society that is more accommodative to plural interests. The requirement of such an identity politics will need to find a commonality that would address the demands of discrete social groups under a larger identity, but nevertheless possess what Mouffe (1999) would call 'a constitutive pluralism' that is accommodative of difference.

Yet, further questions emerge here. What sort of difference can be tolerated and what cannot? To Fanon, the colonial has to be annihilated before any discussion of recognition can begin. To Periyar, the Brahmin, not as a human being, but as a symbol, needs to be done away with before a rational, egalitarian society can emerge. One of the main arguments of Periyar against the Brahmin identity is that as long as there is a social category called the Brahmin, there will always be someone inferior to it. Likewise, if the Dalit is recognised in their particularity, it still is an identity that is based on the recognition that there is someone above them. So, the constitutive pluralism will have to be a conditional pluralism, that is, one that is tolerant to difference based on certain conditions. Pragmatically speaking, it would be hard to convince the Brahmin, the most privileged group in the caste system, and the Dalit, the most exploited group in the caste system, to give up the uniqueness of their identities unless there is another identity that provides them the incentive to cease identification with their erstwhile identities. There has to be an 'empty signifier' identity that enables the suturing of the identities of all the groups involved, while also avoiding the either extremes of appearing aggressively assimilative or being tolerant to sectarianism.

The unconditional anti-colonialism of Fanon and the anti-Brahmin mobilisation of Periyar fail to satisfy this requirement—the former is far too generalising and the latter respects particulars too much. Periyar's fixation on the Brahmin Other and Fanon's creation of a unified colonised Self both come with their sets of problems, but also allow some glimpses into a solution. Is there a possibility of reconciliation of what appear to be two divergent viewpoints? It will have to be a discourse based on a different narrative that would have to serve the purpose. The real success of such a narrative would be in its inherent potential to enable, without superficially suturing differences, discrete social groups to transcend their particularities to something larger, universal.

Notes

[1] Of course, one does not fault Fanon for not being informed of such empirics. The problem is theoretical.

[2] Muhammed Ali Jinnah, the founder of Pakistan, was initially a Congress leader who later became convinced that Muslims and Hindus were two nations and that the future of Muslims could be secured only by demanding a separate state of Pakistan.

The so-called 'Partition of India', which happened in 1947, involved large-scale communal pogroms where hundreds of thousands of Hindus and Muslims perished. The complexities of discourses around Partition are also covered in Anderson's *The Indian Ideology* (2012). Incidentally, Periyar had written to Jinnah in 1944, calling on the latter to support the demand for a separate Dravidian state. Jinnah's response to Periyar was lukewarm and he gave no concrete commitment of support.

[3] Excerpts from the essay, 'Meyo Kutru Moyya Poyya' (Mayo's Charges: True or False?), are published as an appendix to the abridged version edited by Sinha (2000).

[4] For more elaborate criticisms of Fanon's approach to women and sexual politics, see Young (1996) and Mercer (1996). For a defense of Fanon's 'feminism', see hooks (1996), as well as Luste-Boulbina (2011).

[5] For a discussion on this, see Slisi (2008).

References

Ambedkar, B. R. 2006. *Mr Gandhi and the Emancipation of the Untouchables*. New Delhi: Critical Quest.

——— 2007. *Annihilation of Caste*. New Delhi: Critical Quest.

Anderson, P. 2012. *The Indian Ideology*. New Delhi: Three Essays Collective.

Aronson, R. 1980. *Jean-Paul Sartre: Philosophy in the World*. London: Verso.

Bharadwaj, A. S. 1991. 'Women's Question in the Dravidian Movement c. 1925–1948'. *Social Scientist* 19(5–6), May–June: 24–42.

Castells, Manuel. 2010. *The Power of Identity*, 2nd edition. Malden, MA: Wiley-Blackwell.

Dirks, N. B. 2004. 'Recasting Tamil Society: The Politics of Caste and Race in Contemporary South India'. In *Caste Today*, ed. C. J. Fuller, 263–95. New Delhi: Oxford University Press.

Fanon, F. 1963. *The Wretched of the Earth*, trans. Constance Farrington. New York: Grove Press.

——— 1965. *A Dying Colonialism*, trans. Haakon Chevalier. New York: Grove Press.

——— 1988. *Toward the African Revolution: Political Essays*, trans. Haakon Chevalier. New York: Grove Press.

——— 2008. *Black Skin, White Masks*, trans. Charles Lam Markmann. London: Pluto Press.

Ghurye, G. S. 1950. *Caste and Class in India*. Bombay: Popular Book Depot.

hooks, bell. 'Feminism as a Persistent Critique of History: What's Love Got to do With It?'. In *The Fact of Blackness: Frantz Fanon and Visual Representation*, ed. Alan Read, 76–85. London: Institute of Contemporary Arts.

Howarth, D. R. 2013. *Poststructuralism and After: Structure, Subjectivity and Power*. New York: Palgrave Macmillan.

Laclau, E. 2000. 'Constructing Universality'. In *Contingency, Hegemony, Universality: Contemporary Dialogues on the Left*, eds J. Butler, E. Laclau and S. Žižek, 281–307. London: Verso.

Luste-Boulbina, Seloua. 2011. 'Fanon and the Women of the Colonies against the White Man's Burden'. In *Living Fanon: Global Perspectives*, ed. Nigel C. Gibson, 139–48. New York: Palgrave Macmillan.

Manoharan, K. R. 2017. 'Anti-casteist Casteism?'. *Interventions* 19(1): 73–90.

Mercer, Kobena. 1996. 'Decolonisation and Disappointment: Reading Fanon's Sexual Politics'. In *The Fact of Blackness: Frantz Fanon and Visual Representation*, ed. Alan Read, 114–31. London: Institute of Contemporary Arts.

Mouffe, C. (ed.). 1999. *The Challenge of Carl Schmitt*. Verso: London.

Nehru, J. 1969. *The Discovery of India*. Bombay: Asia Publishing House.

Pandian, M. S. S. 1995. 'Beyond Colonial Crumbs: Cambridge School, Identity Politics and Dravidian Movement(s)'. *Economic and Political Weekly* 30(7–8): 385–91.

Ramasamy, E. V. 1998. *Dear Youths*, trans. A. S. Venu. Chennai: Periyar Self-respect Propaganda Institution.

____ 2009. *Thoughts of Periyar E. V. R.: Speeches and Writings of Periyar E. V. Ramasamy*, Volume 6 (Agitations and Messages I), ed. V. Anaimuthu. Chennai: Periyar E. V. Ramasamy–Nagammai Education and Research Trust.

____ 2011a. *Periyar Kalanjiyam: Jaathi-Theendamai Paagam*, Volume 4. Chennai: Periyar Suyamariyathai Prachaara Niruvanam.

____ 2011b. *Tamizhum, Tamizhargalum*. Chennai: Periyar Suyamariyathai Prachara Niruvana Veliyeedu.

____ 2011c. *Thoughts of Periyar*, ed. K. Veeramani. Chennai: Dravidar Kazhagam Publications.

Sartre, J. P. 2008. *Between Existentialism and Marxism*, trans. John Matthews. London: Verso.

Savarkar V. D. 2007. 'Hindutva: Who is a Hindu?'. In *Hindu Nationalism: A Reader*, ed. C. Jaffrelot, 87–96. Princeton, New Jersey: Princeton University Press.

Schmitt, C. 1999. 'Ethic of State and Pluralistic State'. In *The Challenge of Carl Schmitt*, ed. C. Mouffe, 195–208. Verso: London.

Sinha, M. 2000 (ed.). 'Introduction'. In *Mother India: Selections from the Controversial 1927 Text*, 1–10. Ann Arbor: University of Michigan Press.

Slisi, Fouzi. 2008. 'Islam: The Elephant in Fanon's *The Wretched of the Earth*'. *Critique: Critical Middle Eastern Studies* 17(1), spring: 97–108.

Spivak, G. 1987. *In Other Worlds: Essays in Cultural Politics*. New York: Methuen

____ 1988. 'Can the Subaltern Speak?'. In *Marxism and the Interpretation of Culture*, C. Nelson and L. Grossberg, 271–313. Champaign, Illinois: University of Illinois Press.

____ 1993. *Outside in the Teaching Machine*. London: Routledge.

Young, Lola. 1996. 'Missing Persons: Fantasising Black Women in Black Skin, White Masks'. In *The Fact of Blackness: Frantz Fanon and Visual Representation*, ed. Alan Read, 86–101. London: Institute of Contemporary Arts.

Part IV

Political Economy

8. Re-envisioning a City

Chennai as Exhibition/Museum/Backyard[*]

A. Srivathsan and M. S. S. Pandian

[*Pandian and I shared a keen interest in the politics of Chennai city and its urban history. Our conversation started about two-and-a-half decades ago, when I first approached him to comment on my paper on how DMK had reinscribed Chennai. We looked at Dalit settlements in Chennai, their multiple displacements, the political geography of statues, the making of civic spaces and many more episodes of the city. These unstructured conversations eventually led to a successful research proposal aimed at studying how Chennai was staged as a global city between 2000 and 2006. Three years of our work resulted in a report, a visual book and a documentary, and in each of these ventures, we collaborated with other friends. His move to Delhi and me shifting to journalism almost shut down our efforts to publish the work. Now, drawing substantially from our unpublished work, I write, in Pandian's remembrance, about how Tamil Nadu, through its envisioning, stages parts of the city as an exhibition, leaving others as museums and backyards. These propositions, though drawn from our global city project, resonate and remain valid even with the current envisioning of Chennai as a Smart City.*]

I

Starting from the late 1990s, in the reckoning of state and industry, it was necessary to reinvent Chennai both aesthetically and

*This study was made possible by the support of Indo-Dutch Programme on Alternatives in Development (IDPAD) and Indian National Trust for Art and Cultural Heritage (INTACH).

otherwise in a way that it becomes a preferred destination for foreign direct investment and the global business traveller. This new vision for the city envisaged and carried out by those who have access to power dichotomised the city into exhibition and museum. We draw the metaphors of exhibition and museum from the well-known work of Timothy Mitchell on colonial Cairo (Mitchell 1991: 82). The already-built state-of-the-art East Coast Road, a site of consumption for the urban elite, and the ultra-modern multi-lane Information Technology Expressway are the most visible examples of showcasing Chennai as a global entity. In general, this new urban vision imposed a new aesthetics over the city, which is considered to be commensurate with other global cities. For example, cows are prohibited within the city, even if it amounts to displacing many dependent livelihoods; rivers within the city are overlooked while waterways in south Chennai are planned for promenades and leisure tracks; slums are rendered invisible and roads are cleared of hawkers. The city asserts here as an exhibition. Envisioning the city as an exhibition necessarily reduces the inassimilable and the resistant living city as a museum, an inventory of the past, things frozen in time and without a future. The old industrial district of north Chennai and the multitude of fragments such as urban slums, fishing settlements and cowsheds that mark the south Chennai urbanscape, in this understanding, belong to the museum. In treating the exhibition and museum as different stages of urban history, it names the inassimilable as residues of the past which time will necessarily erase (Prakash 2002: 5). Given the violence which is central to this historical vision, which is intolerant to the simultaneous co-presence of different temporalities as part of any reality, the new vision for the city tries its best to shut down the museum and stage the city exclusively as an exhibition. As an instance, Justice S. Jagadeesan of the Madras High Court in 2000 remarked: 'When a person traveling by car stopped for a few minutes for shopping, the vehicle was towed away. But we see vendors with their carts standing permanently on the roadside and they are not removed' (*The Hindu* 2000b).

But the existing city resists because what are being viewed as museums are, in fact, not. They do not belong to the past but indeed live in the present. This lived, and resistant, quality of the inassimilable makes it a backyard. It is a place of diversity in opposition to the desired homogeneity of the spaces and practices informed by the global-city desire. Humans and non-humans, the living and memories of the dead, jostle in the backyard. Playing hide-and-seek with the surveillance of the state, backyards are places of improvisation, resistance and energy. They show up in unexpected places and in unexpected times, and unsettle the much sought after convergence among urban form, space and function. In the process, the backyards constantly frustrate and subvert the globalising desire of the elite. Thus, the backyard is a key *actant*, to borrow a term from Bruno Latour, shaping the future of the city. It is also important to underscore here that in a mass democracy, the backyard decides political outcomes at least in certain critical arenas. This tempers the drive to align the city with the elite vision and, in consequence, the elite tends to see democracy as opposed to modernisation. In capturing the tension, dialogue and resistance among the triad, that is, exhibition, museum and backyard, certain formulations by Partha Chatterjee are most useful. These formulations centre around the opposition between the political society and civil society. At the cost of brevity, let us quote him on political society:

> Many of these groups, organized into associations, transgress the strict lines of legality in struggling to live and work. They may live in illegal squatter settlements, make illegal use of water and electricity, travel without tickets in public transport. In dealing with them, the authorities cannot treat them on the same footings as other civic associations following more legitimate social pursuits. Yet state agencies and nongovernmental organizations cannot ignore them either since they are among thousands of similar associations representing groups of population whose very livelihood or habitation involve violation of the law. (Chatterjee 2004: 40)

In sharp contrast, the civil society, 'restricted to a small section of culturally equipped citizens, represents in countries like India the high ground of modernity' (ibid.). In other words, the contestations and compromises among the urban metaphors of the exhibition, the museum and backyard are contestations and compromises between the civil society and the political society. These are largely mediated by democracy and its violation. This chapter maps the contours of these contestations through a series of urban stories drawn from the contemporary experience of Chennai, and makes a set of general propositions at the end. These propositions might be useful in reconceptualising the city form and innovating new ways of intervening in the urban.

II

Exhibiting the City

Since post-liberalisation 1990s and after, both the government of Tamil Nadu and the leaders of the corporate sector have been representing Chennai, which earlier carried the dominant image of a tradition-bound city with its innumerable temples and grand colonial monuments, as the right destination for the international business traveller and foreign direct investment. For instance, in 2002, the Confederation of Indian Industries (CII) constituted a set of panels headed by prominent industrialists to rebrand Tamil Nadu as an investor-friendly destination. This vision of the corporate sector was fully endorsed by the government of Tamil Nadu. The then chief minister, J. Jayalalithaa, while addressing a CII meeting in 2003, made it clear that, 'Our aim is to reposition Chennai as the premier destination [for investment] in the south, as a gateway to South East Asia' (*Times of India* 2003).

Significantly, the new vision, which was incessantly drummed up and enforced on Chennai by the state government and the industrial lobbies, prioritised certain activities, places, facilities and people; and as a result, discounted others. IT and IT-enabled services (ITES), and the knowledge industry in general, were the new economic activities that were privileged as part of the new vision.

In order to promote the growth of the IT industry, the cash-starved government of Tamil Nadu announced a slew of subsidies and incentives. The IT Policy of Tamil Nadu (2002) is illustrative here.[1] The IT policy offered substantial financial incentives, exempted all software industries from the purview of the Tamil Nadu Pollution Control Act and permitted IT companies to self-certify that they were maintaining the registers and forms as contemplated under various Acts of the state (Government of Tamil Nadu 2003). Significantly, most of these Acts relate to labour.[2] It also granted a 50 per cent exemption of stamp duty and registration fees to the IT industry at the time of purchase of land or building. The policy was brought into effect in May 2003.[3] The state extended these subsidies and incentives in its Information Technology Enabled Services Policy of 2005.[4] Importantly, the DMK, which displaced the All-India Anna Dravida Munnetra Kazhagam (AIADMK) government following the state assembly election of 2006, continued to bolster the trend. Tellingly, the DMK chief minister, M. Karunanidhi, himself administered the IT portfolio.[5]

Though various pronouncements of the government of Tamil Nadu on the IT sector and its IT policy mostly talk about Tamil Nadu as a whole,[6] for all practical purposes, IT remains a Chennai phenomenon.[7]

The state-sponsored study by the Harvard University envisaged Chennai not only as the IT leader of India, but also as the regional gateway to Asia in this sector. Subsequently, various memorandums of understanding (MoUs) were signed, such as the one between the Electronic Corporation of Tamil Nadu and Science and Technology Board and the Trade Development Board of Singapore (*The Hindu* 2000a). The Chennai Metropolitan Development Authority (CMDA) for its part exempted all IT buildings from many of the norms of the City Master Plan.[8] Two key projects 'monumentalised' the government vision to turn Chennai to a global city. The first was Tidel Park, a 12-storeyed state-of-the-art IT park located at Taramani in south Chennai. The park, which cost Rs 338 crores and had 1.28 million square feet of floor space, was completed in a record time of 68 weeks (*The Hindu* 2000c). Inaugurated on 4 July 2000, it employed over 12,000 people.[9] A second, grander project was the building of the 35-km long IT corridor, which had cascading effects that further fragmented the city into the privileged south and overlooked north.

In 2002, a working committee, consisting of the secretaries of the IT and industries departments, and representatives from the highways department and the Metrowater, was constituted to convert Old Mahabalipuram Road (OMR), stretching from Taramani to Siruseri, into an expressway of 'global standards for attracting investments [in IT industries]' (Shankar 2002). This stretch was designated as Chennai's IT corridor. The project was also meant to interlink the East Coast Road with the IT corridor by means of three bridges. We may note here that the East Coast Road has been developed and projected as a site of elite consumption.

In February 2005, the IT Express Limited (ITEL), a 100 per cent subsidiary of Tamil Nadu Road Development Corporation (TNRDC), and the State Highways Department signed an agreement to construct the express highway (Ramakrishnan 2005). The expressway was to have six lanes for traffic flow, two service lanes, two cycle tracks and two walking tracks for pedestrians. According to Rohit Modi, the enthusiastic CEO of the TNRDC,[10] the 20-km IT corridor, will 'singlehandedly alter the fulcrum of development within Chennai city, and within Tamil Nadu. Possibly, even the whole of South India' (Menon 2005). Elaborating the concept behind the expressway, he added:

> Earlier, roads have been looked at as only engineering solutions. But here, it is conceptualised differently. If you want to attract investors in an intangible field like IT, you have to focus on providing the aesthetics, the quality, and ambiance that conveys a sense of world-class character which is what the proposed corridor will do. (Ibid.)

Apart from a

> world-class, 10-lane automated toll plaza, the IT expressway would have a number-plate reading system; information kiosks with internet access; phone-based enquiry system to serve road-users; broadcasting of SMS messages on traffic conditions; web-based frequent-user pass management; video surveillance and incident monitoring; and request switches with speakers at pedestrian crossings to assist the visually challenged.'[11]

The aesthetical content of the expressway included public art, landscaping both sides of the road and along the median, ornamental street lights and cascading water fountains.

Interestingly, TNRDC's presentation on the expressway prefaces its vision with a quote from Oscar Wilde: 'Art never expresses anything but itself.' It is art's innocence at its best. However, others who have done extensive work on urban aesthetics and its power dynamics have other things to say. For instance, Zukin (1999) notes:

> Building a city depends on how people combine the traditional economic factors of land, labour, and capital. But it also depends on how they manipulate symbolic languages of exclusion and entitlement. The look and feel of cities reflect decisions about what – and who – should be visible and what should not, on concepts of order and disorder, and on uses of aesthetic power.

> In this primal sense, the city has always had a symbolic economy. (Ibid.: 7)

The new aesthetics of IT corridor was not only meant to produce visible signs of success, but also affirm it as an enclave—a specially marked territory with the sameness of activity and people. It housed the sprawling campuses of important IT firms such as Infosys, Wipro, Tata Consultancy Services, Polaris, Cognizant Technologies, Pentamedia and Pentasoft. Further, Tidel Park, American International School, Women's Biotech Park, Design and Fashion Centre of the National Institute of Fashion Technology and Siruseri Software Park were all located in the corridor.

Many exclusive townships mushroomed in the entire area. These apartment complexes presented themselves as self-contained spaces similar to the gated communities in the West. Clustering together various facilities, they fostered and catered to the desire of the urban elite to secede from the existing city. For instance, the promotional literature of Southlands, a township proposed to be developed in Chennai's IT corridor by Singapore Realty Pvt. Ltd[12] offered the following to its potential residents: barbeque pits, children's playground, Cineplex, clinics, entertainment and food malls, food courts, function halls, gymnasium, petrol station, restaurants, retail shops, sauna, schools, supermarket, swimming pool and tennis courts. It further claimed, 'Best of all, these amenities are merely a walk away! For the convenience of our residents, a prestigious school and clinic can also be found within walking distance. In addition, commuting to and from Southlands will be a breeze with the air-conditioned bus services ....' The term that summarises the desire for a globalised lifestyle evoked by Southlands is 'world-class'. It promised: 'As a resident here, you'll be enjoying all the unique advantages of a world-class garden city living concept.'[13] Southlands is no exception; it is merely an instance. In another instance, the clientele for a villa project promoted by Chaitanya Builders and Leasing on the East Coast Road (which parallels the IT corridor) at Rs 1.1 crores per unit were to be waitlisted even before the official launch of the project (Nagarajan 2006).

In keeping with the Western imaginary that gives birth to and sustains these housing projects, many of these flaunted outlandish names. The following assortment of names gives us a flavour of the mimetic nature of these projects: The Pacific City, Blue Mont, Midtown, Les Maisons, Sunciti, Brook Dale, Lakeview County, Riverview County, Claremont Court, Wood Bridge County and Daffodils.[14] 'Old world' names of apartment buildings such as Kavyam, Vadhabi Nagar, Sri Mahalakshmi Malika, Veda Vilas, Manoranjitha, Sai Brindavan, Sai Skanda and Astalakshmi continue to have their hold since the housing market is segmented along classes. The explicit religious colouring of most of the latter set of names keeps them out of the freshly minted modernity of the new housing projects (which mark their claim to modernity by adorning Western/secular names). The subalternity of the owners of these old-world housing units is marked by their lack of control over their destinies. For most of the city dwellers, help from the gods is a necessary and much sought after resource to navigate urban problems and desires.

If the diversity of human and non-human encounters has been and is what defines urban distinctiveness, the new vision for Chennai was about producing exclusive spaces. Both exclusivity and its exhibition were achieved by seceding from the existing city. It may be instructive to take a brief look at the townships planned by the State in the pre-liberalisation period to appreciate this point. Navi Mumbai, conceived as the 'city of the twenty-first century' (Shaw 2004: 1), is a case in point. Conceptualised in the 1960s and implemented over a period of 50 years from 1971, the state-sponsored Navi Mumbai township did not visualise the twenty-first century as a time of social homogeneity but one of heterogeneity. It provisioned housing units for the differentially entitled—the lower-income, middle-income and higher-income groups. Its housing schemes included basic tenements, cooperative housing, bungalows, row houses and bulk residential plots (ibid.: 162–88). In the existing city, one needs to traverse different parts of the urban landscape, encounter people of different social backgrounds and engage in different types of negotiations to access these facilities. Naming these urban encounters as 'multiplicity of contact points', Sennett (1973) captures their richness thus:

> Each piece of the city mosaic had a distinct character, but the pieces were "open", and this was what made life urban. Individuals had the capacity and the need to penetrate a number of social regions in the course of daily activities, even though the regions were not harmoniously organized and may even have been at warring ends. (Ibid.: 54)

It is such a complex and rich diversity that marks the existing city. Consider the following description of the Triplicane High Road by a visitor to Chennai:

> ... I was hanging over a balcony, looking out over Triplicane High Road. It was dusk in Chennai. Lumbering bullocks were pulling carts and buses were weighted down at one side with people hanging on. Cows were stationary, and mopeds, cars, and autorickshaws were competing for space. Men were making their way to the Big Mosque in response to the call to prayers which echoed throughout the neighbourhood. Others were making their way to wherever it was they were going while street-dwelling families were arguing among themselves. On the opposite side of the road *sari*-clad women sat selling hair flowers, and others filled plastic pots with water from a municipal wagon ... (Todhunter 2003: 72)

While one needs to avoid romanticising such street life, it does offer a template for urban diversity which can be seized upon and improved. Clustering of urban facilities negates the possibility of a diversity of urban experience and gives rise to the situation of residents not requiring to 'to step out of their home'. This withdrawal of the elite from the existing city produces the city as a heterotopic space of otherness in opposition to the showcased new housing complexes and office spaces.[15] Strikingly, none of these new townships offer a burial ground or a crematorium. They celebrate life and living. While Southlands showcases its project as 'designed for modern living' and 'where quality living begins', the variety of facilities offered by these townships such as jogging tracks, swimming pools and tennis courts are meant to enhance one's longevity. In contrast, the dead will return to the city. The city is thus reduced to a necropolis.

III

The new vision for Chennai was built on the premise that a break from the city is necessary to advocate for the exceptional. And unlike the existing city, which is a proliferation of hybrids, the exceptional spaces had to be free of heterogeneity. Within this framework, the existing spaces within the city cannot qualify as the exceptional. They could become spaces for capital only by giving up their hybrid nature or, as in most cases, by the state rendering them invisible. This is often done, as Latour (1999: 51) has eloquently shown, through an epistemological purification. First, create dichotomies such as rural and urban, and then assert that the rural cannot exist within the urban and purge it. Where it cannot be purged, it is allowed to exist as a vestige of the past. In Chennai, two cases illustrate this: an attempt to cleanse of the city of cattle and displace fishermen from the beachfront.

Cows

The Tamil Nadu Animals and Birds in Urban Areas (Control and Regulation) Act, which was passed by the state legislature in 1997, led to enormous contestations between the cattle-keepers in the city and the state. The Act was brought into existence following an election promise by the then mayor of the Chennai Corporation, M. K. Stalin, that animals from congested localities in the city would be relocated elsewhere. As a mayoral candidate, he promised to make the city free of the ubiquitous mosquitoes that relentlessly harass city dwellers. He reasoned that rearing-cattle in the city was the chief source of mosquito breeding (*Junior Vikatan*, 10 October 1996). However, that was not the only reason. Stalin, immediately after taking over as the mayor of the city, aggressively pushed the idea of Sinagara Chennai or Beautiful Chennai. As a part of this vision, various projects were pushed—flyovers, parks, river restoration and many others. Removing the cattle was the important one among them. This became evident when the Act was challenged by the cattle-keepers in the Madras High Court. The Corporation claimed in a counter-affidavit that '... animals were causing public nuisance and traffic hindrance. Poor maintenance of the animals and sheds paved the way for mosquito breeding. Scores of animals were seen occupying road margins and pavements, creating problems for pedestrians' (Subramani 2003c).

The impounded cattle were released to the owners after collecting a fine of Rs 1,250 per animal and Rs 100 per day per animal as feed and maintenance charges. At that point, significantly, the penalty was several-folds higher than what was charged for violations such as 'erection of building or change in use of land without permission', 'failure to apply for permission and get permission', and 'obstruction to the exercise of the power of entry by the government servants or the servants of the planning authority' under Section 83 of the Tamil Nadu Country and Town Planning Act 1971.

Table 8.1 gives us an idea of the number of cattle impounded and the fine collected by Chennai Corporation between 2000 and 2005.

Table 8.1 *Cattle Impounded by the Chennai Corporation (2000–05)*

Year	No. of cattle	Impounding charges (in Rs lakhs)
2000–01	3,203	19.65
2001–02	2,308	15.69
2002–03	2,782	17.11
2003–04	3,231	6.35
2004–05	1,375	17.95

Source: Taken from http://mpvijayakumar.info/pdf/Removal%20__%20of%20cattle%20from%20chennai%20city.pdf (accessed 1 October 2019).

In its initial years of existence, the Act remained rather dormant. However, five years after it was passed, that is, in June 2003, the Chennai Corporation invoked the Act and declared a total ban on cattle and pig-rearing in 144 out of the 155 Corporation wards from 1 August.[16] The Corporation commissioner, M. P. Vijayakumar, declared that if the owners of impounded animals did not claim them within a month, they would be auctioned off. The Corporation also wanted to expand the scope of the Act and approached the state government to revoke the exemption given to 11 wards (Bhattacharya 2003a).

The ban on cattle-rearing provoked the cattle-keepers of the city immediately. Challenging the ban, they filed a batch of writ petitions in the Madras High Court. The first bench of the high court directed the cattle-keepers to obtain permits from Chennai Corporation within a period of two months. It declared:

> The status quo with regard to the keeping of the animals shall be maintained for a period of two months by which time all those who want to keep the animals shall make applications by complying with the required formalities. Within two months thereof, the authorities shall dispose of the applications. (*The Hindu* 2004)

It also noted that 'the prohibition could not be a blanket in nature but could be exercised on a case-by-case basis' (ibid.).

Though the high court bench was critical of the Tamil Nadu Animals and Birds in Urban Areas Act, it upheld it. Referring to Section 8 of the Act, it noted that this section gave power to the government to enact total prohibition and that the relevant clause must be struck down. The bench, however, said that Section 8 had to be read in harmony with Section 4, which would then balance environmental concerns and prevent traffic hazards (ibid.). While Section 8 of the Act empowered the Corporation to impose a blanket ban on keeping animals within the city limit, Section 4 provided for the cattle-keepers to get licences from the Corporation.

Meanwhile, the city councillors from various political parties, irrespective of their ideological differences, raised objections to the Corporation's auctioning of the impounded animals. They claimed that the possibility of the auctioned-off cattle ending up with butchers was very high, and pointed out that the earlier resolution of the Corporation did not authorise the auctioning, but only the relocation of animals outside city limits. The Corporation council passed a resolution not to auction the impounded cattle (Bhattacharya 2003b). In any case, the earlier moves of the Corporation to auction the impounded cattle ended in failure in the face of stiff resistance from irate cattle-keepers. On 16 July 2003, the Corporation was forced to call off its auctioning of the cattle at the Pudupet cattle pound. Cattle owners congregated at the site of the auction and prevented the bidders from buying any of the animals (Subramanian 2003b). Similar was the fate of the effort by the Corporation to auction cattle at the Perambur cattle depot on 19 July. Opposed by the determined cattle-keepers who gathered in large numbers, none of the potential buyers came forward to deposit the earnest money. Failing to auction off the impounded animals, the Corporation handed over 35 cows to the Blue Cross, an animal welfare charity, to be located outside the city (*The Hindu* 2003h).

On 31 July, the Madras High Court directed the Chennai Corporation to release all the impounded cattle. The Chief Justice asked the additional advocate-general, who represented the state:

> What wrong have they committed? They have not committed any economic offence. They are eking out their livelihood. Why the prosecution threat? Make the scheme known to the

> petitioners. We have to hear their objections and opinions. Till then we will have to wait, and no civil or criminal action shall be taken against them. (Subramani 2003c)[1]

While the language of the judiciary in India had overall shifted in favour of the rich during the 1990s (Shukla 2006), the Chief Justice's queries partook in the earlier language of pro-poor welfarism. The additional advocate-general claimed in court that a scheme had already been framed, and the affected people would be rehabilitated. Turning to the specifics of the so-called scheme, he noted, 'We have identified people below the poverty line, and an estimated 807 families would get the benefits under a Central scheme (Swarna Jayanthi Shahari Rozgar Yojana). We will arrange for financial assistance through banks for self-employment in trades such as tailoring, petty shops or tea stalls' (ibid.: 3757). It was as if switching from one occupation to another was merely a matter of financial assistance. Taking up the case once again on 8 August, the high court authorised the Chennai Corporation to prohibit stray cattle in the city. Excluding from such action those animals which were kept in the houses of the owners, the court said:

> We permit the authorities under the Act in question to prohibit stray cattle in the prohibited areas and also take action for impounding. Insofar as the other cattle which are kept in the respective houses of the owners, status quo as of this day shall be maintained, provided the owners take care of the cattle from not straying on the streets and maintain them in hygienic condition. Meanwhile, the respective parties shall consider the feasibility of the schemes exchanged in between them and submitted to this court their views and suggestions. (*The Hindu* 2003i)

Beautifying Marina

Connolly (1999: 143), engaging with the multiple ramifications of identity politics, shows that the 'imagination of wholeness'—in our case, the anxiety to do away with the so-called rural in the urban and the desire to recover a putatively uncontaminated urban—'readily spawns arbitrary violence ...'. The scant regard for the livelihood of the fisherpeople, who depend on the sea, is indeed an instance of such violence. When seen along with the story of the contestation to demolish Queen Mary's College on the beachfront (Subramani 2003a), such instances show us how the logic of capital, which in the urban context searches out spaces of exchange value, endorses only certain forms of aesthetics. These are forms of aesthetics that further its profit-seeking drive.

The fisherpeople who live close to the beach and fish in the sea have been treated by various governments at different points of time as marring the beauty of the beach, and there have been efforts to remove them. One of the early violent encounters happened in 1985. In November of that year, the police and the officials of the Public Works Department removed, without any prior notice, the catamarans, nets and other fishing gear of fishermen from the beach. Following this, a month later, the fishermen attacked the local police station and the office of the Slum Clearance Board. The immediate provocation was the effort by the Slum Clearance Board to evict them from their tenements for non-payment of rent arrears, but it was an explosion of long-simmering resentment. This led to a police firing, and six fishermen were killed. Finally, the Supreme Court had to intervene and ordered the state government to return the catamarans to the fishermen (*New Indian Express* 2012).

The intention of the state government to convert the Marina beachfront into a developer's dream never ceased. A more ambitious form evolved in the post-liberalisation phase, when the CMDA signed an MoU with the Construction Industry Development Board of Malaysia on 14 January 2003. According to the MoU, the board, apart from preparing a feasibility study of a 2,000-acre administrative city, was also to explore the feasibility of 'beautification of the Marina beach with shoreline corporate complexes at the cost of Rs 1,000 crores'. The project was to cover a 1.5-km stretch of the Santhome beachfront and build 'complexes of international standards to provide office accommodation for multinationals and embassies' (*The Hindu* 2003a). According to the proposed project, the displaced residents of the fishing hamlets would be relocated to a newly built residential complex. Referring to the Marina beautification project, the then chief minister, Jayalalithaa, said that the government would only 'give permission' and not make any investments. Thus, it was an open invitation to private developers to take over the Marina beachfront. It should also be remembered here that one of the arguments of the advocate-general before the high court bench in defence of government's decision to demolish the Queen Mary's College, a heritage building on the beachfront, was that it should be considered an economic policy (Subramani 2003a). Threatened with the possibility of losing their livelihoods, residents of the fishing settlements of Mullaikuppam, Srinvasapuram, Doomingkuppam, Nochikuppam and Ettukattidam—supported by the Chennai Coastal Fisher People Protection Committee and the Pennurimai Iyakkam—demanded that the state government revoke the MoU. They also demanded that Marina be classified a Coastal Regulation Zone-I, 'so that the ecosystem [is] protected from further degradation' (*The Hindu* 2003g).

The government set up a State Beach Management Authority with the chief minister as the chairperson, and the Chennai Metropolitan Beach Committee was created to take control of city beaches. A few initial steps, such as the demolition of Seerani Arangam, a permanent stage used for public meetings, were taken (Manikandan 2003). All public meetings were banned on the Marina, and the entire stretch was declared litter-free (Subramanian 2003a). However, the ambitious proposal to build corporate complexes in place of fishing hamlets had to be given up in the face of stiff protest (Subramani 2003b). Not much seems to have changed for fisherpeople in Chennai. Till date, they continue to face threats of eviction.

Tellingly, the Marina beautification project set in opposing notions of what the city was and what it ought to be. The city, as it is, is marked by enclaves such as fishing hamlets which can signify the occurrence and persistence of what is considered 'rural' within the urban space. Viewed in this way, the existing city is not yet fully urban and carries strong traces of incompleteness. This is most often a source of angst for the urban elite. Another instance of this vision seeking an urban wholeness by purifying places was evidenced in the fight to save the heritage buildings on the Marina.

On 31 January 2003, Jayalalithaa announced that the present state secretariat, a 10-storey building constructed in 1974 and located on the campus of Fort St George, would be relocated to a space opposite the Marina beachfront (*The Hindu* 2003b). The inadequacy of space and that the proposed administrative city near Sholinganallur would take 15–20 years to be completed were offered as reasons for the move. The space between Queen Mary's College and Vivekananda House was chosen for the new secretariat building.

Queen Mary's College, Chennai's first women's college founded in July 1914, was on the CMDA's list of heritage buildings. Further, the Development Control Rules (DCR) of the CMDA prohibits multi-storeyed buildings on the Marina beachfront stretching from Queen Mary's College to Napier Bridge. This stretch of the beachfront houses a number of heritage buildings such as Presidency College (inaugurated in 1870) and Senate House (completed in 1879).[17] While the state government refused an amendment to the DCR, which was sought by the CMDA so as 'to prevent modifications, disfigurations or demolitions of heritage buildings without the Authority's approval' (Ahmed 2003b), it asked the CMDA to amend the DCR to allow multi-storeyed buildings on the beachfront. Both the moves were meant to facilitate the demolition of Queen Mary's College and to build a multi-storeyed new secretariat. Significantly, it was also to set the precedent and make other heritage buildings on the beachfront available for development in the course of time.

The decision of the government to raze the college provoked widespread protest from the students and teachers of the college. There were student demonstrations in front of the college, and the Left-wing student organisations such as the Students' Federation of India (SFI) and All-India Democratic Students' Organisation (AIDSO) supported the agitation. The Tamil Nadu Government Teachers' Association also opposed the government's plan and, recalling the college's history, declared, 'The QMC was the first women's college in the country and one of the biggest colleges in the state, with more than 4,000 students and 200 teachers. The college symbolises the pride of womanhood in society, which still basks in male chauvinism' (Ahmed 2003d). Despite protests, which attracted widespread media coverage, the state government formally announced on 4 April that the college building would be demolished (Ahmed 2003a). As Zukin (1991: 18) reminds us, 'With modernism, "old" was rarely "better." The tortured visibility of older landscapes was viewed as an irritant or a stimulant to an additional and ultimately homogenizing round of structural changes.'

Less than an hour after the formal announcement was made by the chief minister, the students and teachers of Queen Mary's College staged a three hour–long road-block in front of their college. They were also joined by the alumni. The staff and students staged 'in-college vigils' to resist the government's effort to evict students from hostels (Ahmed 2003c). All the major political parties in the state came out in support of the students' demand (*The Hindu* 2003c). On 6 April, the Madras High Court issued an interim order staying the demolition of the college building. Writ petitions from NGOs such as Citizen, Consumer, Civil Action Group and Indian National Trust for Art and Cultural Heritage (INTACH), and political organisations such as the SFI and All-India Democratic Women's Association, were filed in the Madras High Court challenging the government's decision. The only substantive argument that the advocate-general placed before the high court bench defending the government was at best evasive. He argued that it was only a cabinet decision, which was yet to culminate in a government order (Subramani 2003a). On 11 April, when the contending parties concluded their arguments, the high court bench reserved its orders.

In a dramatic step, on 22 April the Union environment ministry amended Section 5 of the Environment Protection Rules and banned the demolition and reconstruction of 'buildings of archaeological and historical importance', 'heritage buildings' and 'buildings of public use', such as the ones used for worship, education, medical care and cultural activities, on coastal stretches. It also prohibited all activities on coastal stretches involving an investment of Rs 5 crores or more (*The Hindu* 2003d). The amended Environmental Protection Rules foreclosed the possibility of demolishing Queen Mary's College and substituting it with a grand multi-crore secretariat building. The Union environment minister, T. R. Baalu, belonged to the opposition party, the DMK, which supported the students' agitation against the demolition. Characterising the environment ministry's notification as arbitrary and an infringement of the rights of the state government, the chief minister sought the intervention of the president, the prime minister and the deputy prime minister to get the notification annulled (*The Hindu* 2003e).[18] However, forced by circumstances, the state government finally decided to build a new secretariat and state legislative assembly in the Anna University Campus in Kotturpuram in south Chennai (Ramachandran 2003).

Studies have criticised heritage movements in Chennai as 'first-world indulgences' and dubbed them as elitist (Arabindoo 2010). But the alliances such resistances have produced require a more nuanced reading. Memories indeed pluralise. All remembrances need not produce a future city wherein competing claims on the city can be accommodated and negotiated. Some remembrances desire exclusion and dream revenge. What spirits from the past are resurrected, what memories are invoked are as important to the future of the city as the fact that memories have the potential to contest singular visions for the city.

IV

Uneven spatial developments are not new. Chennai's long history shows that cities grow incrementally and unevenly, with some parts of the city privileged over the others. One may argue that the celebrated variety and hybridity of the city has been an outcome of its long history of urban development. Citing Gandy (2013: 86), one may hope that a 'city is just a process of urbanization', and the new peripheries of Chennai such as the IT corridor which are currently 'operational landscapes' would soon agglomerate to become the city with the characteristics that one may seek. For many reasons, this is unlikely to happen. Starting from 1798, when Chennai's city limit was fixed for the first time, parts of the city have been viewed as periphery and core. City development, both the incremental type ushered in by the City Improvement Trust and the grand comprehensive master plans prepared by CMDA, attempted to stitch the new and the old, and the periphery and the core. In contrast, developments since the 1990s are premised on fragmentation and exclusivity. If the state-sponsored plans have supported this to make spaces attractive for investment, the real estate market has propped it as a means to protect and enhance property values. Not much has changed even in the current envisioning of Chennai as a Smart City. The pan-city component of smart-city development has only a marginal impact, with the bulk of the investment and attention on the most revenue-earning areas of the city, leaving out the remaining parts.[19] In the new visions, the displaced and the hybrid can only make a claim to the spaces through resistance, playing hide-and-seek, and improvising. One may acknowledge and admire their agency and tenacity, but that cannot be the solution.

It would be worthwhile to consider the following propositions as a way forward. First, the urban planning practices have very little to do with the notion of the citizen, though it is evoked relentlessly. Instead, we need to work with the concept of populations. Clarifying the distinction between citizens and populations, Chatterjee (2004) notes:

> ... Citizens inhabit the domain of theory, populations the domain of policy. Unlike the concept of citizen, the concept of population is wholly descriptive and empirical ... Populations are identifiable, classifiable, and describable by empirical or behavioural criteria and are amenable to statistical techniques ... the concept of the population makes available to government functionaries a set of rationally manipulable instruments for reaching large sections of inhabitants of a country as a target of their "policies" ... The regime secures legitimacy not by the participation of citizens in matters of state but by claiming to provide for the well-being of the population. (Ibid.: 34)

In other words, citizens are treated as homogenous, and populations are conceived as socially variable. Given the social variability of the population, they get classified under different heads such as slum-dwellers, hawkers, cattle-keepers, pedestrians, traders, etc. Such classifications make them targets of different policies. An explicit recognition that policies are based on the concept of populations instead of the citizen is important for more than one reason. The concept of citizen tends to frame policy demands in general terms, that is, in terms of the city as a whole. Citizens, being undifferentiated and homogenous, cannot make sectional demands on the State. Their claims can only be based on the claim of the common good. However, most often the invocation of 'common good' veils power interests and presents the interests of the powerful as those of the society as a whole.

The second proposition is to recognise the violence that grand visions impose, and explore micro-possibilities of city growth. The ground reality is that large visions do not necessarily produce comprehensive or inclusive development. They often masquerade as doing so, but in reality fragment the city. The mirco-possibilities could be incremental, tactical, strategic and collaborative, and can pave the way for inclusion. This, however, does not mean that larger, city-level strategies such as mobility or ecological systems are to be left out.

The third proposition is connected with the question of language. We often find stories of failed or non-implemented urban projects sitting along with an excessive talk about planning for the city. The State often issues statements on urban planning which evoke a theatrical sense of grandeur. For instance, when the eco-park project in the Adayar creek was announced, the description ran as follows:

> According to a senior government official, the park is being developed to become the "hallmark of Ezhilmigu Chennai" [Beautiful Chennai] – as envisioned by the Chief Minister, Jayalalithaa. "She has seen the plan layout and given her approval. It has been one of her long-pending proposals to develop a huge park for the city" ... It will be modeled on the Tezozomoc Park in Mexico ... Among other facilities, the park will have a jogger's track and a roller skating rink. It is being envisaged as a place where school students could learn about eco-diversity. (Subramanian 2003c)

Similarly, one can see the sense of grandeur that was evoked about the new secretariat project, which the CMDA claimed to be an 'architectural marvel', which never took off.[20]

Both the failure and non-implementation of urban projects and statements of theatrical grandeur of new urban projects point to the fact that there is an excess of words in circulation about policies, while policies themselves seem to have minimal impact. Surely this is a sign of policy failure. But our explanation cannot stop at policy failures alone. This excess of words about urban policy performs a critical function for the State. Both State-making and State-legitimisation require this excess of words. Being talkative is the way of the State trying to gain legitimacy in the eyes of the people; whether it works or not is a different matter. This is a process which Caldeira and Holston (2005: 396) felicitously refer to as 'stagecraft-as-statecraft'. In other words, policy-talk need not always be about policies, but about the politics of the State. This calls for a wider critique of the policies, by placing them both within and outside the realm of policy. This has acquired a sense of urgency in the light of the recent smart city policy,[21] which is more of a shrill noise than an empowering form of city planning or living.

Notes

[1] The fiscal incentives announced in the policy note include the following:

> An industry set up anywhere in Tamil Nadu having an investment of (a) Rs. 50 crores and above and below Rs. 100 crores is eligible for a capital subsidy of Rs. 25 lakhs;

(b) Rs. 100 crores and above and below Rs. 200 crores is eligible for a subsidy of Rs. 50 lakhs; (c) Rs. 200 crores and above is eligible for a subsidy of Rs. 100 lakhs. (Government of Tamil Nadu 2003)

[2] The Acts included were the Tamil Nadu Shops and Establishment Act, Payment of Wages Act, the Minimum Wages Act, Workmen Compensation Act, Contract Labour Act, Employees' State Insurance Act, Employment Exchange Compulsory Notification of Vacancies Act, Payment of Gratuity Act and Equal Remunerations Act.

[3] It announced: 'IT policy 2002 and all the concessions therein, except the 50 per cent concession on stamp duty and registration fee, be given from September 19, 2002.'

[4] It offered to provide a cash payment of Rs 5 lakhs as incentive to encourage ITES companies to acquire international process quality certification like the certificate of proficiency (COP), International Standards Oganisation (ISO) certification, etc. (Government of Tamil Nadu 2005: 8).

[5] Interestingly, in an effort to cash in on the IT mantra, the AIADMK manifesto for the 2006 state assembly elections declared:

> In keeping with the maxim, "Innovation for people's welfare" by our relentless and ceaseless efforts and clear policies, we have taken Information Technology and IT Enabled Services in Tamil Nadu to new heights of development. IT exports which stood at Rs. 3,116 crores in 2000–2001 is expected to touch Rs. 15,000 crores during 2005–2006. Likewise the number of software firms at the end of 2005 has gone up to 1266. (AIADMK 2006: 34)

The party promised 500,000 IT-sector jobs to the youth during the next succeeding five years. Ironically, the AIADMK lost the election to the DMK, whose manifesto was silent on IT.

[6] Frequently it invoked the so-called Tier-II cities such as Coimbatore, Madurai and Tiruchirappalli as important destinations for the IT industry. For instance, in 2003, the then finance minister of the state, C. Ponnaiyan, claimed: 'The Chief Minister is clear that the IT development should not be limited to Chennai alone.' After all, he was addressing a meeting in Coimbatore. Similarly, Demand No. 31, 2006–07, of the IT Department of Tamil Nadu notes: 'The Government is keen that the IT revolution should not be confined to Chennai alone. It is fully committed to spread the IT revolution to other towns of Tamil Nadu. It has therefore decided to set up IT parks in Coimbatore, Madurai, Trichy, Salem and Tirunelveli, apart from Chennai.' See Policy Note 2005–06, available at http://cms.tn.gov.in/sites/default/files/documents/Information%20Technology%20Department.pdf (accessed 1 October 2019).

[7] IT exports from the state have grown to Rs 14,115 crores in 2005–06 from Rs 10,703 crores in 2004–05 (and Rs 7,621 crores in 2003–04). However, most of it comes from Chennai. Of exports worth Rs 10,703 crores in 2004–05, less than Rs 60 crores came from the rest of the state. At the end of 2004–05, while Chennai had 845 units, Coimbatore had 46, and all others, including Madurai, Trichy and Sivakasi, had 24 (Balachandar 2005).

[8] In a wilful transgression of the provisions of the Chennai City Master Plan, the IT policy offered a relaxation of the floor space index (FSI) to the extent of 100 per cent to designated IT parks. See https://www.elcot.in/incentives.php (accessed 15 October 2019).

[9] See http://cms.tn.gov.in/sites/default/files/documents/Information%20Technology%20Department.pdf (accessed 1 October 2019).

[10] A former Indian Administrative Services (IAS) officer, who dealt with the World Bank, Asian Development Bank (ADB) and International Monetary Fund (IMF) assistance in the Department of Economic Affairs, Ministry of Finance, Government of India.

[11] See the TNRDC PowerPoint Presentation on the IT Expressway.

[12] Singapore Realty Pvt. Ltd is a company incorporated in India in April 2003 with a paid-up capital of $5,108,818. See the list of Companies/LLPs registered during the year 2003, available at http://www.mca.gov.in/Ministry/pdf/llpreg_2003.pdf (accessed 15 October 2019).

[13] Taken from the advertisement brochure for Southlands, 2005, available at http://www.singaporerealty.net/southlands/ (accessed 1 October 2019). One may note here that the scale of these private-sector housing projects in Chennai is nowhere close to similar projects envisaged in other metropolitan cities of India, in particular, in Mumbai. For instance, the city planned by Reliance at the outskirts of Mumbai is planned to be built over 14,000 hectares of land to accommodate about a million people (Das Gupta and Gadgi 2006). This brand new city will have many offices, hi-tech corridors, acres of lawn and pools and lakes and gardens. What is more, it will have a private seaport and airport as well.

[14] From *India Today Buyers Guide to Homes in Chennai*, May–October 2005.

[15] On the concept of heterotopias (Foucault 1997).

[16] The wards excluded from the ban were 1, 2, 62, 63, 64, 65, 128, 129, 153, 154 and 155 (*The Hindu* 2003i).

[17] Tracing the history and grandeur of Presidency College and Senate House, Muthiah (1987) notes:

> The Presidency College buildings, which combined the Italianate with Saracen, were begun in 1867 and completed in 1870, when the campus was inaugurated by the Duke of Edinburgh. In 1874 work was started on Senate House, where the Byzantine was teamed with the Indo-Saracenic, and the building, with its huge, raised hall and high ceiling, was completed in 1879. Giant Senate Hall, 130 feet by 50 feet and 54 feet high, was built to seat 1600 persons. Massive chiselled stone pillars flank the corridors to the east and west of the hall. The ceiling is elaborately carved and stained glass windows were, in their day, the finest in Madras. Light streaming through this window used to make Convocations of yesteryears a colourful experience ... (Ibid.: 106)

[18] Jayalalithaa tried to portray the Queen Mary's College building as dilapidated and worthy of demolition. In a *suo motu* statement in the state assembly, she announced a compensation of Rs 9 lakhs from the Chief Minister's Relief Fund to a former student of the college who was grievously injured when a verandah of the college collapsed in 1991 (*The Hindu* 2003f).

[19] See 'Smart City Challenge, Stage 2', India Smart City Mission, Ministry of Urban Development, Government of India, available at https://smartnet.niua.org/sites/default/files/resources/ChennaiSCp.pdf (accessed 1 October 2019).

[20] In the official invitation for the foundation stone–laying function, the executing agency, CMDA, said:

> The "architectural marvel" will be a crown, which will add further glory to the city ... A sprawling complex with an expansive visage will have the most modern legislature building, separate rooms for legislative committees, a 2000-seater conference hall,

which will rival the Vigyan Bhavan in New Delhi ... Other amenities promised are a dispensary, a pharmacy, a computerised closed circuit television system, libraries, security blocks, fire-fighting systems, recreation and relaxation rooms, canteens, shops, a crèche, vehicle service and fuel dispensing stations, and separate parking lots for different categories of occupants of the building and visitors practices' (*The Hindu* 2003j).

[21] For details, guidelines and projects, visit http://smartcities.gov.in (accessed 1 October 2019).

References

'Fisherfolk Commemorate '85 Firing Victims'. 2012. *New Indian Express*, 5 December.

'Per Capita Income to be Doubled before National Target'. 2003. *Times of India*, 19 March.

'ELCOT Ties Up with Singapore Firms'. 2000a. *The Hindu*, 22 January.

'Evolve a Scheme, HC Tells Corpn.'. 2000b. *The Hindu*, June 10.

'Madras Miscellany: Must They Move?'. 2000c. *The Hindu*, 24 July.

'MoU on Dream Projects with Malaysia'. 2003a. *The Hindu*, 15 January.

'Secretariat on Marina in 2 Years'. 2003b. *The Hindu*, 1 February.

'Parties Unanimous in Flaying Demolition Move'. 2003c. *The Hindu*, 6 April.

'Ban on Demolition of Public Use Buildings'. 2003d. *The Hindu*, 23 April.

'Jayalalitha Flays Baalu: Notification an Act of Vendetta'. 2003e. *The Hindu*, 6 May.

'Environment Ministry Notification "arbitrary"'. 2003f. *The Hindu*, 9 May.

'Revoke MoU on Marina Project'. 2003g. *The Hindu*, 22 May.

'Corporation Hands Over 35 Cows to Blue Cross'. 2003h. *The Hindu*, 20 July.

'HC Permits Authorities to Prohibit Movement of Stray Cattle'. 2003i. *The Hindu*, 9 August.

'"Secretariat Will Be an Architectural Marvel"'. 2003j. *The Hindu*, 30 October.

'Cattle Owners Get Two Months to Obtain Permit'. 2004. *The Hindu*, 9 July.

Ahmed, Feroze. 2003a. 'Agitated QMC Students to Boycott Exams'. *The Hindu*, 5 April.

——— 2003b. 'Govt. Decision a Threat to Heritage'. *The Hindu*, 2 April.

——— 2003c. 'High Court Stays QMC Demolition'. *The Hindu*, 7 April.

——— 2003d. 'Teachers, Architects Flay Plan to Demolish QMC Building'. *The Hindu*, 26 March.

AIADMK. 2006. 'All India Anna Dravida Munnetra Kazhagam Election Manifesto: Tamil Nadu Legislative Assembly General Elections, 8th May 2006'. AIADMK headquarters, Chennai.

Arabindoo, P. 2010. 'Isolated by Elitism: The Pitfalls of Recent Heritage Conservation Attempts in Chennai'. In *New Architecture and Urbanism: Development of Indian Traditions*, ed. D. Prashad, 155–60. New Castle upon Tyne: Cambridge Scholars Publishing.

Balachandar, G. 2005. 'IT, ITES Boom in Tamil Nadu'. *Business Standard*, 29 November. Available at https://www.business-standard.com/article/technology/it-ites-boom-in-tamil-nadu-105112901084_1.html (accessed 1 October 2019).

Bhattacharya, Saptarshi. 2003a. 'Ban on Cattle, Pig Rearing in City from August 1'. *The Hindu*, 12 June.

Bhattacharya. 2003b. 'Civic Body Won't Auction off Seized Cattle'. *The Hindu*, 25 July.

Caldeira, T. and J. Holston. 2005. 'State and Urban Space in Brazil: From Modernist Planning to Democratic Interventions'. In *Global Assemblages: Technology, Politics and Ethics as Anthropological Problems*, eds A. Ong and S. J. Collier, 393–416. Malden: Blackwell Publishing Ltd.

Chatterjee, Partha. 2004. *The Politics of the Governed: Reflections on Popular Politics in Most of the World*. Permanent Black: Delhi.

Connolly, W. E. 1999. *Why I Am Not a Secularist*. Minneapolis and London: University of Minnesota Press.

Das Gupta, Surajeet and Makarand Gadgi. 2006. 'Mukesh Ambani's Great Gamble'. *Rediff India Abroad*, 15 April. Available at http://ia.rediff.com/money/2006/apr/15spec1.htm (accessed 1 October 2019).

Foucault, M. 1997. 'Of Other Spaces: Utopias and Heterotopias'. In *Rethinking Architecture: A Reader in Cultural Theory*, ed. N. Leach, 348–79. London and New York: Routledge.

Gandy, M. 2013. 'Where Does the City End?'. In *Implosions/Explosions*, ed. N. Brenner, 86–89. Berlin: Jovis.

Government of Tamil Nadu. 2003. 'Information Technology Policy of Tamil Nadu 2002'. G. O. Ms. no. 15, 22 May. Information Technology Department, Chennai.

——— 2005. 'Information Technology Enabled Services Policy of Tamil Nadu 2005'. Information Technology Department, Chennai. Available at http://cms.tn.gov.in/sites/default/files/documents/ITES2005-TN.pdf (accessed 1 October 2019).

Latour, B. 1999. *We Have Never Been Modern*. Cambridge, Massachusetts: Harvard University Press.

Manikandan, K. 2003. 'Seerani Arangam Demolished'. *The Hindu*, 10 August.

Menon, Shoba. 2005. 'Work to Start Soon on Landmark IT Corridor'. *Madras Musings*, 1–15 March.

Mitchell, T. 1991. *Colonising Egypt*. Berkeley: University of California Press.

Muthiah, S. 1987. *Madras Discovered: A Historical Guide to Looking Around, Supplemented with Tales of 'Once Upon a City*. New Delhi: Affiliated East-West Press Pvt. Ltd.

Nagarajan, V. 2006. 'Growing Clientele for High-end Property: Demand Zooms'. *Economic Times*, 2 September.

Prakash, G. 2002. 'The Urban Turn'. *Sarai Reader 2002: The Cities of Everyday Life*. Sarai and Society for Old and New Media, Delhi and Amsterdam.

Ramachandran, K. 2003. 'Govt. Decides on Kotturpuram Site'. *The Hindu*, 4 September.

Ramakrishnan, T. 2005. 'Accord Signed for Chennai IT Corridor Improvement Work'. *The Hindu*, 24 February.

Sennett, R. 1973. *The Uses of Disorder: Personal Identity and City Life*. Harmondsworth: Penguin.

Shankar, T. S. 2002. 'Plans to Make Carriageway on Mahabalipuram IT Corridor'. *The Hindu*, 30 November.

Shaw, Annapurna. 2004. *The Making of Navi Mumbai*. Hyderabad: Orient Longman Pvt. Ltd.

Shukla, R. 2006. 'Rights of the Poor: An Overview of Supreme Court'. *Economic and Political Weekly* 41(35): 3755–59.

Subramani, A. 2003a. 'Judgment Reserved in QMC Demolition Case'. *The Hindu*, 12 April.
——— 2003b. 'No Move to Demolish Memorials: Govt'. *The Hindu*, 21 August.
——— 2003c. 'Release Impounded Cattle, HC Tells Chennai Corpn.'. *The Hindu*, 1 August.
Subramanian, K. 2003a. 'Aquarium, Library on the Marina to be Demolished'. *The Hindu*, 19 August.
——— 2003b. 'Corporation Forced to Put off Cattle Auction'. *The Hindu*, 17 July.
——— 2003c. 'Government Hands Over Land for Eco-park'. *The Hindu*, 23 December.
Todhunter, C. 2003. *Chasing Rainbows in Chennai*. Vancouver: Hacktreks Publishers.
Zukin, S. 1991. *Landscapes of Power: From Detroit to Disney World*. Berkeley: University of California Press.
——— 1999. *The Culture of Cities*. Massachusetts and London: Blackwell Publishers.

9. Emerging Labour Regimes and Mobilities in Tamil Nadu

M. Vijayabaskar

This chapter explores the political economy of emerging labour (im)mobilities in the context of Tamil Nadu. The post-1990s period has been marked by a 'responsibilisation' of regional states in India, entrusting them with greater role for resource mobilisation and promotion of growth. Tamil Nadu is seen to have responded well to this scalar reform, emerging as one of the fastest-growing economies in the country (Kalaiyarasan 2014). This has also been a period of considerable transformations in labour mobilities, with the Tamil worker increasingly being embedded in both internal and international migration circuits of varying scales of time and space. A recent study undertaken at the Centre for Development Studies, Thiruvananthapuram, ranks the state second in the quantum of remittances, next only to Kerala (Irudaya Rajan, D'Sami and Asir Raj 2016). This is significant, as India was the largest recipient of remittances globally in 2013, having received remittances worth \$70 billion (*The Economist* 2015). The study also revealed that nearly one in ten households surveyed in Tamil Nadu had at least one member working outside the country. Internal migration, including interstate migration, has also increased considerably during this period. Tamil Nadu is in fact one of the two relatively better-off states that has a negative net migration rate.[1] The level of urbanisation in the state is also one of the highest in the country, suggestive of an extensive rural to urban movement of labour. Such intensification of mobilities, I argue in this chapter, are rooted in transformations in the rural economy, intensification of rural–urban labour market linkages and emerging structures of opportunity that are partly tied to the processes of neoliberal growth and, importantly, to the regimes of welfare that Tamil Nadu has been noted for.

Development and modernisation theories propose a spatial and economic mobility with economic growth. Increases in incomes are supposed to be accompanied by movement of labour out of agriculture and into non-agrarian urban employment. The agricultural sector's role as a source of income and employment is expected to come down as the non-agricultural sector begins to expand. The transformations taking place in most transitional economies are, however, unlike those anticipated by such teleological narratives. In most parts of this world, since the 1960s, the movement of labourers from the rural to the urban has not been matched by increases in employment in the 'modern' or industrial sector, giving rise to the phenomenon of the 'urban informal'. Other segments continue to labour in agriculture despite low incomes. With the onset of neoliberal reforms, the processes of urbanisation in low-income regions have been accentuated on account of an intensification of the agrarian crises, leading to the phenomenon of 'urbanisation without industrialisation' on a scale large enough to hint at the rise of a 'planet of slums' (Davis 2004). Declining employment elasticities in the manufacturing sector, globally and in India, have revived fears of jobless growth in the modern sector. Sanyal (2007) suggests the possibility of the informal economy lying outside the domain of capitalist accumulation, rendering itself irrelevant to the requirements of capital. On a different register, in countries like India, anti-caste social movements see the urban as a site of freedom, offering various forms of mobility and freedom from 'pre-modern' rural time-spaces ridden with caste and gender hierarchies. Though thinkers like Ambedkar and Periyar have always seen the exit of the lower castes from the village as a key to securing social justice, recent studies point to the presence of caste-based segregation even in urban spaces (Sidhwani 2015). If the urban present and future are as bleak as portrayed and/or anticipated in such studies, how do we understand the labour mobilities that have been generated, and what is the scope for the politics of social transformation and mobilisation? If neoliberal market reforms render urban spaces more exclusionary, what are the politico-economic implications of such mobilities?

Examining state-level secondary data and data garnered through primary fieldwork undertaken in parts of rural Tamil Nadu and in the greater Chennai region, this chapter maps the emergence of multiple forms of labour mobilities and how they are being forged through state (regional) action under a broader neoliberalising regime. Such acts of the state are shaped by competing and often contradictory imperatives. Even as it has to attract private capital through offers of subsidised infrastructure and services, including low-cost labour, it also seeks political legitimacy by appealing to the marginal population groups through welfarist interventions. Such interventions have made possible a colloidal world of labour that straddles the rural and the urban, the agrarian and the non-agrarian. The chapter will highlight the emergence of such new networks of livelihoods that permeate standardised and distinct spatial and economic categories. The chapter also draws attention to the nature of 'truncated agrarian transition' in the region to explain the evolving patterns of mobility. In mapping the mobilescapes of labour, I hope to address, in part, one of the central questions in mobility studies: What are the processes generating specific kinds of mobilities? The chapter is structured as follows. To begin with, it outlines the important socioeconomic shifts taking place in the Tamil region over the past few decades. Starting with the crises in agriculture, I argue that the transition in the rural and the emergent labour processes are reflective of what has been referred to as a truncated agrarian transition (Li 2011; du Toit and de Neves 2014) in contexts of other transitioning economies. I turn next to the politics of welfare in Tamil Nadu and how this welfare regime, in conjunction with patterns of urbanisation, has opened up spaces for constituting a translocal livelihood. Following this, I focus on the changing spatiality of capital accumulation in the industrial sector and its role in labour mobility. Subsequently, I try to map the different worlds of mobile labour that have emerged in the state and ask whether these differential mobilities are tied to gender, caste and class differences. Following this, I highlight a few less-understood aspects of mobility that can constitute elements of a possible research agenda.

Truncated Agrarian Transition and Translocal Livelihoods

Just as in other parts of India, the shift of labour from agriculture has not kept pace with the decline in the share of income from agriculture in Tamil Nadu. Census 2011 indicates that almost 42 per cent of the state's population continues to report themselves as cultivators or as agricultural workers despite the fact that the agricultural sector contributes less than 8 per cent of the state's income. While the share of income from agriculture came down from around 12 per cent to less than 8 per cent during 2001–11, the share of employment fell from close to 50 per cent to 42 per cent in this period (Table 9.1). However, the share of both income from agriculture and those relying on agriculture is one of the lowest in the country.

Importantly, though the share of those reliant on agriculture came down, the absolute numbers within this segment did not fall much between 2001 and 2011 in the state. While the number or even the share of agricultural workers did not fall much, it is the rapid fall in both the share and absolute number of cultivators in the state over 1991–2011 that is striking, possibly suggestive of a process of pauperisation of the peasantry. Agriculture in the state has long been commercialised, and a process of differentiation within the peasantry has been observed (Nagaraj 2006). The extent to which policy shifts have accentuated the process of pauperisation is, however, not clear. Nevertheless, there has been a distinct decrease in the category of large farms in the state, and landholdings above 10 hectares account for only slightly more than 5 per cent of the total lands under agriculture (Table 9.2).[2]

In fact, the average landholding in the state was only 0.83 hectare in 2011, well below the national average of 1.23 hectares, and has consistently declined. The share of land held by marginal farmers increased during this decade (from 31 to 35 per cent) even as the share of land held by medium and large farmers declined. Given that the median annual income for a farmer in Tamil Nadu in 2012–13 was less than Rs 20,000 net of cultivation costs (Government of India 2015), it is obvious that bulk of farming households cannot reproduce themselves. Despite the state registering one of the highest agricultural productivity in the country, returns to agriculture have not been high enough to generate a surplus for the bulk of the farming population. Cost–price differentials in Tamil Nadu are one of the highest in the country (Narayanamoorthy 2006) due to growing resource intensity of cultivation and the absence of compensatory hikes in prices and, hence, incomes. Household indebtedness among rural Tamil Nadu too is one of the highest. Simultaneously, there have also been changes in the agrarian labour regime.

Table 9.1 *Composition of Workforce by Industrial Classification (1981–2011)*

Category	1981		1991		2001		2011	
	Absolute	Percentage	Absolute	Percentage	Absolute	Percentage	Absolute	Percentage
Cultivators	5.82	28.80	6.04	25.00	5.11	18.40	4.25	12.92
Agricultural labourers	6.77	33.50	8.76	36.20	8.67	31.10	9.61	29.21
Household industry and manufacturing	0.97	4.80	0.87	3.60	1.46	5.30	1.36	4.15
Other workers	6.64	32.90	8.53	35.20	12.57	45.20	17.66	53.72
Total workers	20.20	100.00	24.19	100.00	27.81	100.00	32.88	100.00

Notes: (1) Absolute values are in millions. (2) Percentage values are in terms of total worker population.

Source: Census of India (1981, 1991, 2001, 2011).

Table 9.2 *Number of Operational Holdings in Tamil Nadu (2010–11)*

Category	Number of operational holdings	Percentage	Area (in per cent)
Marginal (up to 1 hectare)	6,266,372	77.18	35.30
Small (1–2 hectares)	1,181,797	14.55	25.30
Semi-medium (2–4 hectares)	502,332	06.18	20.90
Medium (4–10 hectares)	150,570	01.85	13.10
Large (10 hectares and above)	17,365	0.21	5.40
All-size classes	8,118,436	100.00	100.00

Source: Government of Tamil Nadu (2014).

There has been a degree of freeing up of agricultural labour from traditional sources of bondage, partly due to the changes taking place within agriculture, partly due to changes in the domain of non-agrarian accumulation and, importantly, also in part due to the emerging welfare regime in the state that we shall elaborate on later.[3] Labour relations are less feudal and approximate free wage labour in most parts of the state—Tamil Nadu is one of the few states where real agricultural wages for male workers have increased during this period. This may, however, not imply better incomes, as the duration of employment may have declined. In other words, agrarian relations are characterised by reduction in traditional sources of dominance even as surplus extraction from agriculture has dwindled during this phase. Agrarian distress accompanied by the freeing up of agrarian labour on the one hand, and pauperisation of sections of the peasantry with little evidence of consolidation of landholdings on the other, best describe the evolution of the agrarian landscape in the state. This has steadily pushed agricultural labour and cultivating households to seek employment avenues outside agriculture. Table 9.2 does not capture such diversification of employment among rural households. This shift constitutes a new phase of pluri-employment in the state.

A recent study of rural non-farm employment in Tamil Nadu indicates this 'hollowing-out' of the villages (Jeyaranjan 2012). The scholar points out that the proportion of workers engaged in non-agricultural employment increased from 26.1 per cent to 42.5 per cent for men, and from just 16.4 per cent to 27.6 per cent for women during the period 1977/78–2009/10 (Table 9.3).

Table 9.3 *Non-agricultural Employment in Rural Tamil Nadu (1977–2010)*

Year	Percentage of workers in non-agricultural employment	
	Male	Female
1977–78	26.1	16.4
1983	31.1	18.2
1987–88	34.8	22.9
1993–94	36.0	21.5
1999–00	37.9	24.8
2004–05	41.3	26.2
2009–10	42.5	27.6

Source: Jeyaranjan (2012).

Sectoral and, hence, spatial mobility tend to be gendered, with a disproportionate share of women continuing to labour in agriculture. The fact that a relatively higher share of Dalit households is found in rural areas also suggests caste-based differences in access to non-agriculture, albeit not too high. Among the farming households in the state, only 30 per cent of the household income came from agriculture which is lower than the all-India average of 45 per cent (Vijayabaskar 2010). A survey in four districts revealed that only 28 per cent of the sample households relied solely on agriculture for their livelihood (Jeyaranjan 2012). In the remaining households, at least one member of the household was engaged in non-agricultural employment. The study points to two contrasting tendencies in non-farm employment of rural households. One strand of this workforce has gained entry into the formal sector with regular waged employment, whereas another segment is increasingly engaged in casualised work. The two trajectories may be indicative of a correlation between progressive diversification on the one hand, and a distress-induced diversification on the other. This de-agrarianisation of livelihoods has fed into the production of new ruralities in the state. This process of de-agrarianisation has also been enabled by the high levels of urbanisation, which is also more decentralised (Rukmani 1996). Well-developed transport networks allow for workers to access non-agricultural employment more easily.

Another dimension of mobility is the rise in the share of the casually employed in the state's workforce. The number of self-employed people, who have formed a major category of the labour force in India and continue to do so in most parts of the country, declined in share in Tamil Nadu over the decade 2000–2011/12 (Table 9.4), suggestive of a process of dispossession.

Importantly, the casualisation of the workforce increased relative to other states over the decade 2000–2011/12, as Andhra Pradesh and Kerala had the same or higher share of casual workers in 2000. The increase in casualisation of employment seems to have happened through reductions in both self-employment and the regular wage/salaried. While the decline in the self-employed may be due to small and marginal farmers exiting agriculture, the decline in share of the regular waged workers is an aspect that I shall address later. The movement from a self-employed to a casual workforce possibly represents the emergence of new mobilities in the countryside. We are thus witnessing two simultaneous processes at work. Segments of labour are neither able to make the transition into the urban completely, nor are they able to sustain themselves within the rural/agriculture.

Such processes are not, however, unique to Tamil Nadu. Li (2009, 2011) describes the confinement of labour within agriculture even as returns are stagnant in a process of 'truncated agrarian transition'. du Toit and de Neves (2014) too draw parallels with developments in rural South Africa. Given the political and economic unviability of this agrarian space, governing these trapped populations has become a major governmental imperative. Sanyal (2007) suggests that even as capitalist processes are dispossessing sections of the rural peasantry, democratic or electoral imperatives push states to counter this process by investing in measures to reintegrate the dispossessed with resources that assure a limited access to livelihoods. Promotion of various welfare programmes, including direct cash transfers to the poor, are all part of an emerging global repertoire of governmental techniques (Barrientos and Hulme 2009). Tamil Nadu too has witnessed such interventions, with an expansion of welfarist interventions since 2006, despite a policy shift towards marketisation of growth.

Table 9.4 *Distribution (per 1,000) of Workers According to Usual Status (PS + SS) by Broad Employment Status, 2000–2011/12 (All-India and Select States)*

	Tamil Nadu		Andhra Pradesh		Gujarat		Karnataka		Kerala		Maharashtra		All-India	
	2011–12	**2000**	**2011–12**	**2000**	**2011–12**	**2000**	**2011–12**	**2000**	**2011–12**	**2000**	**2011–12**	**2000**	**2011–12**	**2000**
Self-employed	317	345	444	403	514	456	478	436	377	359	469	381	522	469
Regular wage/ salaried	255	286	179	228	247	210	225	229	225	238	265	301	179	244
Casual labour	428	369	377	369	239	334	297	335	398	403	266	318	299	287
Total	1,000	1,000	1,000	1,000	1,000	1,000	1,000	1,000	1,000	1,000	1,000	1,000	1,000	1,000

Source: Key Indicators of Employment and Unemployment in India, NSS, 68th round; Employment and Unemployment Situation in India, NSS, 55th round.

State Welfarism and Mobility

The neoliberal turn in India since the early 1990s has fed state-level policies, and Tamil Nadu has been at the forefront of adopting a series of measures that are quite suggestive of a regime of growth premised on privatisation and marketisation (Kennedy 2004). Competing to attract private investments, the state has, over the years, passed a series of legislations that give a greater role to private capital in directing growth in the state. Such initiatives have enabled the state to attract a number of multinational firms to set up operations in the state and also privatised the provisioning of a range of public services like water, roads and urban infrastructure. Growth of sectors such as textiles, garments, leather, auto components and software services during this period has been marked by integration into global production circuits. Even as it has pursued a growth path premised on the agency of private capital, global and otherwise, the state has also been at the forefront of devising a range of social-welfare measures targeted at poorer households (Kalaiyarasan 2014; Vijayabaskar 2010). Recognised for long as a pioneer in welfare schemes (Guhan 1990), the persistence and even expansion of the domain of welfare in the state since the 2006 assembly elections have fundamentally transformed the rural landscape. Campaigning on the offer of a range of welfare provisions, successive governments in the state have succeeded in implementing a set of welfare schemes. The offer of 20 kg of free rice to all ration-card holders; expansion of the range of essential commodities given through the public distribution system (PDS); supply of free gas stoves and subsidised cylinders; free television sets; health insurance scheme for the poor; old-age and widows pension schemes; distribution of free laptops to students enrolled in higher-secondary education in government schools; distribution of cows and goats to the rural poor as a means to support their livelihoods; and opening up of subsidised food canteens in major urban centres are some of the major initiatives enacted by the state. Complemented by the National Rural Employment Guarantee Act (NREGA) of the central government which seeks to provide a minimum of 100 days of employment at minimum wage to all rural households seeking employment, the state appears to have one of the best social-security nets in the country.

Despite the growing vulnerability of agrarian livelihoods, welfare measures led to considerable reductions in rural poverty in the state during the 2000s. What are the implications of such welfarist interventions for labour mobility? My proposition here is that welfarist interventions allow for the production of a translocal livelihood regime. The offer of welfare for resident populations in a specific village allows for members of agrarian households to stay back, even as other members are rendered mobile. Welfare entitlements allow for the mobile members of households to try out new employment ventures, as they offer a degree of income security. Despite a growing informalisation of employment in the state (Vijayabaskar 2017), governmental initiatives may have worked to insulate workers from the income vagaries of casual or informal work. Such interventions have also further incentivised households to continue to be rural as their costs of reproduction are subsidised. Such security nets allow capital to rely on a casualised workforce without having to invest in providing them with social security. The regime of welfare, in conjunction with the changes in the rural, and a growing integration of product and factor markets have led to the emergence of a distinct set of labour mobilities.

Regimes of Mobile Labour: Towards a Typology

Infrastructure expansion and the construction worker

Though incomes from non-agricultural sectors have been growing in terms of their contributions to state income, their contributions to employment absorption has not kept pace except in the case of the non-manufacturing sector within industry (Table 9.5). Construction is the biggest component of this sector, and this is the only component whose share in employment has increased, as Table 9.5 indicates.

The construction economy is highly differentiated, ranging from low-end housing, often in nearby villages and small towns, to high-end apartment complexes in metropolitan locations, and large-scale infrastructure projects. While large-scale projects are undertaken by pan-Indian capital, often employing workers from other states, it is in the remaining segments that Tamil workers appear to be largely engaged. Different durations and different locations also allow for multiple time-spaces of labour and circulation. Ranging from offering

Table 9.5 *Share of Employment across Sectors, 2004–05 and 2009–10 (All-India and Select States)*

States	Sector									
	2004–05					2009–10				
	Agriculture	Manufacturing	Non-manufacturing	Industry	Service	Agriculture	Manufacturing	Non-manufacturing	Industry	Service
Andhra Pradesh	52.8	11.9	7.0	18.9	28.1	51.2	11.0	13.5	24.5	24.3
Gujarat	62.1	12.6	5.1	17.7	20.2	52.2	13.7	7.3	21.0	26.8
Karnataka	64.4	9.4	4.4	13.8	21.7	57.3	9.9	7.7	17.6	25.1
Kerala	40.1	13.5	11.6	25.1	34.8	32.1	12.4	16.3	28.7	39.2
Maharashtra	45.7	14.8	6.2	21.0	34.3	52.9	10.8	6.5	17.3	29.8
Tamil Nadu	46.4	19.6	7.0	26.6	27.1	41 8	17.2	14.0	31.2	27.0

Source: Planning Commission (2014).

themselves in spot-labour markets that are diffused through the Tamil countryside, to forming mobile labour gangs, to working for specific maistries who can move them from one site to another, mobilities and types of labour contracts within a construction sector are varied. Further, segments of skilled labour such as masons, plumbers, carpenters and electricians appear to be plugged into more long-distance circuits that include international labour markets and are part of a different mobility regime. While this segment often consists of young men, unskilled workers also travel as families, but over much shorter distances. At best, they move to construction sites in nearby cities. The multiple rhythms of mobility of different segments of construction labour are, however, not well understood. Outside construction, there have also been changes in the spatial dynamics of manufacturing that has shaped certain kinds of mobility.

The 'company bus' and the commuting worker

Chandrasekhar (2011) makes an important observation about the significance of the 'commuting worker' in India's rural and urban landscapes; workers who stay in rural areas and commute daily to urban areas for work, and workers who stay in urban areas and commute to rural areas for work. Based on the National Sample Survey Organisation (NSSO) data, Chandrasekhar estimates that in 2009–10, over 8 million workers employed in non-agricultural work commuted every day from rural to urban areas to work, while another 4.37 million lived in urban areas and moved to rural areas to work. He goes on to identify an additional 12 million plus workers with no fixed place of work, implying more uncertain employment and higher mobility. In Tamil Nadu alone, more than 7.2 lakh workers commuted from rural areas to work in non-agricultural sectors. This mobility has been accompanied, and to an extent made possible, by a new mobility of capital. Studies indicate a growing ruralisation of the formal manufacturing sector in recent years, with its output increasingly coming from the rural areas, even as urban manufacturing employment is becoming more informal during the period 1989–2005 (Ghani, Goswami and Kerr 2012). Though the primary driving factor is one of lower land costs, formal manufacturing has also been able to tap into new pools of rural labour during this period. In Tamil Nadu, the commuting worker is particularly visible in the case of garments, textiles, leather products and the auto component and electronics sectors.

The 'company bus' has become a feature of rural landscape in the state. Firms run 'company buses' that transport workers from nearby villages, and at times even towns, over a distance of 30–40 km every day between the factories and their villages. Relatively low-tech sectors like textiles and leather have moved to rural areas from the 1990s onwards. While most spinning mills were earlier located in urban locations, the new ones have invariably come up in the villages, some of which are not even on the periphery of urban centres. Leather-product manufacturing units too have dispersed outwards from urban centres to villages located within a radius of 30–40 km.

Such developments have enabled the rise of the commuting worker, a phenomenon that clearly transcends urban–rural distinctions and constitutes a life space that is simultaneously urban and rural. Workers often prefer to stay in their respective villages and commute to their place of work, be it in nearby towns or villages. Garment and shoe factories, and even electronics firms, on the outskirts of Chennai often source labour from within a radius of 60–75 km, sending their buses or vans to transport the commuting workers. This has aided the mobility of women workers in particular whose mobilities were otherwise constrained by gendered divisions of reproductive labour. Access to housing in their villages is another important factor that incentivises this commuting and probably works to subsidise the cost of reproduction of labour. Importantly, this rural preference is encouraged by social welfare regimes that target populations at the place of residence, that is, as members of 'political society' rather than as workers. Ruralisation does not, however, necessarily imply better wage rates or working conditions for the rural population entering into the workforce. There are also variations in the nature and terms of employment. Even though workers in the leather products and in garment factories are offered 'permanent' employment, there is not enough demand for such 'long-term' employment. This is because the minimum wages paid in these sectors are lower than what casual work in the same sector fetches. Hence, the dichotomy between formal and informal employment does not quite overlap with good and bad quality employment.

Despite the process of ruralisation, most of manufacturing is clustered in specific locations, a key feature of post-1990s growth in the state. While there has been a growing concentration of economic activity even across states during this growth phase, growth in Tamil Nadu has been concentrated largely in the greater Chennai region and in the neighbouring districts of Kancheepuram and Tiruvallur, and in districts of western Tamil Nadu. There is also an agglomeration of leather and leather-goods production in the Ranipet-Ambur-Vaniyambadi belt in northeastern Tamil Nadu. Efforts by the state to spread manufacturing to backward regions by investing in infrastructure have not worked. This concentration of economic activity within the state has spawned another kind of mobility.

Clustered economic activity and labour mobilities

In addition to the commuting worker in construction and manufacturing, the concentration of growth in specific agglomerations has led to relatively longer-term migration to these locales. Growth hubs such as Tiruppur, Coimbatore and the greater Chennai region have witnessed migration of labour from the relatively less dynamic districts seeking employment in low end services and manufacturing jobs. While Tiruppur has been long held as a place to go to for unskilled rural youth, Chennai city too has drawn youth into low end services employment of various kinds, particularly as drivers and in retail services. Semi-skilled workers with a diploma in engineering or Industrial Training Institute (ITI) certifications find their way into manufacturing units across these growth centres. Critical to this mobility is networks of access to these jobs. Kinship and family ties are key constituents of these networks, not only in terms of access to information but more critically for access to spaces of reproduction such as housing. While in the case of trade that is largely informal in nature, the role of kinship networks is a lot more obvious; in sectors that are less tied to caste, such as transport, or informal or small-scale manufacturing, such social networks are critical to job access. In a study of workers working along the IT corridor in Chennai, rather than spatial proximity, networks are found to help labour access employment (Vijayabaskar and Suresh Babu 2016). In Tiruppur, distinct slum or informal settlements house migrant workers from distinct regions. Pandian Nagar, for example, is home to migrant workers largely from the Madurai and Dindigul districts. There are also caste-specific settlements but of older vintage.

Despite such high growth and creation of limited employment opportunities, the decade 2000–10 is often described as a period of jobless growth in India (Chandrasekhar and Sharma 2014; Papola 2013). Even the limited number of jobs created has been more in the informal economy. This is true of Tamil Nadu as well. As we saw earlier, since 2000, there has been a gradual increase in the share of casual labour *vis-à-vis* the self-employed and regular salaried work. Growing access to education has not been matched by jobs that are commensurate with such education. Despite the poor growth in employment within the state, Tamil labour has sought to plug itself into pan-Indian and transnational labour markets. Prospects of earning relatively higher incomes and opening of international mobility paths for the low and semi-skilled workers have generated a steady increase in labour mobilities outside the state.

Interstate and international mobilities

Tamil Nadu and Kerala are the only two relatively better-off states that have more people going out of the state to work than people coming in (Chandrasekhar and Sharma 2014). There is limited evidence to suggest that migration from Tamil Nadu takes place to the neighbouring states of Karnataka and Kerala, largely to work in construction and agriculture in the bordering districts. International migration too has been increasing steadily since the early 1990s, with the Gulf countries accounting for the bulk of it, followed by southeast Asia (Irudaya Rajan, D'Sami and Asir Raj 2016). Rough estimates suggest an annual remittance economy of nearly Rs 60,000 crores. While there is some evidence to suggest that mobility capital, that is, the ability to take advantage of such possibilities for movement is unevenly distributed across caste groups, the modes of access to these networks and the nature of barriers to access are not clear. Brokers are key agents who enable these networks, but access to reliable brokers who can arrange their work visas and a job in these countries is conditioned by money and knowledge of the reliability of the brokers. Once again, the bulk of the migrants are male, with only a limited movement of women as domestic workers or nurses. Often, rural or small-town male workers envision a two-stage mobility path. To begin with, in the first stage they seek work in high-growth regions such as Tiruppur. Savings during this phase are then fed into paying a broker for an international work permit.

Mobilities of skilled labour

So far, I have confined myself to the mobilities of those with less access to formal education or those with low-end technical qualifications. Access to tertiary education was much more diffused in Tamil Nadu in 2014–15, with more than 45 per cent of the youth in the age group of 18–23 enrolled in some kind of higher education or the other, according to the All-India Survey on Higher Education 2016. This is the highest among any of the bigger states in the country, and is true even for the Scheduled Castes (SCs), though their enrolment rates are lower at 33.2 per cent. While the urban rates are likely to be higher, even in rural areas accessing higher education is seen as a major route to economic mobility and, importantly, as a means to move out of traditional caste-based occupations, especially in agriculture and in artisanal jobs such as handloom weaving. This relatively broad-based access to tertiary education is tied to new circuits of mobility, particularly in the domain of the software sector.

Tamil labour has been very much part of the post-1990s software boom enabled by the rise of a large number of private engineering colleges and also by positive discrimination policies that have been in place in the state. Given the requirements of knowledge of English and tertiary education, it has been pointed out that the growth of this sector may aggravate labour market inequities given the wide disparities in access to tertiary education and knowledge of English across castes and regions. Though there are no large-scale data on the caste-based distribution of workforce in the IT sector, micro-level studies by and large affirm the predominance of the upper castes in the workforce (Rothboeck, Vijayabaskar and Gayathri 2001; Upadhyay 2007). Tamil Nadu is, however, probably the only state that has seen the entry of students from the backward and most-backward castes in substantial numbers, especially since 2000, into this segment. The entry of Dalits, however, is of a relatively lower magnitude, though we still do not have proper estimates in this regard. These networks that straddle small towns, villages and metropolitan locations in India and the United States are probably the most sought after mobility paths among the formally schooled labour. Drivers of caste and spatial variations, and importantly how the aspirations generated by such social and spatial mobilities generate new anxieties and aspirations among labour outside these networks, are less understood. Also less understood is the nature of associational politics among non-resident Tamil labour in the emigrant countries and their links with Tamil Nadu.

The relationship between access to tertiary education and access to aspirational jobs is, however, highly tenuous. Nearly 30 per cent of Tamil youth from rural areas with a graduate degree report themselves to be neither in employment or training, nor in education, indicating the relatively bleak prospects of securing quality employment in the urban (Vijayabaskar 2017). Aspirational jobs also seem to vary across caste. For the graduate Dalit youth, government jobs either as teachers, police or lower-level bureaucracy are the most coveted. For upper sections of the backward and most-backward castes, low-end government jobs are not seen as the future. These groups prefer to imagine themselves as entrepreneurial workers seeking to make good of the spaces opened up by neoliberal globalisation. The idea of permanent employment is less an ideal compared to a career of temporary jobs that may, in the long run, lead to a high-earning career.

Gendering of mobility

A key phenomenon in Tamil Nadu is the gendering of mobility, especially with the reduction in labour-force participation of women since the early 2000s. Women, particularly in rural areas, are withdrawing from the workforce as household incomes increase. Jeyaranjan (2011), based on a micro-level study, sees this process as a reflection of the household's desire to invest in children's education as a means to escape from rural poverty or out of uncertain agriculture-based livelihoods. This phenomenon, which clearly needs more exploration, seems prevalent more among the backward and most-backward castes in the state. Along with a withdrawal of women from the workforce, there is a feminisation of agricultural labour. The intersection of this process of feminisation with caste and class relations is again unclear. Importantly, the role of welfare regimes that often target women directly or implicitly in shaping their mobility needs to be understood. Among the women seeking work outside agriculture, there appear to be clear limits to their mobility. Apart from commuting, women workers in urban locations are often found to be concentrated in jobs that are relatively more regular but low-paying. Expansion of domestic labour, housekeeping work in large firms, back office processing work, retail and hospitality, education and health services are segments that have witnessed entry of women workers in significant numbers. The interactions of job choices with their life-cycle decisions, and the impact of their relative immobility on their social mobility, again, are aspects that remain unexplored.

Capital *versus* Labour (Im)mobility

The relationship between the need for capital to secure a pliable workforce and labour mobility is often contradictory. On the one hand, capital needs to fix labour to a place if it is to initiate a process of expanded surplus extraction. Simultaneously, it would prefer to be not burdened by costs of reproduction of labour. In other words, while it prefers labour that can easily be shed as per market or demand requirements, excessive mobility may hinder its prospects for accumulation. These twin imperatives have especially become important in the current phase of accumulation that has been marked by rapid turnover of capital, and uncertain and flexible market demand. The emphasis on lower turnaround times, cost-based competition in global markets and, hence, the pressure to reduce the costs of retaining a permanent workforce pushes firms towards what can be termed as 'just-in-time' recruitment of labour. Firms find it more profitable to rely on a pool of casual labour that can be drawn upon as and when orders are procured and shed when there is no or low production. Under such conditions of labour demand, firms rely on a network of labour contractors to source labour as close to the time of production as possible. Labour contractors have become important labour-market intermediaries since the 1990s, enabling firms to rely on numerical flexibility to keep costs down (de Neve 2014; Vijayabaskar 2014). A key technology mediating between the producers, contractors and the workers is the ubiquitous mobile phone. Seldom acknowledged or recognised, cell phones have arguably come to play an extremely significant role in orchestrating production in many a production regime. As soon as a firm indicates the need for additional labour, the network of labour contractors reach out to source areas in rural or small-town Tamil Nadu, or often across the country, through the mobile phone to mobilise labour. The workers are moved from one factory to another once orders are completed or when the demand goes down. This is also a phase that has given rise to large labour contractor firms like UPDATER Services (UDS) that has more than 15,000 workers on its rolls and supplies low-skilled labour to a number of factories in the greater Chennai region (Rajshekhar 2016).

While retaining them as temporary labour, larger firms also resort to housing long-distance workers in dormitories close to the factories to exert greater control over their work time and to temporarily immobilise them. Instances of garment factories resorting to '*sumangali*' type employment schemes that immobilise labour for specific periods are also reported. Young female workers are recruited as apprentices and are paid a monthly allowance. However, the rest of their remuneration is paid in lump sum only if they work for a minimum period, from one to three years, thereby binding the workers to that employer during that period. Such workers are less 'free' and paid less than the more mobile casual workers,[4] who work in several firms. Smaller firms also take up houses on rent to house their workers. Control over spaces of reproduction through debt bondage to tie workers to a specific employer has been observed (Carswell and de Neve, 2014; Guérin 2013). Use of female workers and long-distance interstate migrant workers serves to control labour mobility. We are, thus, witnessing a simultaneous process of capital drawing upon a highly casual and mobile workforce, even as it seeks to restrict labour mobility by a range of strategies.

Towards a Possible Research Agenda

The foregoing discussion has mapped a set of growth processes and state acts that have rendered possible a range of labour mobilities in Tamil Nadu during a period marked by visible signs of neoliberalisation. There are, however, several gaps in our understanding of the worlds of mobile and not-so-mobile labour. While there is evidence of the gendering of mobility, the intersections of caste, class and gender in shaping mobility paths require much greater attention. If unequal access to mobility is a result of uneven distribution of mobility capital, then what are the constituents of such mobility capital? Is it tied to being part of upwardly mobile or upper-caste networks, or is it tied to regional and historical networks? More importantly, are there mobility networks that tend to transcend caste, especially in the case of low-end mobility circuits or in the case of highly skilled migrant networks?

The spread of a range of manufacturing activity in small towns in Tamil Nadu and its diffusion into the nearby villages has spawned new rural–urban and rural–rural mobilities and a move into manufacturing and service-sector jobs among both Dalit and intermediate-caste male youth. While mobility out of agriculture has been relatively even, this has been backed by uneven investments in education and clearly differential access to social networks. How do such differences shape the ability to move and access different kinds of labour circuits? Importantly, how does this uneven access to mobility influence patterns of inequality? The links between labour mobilities and their influence on economic transformations in the state are not quite evident at present. While there are visible signs of change happening in rural and urban Tamil Nadu, the extent and axes along which mobilities engender processes of social and economic differentiation are yet to be understood.

The transformations in the rural and the urban have also generated a pool of youth that appears to be suspended in a space-time that is increasingly appearing to assume a new social fixity—neither able to move back into the rural nor able to be absorbed into spaces of modern capital accumulation. The modes of survival and how those intersect with kinship and other social networks, and state welfare regimes, constitute an important domain of enquiry with implications not only for mobility trajectories but, importantly, for postcolonial developmental trajectories.

The regional state as it negotiates the needs of global capital for a cheap and a flexible workforce has rescaled labour governance to generate a labour regime that straddles the workplace and the place of residence. How does that shape the spaces of collective action? On the one hand, it is possible that the spawning of new mobilities may undermine traditional politics of place given the workers' stakes in multiple spaces, across multiple spaces of work and spaces of reproduction. However, mobility is also held to open up spaces for networked politics that can link up actors across multiple scales (Larsen, Urry and Axhausen 2006; Urry 2012). What kinds of mobilisation can find new salience among such a mobile workforce?

Spatial mobility need not always be tied to economic mobility. Newspaper reports point to the conditions of duress under which segments of low-end internationally mobile Tamils labour in the Gulf and southeast Asian countries. One report points to body bags of Tamil migrant workers being brought into the state (Rajaram 2014). We do not know enough about the conditions of movement, the nature of intermediation and investments required and, importantly, conditions of labour within these circuits. There are also segments that do not move because they do not gain from it or are not required to move.

Finally, mobilities, particularly international mobilities of both software labour and low and semi-skilled labour, have clearly given rise to a new imagination of possibilities of economic and social mobility. How does such an economy of affect play itself out among other labouring youth? Also, how do we envisage a politics of social justice that recognises the legitimacy of such aspirations of mobility in an increasingly unequal economy?

Notes

[1] Implying that people emigrating from the state outnumber those who are coming in.
[2] This is, however, not to deny the new forms of land concentration emerging in Tamil Nadu with several wealthy individuals and institutions buying up agricultural lands.
[3] Carswell and de Neve (2013) point to the decline of bonded labour relations in western Tamil Nadu. This decline is, however, not to deny forms of neo-bondage that have emerged in other sectors in the rural economy (Guérin 2013).
[4] Who tend to be, invariably, young male labour.

References

'Like Manna from Heaven'. 2015. *The Economist*, 3 September. Available at http://www.economist.com/news/finance-and-economics/21663264-how-torrent-money-workers-abroad-reshapes-economy-manna (accessed 10 October 2015).

Barrientos, A., and D. Hulme. 2009. 'Social Protection for the Poor and Poorest in Developing Countries: Reflections on a Quiet Revolution (Commentary)'. *Oxford Development Studies* 37(4): 439–56.

Carswell, G., and G. de Neve. 2013. 'From Field to Factory: Tracing Transformations in Bonded Labour in the Tiruppur Region, Tamil Nadu'. *Economy and Society* 42(3): 430–54.

——— 2014. 'T-shirts and Tumblers: Caste, Dependency and Work under Neoliberalisation in South India'. *Contributions to Indian Sociology* 48(1): 103–31.

Chandrasekhar, S. 2011. 'Estimates of Workers Commuting from Rural to Urban and Urban to Rural India: A Note'. Working paper no. 2011-019, Indira Gandhi Institute of Development Research, Mumbai.

Chandrasekhar, S., and A. Sharma. 2014. 'Urbanization and Spatial Patterns of Internal Migration in India'. Working paper no. 016-2014, Indira Gandhi Institute of Development Research, Mumbai.

Davis, M. 2004. *Planet of Slums*. Verso: London.

de Neve, G. 2014. 'Entrapped Entrepreneurship: Labour Contractors in the South Indian Garment Industry'. *Modern Asian Studies* 48(5): 1302–33.

du Toit, A., and G. de Neves. 2014. 'The Government of Poverty and the Arts of Survival: Mobile and Recombinant Strategies at the Margins of the South African Economy'. *Journal of Peasant Studies* 41(5): 833–53.

Ghani, E., A. G. Goswami and W. R. Kerr. 2012. 'Is India's Manufacturing Sector Moving Away from Cities?'. Working paper no. 17992, National Bureau of Economic Research, Boston.

Government of India. 2015. *Economic Survey 2015–16*, Volume 1. New Delhi: Government of India.

Government of Tamil Nadu. 2014. 'Statistical Handbook of Tamil Nadu 2013'. Department of Economics and Statistics, Chennai.

Guérin, I. 2013. 'Bonded Labour, Agrarian Changes and Capitalism: Emerging Patterns in South India'. *Journal of Agrarian Change* 13(3): 405–23.

Guhan, S. 1990. 'Social Security Initiatives in Tamil Nadu'. Working paper no. 96, Madras Institute of Development Studies, Chennai.

Irudaya Rajan, S., B. D'Sami and S. Asir Raj. 2016. 'Non-resident Tamils and Remittances: Results from Tamil Nadu Migration Survey 2015'. Supported by State Planning Commission, Government of Tamil Nadu.

Jeyaranjan, J. 2011. 'Women and Pro-poor Policies in Rural Tamil Nadu: An Examination of Practices and Responses'. *Economic and Political Weekly* 46(43): 64–74.

——— 2012. 'A Study on the Rural Non-farm Employment in Tamil Nadu'. Report submitted to the Institute of Applied Manpower Research (currently National Institute for Labour Economics Research and Development), New Delhi.

Kalaiyarasan, A. 2014. 'A Comparison of Developmental Outcomes in Gujarat and Tamil Nadu'. *Economic and Political Weekly* 49(15): 55–63.

Kaufmann, V., M. Max Bergman and D. Joyev. 2004. 'Motility: Mobility as Capital'. *International Journal of Urban and Regional Research* 28(4): 745–56.

Kennedy, L. 2004. 'The Political Determinants of Reforming Packaging: Contrasting Responses to Economic Liberalisation in Andhra Pradesh and Tamil Nadu'. In *Regional Reflections: Comparing Politics across India's States*, ed. R. Jenkins, 29–65. New Delhi: Oxford University Press.

Kotwal, A., B. Ramaswami and W. Wadhwa. 2011. 'Economic Liberalization and Indian Economic Growth: What's the Evidence?'. *Journal of Economic Literature* 49(4): 1152–99.

Larsen J., J. Urry and K. Axhausen. 2006. *Mobilities, Networks, Geographies*. Aldershot: Ashgate.

Li, M. T. 2009. 'Exit from Agriculture: A Step Forward or a Step Backward for the Rural Poor?'. *Journal of Peasant Studies* 36(3): 629–36.

——— 2011. 'Centering Labor in the Land Grab Debate'. *Journal of Peasant Studies* 38(2): 281–98.

Nagaraj, K. 2006. 'Tamil Nadu Economy: Contours of Change (A Secondary Data Exploration)'. Mimeo, Madras Institute of Development Studies, Chennai.

Narayanamoorthy, A. 2006. 'State of India's Farmers'. *Economic and Political Weekly* 41(6), 11 February: 471–73.

National Sample Survey Organisation. 2012. 'Key Indicators of Employment and Unemployment in India', NSS, 68th round. Available at http://mospi.nic.in/Mospi_New/upload/nss_report_554_31jan14.pdf (accessed 14 February 2014).

Papola, T. S. 2013. 'Role of Labour Regulation and Reforms in India: Country Case Study on Labour Market Segmentation'. Employment sector working paper no. 147, International Labour Organisation, Geneva.

Planning Commission. 2014. 'State-wise Absolute Employment (in Millions) by Major Sectors and Share of Employment (2004–05, 2009–10)'. Available at http://planningcommission.nic.in/data/datatable/data_2312/DatabookDec2014%20117.pdf (accessed 16 August 2013).

Rajaram, R. 2014. 'Tiruchi Airport Witness to Frequent Arrival of Bodies'. *The Hindu*, 29 September. Available at http://www.thehindu.com/news/cities/Tiruchirapalli/tiruchi-airport-witness-to-frequent-arrival-of-bodies/article6456836.ece (accessed 5 December 2014).

Rajshekhar, M. 2016. 'These Companies are Changing the Way Labour is Hired (and Fired) in India'. *Scroll.in*, 27 September. Available at https://scroll.in/article/815372/these-companies-are-changing-the-way-labour-is-hired-and-fired-in-india (accessed 9 April 2017).

Registrar General and Census Commissioner, respective years. Census of India. Government of India, New Delhi.

Rothboeck, S., M. Vijayabaskar and V. Gayathri. 2001. *Labour in the New Economy: The Case of the Indian Software Labour Market*. New Delhi: International Labour Organisation.

Rukmani, R. 1996. 'Factors Underlying High Dispersal of Towns in Tamil Nadu'. *Review of Development and Change* 1(1): 113–25.

Sanyal, K. 2007. *Rethinking Capitalist Development: Primitive Accumulation, Governmentality and Post-colonial Capitalism*. New Delhi: Routledge.

Sidhwani, P. 2015. 'Spatial Inequalities in Big Indian Cities'. *Economic and Political Weekly* 50(22): 55–62.

Sood, A., P. Nath and S. Ghosh. 2014. 'Deregulating Capital, Regulating Labour: The Dynamics in the Manufacturing Centre in India'. *Economic and Political Weekly* 49(26–27): 58–68.

Upadhya, C. 2007. 'Employment, Exclusion and "Merit" in the Indian IT Industry'. *Economic and Political Weekly* 42(20): 1863–68.

Urry, J. 2012. *Sociology beyond Societies: Mobilities for the Twenty-first Century*. London: Routledge.

Verité Research and Advocacy Initiative. 2010. 'Indian Workers in Domestic Textile Production and Middle East–based Manufacturing, Infrastructure and Construction'. Available at http://digitalcommons.ilr.cornell.edu/cgi/viewcontent.cgi?article=2176&context=globaldocs (accessed 4 October 2015).

Vijayabaskar, M. 2010. 'Saving Agricultural Labour from Agriculture: SEZs and Politics of Silence in Tamil Nadu'. *Economic and Political Weekly* 45(6), 6 February: 36–43.

Vijayabaskar. 2014. 'Emerging Spatio-technical Regimes of Accumulation in the Globalising South and Implications for Labour'. In *Indian Capitalism in Development*, eds B. Harriss-White and J. Heyer, 136–52. UK: Routledge.

_____ 2017. 'The Agrarian Question amidst Popular Welfare: Interpreting Tamil Nadu's Emerging Rural Economy'. *Economic and Political Weekly* 52(46): 67–72.

Vijayabaskar, M., and M. Suresh Babu. 2016. 'The Politics of Urban Mega-projects in India: Income Employment Linkages in Chennai's IT Corridor'. *Economic and Political Weekly* 51(17): 8–92.

10. Politics of Dravidian Populism

Understanding Developmental Outcomes in Tamil Nadu

A. Kalaiyarasan

There is recognition of substantial sub-national differences in economic and social outcomes in India. The 'multi-tier' decision-making within a nation State, social mobilisation and institutional change have all contributed to these differences in outcome (Sinha 2003; Srinivasan 2010).[1] The states that witnessed mass social movements have seen better provision of social services in India (Varshney 2012). Tamil Nadu is one such state. The studies argue that it is not technical intervention by enlightened individuals that produced better socioeconomic outcomes, but rather collective action from below, that is, from the excluded, marginal, lower castes and classes (Heller and Evans 2010; Drèze and Sen 1991).

There is yet another argument that 'the solidarity that emerges from a sense of shared identity' is the source of differences in social welfare and development across states in India (Singh 2015: 506). Singh argues that the presence of shared identity in the form of sub-nationalism may be likely to bring in education and health in the policy agenda by the regional political elite. In other words, states with strong sub-nationalism are more likely to prioritise the social sector. In the absence of sub-nationalism, even if social policies are introduced, they tend to favour narrow elite groups than being accessible to all. However, sub-nationalism alone cannot account for the differences among the states in social outcome. This is because there are differences in levels of social development even among the states that have a history of sub-nationalism. Thus, significant social mobilisation and institutional change on the ground are important factors that shape outcomes (Srinivasan 2010). Collective action from below is, thus, a key factor in ensuring better delivery of social provisions. Tamil Nadu is the case here. The state has seen better delivery of public services and broad-based development because of the sustained anti-caste mobilisation in various forms (Varshney 2012; Drèze and Sen 2013).

Tamil Nadu has witnessed anti-caste movements and an assertive political mobilisation of the lower castes for over a century (Pandian 2007). The DMK, a political party which came to power in 1967 with a broad social base of lower castes and classes (Hariss 1999), has had a tremendous impact on Tamil Nadu's policy regime and institutions (Joshi and McGrath 2015). One crucial legacy of this history is a spate of populist measures—undertaken since the 1980s—designed to address popular concerns (Wyatt 2013). Setting aside critiques, these populist policies have made a material difference to the living conditions of the traditionally dispossessed lower castes (Vijayabaskar 2010). Tamil Nadu has thus seen both social mobilisation and the institutional change needed for public provision of basic services. This chapter maps the origin of populism in Tamil Nadu and its impact on social sectors.

The chapter is organised into two parts. The first offers a brief history of populism in the state. It also offers insights on the differences in the populist measures of the DMK and AIADMK, both in their content and design. The second part deals with populist schemes; it takes two such schemes, pertaining to the PDS and healthcare, to showcase how populism has worked in the state.[2] Following this, the chapter explores the politics of the PDS, its design, coverage and implementation. It goes on, then, to provide insights into how the state has built an effective, functional and inclusive health system in the state.

The Populism

The good performance of Tamil Nadu on certain socioeconomic indicators compared to other states, including even the developed ones, can be understood in terms of 'path-dependent populism'. First of all, populism, contrary to common understanding, need not be negative, but can have positive implications for the socially and economically disadvantaged sections. Wyatt (2013: 2), who has studied contemporary Tamil politics and policy regimes extensively, defines populism as 'an ideological construct that celebrates the importance of the ordinary people, asserts these people should not be divided by social hierarchy and justifies improvements in their welfare'.[3] Thus, populism assigns centrality to ordinary people.

As Subramanian (1999) argues, such populism took two forms in Tamil Nadu from the 1960s onwards, that is, with the Dravidian parties gaining political power in the state. The first one is called 'assertive populism', and it is defined as follows:

> Assertive populism urges supporters towards militant action to open up hitherto restricted spheres; and creates entitlements to education, jobs, loans, subsidized producer goods and sometimes small pieces of property. Due to the scarcity of such goods, they are usually rationed (perhaps through preferential policies) but not granted freely to all. Groups with some social power, albeit modest, are best able to compete for these entitlements ... (Ibid.: 376)

Primarily, assertive populism was practised by the DMK, and it took the form of (i) extending admission to higher education and government jobs to the Other Backward Classes (OBC) and (ii) expanding the number of castes eligible for the same. In short, it took the form of expanding the scope of affirmative action. This has had socioeconomic consequences for the lower castes.

The second form that populism took in Tamil Nadu is characterised as 'paternalist populism', and it is defined as follows:

> Paternalist populism promises that a benevolent leader, party or state will provide the poor and powerless with subsidized wage goods and protection from repressive elites. The lower strata and women, often unable to assert themselves independently or compete for the more substantial benefits assertive populism provides, are its main supporters. (Ibid.)

Such populism was primarily practised by the political rival of the DMK, that is, the AIADMK, under the leadership of the charismatic M. G. Ramachandran (MGR). A good example of paternalist populism was the noon meal scheme introduced by the AIADMK in 1982.

According to Wyatt (2013: 6), 'The noon meals enhanced MGR's image as the protector of children, women and the poor.' In addition, the AIADMK government also expanded food subsidies and increased the number of ration shops so that the rural poor got better access to their benefits.

While paternalist populism (whose impact in Tamil Nadu is important for the argument of this chapter) is primarily part of the politics and policies of AIADMK, the DMK too from the beginning did not fully avoid such populism in formulating and implementing policies. Giving an account of the DMK's policy regime in the late 1960s, Wyatt (2013: 5) writes: 'Slum clearance was accelerated, subsidised rice was provided in selected urban areas', and not only this, 'college fees were waived for poorer students and prohibition was introduced to protect women from the consequences of over-consumption of alcohol by male members of the household.' Competing with the AIADMK for popular support, DMK over time shifted its emphasis from assertive populism to paternalist populism.

The 2006 assembly election is a significant case in point. The DMK election manifesto promised cheap rice *via* the PDS, free colour televisions for families without one, free gas stoves for poor households, enhanced pension, payment of maternity allowances and an improved noon meal scheme. DMK won the election. Most of these promises were implemented in stages, and in addition, a new health insurance scheme for those earning less than Rs 72,000 a year was introduced. In the 2011 elections, AIADMK responded to the paternalist populism of the DMK by promising (i) 'a free food mixer or a grinder for women', (ii) 'free rice for the very poor', (iii) 'increased pension payments' and (iv) 'free laptop computers for students from the OBC and the SC backgrounds in government colleges' (ibid.: 7–8). This was so despite the fact that both the DMK and AIADMK are not opposed to neoliberal market-friendly policies and, in fact, implement them widely.

The significance of such persistence of paternalist populism (even in the context of neoliberalism) points to the fact that when state paternalism becomes the dominant expectation of the electorate, it becomes difficult for competing political regimes to deviate from such policies. In other words, paternalistic policies become path-dependent. As Wyatt (2013) sums up:

> The Tamil case also shows that populist leaders face certain limits, especially if populist assumptions have been absorbed into wider political culture. The AIADMK attempted, and failed, to re-order its governing strategy between 2001 and 2004. The AIADMK leadership concluded that public support for populist subsidies was too strong to be ignored. (Ibid.: 13)

Let us now turn to the socioeconomic consequences of this path-dependent populism in Tamil Nadu's policy regime. To understand this process, I have taken the health system and PDS for analysis.

Making of the PDS

The functioning of the PDS in Tamil Nadu has been highly celebrated for its efficiency and inclusiveness (Drèze and Sen 2011). The PDS has been a relief for the people affected by the agrarian crisis in rural Tamil Nadu. It has become an important factor in shaping and influencing the way the economy works in rural Tamil Nadu (Vijayabaskar 2011). In addition, the state has also seen a faster reduction in poverty in both rural and urban areas in the state. This section explores briefly the functioning of the PDS in Tamil Nadu, its effect on the state's economy and the potential reasons for its relative success in the state. Before that, a slice of history would not be out of place here.

The history of the PDS in Tamil Nadu is closely linked with the DMK assuming power in 1967. The DMK came into power with the promise of supplying three measures of rice per rupee (Venkatsubramanian 2006). Indeed, the new DMK government then declared food policy to be the central issue of the government.[4] It continues to be the electoral issue even now. The subsequent government in the state, thus, established the Tamil Nadu Civil Supplies Corporation (TNCSC) in 1972.[5] The corporation began procuring paddy directly from farmers, processing and distributing it to various parts of the state through its transport contractors. The government, then, established fair-price shops across the state. It enacted a new guidelines with the promise that no family cardholder was to travel more than 2 km to access a fair-price shop. It used cooperatives as the primary instrument for extending these shops to all villages across Tamil Nadu. As the then governor of the state reported in his address to the state assembly on 7 April 1977:

> It will be my government's endeavour to build up a network of retail points in the public sector including the cooperative sector to ensure equitable distribution of essential commodities at reasonable prices. We propose to extend the scheme of Fair Price Shops so that each of the above 16,000 revenue villages will have at least one Fair Shop in the village itself. (Venkatasubramanian 2006: 273)

As a result, the number of fair price shops in the state increased from 9,300 in 1977 to 17,536 in 1982. The political commitment to the PDS continued to be resilient in the state even when the central government attempted to dilute it. For instance, in 1997, the central government introduced the targeted public distribution system (TPDS) by bringing in the categories of below poverty line (BPL) and above poverty line (APL) to set differential prices. The DMK, which was then in power, rejected the TPDS proposal and reaffirmed its commitment for universal PDS.

Content of the PDS

Along with increased coverage, the basket of commodities provided at the PDS also widened. Initially, the TNCSC provided rice, wheat, sugar and kerosene. Under the PDS, it further included *toor dal* (pigeon pea lentil), *urad dal* (split black gram), palmolein oil, fortified wheat flour, *rava* (semolina) and *maida* (wheat flour) at subsidised prices. In addition, the corporation also started supplying cement at concessional rates and free liquefied petroleum gas (LPG) stoves under the scheme of free LPG connections to poor families. Most importantly, the price of essential commodities under PDS in Tamil Nadu was much lower than that of the open market and even the price fixed by Government of India. For example, the issue price of rice at the PDS as fixed by the government of Tamil Nadu in 2008 was Re 1 per kg. This was against Government of India's issue price of Rs 3 per kg under the Antyodaya Anna Yojana (AAY) allotment, Rs 5.65 per kg under BPL allotment and Rs 8 per kg under APL allotment (Venkatasubramanian 2006).

The PDS, thus, became a source of income support and social protection in the state (Drèze and Khera 2013). Since the PDS is universal in Tamil Nadu, the poor get their entitlement fairly. PDS in

Tamil Nadu has provided 35 kg rice per month free of cost for AAY cardholders and 20 kg rice per month for other cardholders since 2011. The poorest of poor are targeted for the issue of AAY cards. The state also provides wheat, sugar, kerosene and essential pulses at very subsidised prices. Unlike other states, the PDS operated by fair-price shop is run by cooperative societies in Tamil Nadu.[6] A recent study by Drèze and Khera (2013) estimated that the implicit subsidy through the PDS was as high as Rs 113 per month per head for rural and Rs 111 for urban Tamil Nadu. The corresponding figures for all of India were Rs 60 and Rs 72, respectively. Tamil Nadu topped among the states in India in the estimates of implicit subsidies provided through the PDS in both rural and urban areas.

The same study also provided estimates of the potential effect of the PDS in poverty reduction. According to the study (Drèze and Khera 2013: 58), income transfer through PDS accounted for about 11 per cent of total poverty reduction in rural India. For Tamil Nadu, the effect of PDS on poverty reduction was as high as 44 per cent, which was the highest among the states in India. If one uses the distribution-sensitive poverty-gap index, the impact of the PDS on poverty reduction further goes up. The estimated impact of PDS on poverty reduction measured by the poverty-gap index is about 61 per cent for Tamil Nadu, as against 18 per cent of the all-India average. Therefore, the major reduction of poverty that the state has witnessed in recent years is largely attributable to a well-functioning PDS in the state.

Efficiency and Diversion of the PDS

It is argued that the PDS in Tamil Nadu is not just known for universal coverage but also for its efficient and transparent functioning without much leakage and corruption.[7] A recent study has attempted to assess and rank the performance of the PDS across states based on eight parameters (Khera 2011a). The eight parameters are: degree of inclusiveness, integrity of the system, quality of the PDS grain, physical access (distance and time), predictability, reliability, record-keeping and institutional arrangements. Tamil Nadu performed better and topped on most of these indicators.

Similarly, the per capita purchase of PDS grain in Tamil Nadu has been the highest among the states in India. In per capita rice purchase from the PDS, the state tops the other states in India. For instance, in 2007–08, per capita rice purchased per month from the PDS in Tamil Nadu was 4.84 kg in rural and 3.19 kg in urban areas. The corresponding figures for all of India were 1.18 kg and 0.69 kg, respectively (Khera 2011a). Further, Tamil Nadu had a diversion rate (the proportion of grain that does not reach beneficiary households) of 4.4 per cent as against 44 per cent for all of India—one of the lowest among the states compared (see Figure 10.1). The state has an efficient tracking mechanism in place to prevent diversion (Vythiyanathan and Radhakrishnan 2010). It has control rooms established in all the districts to track the trucks, and a database of commodities that the trucks carry and the shop to which the goods are to be delivered. In 2010, the state also introduced a GPS-based vehicle movement monitoring system to track the movement of vehicles carrying the PDS goods. In order to ensure the availability of commodities at fair-price shops, the state established a mobile phone–based stock-monitoring mechanism across districts in the state. This enabled officials to identify stock levels on a daily basis. In addition to technical intervention, the vigilant popular mobilisation from below also contributed to the effective and transparent functioning of the PDS in the state, without too many leakages or corruption.[8]

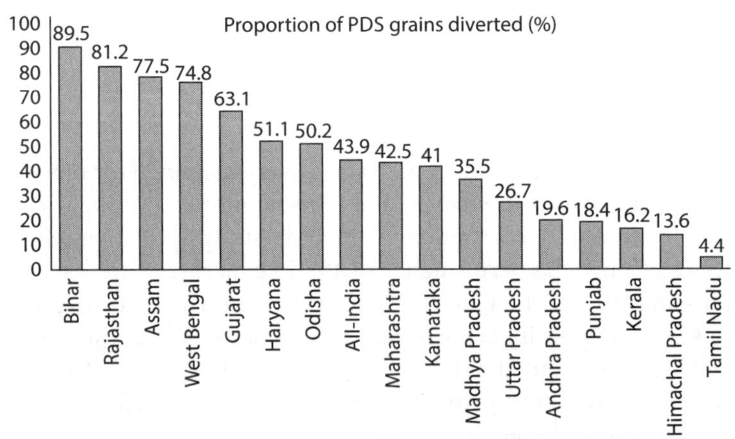

Figure 10.1 *Estimated Diversion of Foodgrains (2007–08)*

Source: Khera (2011a).

Social Inclusivity of the PDS

As stated earlier, Tamil Nadu has been maintaining universal PDS while most of the states in India have adopted targeted PDS since 1997. When targeted PDS was implemented in Tamil Nadu in 1997, the state was forced to reverse its decision within a few months under public pressure (Srinivasan 2010). The coverage of the PDS is also widespread in the state compared to the rest of the country. Tables 10.1 and 10.2 provide details of the coverage of the PDS and the types of ration cards that are used in the state. The coverage of the PDS, measured as a percentage of households availing ration cards, was around 90 per cent in rural Tamil Nadu as against 81 per cent at the all-India level in 2004–05. The coverage in urban areas stood at about 78 per cent for Tamil Nadu, while it was 67 per cent for all of India. At a disaggregated level, about 91 per cent of the poor had access to the PDS in rural Tamil Nadu, whereas the all-India figure stood at 81 per cent. The access to PDS for the urban poor in Tamil Nadu was 82 per cent as against 71 per cent for all of India. The distribution of the type of cards also showed that the percentage of BPL cards in the state was higher than that of all of India, despite the fact that the percentage of the poor was lower in Tamil Nadu. The coverage of different caste groups by the PDS too showed that caste groups that

Table 10.1 *Coverage of the PDS (%), 2004–05*

	Poor		Non-poor		Total	
	Tamil Nadu	All-India	Tamil Nadu	All-India	Tamil Nadu	All-India
Rural	90.9	80.6	88.4	81.9	89.2	81.4
Urban	82.2	71.8	76.6	65.8	77.6	67.0
Caste-wise Coverage of PDS						
Tamil Nadu						
	ST	SC	OBC	Others	Total	
Rural	93.7	91.3	89.0	71.6	89.2	
Urban	68.4	79.2	79.4	81.6	79.4	
India						
Rural	75.6	83.0	81.3	82.0	81.0	
Urban	53.0	70.1	68.8	69.3	68.8	

Source: Calculated from NSSO, 61st Unit Record.

were placed at the bottom in the caste hierarchy, such as the STs and SCs, had better access to the PDS in the state than their counterparts at the all-India level. For instance, about 91 per cent of SC households were covered under the PDS in rural Tamil Nadu and about 80 per cent in urban Tamil Nadu. The corresponding all-India figures were 79 per cent and 70 per cent, respectively.

Table 10.2 *Type of Cards (%), 2004–05*

Type	Rural		Urban	
	Tamil Nadu	All-India	Tamil Nadu	All-India
AAY	01.7	03.6	00.7	01.2
BPL	21.2	32.6	16.4	15.7
APL	77.2	63.7	82.8	83.1
Total	100.0	100.0	100.0	100.0

Source: Calculated from NSSO, 61st Unit Record.

Table 10.3 *Top-performing States in Provision of Public Services (Ranking), 2001*

State	Water	Health	Transport	PDS	Education	Overall
Tamil Nadu	1	4	2	1	1	1
Andhra Pradesh	7	16	4	2	4	5
Karnataka	2	6	3	3	3	3
Kerala	13	7	7	5	8	6
Maharashtra	5	2	5	4	4	4

Source: Paul et al. (2006: 93).

According to a study[9] undertaken by the Public Affairs Centre (PAC) on the provision of public services in India, Tamil Nadu topped in provisioning major public services, including the PDS (Table 10.3). In Tamil Nadu, more than 90 per cent of rural households had access to the PDS. In addition to access, 73 per cent of households in Tamil Nadu in the survey responded that services were reliable, as compared to the all-India average of 23 per cent (Paul et al. 2006: 87).

In sum, the PDS has been functioning exceptionally well in Tamil Nadu. The political commitments nurtured through paternalist populism, coupled with collective action by the people, have contributed to this success.

Building Health

Social mobilisation has facilitated the upward mobility of the lower caste populations in the state. They have not only come to prominence in public policy design, but have a greater say in decision-making too. It is argued that since historically marginalised caste groups could influence institutions in Tamil Nadu, it is they who pushed the successive political regimes to provide public services such as health. Public health in Tamil Nadu has been the model to be emulated in other states in India (Desikachari et al. 2010). These policies are not just technical interventions with budgetary allocation by the state. They are the outcome of the changes in the state. Political will, coupled by social mobilisation, has sustained such policies and ensured their effective delivery (Rajivan 2006; Mehrotra 2006; Sinha 2012). As Drèze and Sen (2011) argue:

> Less well known, but no less significant, is the gradual emergence and consolidation of universalistic social policies in Tamil Nadu ... Tamil Nadu, unlike most other states, also has an extensive network of lively and effective healthcare centres, where people from all social backgrounds can get reasonably good healthcare, free of cost. (Ibid.: 2011)[10]

Tamil Nadu has indeed introduced a series of policies with universal characteristics and such policies have produced far-reaching health outcome.

Basic Health Indicators

Table 10.4 provides details of basic health indicators for both Tamil Nadu and all-India. Tamil Nadu performed better on certain basic health indicators compared to all-India. For instance, the life expectancy rate for Tamil Nadu for 2006–10 stood at 67 for males and 71 for females. The corresponding all-India figures were 65 and 68, respectively. The maternal mortality ratio (MMR) for the state stood at 97 against 212 for all-India. Similarly, in measures such as infant mortality ratio (IMR) and under-5 mortality ratio (U5MR), the state performed better than the all-India average. The IMR for Tamil Nadu stood at 22 in 2011, while the corresponding all-India figure was 55.

Table 10.4 Basic Health Indicators (2005–06)

Indicators	Tamil Nadu	All-India
Male life expectancy (2006–10)	67.1	64.6
Female life expectancy (2006–10)	70.9	67.7
IMR (per 1,000 live births, 2011)	22.0	44.0
U5MR (per 1,000 live births, 2011)	25.0	55.0
MMR (per 100,000 live births, 2007–09)	97.0	212.0
Total fertility	1.7	2.4
Children who are undernourished (stunted) (%)	31.1	45.8
Vaccination (%)	80.9	43.5
Antenatal care (%)	99.0	77.2

Source: International Institute for Population Sciences (2007); Registrar General of India (2012).

Table 10.5 Performance of Tamil Nadu and Major States of India in Key RCH Indicators (2005–06)

State	Unmet need (%)	Any antenatal check-up (%)	Safe delivery (%)	Percentage of children who received full immunisation
Andhra Pradesh	12.0	94.0	69.0	63.0
Assam	23.0	61.0	33.0	19.0
Bihar	37.0	38.0	29.0	24.0
Gujarat	16.0	88.0	62.0	58.0
Haryana	15.0	88.0	43.0	63.0
Himachal Pradesh	12.0	91.0	51.0	79.0
Karnataka	15.0	91.0	67.0	74.0
Kerala	15.0	100.0	98.0	81.0
Madhya Pradesh	21.0	74.0	36.0	33.0
Maharashtra	13.0	93.0	63.0	74.0
Odisha	24.0	76.0	44.0	55.0
Punjab	10.0	89.0	64.0	75.0
Rajasthan	22.0	68.0	44.0	25.0
Tamil Nadu	18.0	99.0	89.0	92.0
Uttar Pradesh	34.0	58.0	29.0	28.0
West Bengal	11.0	91.0	54.0	54.0
India	21.1	73.4	47.6	47.6

Source: International Institute for Population Sciences (2017).

The state also performed better on key reproductive and child health (RCH) indicators. The topmost priorities of the RCH programme in India are: (i) ensuring safe motherhood and improved child health and (ii) raising contraceptive prevalence rates (Mehrotra 2006). Secondary literature shows that on both demands, the state performed better compared to other states (ibid.). Table 10.5 provides some details on the status of RCH indicators for some of the states. In Tamil Nadu, antenatal check-up was done in 99 per cent cases in comparison to 73 per cent all-India. The rate of safe deliveries in Tamil Nadu was about 89 per cent, and the corresponding all-India figure stood at 48 per cent. Child immunisation for Tamil Nadu was 92 per cent, whereas for all of India, it was just 48 per cent. Therefore, the state faring better on health indicators has been the result of the performance of process variables, access and state provision.

Access to Health Services

The good performance of Tamil Nadu on health indicators compared to other states has to be located in the access to health services that have been provided by the state. It is widely known (Khera 2012) that the state has been leading in the provisioning of free primary healthcare (which includes immunisation, antenatal care, postnatal care and eye care), with an emphasis on preventive healthcare. Primary health centres (PHCs) are well-equipped and function better in Tamil Nadu in comparison to other states.

Table 10.6 provides details of health infrastructure and access to health services. Tamil Nadu has more PHC density than all of India. For instance, the population covered by PHCs in Tamil Nadu in 2005–06 was 32,100, whereas the corresponding all-India figure was 49,200. The wide coverage of the PHCs in the state becomes clearer when we look at its coverage in villages. More than 79 per cent of the villages in Tamil Nadu had access to at least one PHC within 10 km, whereas for all-India, it was only 71 per cent. Similarly, the percentage of villages with a sub-centre within 3 km was 84 in Tamil Nadu, as against 71 per cent all-India. The proportion of villages with some government health facility in Tamil Nadu was 62 per cent, while the corresponding all-India figure was 46 per cent.

Infrastructure within the PHCs plays a major role in delivering better health outcomes. Tamil Nadu's PHCs are better equipped than

Table 10.6 Inequities in Availability and Accessibility of Health Services for Tamil Nadu and All-India (2007–08)

	Tamil Nadu	All-India
Population covered by a sub-centre	4,022	5,111
Population covered by a PHC	32,100	49,200
Proportion of villages with any government health facility	62	46
Villages with sub-centre within 3 km	84	71
Villages with PHC within 10 km	79	71
PHCs with the following facilities		
Medical officer (% of PHC)	85	76
Pharmacist (% of PHC)	94	69
New-born equipment (% of PHC)	64	28
Functional operating theatre (% of PHC)	90	61
Essential drugs (% of PHC)	98	68
Population served per government hospital	15,391	156,556
Population per government hospital bed	1,498	2,336

Source: International Institute for Population Sciences (2010).

those in other states in India. For instance, the percentage of PHCs with a medical officer in Tamil Nadu was 85 in 2007–08, as against 76 for all-India. The percentage of PHCs with pharmacist in the state was 94 as against 69 for all-India. Similarly, 90 per cent PHCs had functional operating theatres in Tamil Nadu as against 61 per cent in all of India. The percentage of PHCs with essential drugs was as high as 98 per cent in Tamil Nadu, while the corresponding all-India figure was 68 per cent. On indicators such as population per government hospital and governmental hospital bed, Tamil Nadu had a better score than all-India.

Caste and Health Indicators

Following the overall trend, in caste-wise performance on health indicators too Tamil Nadu fared better than all of India. In 1992–93, the IMR for SCs in Tamil Nadu was 90 points, and it came down to 37 points in 2005–06 (see Table 10.7). The corresponding all-India figures stood at 107 and 66 points, respectively. Thus, SCs gained

Table 10.7 *Key Health Indicators for Caste Groups in Tamil Nadu and All-India (1992–93 and 2005–06)*

	1992–93			2005–06		
	SC	Others	All	SC	Others	All
IMR						
Tamil Nadu	90	65	71	37	38	38
All-India	107	82	86	66	49	57
U5MR						
Tamil Nadu	127	85	95	48	45	45
All-India	149	112	119	88	59	74
Under-nutrition of children cross caste groups (%)						
Tamil Nadu	53	45	49	40	28	31
All-India	58	52	53	54	41	46
Child immunisation among caste groups (%)						
Tamil Nadu	59	67	65	72	85	81
All-India	27	38	35	40	54	43
Mother's antenatal care (%)						
Tamil Nadu	92	95	94	98	99	99
All-India	58	66	53	74	85	77

Source: International Institute for Population Sciences (1994, 2007).

about a 53-point reduction in the IMR in Tamil Nadu during 1992–93 to 2005–06, while the SCs all over India gained only about a 41-point reduction in the same period. On the U5MR indicator too, SCs in Tamil Nadu did better than all-India. The U5MR among the SCs stood at 127 in 1992–93 in Tamil Nadu, and it drastically came down to 48 in 2005–06. The corresponding all-India figures for the SCs were 149 and 88, respectively. The gain the SCs made in Tamil Nadu in reducing the U5MR during 1992–93 and 2005–06 was 79 points, while SCs at the all-India level gained a reduction of 61 points. The percentage of children suffering under-nutrition among the SCs was 53 in 1992–93, and it came down to 40 per cent in 2005–06. The corresponding all-India figures were 58 and 54 per cent, respectively. In the case of indicators such as child immunisation and mother's antenatal care, too, deprived caste groups in Tamil Nadu performed better than all-India. Child immunisation in Tamil Nadu was about

80 per cent, while it was merely 43 per cent for all-India in 2005–06. On many of the health indicators, deprived caste groups in Tamil Nadu performed better than the dominant caste groups at the all-India level. A comparative study of the performance of different caste groups in terms of health indicators done by different scholars endorses the argument advanced here.[11]

Health Expenditure

There is no marked difference between health expenditure patterns in all of India and Tamil Nadu, but for the average per capita health expenditure in the period 1990–2010 (see Table 10.8 and Figure 10.2). The average per capita health expenditure in Tamil Nadu was indeed higher compared to all-India. The average per capita health expenditure during 2005–06 to 2009–10 was Rs 382 in Tamil Nadu, and the corresponding all-India expenditure was Rs 302. However, what is significant in Tamil Nadu is the utilisation pattern and access to government health services. It is now argued that the implementation and utilisation of services matter more than actual expenditure on health in deciding outcomes (Sinha 2016). This is particularly evident if we look at the expenditure pattern where both the state and all-India move in tandem across time. An additional dimension explaining the better implementation of healthcare at the rural level is

Table 10.8 *Key Expenditure Details for Tamil Nadu and All-India (1990–2010)*

	1990–91 to 1994–95	1995–96 to 1999–2000	2001–01 to 2004–05	2005–06 to 2009–10
Per capita health expenditure in Rs (at 1999–2000 prices)				
Tamil Nadu	149.50	175.60	181.00	382.70
All-India	124.80	141.10	153.40	301.80
Health expenditure to total expenditure				
Tamil Nadu	5.33	5.50	2.78	0.82
All-India	5.03	4.90	2.75	0.95
Health expenditure to NSDP				
Tamil Nadu	1.07	0.99	0.87	0.97
All-India	1.02	0.95	0.86	1.04

Source: Reserve Bank of India (2011).

the reservation policy in professional education that the state has been practising. As a result, since the 1970s, higher professional education has become available to the middle castes and classes from district towns. Consequently, a cadre of doctors with roots in small towns and willing to work in PHCs in the villages has emerged in Tamil Nadu (Sinha 2012).

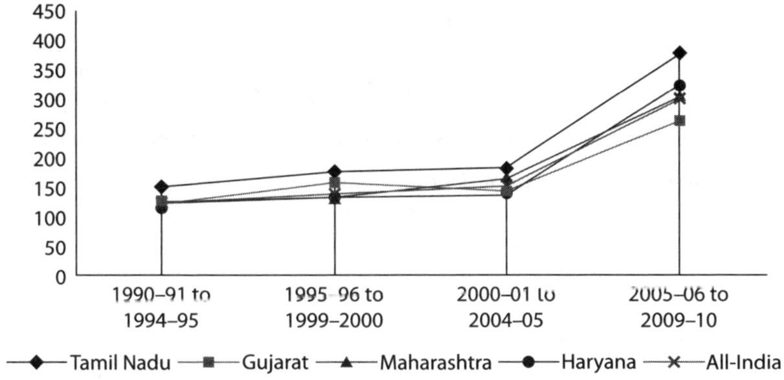

Figure 10.2 *Per Capita Health Expenditure (in Rs at 1999–2000 Prices), 1990–2010*

Source: Reserve Bank of India (2011).

An important aspect of Tamil Nadu's success in public health is the supply of free medicines in government-run health centres.[12] The state has set up an elaborate network consisting of a pharmaceutical corporation, the Tamil Nadu Medical Services Corporation (TNMSC), and a well-developed supply chain with computerised records to ensure affordable medicines to all.[13] The result of such measures is reflected in the secondary data. For instance, the National Sample Survey, 60th round (2004), indicates that the average expenditure a household incurred for hospitalisation in a government health facility was lower in Tamil Nadu. As shown in Figures 10.3 and 10.4, the expenditure per household incurred in availing hospitalisation in public health institutions in Tamil Nadu was Rs 637 in rural areas and Rs 1,666 in urban areas. The corresponding all-India figures were Rs 3,238 and Rs 3,877, respectively.

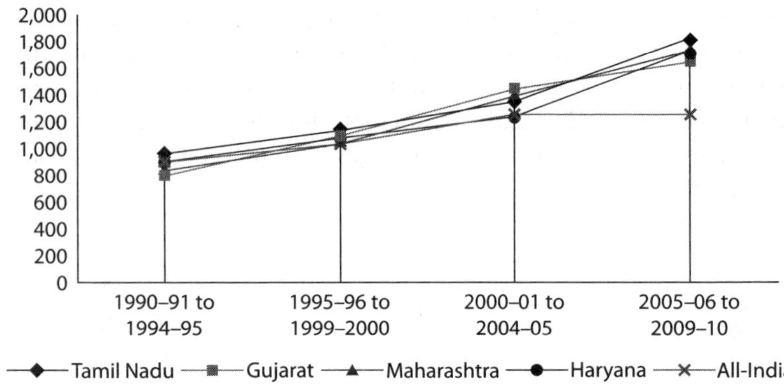

Figure 10.3 *Per Capita Social Expenditure (in Rs at 1999–2000 Prices), 1991–2010*

Source: Reserve Bank of India (2011).

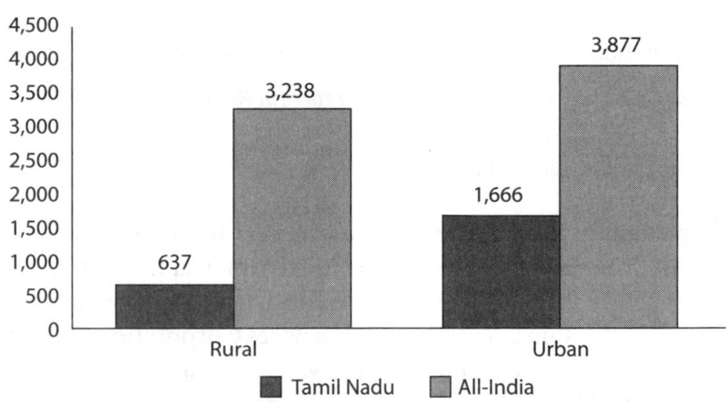

Figure 10.4 *Average Expenditure for Hospitalisation in Government Institutions in Tamil Nadu and All-India (in Rs), 2004*

Source: National Sample Survey (2004).

Further, Drèze and Sen (2013) show that the private costs of obtaining healthcare in public institutions are lower in Tamil Nadu as compared to other states; in the case of out-patient care in rural areas, the costs are actually zero. Similarly, loss of household income due to hospitalisation is the lowest in Tamil Nadu as compared to other states (National Sample Survey 2004). As is shown in Figure 10.5, the average loss of household income in Tamil Nadu in 2004 was Rs 369 in rural Tamil Nadu, while it was Rs 367 in urban Tamil Nadu. The corresponding all-India figures were Rs 636 and Rs 745, respectively, which is double of what households in Tamil Nadu incurred. Tamil Nadu also had a higher share of people going to government health facilities in both rural and urban areas compared to all-India. The presence of healthcare facilities does not by itself guarantee improved health outcomes; these facilities have to be used for them to influence health status (Goyal 2006). Better access and delivery of basic healthcare in Tamil Nadu, thus, needs to be located in the evolution of public health in the state.

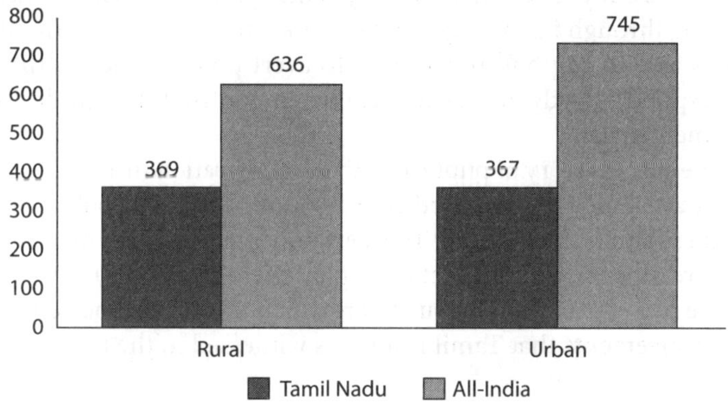

Figure 10.5 *Average Income Loss per Household for Hospitalisation in Tamil Nadu and All-India (in Rs), 2004*

Source: National Sample Survey (2004).

Public Health

It is widely recognised that good public health service is key in improving health outcomes. Tamil Nadu's improved performance in maternal and child care can be attributed to the efficient, well-functioning public health system in the state. The state has seen great improvements in measures such as MMR and IMR. Public health in Tamil Nadu has been appreciated by academics and policymakers in India, and it is being suggested as a model worth emulating in other states in the country (Basu 2010; Desikachari et al. 2010). It is also said that Tamil Nadu's success in public health lies mainly in efficiency gains, than the quantum of expenditure spent by the state. The efficient functioning of public health is often attributed to the organisational and functional structure of public health in Tamil Nadu. One of the key aspects of such organisational structure is the separation of public health from medical services. Public health professionals have to secure a public health qualification in addition to their medical degrees. It is important to note here that health is a state subject in the Indian Constitution. Therefore, it is the leadership at the state level that makes all the difference in the health system. Tamil Nadu has a Public Health Act in place.[14] Unlike in other states, where action is taken only after an outbreak in health disorder occurs, Tamil Nadu has successfully been maintaining anticipatory/preventive health planning through its management of public health services. The state, thus, is able to respond proactively to avert potential health threats, and respond quickly and effectively when confronted with disasters and emergencies.

The success story of public health administration in Tamil Nadu is usually attributed to organised coordination among the public health managers and technical staff. This certainly makes a contribution, but there are other significant factors at play. Mehrotra (2006) has argued that the real explanation for such performance has to be located in the social movements that Tamil Nadu has witnessed in the past century.

Conclusion

Tamil Nadu has introduced a series of universalistic social policies. As a result, the state has achieved socially inclusive outcomes in key development indicators. The rise of Dravidian parties in the state has brought in political regimes, which follow such populist policies. For electoral and other reasons, the regime has acquired a path-dependency in sustaining those policy measures. Hence, the state has become one of the few states that provides basic public services universally and in the most efficient way.

The history of these policies coincides with the DMK coming into power in the state. The poor get their entitlement fairly here. The caste groups that are placed at the bottom of the caste hierarchy get better access to basic services in the state. Tamil Nadu tops the states in the estimates of implicit subsidies. In addition to technical intervention, vigilant popular mobilisation from below has also contributed to the effective and transparent functioning of these services. As a result, the development indicators of lower castes in Tamil Nadu are much better even in comparison to those of the dominant caste groups in the rest of the country. Century-long reservation policies, both in education and profession, have helped many deprived caste groups access basic services and, hence, facilitated better social outcomes. If the populist political regimes are supported by broad-based social mobilisation, they can indeed bring in better social outcomes. The story of Tamil Nadu stands as an example.

Notes

[1] The Indian Constitution divides the legislative power between the centre and the states through three subject lists: the Union (central government) list, the state list and the concurrent list. States can enact legislation in areas such as agriculture, land and labour markets, water supply and sanitation and, most importantly, education and health (Panagariya, Chakraborty and Rao 2014). The states account for about 90 per cent of total government expenditure on education and health in India (Mehrotra and Panchamukhi 2006). The development expenditure incurred by the state governments has an impact on socioeconomic outcomes, particularly on poverty reduction in India (Dutt and Ravallion 2002).

[2] We have taken the PDS and health sectors for analysis here. Both these sectors are known for their universal coverage, good design and good implementation in the state. These sectors also have seen a range of innovative schemes and creative state intervention in implementation.

[3] There are other scholars too who take a similar position. For example, see Subramanian (1999).

[4] The state was indeed facing serious food crisis. The government could not deliver its promise. Instead of three measures of rice for a rupee, it could give one measure. These had serious implications for electoral outcomes.

[5] The policy on food supply was designed by the central government. The state government was dependent on the central pool for foodgrains, and permission of the central government was needed even if the state government had procured them from other states. Guided by its ideology of state autonomy, the DMK, thus, decided to establish TNCSC in 1972 to manage the foodgrain supply of the state.

[6] See http://www.tncsc.tn.gov.in/html/pds.htm (accessed 16 May 2014).

[7] For provision of public services in Tamil Nadu, see Srinivasan (2010).

[8] Ibid.

[9] The study was carried out by the PAC covering all the states in India to assess the performance of essential public services provided in each state. Opinions were collected from 37,000 households on five services such as drinking water, primary healthcare, primary education, PDS and public transport.

[10] The authors note that the relative success of Tamil Nadu in comparison to that of other states lies in a set of universal social policies, including universal PDS, integrated child development services (ICDS) and mid-day meals, that the state has been providing to its people. They also attribute the better performance of health systems to

robust administrative regulation and accountability, due to pressure from the below. For further details, see Drèze and Sen (2011).

[11] See Mehrotra (2006) for a detailed comparison in health performance of different caste groups between Tamil Nadu and Uttar Pradesh. The author locates the relative success of Tamil Nadu in the creative technical interventions by the state in public health and social mobilisation which has provided a conducive environment for such interventions to work better.

[12] The Planning Commission (2011: 10) expert group on universal health coverage too acknowledged the success of Tamil Nadu in providing essential drugs, and proposed to Government of India that 'an increase in the public procurement of medicines from around 0.1% to 0.5% of GDP would ensure universal access to essential drugs, greatly reduce the burden on private out-of-pocket expenditures and increase the financial protection for households'.

[13] The setting up of the TNMSC, a state-owned company, was seen as a key to ensure essential drugs at affordable price. The TNMSC built its procurement and distribution system on a well-designed IT architecture, ensuring a supply chain from manufacturer to warehouse to pharmacy and finally to the patient. For further details, see Basu (2010).

[14] The Act specifies the legal and administrative structures for the public health system in the state. It provides the framework of well-defined responsibilities to different government agencies within the structure with corresponding budget allocations.

References

Alamu, R. 2011. 'It Just Works in TN'. *The Hindu*, 24 September. Available at http://www.thehindu.com/features/magazine/it-just-works-in-tn/article2475948.ece (accessed 2 June 2014).

Basu, R. 2010. 'Leadership in the Health Sector: The Importance of the Tamil Nadu Model for a Universal Public Health Care System in India'. Annual Conference, Network of Asia Pacific Schools and Institutes of Public Administration and Governance (NAPSIPAG), New Delhi. Available at www.napsipag.org/pdf/d_ab_18.pdf (accessed 10 April 2015).

Desikachari, B. R., K. K. Datta, Monica Das Gupta, P. Padmanaban, Rajendra Shukla and T. V. Somanathan. 2010. 'How Might India's Public Health Systems Be Strengthened?: Lessons from Tamil Nadu'. *Economic and Political Weekly* 55(10): 46–60.

Drèze, Jean and Amartya Sen. 1991. *Hunger and Public Action*. New York: Oxford University Press.

——— 2011. 'Putting Growth in Its Place'. *Outlook*, 14 November.

——— 2013. *Uncertain Glory: India and Its Contradictions*. Princeton, New Jersey: Princeton University Press.

Drèze, Jean and R. Khera. 2013. 'Rural Poverty and the Public Distribution System'. *Economic and Political Weekly* 48(45–46): 55–60.

Dutt, G., and M. Ravallion. 2002. 'Has India's Post-reform Economic Growth Left the Poor Behind?'. *Journal of Economic Perspectives* 16(3): 89–108.

Evans, P., and P. Heller. 2014. 'Human Development, State Transformation and the Politics of the Developmental State'. In *The Oxford Handbook of Transformations of the State*, eds Stephan Leibfried, Frank Nullmeier, Evelyne Huber, Matthew Lange, Jonah Levy and John Stephens. UK: Oxford University Press.

Goyal, Sangeeta. 2006. 'Human Development in Tamil Nadu and Karnataka'. In *Reinventing Public Service Delivery in India*, ed. Vikram K. Chand, 294–332. New Delhi: Sage.

Harriss, Barbara. 1984. 'Meals and Noon Meals in South India: Food and Nutrition Policy in the Rural Food Economy of Tamil Nadu State'. Occasional paper no. 31, School of Development Studies, East Anglia.

Harriss, John. 1999. 'Comparing Political Regimes across Indian States'. *Economic and Political Weekly* 34(48), 27 November: 3367–77.

Heller, P., and P. Evans. 2010. 'Taking Tilly South: Durable Inequalities, Democratic Contestation, and Citizenship in the Southern Metropolis'. *Theory and Society* 39: 433–50.

Himanshu. 2011. 'Growth versus Redistribution'. *Live Mint*, 19 July.

International Institute for Population Sciences. 1994. 'National Family Health Survey 1992–93 (NFHS-1)'. Ministry of Health and Family Welfare, Government of India, Mumbai.

——— 2007. 'National Family Health Survey 2005–06 (NFHS-3)'. Ministry of Health and Family Welfare, Government of India, Mumbai.

——— 2010. 'District-level Household Survey 3 (DLHS-3) (2007–08)'. Ministry of Health and Family Welfare, Government of India, Mumbai.

——— 2017. 'National Family Health Survey 2005–06 (NFHS-3)'. Ministry of Health and Family Welfare, Government of India, Mumbai.

Joshi, Devin K., and Kathleen McGrath. 2015. 'Political Ideology, Public Policy and Human Development in India: Explaining the Gap between Gujarat and Tamil Nadu'. *Journal of Contemporary Asia* 45(3): 465–89.

Kapoor, Radhicka. 2012. 'Inequality Matters'. *Economic and Political Weekly* 48(2), 12 January: 58–65.

Khera, Reetika. 2011a. 'Trends in Diversion of Grain from the Public Distribution System'. *Economic and Political Weekly* 46(21), 21 May: 106–14.

——— 2011b. 'Revival of the Public Distribution System: Evidence and Explanations'. *Economic and Political Weekly* 46(45), 5 November: 36–50.

——— 2012. 'Tamil Nadu's Striking Progress in Welfare'. *India Together*, 10 September. Available at http://www.indiatogether.org/2012/sep/gov-tnwelfare.htm (accessed 3 June 2016).

Mehrotra, Santosh. 2006. 'Well-being and Caste in Uttar Pradesh: Why UP is Not Like Tamil Nadu'. Economic *and Political Weekly* 41(40), 7 October: 4261–71.

Mehrotra, Santosh and Parthasarthi R. Panchamukhi. 2006. 'Private Provision of Elementary Education in India: Findings of a Survey in Eight States'. *Journal of Comparative and International Education* 36(4): 421–42.

National Sample Survey. 2004. 'Morbidity, Health Care and the Condition of the Aged'. NSS, 60th round, report no. 507 (60/25.0/1). Ministry of Statistics and Programme Implementation, Government of India.

Panagariya, A., P. Chakraborty and G. Rao. 2014. *State Level Reforms, Growth, and Development in Indian States*. New Delhi: Oxford University Press.

Pandian, M. S. S. 2007. *Brahmin and Non-Brahmin: Genealogies of the Tamil Political Present*. New Delhi: Permanent Black.

Paul, S., S. Balakrishnan, G. T. Thampi, S. Sekhar and M. Vivekananda. 2006. *Who Benefits from India's Public Services?: A People's Audit of Five Basic Services*. New Delhi: Academic Foundation.

Planning Commission. 2011. 'High Level Expert Group Report on Universal Health Coverage for India'. Government of India, New Delhi.

Rajivan, Anuradha. 2006. 'Tamil Nadu: ICDS with a Difference'. *Economic and Political Weekly* 41(34), 26 August: 3684–88.

Registrar General of India. 2012. 'Sample Registration System Statistical Report'. Ministry of Home Affairs, Government of India, New Delhi.

Reserve Bank of India. 2011. 'State Finances. A Study of Budgets, 2010–11'. Government of India.

Sharma, Sandeep. 2012. 'Rich State with Poor Health: Disappointing Status of Public Health in Gujarat'. In *Poverty amidst Prosperity: Essays on the Trajectory of Development in Gujarat*, ed. Atul Sood, 199–213. New Delhi: Aakar.

Singh, P. 2015. 'Subnationalism and Social Development: A Comparative Analysis of Indian States'. *World Politics* 67(3): 506–62.

Sinha, Amarjeet. 2012. *An India for Everyone: A Path to Inclusive Development*. Noida: Harper Collins.

Sinha, Aseema. 2003. Rethinking the Developmental State Model: Divided Leviathan and Subnational Comparisons in India. *Comparative Politics* 35(4): 459–76.

Sinha, Dipa. 2016. *Women, Health and Public Services in India: Why are States Different?*. New York: Routledge.

Srinivasan, Vivek. 2010. 'Understanding Public Services in Tamil Nadu: An Institutional Perspective'. Ph.D dissertation, University of Syracuse, New York.

Subramanian, Narendra. 1999. *Ethnicity and Populist Mobilization: Political Parties, Citizens and Democracy in South India*. New Delhi: Oxford University Press.

Tilly, Charles. 1998. *Durable Inequality*. Berkeley: University of California Press.

Varshney, Ashutosh. 2012. 'Two Banks of the Same River?: Rising North–South Economic Divergence in India'. In *Anxieties of Democracy: Tocquevillean Reflections on India and the United States*, eds Partha Chatterjee and Ira Katznelson, 225–56. New Delhi: Oxford University Press.

Venkatasubramanian, A. K. 2006. 'The Political Economy of the Public Distribution System in Tamil Nadu'. In *Reinventing Public Service Delivery in India*, ed. Vikram K. Chand. New Delhi: Sage.

Vijayabaskar, M. 2010. 'Saving Agricultural Labour from Agriculture: SEZs and Politics of Silence in Tamil Nadu'. *Economic and Political Weekly* 45(6): 36–43.

_____ 2011. 'Global Crises, Welfare Provision and Coping Strategies of Labour in Tiruppur'. *Economic and Political Weekly* 46(22), 28 May: 38–46.

Viswanathan, Brinda. 2006. 'Access to Nutritious Meal Programmes: Evidence from 1999–2000 NSS Data'. *Economic and Political Weekly* 41(6), 11 February: 497–505.

Vythiyanathan, S., and R. K. Radhakrishnan. 2010. 'Behind the Success Story of Universal PDS in Tamil Nadu'. *The Hindu*, 10 August. Available at http://www.thehindu.com/opinion/op-ed/behind-the-success-story-of-universal-pds-in-tamil-nadu/article562922.ece (accessed 2 June 2014).

Wyatt, Andrew. 2013. 'Combining Clientelist and Programmatic Politics in Tamil Nadu, South India'. *Commonwealth and Comparative Politics* 51(1): 27–55.

11. Tenancy Reforms in Tamil Nadu

*A Study from the Cauvery Delta Region**

J. Jeyaranjan

Despite Tamil Nadu having emerged as a model state in recent years, it has often been critiqued for its poor implementation of land reforms. Despite passing of many laws, existing literature on these measures repeatedly highlight the enormous loopholes and poor implementation of the provisions of these laws (Ladejinsky 1972; Sonachalam 1970; Thorner 1973; Thangaraj 1995). Low levels of surplus-land identification, and vast proxy and *benami* holdings[1] of land have been observed (Badrinath 1972). How the big landlords floated bogus trusts/organisations to retain their surplus land

*This research was made possible with financial assistance from National Institute of Rural Development and Panchayati Raj (NIRD & PR). Professor Suman Chandra, Centre for Agrarian Studies and Disaster Mitigation, was a source of support and encouragement throughout this study. Professor D. Narasimmha Reddy gave valuable advice at various stages of this work. Dr Saravanan helped throughout my fieldwork. Dr Rukmani and Dr Gopinath too helped in various ways. Mr Darmaperumal skilfully processed the data. Mr Suresh and Mr Arivazhagan helped with word processing. The revenue department officials of the Thanjavur district at all levels cooperated in sharing the data. The registration department officials threw open the safe room for me to gather the land transfer data for the selected village. Mr Karthikeyan, Mr Arumugam, Mr Xaviour and Mr Srinivasan of the VP village spent enormous amounts of time providing the oral history of the various aspects of the village. Many respondents spent hours recollecting family history, especially relating to their land purchases and sales. Mr Murugaperuml, Mr Aarumugam, Mr V. Durairaj, Mr S. R. Venkatesan, G. R. Venugopal and Mr K. Ashok of the Palakurichi village were very helpful with long interviews to understand the changes in that village. I owe gratitude to all of them.

(Sivaprakasam 2009) and how laws led to landlords evicting their tenants are also documented (Gough 1989).

In this context, one would therefore naturally presume that landlordism would have thrived in its earlier form with high levels of tenancy and stiff rents, particularly in areas like the Cauvery delta region that has been noted for high incidence of tenancy. However, landlordism has declined in the delta in general and tenancy conditions have eased enormously. The power relation between the landlord and the tenant is completely reversed with the tenant enjoying certain powers to negotiate compensation for giving up the right to cultivate. How did this change in tenancy relations come about in the Cauvery delta? What were the processes at work that brought about such a change? We argue that mobilisations by the Communist Party and the Dravidian movement, the Dravidar Kazhagam in particular, have been critical to the creation of a culture of collective action and resistance to landlord power. Further, the coming to power of the Dravidian parties in 1967 created conditions for consolidating the power of the lower-caste tenants, who benefited both from a set of state initiatives launched by the DMK soon after its coming to power and the culture of collective action against Brahmin landlords. This chapter addresses these questions through careful empirical examination of land-transfer documents and primary fieldwork in one village in the western part of the delta, known for high levels of tenancy in the past, but at present dominated by farmer cultivators. The secondary data collected include landholding data from the revenue department to assess the present landholding pattern, tenancy data from the revenue department to assess the level of registered tenancy in that village and land-transfer data collected from the registration department for the period 1967–2014 to capture the change in the land ownership pattern. Primary information consisted of interviews various actors involved in the process of change, such as district and subdistrict revenue officials, temple officials, lawyers, political party office bearers, tenants and landlords across the delta, to construct a macro-picture of tenancy relations in the delta at present. In addition, a detailed questionnaire was administered to collect data from the tenancy households, followed by several detailed interviews in the village to understand the decline of tenancy in the case village.

Study Area

The Cauvery delta had evolved an elaborate agrarian relation over a very long time, as it is one of the oldest deltas. Another notable feature of the delta was the predominance of Brahmin land ownership, particularly in the upper part of the delta.[2] Land distribution in the delta was highly unequal with both large family-owned landed estates and Hindu temples and mutts owning vast tracts of land. Apart from direct cultivation, the landlords leased out their land to the tenants. There were various arrangements under which lands were leased out for cultivation. Such land tenure arrangements along with the *pannaiyal* relation[3] defined the agrarian relations of the Cauvery delta production system. Land tenure systems involved both fixed-rent (*kuthagai*) and share-cropping (*varam*) arrangements. Gough (1981: 47) found in 1952 that the tenant could get only 7 to 10 per cent of the produce as the net share after meeting all the expenses, in a village in the western delta.

In response to such unequal distribution and exploitative land relations, the Communist Party of India (CPI) formed the Agricultural Association in the district in 1943. The initial support for the party came from the untouchable labourers in the coastal delta, particularly from the Mannargudi and Thiruthuraipoondi taluks of the Thanjavur district, where they organised around issues of higher wages and protection of the rights of the tenants. The formal organisation of tenants began in the Thenparai village in the Thanjavur district in 1943. These Communist agitations were the main force propelling the government towards instituting first the Mayuram Agreement in 1948 and the Thanjavur Tenants and Pannaiyals Protection Act in 1952 (Gough 1981: 149–50). While the struggle between the landlords and the tenants and labourers was intensifying, the state tacitly supported the landlords. It used its police and judiciary to foist numerous false cases against the agitating members of the Kisan Sabha and its leaders (Menon 1979: 63). Despite Congress Party passing many resolutions in support of the tenants and agricultural labourers in various forums, none of them were implemented. Following a decision to abandon the militant struggles of the previous years and to contest the general elections, with support from the Dravidar Kazhagam, Communist Party won five seats in the Madras[4] assembly and one in the Lok

Sabha in Thanjavur out of a total of 12 Communist assembly seats and one Lok Sabha seat won in Tamil Nadu as a whole, in the elections held in 1952. The Community Party, thus, embarked on a long period of parliamentary democracy and peaceful trade-union struggles (Gough 1981: 150).

While the organisation grew in size, the focus was more on agricultural labour–related issues than on the issue of tenancy. Though the charter of demands included demands related to the security of tenancy rights and fair rents, actual struggles were organised more around wages and employment protection. While the struggle by the Left did result in some improvements in the lives of tenants, the legislations that were enacted to protect the tenants led to the ouster of a large number of them from the lands. A less-recognised aspect of mobilisation in the region is that undertaken by the Dravidar Kazhagam.

Role of Dravidar Kazhagam in Agrarian Struggles in Thanjavur

Even before the Communist Party found its roots in east Thanjavur, caste oppression of the Parayars and Pallars by the Brahminical order was challenged by Periyar. His virulent opposition to Brahminism (which was the ideological plank of landlordism) attracted the attention of a large number of peasants and workers in east Thanjavur. Dravidar Kazhagam was becoming increasingly popular. It was very strong in the Nagapattinam and Thiruvarur taluks, and in the coastal belt. The Dravidar Kazhagam formed the Dravidar Vivasaya Thozilalar Sangam (DVTS) (Dravidian Agricultural Workers Union) in 1952. The union had 15,000 Dalit agricultural workers and another 5,000 backward-caste workers as members in Nagapattinam area alone (Kasthurirangan 2013: 33). The union was stronger in the Kilvelur region with more than 50,000 members (ibid.: 36). The DVTS struggled for the rights of Dalit workers and, therefore, was in direct conflict with landlords. While in some places they unitedly struggled against the landlords, in others there were problems between the Communist and the Dravidar Kazhagam–led unions.

The fact that the Dravidian movement sought to undermine the hegemony of Brahminical power led to Periyar extending his support to the K. Kamaraj–led Congress government from the outside, as it was the first government to have a Shudra as the head. This decision, while it had political legitimacy at the level of the state, however, was contradictory to the conflicts at the local level in Thanjavur between the DVTS and the Congress-supporting land owners. When this conflict of interest was ignored by the Dravidar Kazhagam, the DVTS decided to function independent of the Dravidar Kazhagam and also to secede from it. Under these circumstances, the DVTS of Nagapattinam decided to merge with the Communist Party. The Communist Party welcomed the decision of DVTS, and the merger happened in the beginning of 1963. In fact, after the merger, the erstwhile secretary of DVTS's Nagapattinam unit was appointed as secretary of the Communist Party unit in Nagapattinam (ibid.: 6–57). While this led to further consolidation of the movement against Brahmin landlordism, the coming to power of the DMK decisively tilted the struggle in favour of tenants, both through the passing of a series of legislations and through a further consolidation of political power among the lower castes. The persistent struggle by the Left in east Thanjavur forced the government to bring about reforms in the laws that governed the welfare of the tenants.

Legislations Under the DMK Regime

To be sure, as stated earlier, several legislations were passed during the Congress period, such as the Thanjavur Tenants and Pannaiyals Protection Act 1952, the Tamil Nadu Cultivating Tenant's Protection Act 1955 and the Tamil Nadu Cultivating Tenants (Payment of Fair Rent) Act 1956, to address issues of rent control and security of tenure. Further, the Tamil Nadu Land Reforms (Fixation of Ceiling of Land) Act 1961 allowed a family with five members to hold no more than 30 standard acres.

The DMK was responsible for passing the Tamil Nadu Cultivating Tenants (Special Provisions) Act 1968 that allowed for payment of rental arrears in easy instalments, thus easing the process of paying rent for the tenants. It also opened a window for the tenant to buy time in paying the rent. The landlords had to wait and could not push the tenants for their rent. The earlier tenancy protection Acts were not effective, as there was no registration of tenants. It became a huge task for tenants to prove their case in revenue courts and in other judicial forums. The DMK government brought about a law to rectify this lacuna in the existing tenancy protection laws. The Tamil Nadu Agricultural Lands (Record of Tenancy Rights) Act 1969 provided for the registration of tenants. A register of tenants was prepared for each village by the revenue officials of the taluk. The list was gazetted and the tenant was issued a document conferring the tenancy. In theory, this document provided a legal right to the tenant and to pay a fair rent.

An important aspect of the law was that it did not insist on any documentary evidence from the tenant to confer the tenancy right. Local inquiries, oral evidences and depositions by the neighbouring cultivators were sufficient evidences to include a tenant's name in the register of tenants. The Left unions printed thousands of required applications and distributed them among tenant farmers in the district. This effort resulted in the registration of more than 100,000 tenant farmers as tenants under this Act (Veeraiyan 2011: 15). Nearly 5 lakh tenants and about 7 lakh acres of land were registered in tenants' names in the Thanjavur district under this law (Sivaprakasam 2009: 73).

The Land Reform Act was amended in 1970, bringing down the ceiling from 30 standard acres to 15 standard acres. The rate of compensation for the surplus land was also drastically reduced (Gough 1989: 24). Tenancy Act amendments in 1979 reduced rent further to 25 per cent and protected tenants against eviction, even if they fail to pay rent during natural calamities. Another important legislation that gave enormous foothold to the tenants and agricultural labourers was the Conferment of Ownership of Homestead Act 1971. Anyone living in a homestead belonging to someone else or on land belonging to the government as on 19 June 1971 was conferred ownership absolutely free from all encumbrances. This important legislation freed the landless from the control of the landlords. Next year, in 1972, the government of Tamil Nadu passed another legislation that waived all the rental arrears of the tenants.

Three other important legislations were passed in the assembly but did not get presidential assent. One bill gave the right to the tenant to purchase the rented land by paying 12 times the fair rent to the owner, and the payment could be made in instalments. If the tenant was paying a lump sum, it was enough that they paid 75 per cent of the purchase price as a consideration. Most of the religious mutts objected to this legislation and presented their case to the Union government and the president. The bill was never returned to the state and, therefore, the legislation never saw the light of day. Two other legislations, which tried to declare void the transactions that had taken place in the immediate past prior to the passing of the legislation, also never saw the light of day at Rashtrapati Bhavan in New Delhi.

Tenancy in Western Delta in 1976

Gough (1989) revisited Kumbapettai in 1976 and documented the changes in land ownership, tenancy arrangements and various other socioeconomic aspects of the agrarian society. It is evident from her account that the ownership pattern of land has changed significantly in Kumbapettai. The Brahmins from within the village have lost land quite rapidly, from 32 per cent of its cultivable land to 9 per cent in 1976, while the non-resident Brahmins have held on to nearly 21 per cent of the total cultivable land. During this time, the SCs have, in fact, lost land, going down from 3.4 per cent in 1952 to 0.2 per cent in 1976 (ibid.: 84). Merchants from outside have bought more land in Kumbapettai while the small traditional non-cultivating landlords and tenants have lost their land. The rate of rent was the same in 1976 as it was in 1952 for unregistered tenants without tenancy documents. However, those who got protection through registration paid only 36 *kalams*[5] per acre per year. Thus, apart from protecting tenants from eviction, the law ensured fair rent for the tenants. Moreover, at the time of distress, registered tenants could benefit from rent remissions, whereas the unregistered tenants were left to the mercy of the landlords (ibid.: 293).

While nearly half of the land leased out in Kumbapettai, where the Left had no presence, was registered, the fact that registration was so poor in Kirippur, where there was a strong peasant union, is another aspect which remains unexplained in Gough's work. Her discussion about the activities of the Left parties in the village is entirely on struggles for better wages and work conditions. There is no discussion on tenancy relations, which goes to suggest that the Left unions seem to have directed little or no effort towards tenancy relations.

Differences in Tenancy Conditions in Eastern and Western Delta

K. Gough, in her work, explored the differences in the agrarian structure in the western and eastern delta. This was further explored by Bouton (1980). He marshals evidence and argues that there was polarisation of the institution of tenancy in Thanjavur: '... there was improvement in the status of tenants who were already relatively powerful *vis-à-vis* the landlord, and deterioration in the status of tenants who were relatively powerless *vis-à-vis* the landlord' (ibid.: 223). The Non-Brahmin Movement piloted by Periyar gained strength during 1920–45 (Irschick 1969; Barnett 1976). The movement had weakened the power of the Brahmins in the villages in the delta. With the gains made through kuthagai cultivation, the political capital provided by the spreading Non-Brahmin Movement, the non-Brahmin tenants were turning out to be more assertive.

M. Bouton, with the support of other studies and data, argued that the tenants in the western delta were in a stronger position in relation to their landlords. Therefore, they could negotiate from strength and negotiated better deals.

The DMK, which had captured power in the state in 1967, wanted to build a strong base among the agricultural workers and peasants in the Thanjavur district, particularly in east Thanjavur. Karunanidhi, who hails from the heartland of east Thanjavur, became the president of the DMK and chief minister of Tamil Nadu in 1969, and he made conscious efforts to break into the strongholds of the Communist Party in the district. Finding a firm foothold for his party among the peasants and agricultural labourers was on top of his agenda. Apart from bringing in legislations which would benefit the agricultural labourers and tenants, he realised that Dalits held the key to this political segment in the delta. The Left parties had organised Dalit workers, and were known as the Pallar/Parayar party in the past. He saw to it that the DMK party secretary of the district in the eastern delta was always a Dalit. It is evident that he succeeded in his efforts, as he contested from Thiruvarur constituency in the 2016 assembly elections and won with the highest margin in the state. Hence, the party mobilised people on the ground that led to their greater empowerment along with legislative policies around concerns of the tenants and agricultural labourers.

An important law enacted by the DMK was the Tenancy Land Record Act of 1969. It was an important step that strengthened the tenants in their negotiations against the landlord. DMK appointed a select committee of the legislative assembly and sought the views of the landlords and tenants. The process of preparing the tenant register was liberalised. The presiding officers visited the village and held public hearings to record the leaseholders in the register. The sub-tenants were also to be recorded as tenants. The initiative to record the tenancy right was to originate from the tenant. There was an amendment to the Act in 1972 which authorised the record officer to conduct inquiries *suo moto*. The number of revenue courts was increased from two to five. The 1972 legislation wrote off all rent arrears that were due till 30 June 1971. In 1973, the DMK government introduced a law that gave the tenant the right to purchase all or part of the land not exceeding five standard acres. Simultaneously, the landlord could resume self-cultivation on half of the leased out land not exceeding five standard acres. The law also had provisions for making payment in instalments and fixed the price based on fair rent.

All these legislations led to 'the "bifurcation" of tenants into "high-end" and "low-end" sectors, based on subtle but important distinctions in the terms and conditions of tenancy, caste status and political climate, all of which contributed to important differences in the quality of landlord-tenant relationship' (Bouton 1980: 258). Thus, the ascendency of the DMK to power led to refinements and innovations to laws, which empowered the tenants and agricultural labourers in important ways. Registration of tenancy, remission of rent, more revenue courts, and provisions to buy leased-in land and conferment of ownership title over the homestead increased the negotiating position of the tenants manifold.

Ascendancy of DMK to Power and Change in Village Power Relations

It was noted in an earlier section that at one point of time, the Dravidar Kazhagam–led labour union was very strong in east Thanjavur. Subsequently, most of the tenants and agricultural labourers drifted towards the Left unions. The DMK was in its infancy at that time, but it gained enormous foothold very rapidly and grew in strength in other parts of the state, including in the western delta. Since 1962, most of the constituencies in the western delta were returning DMK candidates to the assembly. However, it took the party some time to spread to the inner parts of the eastern delta. Very soon, by a combination of policy interventions and organisational acumen, it spread its wings in the eastern delta. To begin with, it got cadres from its parent organisation, the Dravidar Kazhagam. Subsequently, it broke the strongholds of the CPI and Communist Party of India (Marxist) [CPI(M)]. Two prominent members of legislative assembly (MLAs) from CPI joined the DMK in the mid-1970s. Such poaching by DMK continued unabated at the lower levels. When the AIADMK was formed, it also started gaining strength in the delta, but not as much as the DMK. The DMK, which contested alone in the 1977 assembly elections, won the second largest number of seats from the Thanjavur district, next only to Chennai city. The delta continuously returned more numbers of DMK MLAs in all the subsequent elections, except during waves like those seen during the 1991 assembly elections immediately after the assassination of Rajiv Gandhi. However, the AIADMK also started gaining strength in the delta districts and, as of now, both DMK and AIADMK bag all the assembly seats between themselves.

The dominance of the two parties coincided with the growing power of the backward castes. The Kallars, a dominant backward caste in the western delta, have been the office bearers in both the parties (AIADMK and DMK) in the district from 1967 onwards. They have been the ministers representing the district, except in one or two instances. The dominance of this caste in both the Dravidian parties reflects in the polity at the village level. More importantly, the state bureaucracy and police are at their command. Consequently, they have a huge presence in the dispute settlement mechanism. Other landed castes in the old delta resent the dominance of the Kallars. Even within the political parties, the caste politics orchestrated by the Kallars is very pronounced. As a result, Brahmins within agriculture have found controlling the tenant and the agricultural labour through caste superiority increasingly difficult.

Tenancy in Cauvery Delta: The Contemporary Macro-picture

The most prominent feature of tenancy today in the delta as compared to the past is the complete decline of Brahmin dominance in most of the villages. Brahmins have lost their land either through sale or through appropriation by the lower-caste tenants.

There was a general consensus among the respondents who were interviewed in this study about landlordism in Thanjavur. All of them opined that landlordism is a relic of the past and that the Communist and Dravidian parties have successfully fought against it. The benami holders, who were entrusted with the land fearing land-ceiling laws, could easily get away and, thus, many landlords lost their lands further. Most of the landlord families experienced emigration of their next generation to urban jobs. All these factors combined and resulted in the decline of landlordism in general in the district. It was surprising to see that some of the landlords, classified as quite aggressive by an activist in the 1960s and 1970s, were living on modest means during our field visits. Only a few have managed to retain a part of the landed estate intact.

Apart from individual landlords, religious *matams* (Hindu monastic establishments) and temples owned vast tracts of land and all these lands were necessarily cultivated by tenants. Earlier, the matams and temples were as oppressive as the individual landlords. While the landlords have lost considerable power due to law, politics and social changes, what the status of these religious institutions is regarding the tenancy arrangements is discussed in the following section.

Near-ownership of Temple Lands

It was noted earlier that the temples and mutts owned vast tracts of land and were exempted by all land reform legislations. However, the Tenancy Protection Act protects the tenants of these lands. In the course of interviews with tenants, the following narratives emerged.

Uthirapathy, a Mutharayar by caste (a most-backward caste) cultivates 1.5 acres of land owned by Sri Brahmma Gnaneswara Swami Temple of Kovilur. He is a fourth-generation tenant. Earlier, the rent for the land was 11 bags of paddy per acre per annum. When he filed a petition in the revenue court, the court ordered a payment of five bags of paddy per acre per annum. He has been paying this rent for the past 11 years to the temple. The land is fit for raising only one crop in a year, as there is no ground water. Canal water is available for only five months in a year and, hence, only one crop can grow. He was able to register the land under the Tenancy Act only during the time of special officers. Otherwise, the Kallars, the dominant backward caste group in the region and the village, are usually appointed as trustees to this temple. They would not have allowed the registration of tenancy during their time. The Kallars, as trustees, force tenants from other lower castes to pay the rent regularly but cannot force fellow Kallars to pay rent. In the neighbouring village of Nallavanniyan Kudikadu, this temple owns more than 70 acres of land. The Kallars from that village are the tenants and none of them pays any rent to the temple, and the Kallar trustees of the temples never attempt to collect rent from Kallar tenants of that village. The trustees do not even try the legal course to collect the rent, nor are they able to retrieve the land.

Since the land is registered, Uthirapathy, the tenant, says that he can exchange the land, pledge it or even sell it at the market rate. The registration will remain in his name. The buyer can enjoy the land but does not have the alienable right in law. Generally, eviction of a tenant from temple lands is next to impossible. There are so many legal provisions to protect a tenant, and plenty of opportunities are provided by law. This is the reason why the rent arrears to temples, mutts and other such establishments run to several crores in the state. Even if they manage to get a favourable verdict, the eviction of a tenant is impossible and finding another tenant still more difficult. The reason is that there is a social consensus about the right of the tenant over cultivation rights. This consensus is all-pervasive.

Futility of Court Directions

Our research team came across several cases where the land owner, after a prolonged litigation, may have got a favourable verdict to evict the tenant for non-payment of rent over a long period of time. Such verdicts remain on paper and can hardly be enforced. Taking physical possession of the land, particularly in another village, proves impossible. The tenant gets the support of other cultivators. They threaten the land owner that the land cannot be cultivated without their cooperation and support. Irrigation without the cooperation of other land owners is impossible. Similarly, the crop cannot be protected from the marauding cattle if fellow land owners do not cooperate. The land owner cannot even sell the property to others. Potential buyers also face the same boycott and threat from local land owners. The local land owners will join together and prevent the owner from entering the land. If the land owner approaches the police for protection, the police in turn will advise negotiating a settlement with the tenant rather than assuming the judicial route. This reversal of power is best illustrated in the case of Venugopal Iyyer of VP, the village selected for our study, who leased out eight acres of land in the neighbouring village to a Pallar tenant. The tenant had not payed any rent for six years and no cajoling could persuade him to do so. Iyyer went to various courts and got an eviction order. Using his high-level connections, he got the support of the police. Despite such marshalling of his connections, he could never enter the field, nor could he sell the land to anybody. Finally, he gave up and emigrated to Tiruchirappalli. The tenant continued to enjoy the land. His fellows from the same caste supported him and told the police that if they forced the issue, they would face a huge law-and-order issue. The police quietly withdrew from the scene and advised Iyyer to negotiate a deal with the Pallars.

Innumerable such cases are cited as evidence of the power of the tenants and the risks associated with leasing out land throughout the Cauvery delta. What has empowered the tenants? Apart from formal rules that can be flouted on the ground as we saw earlier, there are informal conventions fostered by collective mobilisation in the region that sustains the power of the tenants.

Uzhavadai Pathyadai (Right to Cultivate) to the Tenant

The law protects the tenant from eviction under normal circumstances. However, a convention has evolved throughout the delta whereby the tenant has the right to cultivate. The right is unconditional. If the tenant has to give up that right, then a compensation is due to the tenant. The minimum compensation is one-third of the land that the tenant had been cultivating. Once the landlord settles one-third of the land or its money value on the tenant, the tenant gives up the right over the rest of the lands.

All mediations in the disputes between a landlord and the tenant have this convention as the basis. If the landlords are powerful, they can reclaim two-thirds of the land by giving up ownership rights over one-third of the land. The share of the tenant is inversely related to the power of the landlord. At the extreme, the tenant will not give a cent of land if the landlord is a non-resident and does not have any caste power within the village. Thus, the caste and power of the tenant and the landlord define the outcome of the negotiation. Registered tenants hardly give up without compensation. Unregistered tenants have an equal right by convention and this convention is quite pervasive. Thus, while the law has protected only against the eviction of tenants, the convention has bestowed a compensation for the tenant.

Thus, dispute resolution is a complex process with several layers of power-play. This is particularly true of the landlord–tenant disputes, and the right of the tenant to cultivate has come to stay as a norm throughout the district. Many Left leaders have claimed credit for this 'law', which has been firmly established and widely invoked to ascertain the right of the tenant. Many studies that have attempted to evaluate the land reform legislations in Tamil Nadu have failed to capture the operational part of his unwritten law, which is not found in any legislation. Because of the implementation and acceptance of this unwritten law, the institution of tenancy has definitely declined in the Cauvery delta.

The political power enjoyed by the backward castes and the new assertion by the Dalits have all combined to stabilise the *de facto* right of the tenants. As a result, rent has fallen steeply over time. Non-payment of rent over a long period of time cannot be penalised in most cases. The inability to enforce the court directives, which are difficult to implement, has emboldened the tenants. It is, therefore, not surprising when K. Balakrishnan, the leader of the peasant wing of the state unit of the CPI(M) opined that tenancy is a dead issue in the delta. No tenant from the district raises the issue of tenancy protection anymore in party forums. So much so, that when it was suggested in the All-India Kisan Sabha meeting that the tenancy question could be taken up, Balakrishnan rejected the suggestion on the ground that it was a non-issue in the delta.[6]

Thus, a combination of historical, political and social factors has led to the decline of landlordism in the Cauvery delta and tenancy has become a non-issue. How this combination works in a concrete way is important in understanding the outcomes of these macro-processes.

Decline in Tenancy in the Cauvery Delta: A Micro-study of VP

For a micro-level study, we selected VP, a village in the western delta, a region in which existing studies indicate the predominance of Brahmins as landlords. Initially, we attempted to select a village that had been studied earlier. However, a preliminary visit to the village studied by Gough (Kumbapettai being a pseudonym) indicated that the entire system had changed beyond recognition and the current residents had little knowledge about the past. Scouting for a suitable village in the western delta, we narrowed upon the VP village that had a sizeable Brahmin population that continued to be in agriculture. Importantly, tenancy had transformed predominantly into owner cultivation by the lower castes, replacing tenancy cultivation for Brahmin landlords.

We were also able to provide details about the past. Importantly, the office assistant of the local revenue office, who was in his late fifties, was still in service. He is a native of the village and had served the department's village office since 1970. He was a crucial informer who could later provide a link to the past from the present-day revenue records, as well as the land transfer data collected from the registration department.

We listed all the houses followed by a detailed survey undertaken among the identified tenants in both the villages. However, we focused more on the status of tenancy arrangement in the delta. The research team wanted to map this process in VP, as it had a high level of tenancy at one point and much of the land had been transferred to lower-caste men. We used the tenancy register to get the list of tenants and traced the changes in ownership of such lands over time. With the help of the revenue official and other informed persons in the village, we tried to map the process of land transfer at the level of the individual.

Physical Features of VP

VP is on the north bank of the Cauvery river, 16 km downstream and east of Grand Anicut. The village is bound by Cauvery in the south and the Kollidam river in the north. Kollidam is a massive drainage system that takes the surplus water of the Cauvery and saves the delta during floods. The natural gradient from the south to the north enables quick and sufficient flows in the channels that take off from Cauvery and irrigate the fields in VP. Given its location in the upper reaches of the delta, which ensures early flow of water, and the soil type, which absorbs and stores water in the sub-soil, the water table is very good. The scope for ground-water irrigation enables cropping throughout the year. VP has more than 200 shallow tube wells fitted with a large number of electric pump sets. Since electricity is free for agriculture, irrigation is not an issue in VP. The normal crop pattern is two paddy crops (from June to February) and a summer crop of either oil seeds or pulses. Cultivation is highly mechanised with hardly any manual labour except in a few operations like ploughing. VP, however, is dominated by numerous smaller holdings.

Social History of VP

Smarta Brahmins were the dominant land owners. They were living in an exclusive habitation of two streets. The Kallars (OBCs) were their tenants and farm servants. They lived on a separate street. The Parayars and Pallars (both SCs) were the permanent farm servants of the landlords. There were few carpenters and blacksmiths serving the village apart from other service castes. All the village artisans and the service-caste folks were paid in grain during harvest in return for their services.

Taking to formal education early, Brahmins emigrated in search of urban employment all over the country. There were many Iyyers who were identified by the city where they lived in North India, or by the companies that they were working for. There were numerous such Iyyer names in the land registration documents and revenue records. They leased out their lands on a fixed rent when they migrated out of the village in search of employment. They either collected the rent in person or entrusted the task to their relatives. Some of them leased their lands to the Pannaiyals (permanent servants from the SC) or their *kariakarans* (managers from the Kallar caste). Apart from the migrant land owners, local Brahmin land owners also rented out their land. However, there were a few families who cultivated their land directly with the help of permanent farm servants from the SCs.

Importantly, VP has not witnessed the rapid out-migration of all the Brahmins of the kind that happened in other Brahmin villages in the delta. Some of the large land owners have stayed back, or at least one or two members of their families have. Similarly, the *agraharams* (secluded habitation of Brahmins) are not deserted completely, though they do not remain exclusive anymore. While the smaller agraharam has only one Brahmin house, the larger agraharam has a mix of both Brahmin and non-Brahmin houses. The remaining Brahmins have land and cultivate it directly. In that sense, VP has not converted entirely into a non-Brahmin village from a Brahmin village. Some of the remnants of the past are still there with sizeable Brahmin land owners, and their streets, houses, temples and festivals.

Migration of Brahmins in Search of Employment

Migration for work among Brahmins increased from the 1960s onwards when the anti-Brahmin movement gained enormous strength along with DMK's coming to power. The Kallars and Pallars became very assertive. The Pallars started contesting the local elections and the VP Brahmins were openly challenged for the first time. A Pallar contested and won the village election, defeating a Brahmin landlord in the late 1960s. The Brahmin landlord had vast tracts of land in the village as well as outside, and all his brothers were either in Chennai or Delhi with connections in the judiciary, legislation, central secretariat, etc. The local panchayat election clearly indicated the shifting power. The 1963 election to the assembly returned a local school teacher, a Kallar, who was nominated by the DMK. For the first time, a person with humble resources could win against an opponent with money bags. Several DMK MLAs had similar ordinary backgrounds. Tea-shop owners, cycle mechanics, barbers, carpenters and so many others were elected. For the first time, political power went from the elite to the downtrodden. The opponent of the Kallar school teacher was a big landlord supported by all the Brahmins in the village. The Kallars came to occupy the assembly seat as well as the panchayat union chairmanship. They became district secretaries of the DMK, AIADMK, Congress and other parties. Thus, a Kallar network came to power in all public spheres in the late 1960s, and this dominance continues even today. However, the Pallars did not get such political power. But as a militant caste, they could break free from the hold of the Brahmins rather easily and emerge as an independent economic and social group in the village. The laws introduced by the new DMK government too protected the tenants from eviction and gave complete ownership of homestead land. The material foundation of the social order built up by Brahmins by owning and controlling the land was shaken. As a numerical minority and without their socially approved superordinate position, their power diminished.

Changes in Tenancy Relations in VP

A fixed-rent system of kuthagai was widely adopted in VP given its assured irrigation. Crop failures were rare and the yield was also better in VP compared to most parts of the Cauvery delta. The tenants were regular in paying rent to the landlords. Over time, backed by political mobilisation and the coming to power of the DMK, tenants started asserting their right to cultivate the lands. The widespread practice of demanding a compensation for vacating the land under tenancy came into practice on a much larger scale in VP. As Brahmins did not have any support, either on their own or from the outside, they could hardly reclaim their land. At best, they could pay compensation and reclaim the land leased out only to sell it to others. Under these circumstances, they started selling the land to the tenant or to anybody whom the tenant suggested. A substantial part of the money went to the tenant. Whatever came to the legal owner was a windfall. Many of them sold their houses and quit VP for good. Brahmins are, therefore, no longer the dominant land owners in VP at present. The erstwhile tenants, the Kallars and Pallars, have gained the land from the Brahmins and the Brahmins have lost their land to a significant extent.

Land Distribution Pattern in VP, 2014

The study team collected land revenue records for VP from the revenue department and identified each title by the caste of the titleholder and the operational category (owned or rented in). An analysis of the data indicates that 76 per cent of the land in the village was owner-operated, whereas about 23.4 per cent was operated by tenants in 2014 (Table 11.1).

Table 11.1 Distribution of Land in VP across Types (2014)

Type	No. of titles	Percentage	Extent (in hectares)	Percentage
Government	8	1.30	1.31	0.37
Own	495	81.40	263.93	75.90
Tenants	104	17.10	81.65	23.40
Temple	1	0.10	0.80	0.20
Total	608	100.00	347.69	100.00

Source: Government of Tamil Nadu (2014).

In terms of titles, about 81 per cent were ownership titles and 17 per cent were operated by tenants. The data have been disaggregated by caste, and also exclude the government land and the land on which a temple is located. Lands belonging to temples are leased out and, hence, are identified as lands operated by tenants.

In 2014, the Kallars operated about 62 per cent of the land in VP, followed by the SCs, who operated about 22 per cent of the land (Table 11.2). The Iyyers, who owned almost the entire land in the past, operated only about 10 per cent of the land. The other castes had negligible land. The titles (*pattas*) are distributed in the same pattern across these caste groups. The largest share of owned land was with the Kallars, followed by the Iyyers.

Table 11.2 Distribution of Land by Caste in VP (2014)

Caste	No. of pattas	Percentage	Extent (in hectares)	Percentage
Aasari	4	0.60	1.44	0.42
Iyyer	55	9.20	82.60	9.40
Kallar	386	64.30	214.41	62.10
Naidu	3	0.50	1.31	0.37
Pillai	18	3.00	18.89	5.50
SC	132	22.00	76.01	22.10
Thevar	2	0.30	0.93	0.26
Total	600	100.00	345.57	100.00

Source: Government of Tamil Nadu (2014).

While the law on land reforms failed to identify the surplus lands, acquire it and then redistribute it among the landless, the specially enacted state law empowered the tenants in the delta to evolve a compensation system. This, in turn, led to the transfer of land from the landlords to the erstwhile tenants.

The resultant land transfer from the upper to the lower castes can be understood better with an analysis of the data relating to registered land sales in the village. Land registration data can indicate only the transfer of land (the extent, claimant, executioner and the date of registration), but the nature of transfer needs to be gathered independently. We noted that the land transfer did not take place as a pure market transaction. There were several types of transfers. Tenants asserted their rights and were compensated at different levels. This was one type of transaction. In fact, there are many entries in the register which explicitly state that the deal between the tenant and the landlord was for the tenant to give up the right to cultivate, after being compensated with money or a portion of land. While such transfers can easily be identified, there are other kinds of transfers that require further queries to establish the nature of transfer. A tenant will buy the entire land leased out, at half of the market rate. Or a tenant may arrange for the sale of the land and take a substantial part of the sale proceeds. All such transfers take place under the tenancy hold and the tenant benefits immensely out of such sale proceeds, which in turn is the tenant's compensation. Such deals need to be mapped to classify different types of land transfers in the village.

The research team collected the land transfer data for VP from 1967 to 2014 from the registration department. Discussions in the field both in VP and in other places indicated that the ascendency of DMK to power in 1967 and the Tenancy Act of 1968 were the important milestones in the land transfer history of VP and the delta in general. Land transfers would have taken place earlier. But the specific types of transfers from the landlords to the tenants could have started only since 1967, as the legislation came into effect around that time and the empowerment of the non-Brahmins was symbolised by the DMK rule since 1967. The social norm of compensating the tenant evolved around this time. Hence, 1967 was chosen as the base year. After collecting the land transfer data from the registration department, the transactions regarding mortgages, family attachments, acquisitions and housing sites were weeded out from the database. Finally, only the land sale and settlement transactions related to tenancy were retained. Subsequently, qualitative data were recorded about each of these transfers regarding the castes of the executioner and the claimant, along with the types of transfer. Very broadly, the transfers were identified as market transfers and tenancy-related transfers. Through this process, we were able to arrive at a social map of land transfer in VP between 1967 and 2014 by superimposing the qualitative data on data from the registration department. The discussion in the following section focuses on such land transfers.

Land Loss for the Iyyers and Land Gains for the Lower Castes

The land transfer register has 786 entries on sale and settlement for tenancy in VP between 1967 and 2014. Altogether, 570.99 acres of land have changed hands between these two points of time.

Which castes have gained land over time and which castes have lost land? There is a need to analyse the net transfers to understand this. The Iyyers executed more sale deeds than purchase deeds. Similarly, the Pillais had a negative net transaction. Both the Kallars and SCs purchased more number of times than they registered sales (Table 11.3). In terms of area, the Iyyers have sold 197 acres of land over what they had purchased (Table 11.4). 'Other' castes also sold more than what they purchased.

Table 11.3 *Net Transfers in Land Transactions among Various Castes in VP (1967–2014)*

Caste	No. of purchases	No. of sales	Net
Iyyer	136	417	–281
Kallar	437	234	203
SC	161	77	84
Pillai	8	17	–9
Others	44	41	3
Total	786	786	0

Source: Government of Tamil Nadu (1967–2014).

Table 11.4 Net Transfers in Extent of Land in VP (1967–2014)

Caste	Extent of purchase (in acres)	Extent of sale (in acres)	Net (in acres)
Iyyer	124.84	322.31	−197.47
Kallar	308.44	167.94	140.50
SC	101.54	48.23	53.51
Pillai	20.65	7.28	13.37
Others	15.52	25.18	−9.66
Total	570.99	570.99	0

Source: Government of Tamil Nadu (1967–2014).

In sharp contrast, the net gain for the Kallars was 140 acres and the net gain for SCs during this period was 53 acres. This pattern of net gain holds good for the Pillais as well. Land has been thus moving from the landlord and 'other' castes to former tenants and agricultural labourers during 1967–2014 in VP.

When we look into the pattern of sales and purchases in VP across important caste groups, we find that 52 per cent of the sale deeds executed by Brahmins were in favour of the Kallars. Another one-fifth of the transactions of Iyyers were in favour of SCs. Nearly 23 per cent of the sale deeds executed by the Iyyers went in favour of intracaste transfers (Iyyer–Iyyer).

However, transactions executed by the Kallars were predominantly intracaste. Nearly three-fourths of the sale deeds executed by Kallars were in favour of fellow Kallars. About one-tenth went in favour of SCs and Iyyers. Thus, while the Kallars were buying land from the Iyyers, they were also buying from among their caste members. The Kallars were thus consolidating their landholding. A similar pattern is discernible among SCs but it is not as pronounced as it was among Kallars. Nearly half the number of sales of land by SCs was to their fellow SCs. About one-third of their transactions were in favour of the Kallars and about one-fifth in favour of Iyyers.

It is clear from the analysis of the land transfer data that land was acquired by the Kallars and SCs from the Iyyers between 1967 and 2014 in VP. The Iyyer land owners sold their land to their tenants or to some other buyer arranged by the tenant after receiving some money which was lower than the market rate. In some cases, they had to part with a portion of the leased-out land as compensation. Thus, tenancy was a means of acquiring land for the non-Brahmin tenants.

Land transfer data, thus, can be broadly classified into (i) market sale land and (ii) sale of lands that were rented out to tenants. The oral history collected from various persons in the village informed this identification. While some information was available from the Kallars and the SCs, the revenue assistant, who is from the village and who had been serving the department, and has been charge of revenue collections for a long time, helped us with information about the nature of such land transfers.

When the research team looked into the number of sale deeds executed, they found that about 70 per cent of transactions were market-based transactions. The remaining 30 per cent were transactions between the landlords and tenants. When disaggregated by caste, it emerged that 45 per cent of the transactions executed by Iyyers was between the landlords and their tenants. They could manage only 55 per cent transactions under market conditions. However, among the Kallars and SCs, the market transaction was much higher at 91 and 83 per cent, respectively. Even the tenant transactions executed by them were release settlements where they would have received cash compensation from Iyyer landlords. A very insignificant number of land owners from among Kallars and SCs, and other castes, have leased out their land. Thus, one can safely deduce that the entire tenant transfers were from Iyyers to non-Iyyers in VP.

When the extent of land transacted was analysed, the picture emerged that nearly more than half of the land sold by Iyyers was on market terms and the other half of was to their tenants. However, for the Kallars and SCs, market transactions predominated. Nearly 85 per cent of the land sold by Kallars was on market terms and the rest on tenancy terms. The incidence of tenancy-related transaction was higher (at 29 per cent) among SCs. Other castes transacted 64 per cent of their transactions under market conditions and 36 per cent under tenancy terms. The overall picture for all the castes together indicates that more than one-third of the land sold was under tenancy terms.

Chronology of Land Transfers in VP

Kallars from this region went with the DMK in large numbers. A Kallar from a neighbouring village, a school teacher by profession, was elected to the assembly on a DMK ticket twice in 1967 and 1971.

Since then, the Kallars have occupied the MLA position (either from DMK or AIADMK) from the constituency. Similarly, district-level party functionaries from both the parties had always been Kallars. Does this ascendency of Kallars along with the DMK and AIADMK reflect the decline of Brahmins in land ownership in the village? When we mapped the chronology of land transfer in VP, we could discern that the change in land ownership was concentrated during the time between the mid-1970s and mid-1990s.

An examination of the year-wise number of executions of sale deeds in VP indicates that nearly 70 per cent of them were executed by Brahmins during 1974 and 1994. Nearly 63 per cent of all executions happened during this time. Further, nearly 80 per cent of the tenancy transactions took place during 1974 and 1994, while only 55 per cent of the total market transactions took place during this period.

Changes in the Status of Registered Tenancy Lands in VP

The registration department registers only the sale deed and not lease arrangements. What this study has attempted so far is to disaggregate the sale and purchase of land by various types. This process subsumes the tenancy market. Only when the tenancy arrangement metamorphoses into a sale does it get reflected in the sale and purchase data. However, tenancy lands are not officially registered either in the revenue records or in the registration records. The Tamil Nadu Agricultural Lands (Record of Tenancy Rights) Act 1969 has mandated the special *thasildar*s (revenue official) in each district to act as the record officers for registering the record of tenancy. By registering, the tenants' rights as cultivators are protected. Based on this Act, the tenancy record of VP was prepared and published in the district gazette on 24 May 1971. It was publicised and displayed in the village on 18 June 1971. The registered information was conveyed to the landlord and the tenant in writing, and their acknowledgement was received. Both tenants and landlords were given 30 days of time to add or delete information in the register. Representations were enquired further into in the field and the registration was finalised. Further additions and deletions were possible by representing the issue to the special thasildar. The Record of Tenancy Rights (RTR) for VP had 139 tenants and the total area registered was 173.52 acres.

Based on this, we mapped the present-day status of each of these registered tenancy lands and the caste of the owners from the register. Most of the entries mention the caste of the landlord and the tenant. This can also be deduced from the surnames of the tenants. Three-fourths of the land leased out belonged to the Iyyers. Temples were the second largest lessor of land, and they accounted for the remaining one-fourth of the land leased out. There was one carpenter and one Kallar who had leased out about 3.5 acres of land together (Table 11.5).

Table 11.5 *Distribution of Lessors of Registered Tenancy Lands by Caste in VP (1971)*

Caste	Number	Extent (in acres)
Iyyer	112	127.31
Temples/trusts	25	42.78
Aasari	1	1.72
Kallar	1	1.71
Total	139	173.52

Source: Record of Tenancy Rights Register, Taluk Office, Thiruvaiyaru.

When we looked into the caste of the tenants, we found that in 1971, the Kallars were the largest number of tenants (60 per cent), followed by SCs (30 per cent). There were 10 Iyyer tenants and six 'other' caste tenants (Table 11.6). The Kallars were tenants for 57 per cent of the land rented out. The SC tenants accounted for one-fourth of the total land rented out, followed by Iyyers (10 per cent), with the remaining land leased by 'other' caste tenants.

Table 11.6 *Distribution of Registered Tenants by their Caste in VP (1971)*

Caste	No. of tenants	Extent (in acres)	Percentage
Kallar	100	98.54	56.6
SC	50	44.49	25.4
Iyyer	10	20.96	11.5
Rayudu	4	6.52	3.4
Vanniyar	2	3.00	1.7
Total	166	173.52	100.0

Source: Record of Tenancy Rights Register, Taluk Office, Thiruvaiyaru.

Current Status of Land under Registered Tenancy in VP

We earlier pointed to the *de facto* social norm of tenancy rights in the Cauvery delta, whereby the tenant claims a minimum of one-third of the extent of land as compensation to forego right to the land. We further observed that nearly one-third of the land transferred to the lower castes by the Iyyers was on tenancy terms, and included both registered and unregistered tenancy lands. Landlords of VP could hardly retrieve any significant extent of land that was rented out to tenants and registered in the 1970s. Though the Kallars and SCs both benefited from such transfers, the larger benefit had gone to the Kallars. Higher levels of compensation paid by the Brahmin landlords also indicate their poor bargaining position. The net result of the process has been the decline of tenancy to a large extent and also of the landlordism of Brahmins. Erstwhile tenants have acquired land from their landlords and become owner-cultivators. The land transfer data clearly demonstrate that the struggle for fair rent and right of the tenant unleashed a new course, whereby the tenants have become owners. The emigration of Brahmins had aided this transformation. Though the state brought about weak land reform laws, the social and political process used such weak laws as a crutch to evolve a social norm and gave enormous currency to such norms, benefiting the tenants.

These laws *per se* are not effective in addressing the agrarian issues. Many micro- and macro-level studies have indicated the numerous inadequacies of the laws. Importantly, the old agrarian system has failed to reproduce itself due to changes in the society that were extraneous to these laws. None of the tenants feels insecure about their occupancy right except in very rare cases. They are, in fact, confident of securing a compensation for giving up their cultivation right. A socially acknowledged *de facto* compensation right had evolved and was widely acknowledged and practised. What a *de jure* provision could not do has been achieved by evolving *de facto* norm through a social and political process.

Laws enacted by the state of Tamil Nadu, organised struggles by the tenants and workers, the anti-Brahmin movement followed by the emigration of Brahmins, the resultant change in the power relations in the villages, ascendency of Dravidian parties to power and the new crop practices have all led to this transformation. Laws introduced by the state *per se* may be ineffective. But to expect law alone to lead the transformation is highly problematic. This framework excludes the roles of social and political movements that emanate from below and transform the system. When such movements and the law work in tandem, a more widely accepted and easily implemented *de facto* social norm could be evolved. More importantly, such a norm was able to get almost a universal acceptance in the delta region. Added to that is the competing politics between the political formations. While one formation agitates for the rights, the other formation uses its power to legislate laws that would help them poach the base of the agitating formation.

Such a transformation may not have benefited the Dalits as much as it did the non-Dalits in both villages. When negotiations take place in an environment of changed power relations, the character of the dominant power seems to set the tone for the whole process as well as the outcome. The DMK and AIADMK, as parties representing the interests of the OBCs, may have favoured them more than the Dalits. Perhaps, if the state had a more proactive tilt towards the Dalits, they might have benefited more.

Notes

[1] Benami refers to a transaction in which the real beneficiary is not the one in whose name the property is listed or found.

[2] For a detailed discussion of the social dominance of the Brahmin community in the Cauvery delta, see Menon (1979: 52–64).

[3] A pannaiyal is a permanent agricultural labourer attached, along with his family, to one land owner.

[4] Some old city-names have been used in this chapter in the historical context in which they are mentioned.

[5] A kalam is a local weight measure, equivalent to approximately 29 kg of grain.

[6] Personal interview with K. Balakrishnan in Mayiladuthurai on 24 July 2015.

References

Athreya, V. B., Göran Djurfeldt and Staffan Lindberg. 1990. *Barriers Broken: Production Relations with Agrarian Change in Tamil Nadu*. New Delhi: Sage Publications.

Badrinath. 1972. 'A Report on the Implementation of Tamilnadu Agricultural Lands Record of Tenancy Rights Act, 1969'. *Indian Journal of Industrial Relations* 8(2): 279–99.

Barber, C. G. 1940. *History of Cauvery Mettur Project*. Madras: Government of Madras.

Barnett, M. R. 1975. 'Cultural Nationalist Electoral Politics in the Indian States'. In *Party Systems and Cleavages*, eds Myron Weiner and John Osgood Field, 78–83. New Delhi: Manohar Book Service.

—— 1976. *Politics of Cultural Nationalism in South India*. Princeton: Princeton University Press.

Bouton, Marshall M. 1980. 'The Sources of Agrarian Radicalism: A Study of Thanjavur District, South India'. Ph.D. thesis, University of Chicago, Illinois.

—— 1985. *Agrarian Radicalism in South India*. Princeton: Princeton University Press.

Dasgupta, B. 1977. 'India's Green Revolution'. *Economic and Political Weekly* 12(6–8): 241–60.

Ford Foundation. 1959. 'Report on India's Food Crisis and Steps to Meet It'. Agricultural Production Team, New Delhi.

Fuller, C. J. 2013. 'Introduction to the Third Edition'. *Caste, Class and Power: Changing Patterns of Stratification in a Tanjore Village*, André Béteille, *ix–xxxiv*. Chennai: Oxford University Press.

Gough, K. 1981. *Rural Society in Southeast India*. Cambridge. Cambridge University Press.

—— 1989. *Rural Change in Southeast India, 1950s to 1980s*. Madras. Oxford University Press.

Government of India. 1972. 'Report of the Irrigation Commission', Volume 3, Part 2. New Delhi.

Government of Tamil Nadu. 1967–2014. Index II of Vishnampettai Village for various years (1967–2014), Registration Department, Thirukkattuppalli, Thanjavur District.

—— 2014. 'Chitta for Vishnampettai, 2014'. Revenue Department, Village Administrative Office, Vishnampettai Village, Thanjavur District.

Guhan, S. 1983. 'Palakurichi: A Resurvey'. Working paper no. 42, Madras Institute of Development Studies, Madras.

Irschick, Eugene F. 1969. *Politics and Cultural Conflict in South India: The Non-Brahmin Movement and Tamil Separatism, 1916–29*. Berkeley. University of California Press.

Kasthurirangan. 2013. *Ninaivugalum Nigazhvugalum*. Kumabkonam: Revolt Press.

Krishnasamy, S. Y. 1974. *Development of Irrigation under the Cauvery-Mettur Project*. Madras: Government of Madras.

Kumar, Dharma. 1965. *Land and Caste in South India: Agricultural Labour in Madras Presidency in the Nineteenth Century*. Cambridge. Cambridge University Press.

Ladejinsky, W. 1972. 'Land Ceilings and Land Reforms'. *Economic and Political Weekly*, annual number: 401–08.

Menon, S. 1979. 'Responses to Class and Caste Oppression in Thanjavur District, 1940–52'. *Social Scientist* 7(6; 7; 10): 14–3; 57–68; 52–64.

Ramakrishnan, G. 2014. 'Peasant Movement and Dalit Rights in East Thanjavur, Tamil Nadu'. In *Dalit Households in Village Economies*, eds V. K. Ramachandran and Madura Swaminathan, 85–110. New Delhi: Tulika Books.

Sivaprakasam, V. 2009. *Temple Lands and the Agrarian Reforms in Tamilnadu during the Dravidian Rule*. Chennai: University of Madras.

Sonachalam, K. S. 1970. *Land Reforms in Tamilnadu: Evaluation of Implementation*. New Delhi: Oxford and IBH Publishing Co.

Surjit, V. 2014. 'Tenancy and Distress in Thanjavur Region, Tamil Nadu: A Case Study of Palakurichi Village'. In *Dalit Households in Village Economies*, eds V. K. Ramachandran and Madura Swaminathan, 170–96. New Delhi: Tulika Books.

Thangaraj, M. 1995. *Land Reforms in India, Tamil Nadu: An Unfinished Task*, Volume 9. New Delhi: Sage Publications.

Thorner, Daniel. 1973. *The Agrarian Prospect in India*. New Delhi: Allied Publishers.

Veeraiyan, G. 2011. *Sengodiyudan oru Neenda Payanam*. Chennai: Barathi Puthagalayam.

Part V

Cinema and Society

12. Mastering the Traumatic

Hey Ram *and its Cultural Narcissism**

Venkatesh Chakravarthy

Narratives that focus on a harrowing historical experience incessantly struggle to represent something that eludes symbolisation only to erect a fetish that demands reality status. The drive to master the traumatic excess thrown up by the narrative world inevitably leads to an impossible equilibrium. What results from such an exercise is not the realisation of some unattainable intellectual or psychical mastery of the trauma but a compulsive, repetitive

---

*The first version of this chapter was published in 2003 under the title, 'Encountering the Traumatic: *Hey Ram* and its Cultural Narcissism', *MICA Communications Review* 1(1): 52–73, Mudra Institute of Communications, Ahmedabad. Although the initial hypothesis stays as it is, the chapter has been substantially revised. It is republished with permission from MICA, Ahmedabad.

Acknowledgements: First, I wish to thank Ravi Vasudevan, for giving me the necessary encouragement to pursue my hypothesis, and Lalitha Gopalan, for spending a lot of time on the initial draft, raising crucial questions, offering highly important comments and persisting in her demand to publish the article. Many thanks to M. S. S. Pandian and S. V. Srinivas for the promptness with which they responded with their comments and criticisms that helped me highlight some crucial nuances. Special thanks to Rupa Viswanath and Nathaniel Roberts for their warm support, and for sparing their precious time amidst their hectic fieldwork to see the film on my request before reading the draft and subjecting it to a close analysis to offer their valuable comments and criticisms. Recently, before the current revised draft was finished, thanks to Swarnavel Eswaran Pillai for giving me the final boost that was necessary, and to Karthick R. M. for his patient comments and suggestions. Last but not the least, I owe a lot to Pritham K. Chakravarthy, for the important questions she raised during many previews of the film and later during all the drafts.

and aggressive extraction of narcissistic compensation. This kind of narcissism is not merely a preoccupation of some individual psyche, but is collective and cultural in import, as narratives are forms that engage the public sphere.

A pertinent question about *Hey Ram* then is: How does it attempt to master the various traumas it addresses; the constitutive anxiety of Saket Ram, the protagonist; the trauma that triggers his quest or mission; the ordeal of Partition; the disturbing assassination of Gandhi; and the suffering initiated by contemporary Hindu–Muslim riots? Finally, what do the two friends, Saket Ram and Amjad Khan, do after living through horrendous genocide on either side, when they so deliberately but yet so accidentally encounter each other at the climax of the film? Do they share a prolonged and intense moment of silence that could initiate the process of mourning?[1]

I

Presumably, the film narrates a tale of moral redemption. Saket Ram (Kamal Haasan), a South Indian Vaishnavite Brahmin and an archaeologist by profession, loses his Bengali wife, Aparna (Rani Mukherjee), a schoolteacher, in the Calcutta[2] riots of 1946. She is gang-raped and brutally murdered by their tailor Altaf (Sadaf Khan), and some members of his Muslim community on the Direct Action Day called by Muhammed Ali Jinnah. After avenging her sacrilege and death by taking the life of Altaf and killing other Muslims who have no direct connection with his tragedy, Saket encounters the Hindu militant, Sri Ram Abhayankar (Atul Kulkarni), his mentor-to-be, who identifies M. K. Gandhi (Naseerudin Shah) as the arch villain behind the riots.

A year later, Saket weds Mythili (Vasundhara Das), a member of his own south Indian caste and sect at Mannarkudi. Pursued nevertheless by traumatic images of the past, he sets out to assassinate Gandhi, under the tutelage of Abhayankar and patronage of the Maharashtrian Rajah (Vikram Gokhale). Just before he can accomplish this mission, his close friend and erstwhile colleague Amjad Khan (Shah Rukh Khan), a Pathani Muslim, suddenly surfaces in Delhi. He has chosen to return to India despite Partition and the emergence of Pakistan. With the bloody sacrifice of his life, he attempts to restore the sanity of his friend Saket, who then kills Hindu militants in order to protect

Muslim women and children. Five decades later, Saket Ram himself dies in Chennai as the ambulance rushing him to the hospital cannot proceed further owing to a contemporary Hindu–Muslim riot. In the final flashback of the film narrated by his grandson, Saket Ram, Jr (Gautam Kanthadai), to the great-grandson of Gandhiji, Tushar Gandhi (Tushar Gandhi), we learn that the elder Saket tries to confess his sins to Gandhiji by surrendering the box containing his murder weapon. In his hurry to attend his regular meeting, as Gandhiji defers this ritual and continues to proceed on his way, the inevitable happens. Nathuram Godse (Sharad Ponkshe) blocks his path and fires thrice to kill him on the spot. In the epilogue that follows, Saket Ram, Jr, hands over to Tushar Gandhi the murder weapon, Gandhiji's worn-out footwear and the broken glasses brought back by the elder Saket as talismanic relics of that tragedy.

II

The film has been the subject of at least two important and elaborate readings.[3] According to the first reading by Vasudevan (2002: 2917–25), *Hey Ram* signals a shift in the 'perspective on the consensus of leading figures like Gandhi and Periyar in a discourse of secularism, democracy and identity'. In his view, the uncertainty experienced by the viewers of the film is caused by two narrative drives working in opposition to one another: The predominant, 'inflammatory voices that conjure up a narrative of Muslim bloodlust and Hindu trauma on the one hand, and the less forceful narrative move to distance the spectator from an extreme Hindutva perspective on the other'. By way of this, although 'another history surfaces', 'unable to chart a clear path through an erupting unconscious, the film acknowledges a public will to rewrite history' and 'kill the father', and can compensate for the resulting sense of shame and loss only by 'a simulated imbrication in the iconicity of the great other, and a silence thereafter. Ridding oneself of the father isn't all that easy, after all; recovering him is even harder'. In the second reading, according to Gopalan (2002: 187–96), a feminised masochistic drive is displaced by a sadistic masculinity, however, at the closure, rendering 'the excesses of militant masculinity as a futile excursion, choosing instead to close on a male subject whose place in history is assured after a journey through sadism'; and as Saket Ram 'proceeds from a disinterested scholar who becomes a militant Hindu nationalist after encountering the gorier aspects of communal riots in Calcutta and finally turns into a Gandhian pacifist by the end', the story thus becomes 'a conversion narrative that rescues the film from wholly aligning itself with Hindu Nationalism'.

Both the readings, despite their differing engagements, do acknowledge that in the last instance, the film makes an attempt to distance itself from Hindu nationalism, whatever the intensity of such an attempt may be. While it is possible to read it in this manner, as the film itself seems to prefer it to be read that way, other things could be brought into play to contest this conclusion. That is, in my reading these distancing efforts are only indicative of some kind of window-dressing, as the film in no way attempts to recover the father, not because initially it lacks any murderous desire against him, but because any Oedipal resolution of the narrative is foreclosed. In other words, Vasudevan and Gopalan do not interrogate their assumption that the film attempts to resolve its conflicts within a typical Oedipal framework. On the contrary, it is my hypothesis that, unlike the typical Oedipal scenario, *Hey Ram* describes an aborted Oedipal journey verging on psychosis, while traversing the family and the nation. In other words, the protagonist's individual psychosis and infantile narcissism are inextricably anchored in the cultural psychosis or cultural narcissism of the Hindu national imaginary. The question that arises then is whether those distancing moves of the film are a textual strategy to pre-empt criticism such that a launching pad could be provided for the most virulent ideological missile.[4]

III

In Oedipal narratives, the heroic character often eliminates or subdues the *obscene father* and wins the approval of the *symbolic father* by accepting symbolic castration or by paying some symbolic debt to this figure, to emerge as the authorised and authoritative male subject or an ideally interpellated subject of ideology and society of its narrative world.[5] How then can we describe the way the constitutive trauma of Saket is set up in the film?

His separation from his mother is not enacted in the film, but from what other characters say, we learn that he lost his mother in early childhood and that his uncle's wife, Vasantha *maami* (Nagamani

Mahadevan), is his surrogate mother. Often narratives include a traumatic scene to trigger the quest of the hero working as a metaphorical substitute of the castration trauma the heroic subject encounters on his Oedipal journey. In *Hey Ram*, the Calcutta riots sequence could be read as a metaphorical staging of Saket Ram's constitutive trauma. The traumatic loss of his passionate love-object, Aparna, for instance, could then be indicated as metaphorically recapitulating the hero's traumatic separation from his mother or his nourishing agent—Aparna becoming, in that sense, the libidinal substitute for the primal erotic relationship with the mother. Significantly, this scenario occurs within the private space of his apartment at Calcutta than elsewhere. The Oedipal hero would then attempt to recover this lost object by undergoing a long ordeal and by paying his symbolic debt to some father figure to eventually win the hand of a princess in the moment of final reckoning.

Conversely, Saket Ram's second marriage with Mythili, does not take place in this manner as it occurs immediately within a couple of scenes after the Calcutta riots in which he loses Aparna. If we read Saket Ram as a subject susceptible to psychosis, then his trauma, as highlighted by the film in the riot sequence, assumes an entirely different colour. When the intruding gang violates Aparna, Saket Ram, like a helpless child, is unable to do anything. In contrast, when a somewhat elderly Muslim attempts to sodomise him, however, he manages to reverse the situation in an exhibition of utmost violence by inflicting a severe blow right on this man's crotch and sending him reeling across the balcony to his gruesome death below. Only after this event does Saket Ram find that the gang of intruders has slit Aparna's throat to further intensify his trauma.

In this primal scene, it is not a chance occurrence that this somewhat elderly sodomising Muslim is the leader of the rampage. The script emphasises at this point that Altaf refers to him as '*dada*', the chief of the gang, when he invites him to enjoy the honour of feasting upon Aparna first (Haasan 2000, Scene 10: 46).[6] In that sense, he is specifically a castrating figure albeit a degraded vulgar father image. Moreover, by refusing to accept Altaf's invitation and staying behind to meet his fate, this figure does not show his preference for Aparna, but expresses his desire to sodomise Saket Ram. This exercise, if taken to its logical conclusion, would then entirely undermine the masculinity of the heroic subject establishing his *feminised* position in relation to this figure. This is far more inimical and traumatic to the subject than the contest over the love-object, as it would destroy the very identity the subject wishes to possess. Crucially, what distinguishes the psychotic subject, according to psychoanalysis, is this *feminised* subject position he occupies in relation to the sodomising father image, forming the constitutive trauma of his paranoid subjectivity (Freud 2001: 18–29). To confound matters, this subject position does not emerge from without or is inflicted from outside as he imagines, because this subject ambiguously but intensely desires a homoerotic relationship with the father figure. This impulse violently contradicts and threatens the masculine identity of the subject from within; and for this reason he expels this desire with equal force to overcome his anxiety. Nonetheless, this trauma continues to pursue him now in an opposite guise from without as an external threat posed by the desire of a persecuting agent or a degraded father figure. This process, which turns the tables in this way, describes one of the basic features of psychosis, otherwise known as the mechanism of projection wherein what begins as an internal perception ends as an external perception. What needs to be emphasised at this point is thereby that the initiative for the subject's delusion comes from outside, from the symbolic field of the *big Other*. It is this initiative the paranoid subject struggles to seize, but by negating his own homoerotic desire (Lacan 1997: 193). In effect, the traumatic disintegration of the subjective universe of the psychotic, triggered by his own desire, appears to his paranoid perception as a phenomenal world-disintegrating event (see Freud 2001: 3–84) initiated by the fallen other. This is how the Calcutta riots sequence functions for Saket Ram, as it is his expelled homoerotic desire that erupts in the guise of the *sodomising other*, producing its most intense trauma and the reciprocal reactive brutal retaliation aimed at this person. It is in order to overcome this inaugural traumatic and emaciating threat to his masculinity that Saket Ram desperately constructs grandiose and virulent hypermasculine images of himself to seek narcissistic compensations. This *sodomising virile Muslim other*, being a common figure in the collective phobia or fantasy of the Hindu national imaginary, the bloody compensatory aspects of the hypermasculine exercises indulged in by the saffron brigade during various pogroms, shares a similar locus or a traumatic sense of feminisation or loss of masculine authority. Reading this feminisation in the film as, a rape-revenge narrative, Gopalan (2002: 193) does clearly emphasise the fact that 'Saket Ram avenges not his wife's rape but his own'. Her description, however, limits itself to the transformation of masochism into sadism, and as mentioned earlier, does not interrogate the assumption that the film attempts to provide an Oedipal resolution of its conflicts, as against my hypothesis that it entails an aborted Oedipal journey, which thwarts any such typical resolution. Owing to this, the subject cannot emerge as a full-fledged male subject because at a crucial point he is willing to compromise his masculinity with someone. The conflict is over who that object is eventually going to be.

Notwithstanding the scene mentioned earlier, the expelled *feminised* disposition of Saket Ram refuses to disappear, pitching him in incessant battle with its forces. Thus, for instance, in every scene of copulation in the film, a traumatic note enters, before, after or during the process, to disturb its resolution within the typical male–female romantic scenario, producing bizarre masculine expressions on the part of the hero. In the very first scene of copulation in the film, in order to reassure his sense of masculinity, he claims to Aparna that it is he who has 'sexually assaulted her'. In a similar scenario with his second wife Mythili, he covers his posterior with a long-flowing white bed sheet thrusting his chest forward to play the piano. This use of the bed cover is a significant variation of the common instance enacted by female figures in Hollywood cinema where, of course, in similar scenes, the white sheet covering the female body fetishises it by enhancing the mysterious quality attributed to womanhood and triggering the desire to see more. Here, on the contrary, the extended flow of the sheet stretching behind Saket Ram is a metonymic register for the desired contact with the paternal phallus.

We arrive at this lovemaking scene of Saket and Mythili only through a long metonymical detour, as it does not take place on the ordained nuptial night of their wedding. In the nuptial scene, on the contrary, before Mythili arrives, Saket is flipping through her copy of Gandhi's autobiography. The fact that such a book has surfaced in the nuptial bedroom on the night of the wedding in a rather unusual context is a sign that the anticipated coitus is not going to take place. Significantly, this has nothing to do with the moral connotations associated with Gandhi, but with the fact that he is another figure who occupies the disturbing paternal position in relation to Saket, reminding him of his *feminised* position. Subsequently, when Mythili goes into the bathroom to change, she screams because a lizard falls on her shoulder. This triggers Saket Ram's first set of persecutory hallucinations. In this scenario, the emaciating father figure appears as the repulsive lizard wiggling through the streaming blood on the floor, which is another signifier of the paternal phallus. The traumatic images associated with the Calcutta riots that erupt at this moment are not the only cause for the disruption of the ordained coitus of this wedding night. These images of the riots, as metonymical sediments, primarily reinforce Saket's fears about his *feminisation*. The disruption of the coitus in this scene, therefore, has a more important reason. As against this vulgar signifier of the phallus, he must find a worthier one with which he can compromise his masculinity, and that can happen if and only if his quest is elevated to that of a redeemer of the nation. Until then, he cannot indulge in any phallic enjoyment and crucially at this juncture, as such an elevation necessarily entails the renunciation of any preference for Gandhi or his book, given the trajectory of the narrative. The transition to such a state has to be effected by the maternal call to such an elevated task which emerges later in the secret ritual conducted at the Rajah's armoury room. In this scene, once the names of Sri Ram Abhayankar and Saket Ram turn up for the mission of assassinating Gandhi, the Rajah's face morphs into the face of Aparna to utter the command in English, 'Today is Vijayadasami. It seems like it is the will of Bhavani that it shall be a Ram who should do the job' (Haasan 2000, Scene 37: 108). Significantly, it is only after Saket Ram accepts this call of the goddess Bhavani that his persecutory hallucinations cease to trouble him any longer and the devilish but depreciated images of Gandhi occupy the place by becoming the avowed target. Therefore, the last time ever the trauma of Calcutta and its associated guilt assails Saket Ram is briefly before Abhayankar takes him to the armoury room to attend the secret ritual. It is only after his acceptance of the call and by enacting an imaginary murder of Gandhi by shooting at his hallucinatory demonised image that Saket Ram can subsequently indulge in coitus with Mythili.

The scene in the armoury room thus enacts a crucial transformation, wherein one set of hallucinations are displaced by another set of hallucinations, reversing the role of the persecutor and the persecuted, the protagonist thus seizing the initiative from the fallen imaginary other. Specifically, the guilt that assails him in the haunting image of the little blind Muslim girl (metonymically a remainder of Gandhian secular values), giving the persecutory charge to the first set of hallucinations, does not have a similar counterpart in the second set of hallucinations. In them, Saket Ram is the persecutor and the persecuted is, of course, Gandhi. This displacement of a *delusion of persecution* by a *delusion of grandeur* is typical of the deluded subject who has locked himself in an unyielding infantile narcissism. This transformation further indicates that Saket Ram is rebuilding his disintegrated world gradually with a fantasised megalomania, wherein he can emerge as the sole redeemer of his Hindu nation. Moreover, this transition from the first to the second set of hallucinations is mediated by the transformation of the Rajah's face into that of Aparna's. For that reason, the Aparna who pronounces his mission is not the Aparna who died in the riots at Calcutta, but the Aparna recovered through her Durga/Kali portrait in Saket Ram's second visit to Calcutta. The fact that now she wears the Rajah's turban as she pronounces her commandment in a ritual context, specified as an effort to redeem the Hindu nation, makes it obvious that this Aparna is the phallic mother with whom the nation converges. She, therefore, invokes the will of goddess Bhavani/Kali and the just war in Mahabharatha when she indicates that this command is delivered on the day of Vijayadasami, an auspicious moment for such an engagement.

Notably, following this ritual, the other Aparna who died in Calcutta does not remind Saket of any trauma or permanent loss, but appears in the succeeding scene, the Lavani song-and-dance sequence, yet again as an object of his voyeuristic gaze, indicating that now the block against his phallic enjoyment has been temporarily removed. However, in the first event of actual copulation that follows immediately between Saket and Mythili, the expelled desire towards the father figure surfaces again—to tackle which Saket Ram becomes the persecuting agent again, transforming Mythili's body into a gigantic Mauser gun aimed at his avowed target Gandhi, who of course, is physically absent in this scene but metonymically present as the imagined target.

Gandhi thus occupies the position of Saket's principal adversary, since he threatens to rupture both the masculine unity of Saket Ram and the virility of his Hindu nation. Saket's compensatory reactions opposing this trauma are, therefore, gargantuan in proportion and registered, among other things, in the very intensity of the hallucinated images of Gandhi.

The quality of these images of Gandhi is better described by comparing the script version (Haasan 2000, Scene 37: 106–08) and the film version of the ritual scene in the armoury room. It begins when the Rajah says, specifically, in English, 'the misfortune of this Hindu Nation is its worst enemy is a practising Hindu. Right from the beginning he has been taking their side and neglecting the people of his religion'. On this note, as Saket begins to imagine/hallucinate, according to the script, a gold coin rolls down to find its way to a large heap of gold, which is then unloaded from a carriage of a train like rock metal at a quarry. The camera then tilts up from a pair of boots to reveal Jinnah offering his ceremonial salute to formalise Partition and transfer of power. In response to this image, an army parade is led by Louis Mountbatten, formally juxtaposed with a procession of the gold-bearing carriages of a train, but significantly visualised in *black and white* with the telling details, the gold coins alone in their resplendent *colour*. The sole purpose of this formal mechanism is to highlight the narcissistic wounds of Hindutva to ensure that the spectator does not miss their intended significance. The moment the doors of the carriages swing open, the cadres of Congress Party unload the gold at the feet of Jinnah. In the next *black-and-white* image, Gandhi is imitating the ceremonial pose of Jinnah as he witnesses a parade of a refugee train full of dead people with only their *blood revealed in colour*. Now as the engine shrieks, bellowing smoke and expunging steam beneath its wheels, the Rajah declares that 'for centuries we have worshipped in valour and its accompanying instruments. He now wants us to change our form of worship and pray to a new god—himself and a new religion—ahimsa' (Haasan 2000, Scene 37: 107).

Saket Ram's hallucinations return on this note with Gandhi sprinkling gold coins at a cactus plant that transforms itself into the green flag of the Muslim League. The Rajah interrupts, 'Brave men it should be done as a symbolic act, and not as revenge. But, to show the world and the country what a Hindu is capable of' (Haasan 2000, Scene 37: 107). The names of Saket Ram and Sri Ram Abhayankar turn up after this and as the Rajah tries to announce the assignee of the mission, his face is replaced by Aparna's face. Accepting the mission and choosing the required weapon, as Saket takes aim with it, the next series of hallucinated images follow.

A refugee train proceeds with numerous dead bodies but Gandhi is casually witnessing the scene spinning cotton at his wheel. He then turns towards Saket as if someone hailed him. Instantly, as Saket fires at him, an explosion shatters Gandhi's image into smithereens, and from the blaze produced by the bullet, a swastika emerges, it blackens to become a metallic Nazi swastika and transforms itself into a metallic lotus to disintegrate and disappear by way of a transition to the next scene, the Lavani dance sequence (Haasan 2000, Scene 37: 108).

As against this description in the script, these hallucinations are somewhat condensed in the film, and unlike in other instances the published script does not indicate if some of these images were censored. In the film, we first see Gandhi sprinkling gold coins at a greenish cactus plant. Later in the second montage, we see Gandhi at his *charka* (wheel) against the backdrop of the green Muslim League flag looking towards Saket who then fires at him. From the resulting explosion and the subsequent shattering of the image, a Nazi Swastika emerges. Then a Hindu Swastika (not in the script) displaces it followed by the Sangh Parivar's metallic lotus. This last image does not disintegrate in the film on its own or disappear as described by the script, but is replaced with a smooth elliptical wipe that opens on the Marathi Lavani song-and-dance sequence, formally and literally opening the door of phallic enjoyment. What needs to be emphasised at this point is that like the fantasy of the *sodomising Muslim other*, these images of Gandhi and the words spoken by the Rajah share a similar locus in the discourse of the Hindu national imaginary, as outlined by the latter's emphasis on the Hindu worship of valour as against *ahimsa* (non-violence). This principle of non-violence is singled out for attention, as it does not provide any narcissistic compensation to Brahminical or upper-caste authority in the context of a series of threats it faces from below. Therefore, what is more inimical about this principle to these protagonists of the Hindu nation is that it *feminises* their subject position.

A major instance of this distended aesthetic of self-representation in the film is the glorification of Saket Ram's body when it phenomenally weathers a twister of a sandstorm in the weird dream sequence that begins the second flashback of the film. Embellished in full-fledged Brahminical attire, with a silk dhoti outlined by a shining golden-red border and a half-naked torso glossed by an erotic play of light, and an aggressive posture enhanced by the extendable fancy handle of the Mauser gun, Saket perfects his aim at his target. As he gets closer and closer to it, a sandstorm gathers in the horizon. The moment the bullet hits the clay model, a substitute for vulgarised Gandhi's head, the storm attacks Saket Ram and, significantly, precisely at this moment, it comes as a serenely enjoyable occasion for him. Violently but erotically unwinding his mane, and in its wild flow evoking its iconographic similarity to the flowing mane of Ram (as in the deliberate fusion of Siva and Ram deployed in many Sangh Parivar cut-outs during the phase of the Chalo Ayodhya call across the nation to lay the foundation stone for a Ram temple at the Babri Masjid site), the storm caresses his body with all its mighty force. According to the script (Haasan 2000, Scene 48: 127), this gigantic twister is supposed to be dancing in the form of *uduku*, Siva's percussion instrument, and hence could be read as a metonymical substitute for his divine phallus. In addition, because once the storm fully engulfs Saket, according to the script, he becomes its very eye and perhaps because of that 'he is all the more serene', signifying an ecstatic sexual fusion between (Saket) Ram and Siva. Only with this kind of megalomania, Saket Ram is willing to thus compromise his masculine virility.[7]

This dream sequence, in effect, pushes his megalomania to its culminating point, providing the anchoring point for his fantasy as the sole messianic redeemer of the Hindu nation. However, the god of Saket Ram or the Ram of Ayodhya, the way Hindutva locates him, 'is stricken with a sort of feminisation' or suffers from an 'imaginary degradation of otherness' like the protagonist (Lacan 1997: 101) lending a precarious balance to this redeemer fantasy, and hence the necessity to fuse it with an aggressive Siva. With the explosion of this full-blown megalomania, Saket Ram does not hallucinate any longer in the film, as there is no further need to imagine anything greater as he has chosen his object, his divine and mighty imaginary partner. Saket Ram's erotic fusion with Siva provides him with the necessary shield to diffuse the trauma of castration and acquire a monstrous strength towards his adversaries by unrelentingly retaining his narcissism.

IV

How do we then read Saket's ambiguous second phase of relationship with Gandhi, in which apparently there seems to be some recovery of this father figure once Saket Ram decides to confess his sins? Does

Gandhi thereby emerge as the symbolic father of Saket Ram? If he does, will it then not become necessary that Saket Ram give up his relationship with the extraordinary and divine imaginary partner of his, apart from severing the incestual ties with his mother, and all of which would necessarily entail the renunciation of his infantile narcissism and its Hindutva baggage?

In order to unravel these implications, we have to go back to the very first scene of the film. In this scene, the prologue of the film, the grandson, Saket Ram, Jr, in his conversation with the doctor, Munawar (Abbas), reveals three basic features of his grandfather. First, although the rest of the family considers the elder Saket mentally unstable, the grandson thinks otherwise. Second, in opposition to Gandhi who prefers bright light in his room, the elder Saket prefers darkness. Last, but not the least, although the elder Saket Ram may not be a *Mahatma* (great soul) like the former, he is nonetheless a good *atma* (soul) whose story is worth telling. As the grandson insists (Haasan 2000, Scene 1: 10), 'May be my grandfather is a Mahatma or not, but he is a good man. A good average atma! Is that not enough?'.

Enough for whom, is the issue. If being an ordinary atma were sufficient, then there is no need for the story. In that sense, the narrative poses an enigma at the very outset and that is: Is Saket Ram sane or insane? Is he a Mahatma or an ordinary atma?

Significantly, at the threshold of the Oedipal phase, 'Am I a man or Am I a woman?' is the burning existential and hysterical question that assails the human subject.[8] By paying its pound of flesh or accepting symbolic castration, and defining its identity in terms of its similarity or opposition to the symbolic father figure, the child assumes a male or female sexual identity by thus answering this question. In the psychotic subject, this question cannot be resolved as it excludes the authorising symbolic father or the endorsing *big Other* from its subjective world, producing its associated trauma. The film, of course, does not raise this hysterical question directly. Instead, it assumes the shape, 'Am I sane or insane? Am I a Mahatma or an ordinary atma?', in its narrative.

To be a Mahatma, according to the very dynamics of the first scene, is to show a preference for bright light as against the darkness preferred by Saket Ram. Now, as Lacan (1997: 148–49) rightly insists, day and night, brightness and darkness, are not just experiences. They are, above all, signifiers that connote something for someone, wherein the bright luminous sun stands as the symbol of masculinity in opposition to our planet, the dark mother earth, which stands as the symbol of the feminine. Similarly, sanity and insanity are not just experiences but signifiers, as patriarchy often associates women with dark madness and men with shining sanity. These signifiers, opposing each other, thus stand for the presence or absence of the phallus. Provided our discussion on Saket Ram's *feminised* position so far, it is not surprising that in the first scene, the film itself, by way of these signifiers, confers exactly a similar feminised status to Saket Ram, as people regard him mentally unstable and he prefers darkness. It is this inaugural lack that the film or Saket Ram's extended journey through the nation hopes to annul, so that he can possess the light in the end to assert his masculinity, and transform his insane Hindutva discourse into a shining picture of sanity. To achieve this, of course, Gandhi and his discourse of ahimsa have to be castrated and pushed to the feminised/insane position and ejected into the limbo of darkness.

What seems to blatantly contradict this picture is the fact that, once Godse kills Gandhi, Saket Ram who takes aim at Godse, withdraws his gun on Goel's (Om Puri) insistence on non-violence, thereby apparently subscribing to some Gandhian value. The point remains though that Saket Ram, who imagined the murder of Gandhi so many times in the film, cannot imagine his murder of Godse even for a brief second.

Such a thing is not possible, not because Saket Ram has undergone a change of heart and, therefore, prefers non-violence, as the film seems to insist, but because Godse occupies the same position that Saket Ram always so adamantly wished to occupy. The film very clearly equates them in the secret ritual scene, when Aparna declares, 'It seems like it is the will of Bhavani that it shall be a Ram who should do the job' (Haasan 2000, Scene 37: 108). Therefore, it does not matter for the film whether it is Nathuram Godse or Saket Ram who accomplishes the job. The former is simply the double of the latter. Therefore, Saket Ram killing Godse cannot occur in *Hey Ram* even as an imaginary exercise, because there is no contest between the two for the affection of the Hindu phallic mother. In contrast, between Saket Ram and Gandhi, there is no contest for the same maternal object either, and in this case it is so because they do not desire the same thing or the same kind of nation, as Gandhi's idea of a nation threatens the virility of Saket Ram's nation.

Does it imply then that Saket Ram fails to emerge as the heroic figure of the narrative because Godse accomplishes a goal staked out in advance with all melodrama for the hero of the film? On the contrary, out of sheer necessity that the ideology of the film must fit facts, it grants Godse the position to eliminate Gandhi; otherwise, the film does not throw any doubt on Saket Ram's heroic stature. Moreover, as Lacan (1977: 179) points out, what becomes necessary according to the narrative is, 'when you entrust someone with a mission, the *aim* is not what he brings back, but the itinerary he must take'. It is not necessary, therefore, that Saket Ram should kill Gandhi all by himself but only share the same itinerary or journey with Godse.

Yet, Saket Ram brings back something that Godse could not take with him, the broken spectacles and the worn-out footwear of Gandhi. How do we read this? As an expression of his love for Gandhi? He does not bring these objects alone, but also the box containing his much cherished murder weapon, the Mauser gun. If there is any central failure, therefore, on Saket Ram's part, it is the fact that his surrender of the weapon to Gandhi does not transpire because that would have then constituted the payment of his pound of flesh to his symbolic father, recovering Gandhi in the process. By way of a great coincidence, Godse, by killing Gandhi just in time, however, does not provide Saket Ram any such option to pay his symbolic debt. These 'structured coincidences' in the film have a close connection with the desire of Saket Ram and the ideological coherence the film wishes to achieve by way of similar chance occurrences.

For instance, whenever, Saket Ram desires the presence of Sri Ram Abhayankar, he seems to materialise from nowhere, three times at that and always by some coincidence. In other words, if Gandhi in the later part of the film is recovered as a symbolic father, then Saket would have surrendered his weapon and confessed his sins to him. Saket's delusional choice, his pact with the imaginary divine partner, however, rules that out. It is for this reason that once Gandhi moves away from Saket, saying he would listen to his confession later, this briefly revered figure is returned to his earlier vulgar image, flung as he is obscenely on the ground by the impact of the bullets flowing from Godse's gun. The short friendly demeanour of reverence given to Gandhi, therefore, has only one function and that is to name Saket Ram a Mahatma by Gandhi's own words (Haasan 2000, Scene 16: 159), as he does because Saket Ram apparently saves the lives of some

Muslims. The whole Hindu–Muslim trouble towards the end of the film, where Saket Ram suddenly becomes a saviour of Muslim people, however, begins only after he first kills a Muslim, Jalal (Manoj Pahwa), to reclaim his gun from him at the Azad Soda Factory (Haasan 2000, Scene 63A: 158–59). That this man is the uncle of Amjad Khan, and that despite his death right in front of his eyes Amjad Khan is self-effacingly Gandhian, are quickly glossed over by the film in order to establish Saket Ram as a Mahatma.

Nevertheless, the question remains as to how we can reconcile the ambiguous fact that Saket Ram kills Muslims at one point and Hindus at another point in the film. The point is not to reconcile these contradictions or other secular prevarications of the film but to shift the locus elsewhere, because for the hero of the narrative, as Lacan (1997) observes about the deluded subject:

> Reality isn't at issue for him, certainty is. Even when he expresses himself along the lines of what he experiences is not of the order of reality, this does not affect his certainty that it concerns him. The certainty is radical. The very nature of what he is certain of can quite easily remain completely ambiguous, covering the entire range from malevolence to benevolence. But it means something unshakable for him.
>
> This constitutes what is called, whether rightly or wrongly, the elementary phenomenon or, as a more developed phenomenon, delusional belief. (Ibid.: 75)

In effect, then, nothing in the film challenges Saket Ram's unshakeable certainty that he is the sole messianic redeemer of the Hindu nation. There is no space in the film for two messiahs to coexist. Again, it is not merely a coincidence that Saket Ram's death in the film ambiguously precedes Gandhi's assassination and death. According to the *story time* of the film, or the temporal order within the story, if Gandhi dies in 1948 and Saket Ram dies in 1999, then to the contrary, in the *discourse time* or the temporal order of the narration with its flashbacks, Saket Ram dies first. By such a strategy, a film that was widely advertised as a film about Gandhi jettisons his funeral scene. Instead, it invites the spectator to witness the funeral scene of Saket Ram, but mediating it through the presence of Tushar Gandhi. He, however, by proclaiming himself as the fan of Saket Ram, Jr, is ironically oblivious of the fact that he is not receiving the confessions of the sins of the elder Saket Ram, but the castrated entrails of his great-grandfather in the shape of the worn-out footwear and cracked spectacles.

It is important to note at this point what happens once Tushar Gandhi begins to look at these objects, including Saket Ram's Mauser gun, and from whose point of view he does so in the last scene of the film. To frame this event, the camera crosses the imaginary line by violating the 180-degree rule, not to self-reflexively reveal its symbolic mechanisms but to situate an impossible gaze, as we now see the event from the head of Saket Ram's bed. Although he is dead, absent, he is nonetheless present by way of this impossible gaze. This gaze is impossible because only in a fantasy or a dream is it possible for someone to be present as a gaze of one's own birth or death.[9] The last image enacts such a fantasy. We see from that point of view, an unusually large portrait of Gandhiji painted on what are a series of closed windows. If Saket always remained in the dark in this room, which the film and the script takes pain to emphasise, it implies that he could never have looked at this image as we do. Why then now does his grandson, significantly carrying the same name, Saket Ram, Jr, open these windows and the spectator is privileged to share it from the impossible point of view of the dead elder Saket Ram? Because from this point of view, the elder Saket Ram simultaneously possesses the bright light, the signifier of masculinity, the phallus, as his grandson gradually pushes Gandhiji's image into darkness, the signifier of femininity. The compensatory pleasure derived from this gaze is revealed by the fact that it is from this point of view that Tushar Gandhi, before the windows are opened, receives the broken spectacles and the worn-out footwear of Gandhiji, a metonymic signifier for his castrated entrails; and thus Gandhiji's position is doubly *feminised* at the closure. In the foundational traumatic scene of the Calcutta riots, one eye-piece of Saket Ram's glasses is shattered during his struggle with the sodomising other and in the end it is Gandhiji's glasses which receive such a mark at the point of his death, thus resolving Saket Ram's trauma. There is no attempt in the film, therefore, to recover Gandhiji as the symbolic father, but only the opposite effort to push him forever into the abyss and, therefore, there is no 'simulated imbrication in the iconicity of the great other, and a silence thereafter' (Vasudevan 2002) for the shame and loss produced by the killing of the father. Instead, there is ample sadistic pleasure in achieving the target and having produced a double to carry that work further.

Since Gandhi is thus ejected into darkness, is it possible then that Saket Ram has a symbolic father, say, for instance, in other paternal images like Sri Ram Abhayankar or the Maharashtrian Rajah who holds forth on Hindu valour? Seemingly, Sri Ram Abhayankar appears to fit the bill for two reasons. First, the connotations generated by both the names of Saket Ram and Sri Ram Abhayankar provides one argument. The name Saket Ram literally means Ram who hails from Saket in Ayodhya, and the name Sri Ram Abhayankar literally means one who offers refuge to Ram. Moreover, in the very first encounter between these two, Abhayankar quotes his origin in Sanskrit by citing the Kaushikagotra, which thereby makes him a surrogate Viswamitra. Second, after complete paralysis, he obtains a pledge from Saket Ram that the latter would renounce his familial ties to accomplish the avowed mission. Later, at Kashi, Saket Ram ritually renounces his ties. Cumulatively these elements seem to imply that Sri Ram Abhayankar is the actual symbolic father of Saket Ram because the latter pays some kind of symbolic debt to him by renouncing his familial ties. For more than one reason, however, it is not worth rushing into this conclusion, because Saket Ram castrates Sri Ram Abhayankar as well by sending him into his fatal paralysis and death. This event transpires during the tent-pegging game, when riding close to each other, Saket Ram's horse knocks down Abhayankar from his horse causing the fatal accident. Again, it is not mere chance that produces this event. Above all, if Abhayankar remains alive, he would only threaten Saket Ram's megalomania that can permit only himself as the sole redeemer of the Hindu nation. Therefore, when Abhayankar finally hands over the murder weapon to Saket Ram, a comparison is suggested by the metonymical presence on the adjacent wall of the calendar image of Hanuman tearing open his chest to reveal his real love and affection for Ram and Sita. By similarly tearing open the box placed on his own chest, Abhayankar offers the murder weapon to Saket Ram. In this manner, Abhayankar, who begins his journey as a Viswamitra ends up as a Hanuman. The pledge given to him by Saket Ram is, therefore, not equivalent to symbolic castration. Moreover, when Saket Ram renounces his familial ties it is very clear that he is not severing himself from his incestuous ties with his phallic mother. In short, he is not paying any symbolic debt to any father figure. Particularly, when he breaks his sacred thread and abdominal cord, and takes a dip in the Ganges, this image smoothly dissolves into his mother's photograph as if he is merging with her and the nation. Strengthening this link, in a few scenes previous to this event of renunciation, Saket Ram, while perfecting his weapon in his secret chamber, caresses the map of Akhand Bharath and the photograph of his mother with one continuous affectionate stroke of his fingers as both these objects are conveniently placed next to each other.

Why does the film then expend so much drama over this scene of renunciation[10] and takes all that trouble to do so at a great distance from Chennai in a place like Kashi? No doubt, the main purpose is to religiously anoint Saket Ram's mission by turning his quest into a spiritual one, but it simultaneously entails an attempt to overcome other contradictions in the Hindu national imaginary. Within south Indian Tamil Vaishnavism, which prioritises *bhakti marga* (the path of devotion) over *jnanamarga* (the path of knowledge) or the *karma marga* (the path of action), renunciation means giving up family ties and everyday attachments to dedicate oneself to humble service in a temple or related order. If Saket Ram does so, his entire mission would lose its maniacal masculine aura. Saket Ram's Vaishnavite god Ram is 'stricken with a sort of feminisation' (Lacan 1997: 101), and opting for bhakti marga would in no way help him or his god. It would in that sense rob Saket Ram of his masculinity by turning him into a resentless *baul* (mystic minstrel), a sort of a close copy of Gandhi singing his *bhajans* (devotional songs). This is something the hero cannot tolerate and, therefore, chooses to conduct his renunciation according to Saivite rites just as he dreams up the fusion of Ram and Siva in the storm sequence. Consequently, in this renunciation sequence, Saket Ram wears the Saivite sacred ash on his forehead instead of his usual Vaishnavite red mark. Another object thus achieved is the fusing of contradictory traditions into a unified monolithic Hinduism, as it occurs in the choice of his two wives—Aparna, the first, being a Bengali Shakta Saivite, and Mythili, the second, being a Mannarkudi Vaishnavite.

If Sri Ram Abhayankar for the reasons cited above fails to emerge as Saket Ram's symbolic father, what then are the chances of the Maharashtrian Rajah in becoming the chosen one? He loses the race in the crucial scene because exactly when he announces the mission, his face is effaced by Aparna's face. Moreover, Saket Ram yields nothing of symbolic value to him. What then about Saket Ram's absent father, in the film at least? Does he enjoy such a privilege? The first instance we get to know that Saket Ram has a father is by way of his telegram that reaches his son in Calcutta. He tears it up though to formalise his marriage with Aparna. However, he later marries Mythili according to the wishes of this father. How do we read this ambivalence? Although Saket Ram either directly or symbolically annihilates anyone occupying the paternal position in relation to him, he is nonetheless ambiguously quite submissive to these figures from time to time. For instance, when he undertakes the pledge with Abhayankar, in his swift response to the telegram sent by the Rajah to proceed on his mission or in eventually complying with his own father's desire by marrying Mythili, Saket Ram takes a submissive position towards these figures.

As Lacan (1997) observes, such a submissive attitude is revelatory of the conformist side of psychotic delusion:

> The alienation here is radical, it is not bound to a nihilating signified, as in a certain type of rivalrous relation with the father, but to a nihilation of the signifier. The subject will have to bear the weight of this real, primitive dispossession of the signifier and adopt compensation for it, at length, over the course of his life, through a series of purely conformist identifications with characters who will give him the feeling for what one has to be a man. (Ibid.: 205)

It is because of this foreclosure of the *paternal signifier* or the *name of the father*, that signifies symbolic fatherhood and which cannot be internalised by Saket Ram, that his rivalry with all the father figures oscillates between two poles, moving from submission to attack or from attack to submission or from reverence to degradation or *vice versa*. For instance, in the case of the *sodomising Muslim other*, he moves from a position of submission to a position of attack. In the case of Gandhi, he moves from a position of submission in terms of the guilt produced by Gandhian secular values, represented by the haunting image of the blind Muslim girl, to full-fledged attack when he fires at his hallucinated image, to submission again when he briefly kneels down in front of him to offer him his gun box, but in the end he moves into a position of attack once again, by burning Gandhi's effigy, the huge portrait on the wall, with his impossible gaze. In addition, the expulsion of the paternal signifier, going beyond all these figures, is problematic for Saket Ram's own paternal position as well. He cannot, therefore, recognise his own son, M. G. Raman (Chandra Haasan), who is condemned to be an inferior shadow of his father.

This does not imply that Saket Ram lacks any desire to procreate. The storm scene, where his megalomania reaches it full form, as discussed, given the kind of sexual fusion that takes place, involves a final compromise of his virility. This compromise necessarily entails a *pregnancy fantasy*, as without that the purpose of this divine erotic relationship will not be realised within the delusion of Saket Ram. Like his counterpart Daniel Paul Schreber, he thus wishes to father/mother a nation with his God, and proliferate it with an entire race of his doubles. This is 'procreation after the deluge' after the conclusion of the hero's most agonising apocalyptic encounters with the sodomising other and Gandhi (Lacan 1997: 213). His son, Raman, in that sense, is one of the products of the deluge, hence his inferiority. It is significant that in the story of Saket Ram there is a huge temporal gap between 30 January 1948 and 6 December 1999, probably indicating in the interim a long period of hibernation or incubation after the deluge. Hence the pride of place the grandson, Saket Ram, Jr, enjoys. He is the only one authorised to speak on behalf of his grandfather, a status granted to him by the very name he bears as his double. It is not surprising that like his grandfather, he has the ambiguous ability to unnerve the threatening Muslim police officer Ibrahim (Nasser) with all benevolent intentions, by asking him for his name, so that the onus of proving one's secular credentials is always on the other.[11] In the film, when we first see this police officer in the context of the Chennai riots, except for the fact that the role is played by Nasser, we do not know that the character he portrays is, therefore, necessarily a Muslim. In the end, when Saket Ram, Jr, asks for his name, by way of another coincidence his name badge is missing. Searching for it and not finding it, the officer after an embarrassing moment of hesitation announces his name as 'Ibrahim'. Initially, it is this officer who aggressively blocks the ambulance taking the elder Saket Ram to the hospital and forces the stretcher carrying Saket Ram and the others accompanying him into a dry drain, to wait below the surface of the ground until the riots cease. Thereby he enjoys all narrative initiative at this point. During the riot, when predominantly Muslim mobs are shown as engaging in destructive activities, this officer is highly conscientious about his duty, proving his secular credentials for the gaze that judges him. In the end, when Saket Ram, Jr, seizes the initiative by asking for his name, he thus reveals the disarming side of this gaze that was judging this father figure all the time. In that sense, even in the case of Saket Ram, Jr, anyone who occupies the paternal position is degraded in some manner after an initial moment of submission.

V

This ideological fantasy of the film apparently received its ultimate mark of authenticity even before it could acquire any public acclaim elsewhere, by the fact that Tushar Gandhi, the great-grandson of Gandhiji, did not just accompany Kamal Haasan for the grand occasion organised by the Government of Bengal to honour the film in Calcutta, but actually appeared in the film and as himself.

The initial addressee of the story seemingly narrated by Saket Ram, Jr, in the beginning of the film is the young doctor, Munawar, a Muslim and a stand-in for the spectator in this first scene of *Hey Ram*. Surprisingly, however, Tushar Gandhi takes this position at the end to metonymically confer the blessings of Gandhiji on the film. In the world described by its narrative, Tushar Gandhi thus arrives in it, ostensibly to receive the confession of the sins of the elder Saket Ram that his illustrious great-grandfather could not do because of his untimely death. As Tushar Gandhi appears as himself, however, as if he is from outside the realm of its fictional characters, on the one hand, his presence is included to pre-empt any criticism of the film by obtaining a Gandhian validation of it and, on the other, to double its reality effect. The film cannot achieve these ends without inadvertently creating one of its major ambivalent components, as it raises the issue whether Tushar Gandhi belongs to the object world of the narrative of the film or stands outside it.

The crucial question then is: What is the actual status of Tushar Gandhi in the film? Is he real or fictional? It seems obvious that he appears as himself and not as characters normally do in fiction because he carries his actual name within the film, and in which case he is real. If then, how can he make the impossible claim that he is a fan of the writings of Saket Ram, Jr, who is obviously a fictional character, and in which case Tushar Gandhi's status is then as fictional as that of Saket Ram, Jr. In other words, the film cannot achieve its ends without denying the fictional status of Tushar Gandhi in its narrative. This process is derailed as the repressed fictional status of his character returns, not just in the visual construction of the scene where he meets another fictional character, but in the very utterance of Tushar Gandhi to Saket Ram, Jr—'I have read your books. I am your fan' (Haasan 2000, Scene 71: 182)—that locates the speaker of this statement as an equally fictional character. His presence thus gives rise to two incompatible statements at the same time, like saying, although he is actually an imaginary character, he is nonetheless real. The fact that the film cannot control the emergence of his fictional status on its own surface, however, makes evident that Tushar Gandhi's presence in the film is nothing more than that of the creation of another double that is in service of its death drive. The fact, however, remains that in the process it cannot efface the yawning gap between reality and representation.[12] What appears in the film, therefore, contrary to its claims, is not history in all its impossibly unsullied archaeological being, but something that takes its place with all the fascinating powers of the cinema to claim reality status.

Ambivalences (pairs of opposites) or disavowals (simultaneously holding or asserting two incompatible beliefs) of this kind proliferate in the film to produce other devious contradictions, conferring reality status to what the film finds desirable and fictional status to what it does not find desirable. In Scene 19, immediately after the wedding ceremony, where Saket Ram is becoming a little more acquainted with Mythili in their nuptial bedroom, he refers to Gandhi's autobiography, *The Story of My Experiments with Truth*, as 'biography' and, therefore, in his opinion, as 'semi-fiction'. To Mythili, on the contrary, because it is a 'biography', it is 'history' (Haasan 2000, Scene 19: 74). The issue here is whose words carry the necessary authority and power of truth within the film, and, therefore, it is what Saket Ram says that carries all the weight. In direct contrast to Gandhi's book, 'Veer' Savarkar's unidentified book, about which a great deal of secrecy and curiosity is aroused in the film, is 'history' to Saket Ram but 'semi-fiction' to Mythili (Haasan 2000, Scene 32: 95).

Intriguingly, the film introduces Savarkar's book for the first time to the spectator as if it is an equivalent of *Everything You Wanted to Know about Sex (Indian History) but Forgot to Ask 'Veer' Savarkar*. It is Sri Ram Abhayankar who gives the book to Saket Ram in a hush-hush tone uttering, 'read this book ... this is a banned book ... this is Veer Savarkar's ...', and saying nothing more on it (Haasan 2000, Scene 11B: 55). Later in the aircraft on their way to Poona, noticing Saket Ram's absorption in the book, Mythili suggests in Tamil that he may be reading 'pornography' because the brown wrapper on the book deliberately hides its identity (Haasan 2000, Scene 32: 93–94). Does Mythili's comment interjected at this point in the film work as a subversive remark on 'Veer' Savarkar's book? The facts are to the contrary. Her statement is neither a dialogical contestation of Saket Ram's position on the book nor a self-reflexive instance in the film aimed to deconstruct its fetishism. Moreover, the possibility for such a reading does not arise because Saket Ram at the conclusion of the scene washes the book clean of its historical sins by equating it with the very moral principle of Gandhi's three monkeys before Mythili can half-heartedly deny it by saying, 'I hate semi-fiction':

> **Mythili**: I am like the three monkeys of Mahatma. I would see no evil, speak no evil and hear no evil. For good things, these three senses will always remain open.
> **Saket Ram (offering the book to her)**: Good! Then you can read this book. History!
> **Mythili**: I hate semi-fiction!

Thus, what emerges as pornography contradictorily ends up as a morally worthy history. The film registers Mythili's claim, 'I hate semi-fiction', only as a naïve remark and as a partial denial. Hence, her voice is not the dominant one in it; or woman as woman do not exist or enjoy any speaking position within the film. They can only masquerade as ideological constructs,[13] and the greater their agency, the more severe the narrative punishment. It is not by chance that the first woman Saket Ram loves is brutally eliminated and the next one is condemned to live the life of a widow much as she is married to him. Their very existence is inimical to his identity as they constantly remind him of his feminisation. Mythili's initial comment on the book, therefore, is an important index of the texual strategies of the film. By metonymically introducing the suggestion of pornography, by its wrapper giving it a secrecy, the film doubles the sense of curiosity in the spectator about Savarkar's book, triggered as it is in its first instance in the film by Abhayankar—which then makes it easy for Saket Ram to emphatically assert the enhanced status of it as the missing link in the history of the nation or give that problematic representation of history the necessary phallic consistency and desirability, and thus valorise its significance over Gandhi's book.

Crucially, the fact that Saket Ram is in love with Sarvarkar's book because it is history, and Mythili hates it because it is semi-fiction, does not entail an absolute polarisation of views between the two, because the ambivalence of love and hate expressed towards the same object often strengthens its libidinal attachment. Significantly, if Mythili objects to Saket Ram's desire for hunting by pointing out that it is a sin at one time, and quite elaborately at that (Haasan 2000, Scene 33: 97–99), then later on she says to Saket, that is, after she has been thoroughly subdued in bed in an extravagant demonstration of hypermasculinity, 'You like hunting. That is not a sin. It is the Tiger's dharma to do so. I love you my Tiger' (Haasan 2000, Scene 42: 116). Implying that she has already come around to Saket's point of view and would eventually read the book he recommended.

In comparison to 'Veer' Savarkar's book, Gandhi's autobiography in the film does not enjoy the same status despite the contradictory statements made about it. The film includes it, therefore, to only reject it, valorising Saket Ram's experiments with truth against Gandhi's experiments with truth. Moreover, the narrative clearly identifies it by its name and provides no cause for any excited secrecy or curiosity about it. Second, it is Mythili's copy and, in the scene in which it appears, as it is her initial sense of history, Saket Ram wishes to overcome it when he flippantly dismisses it as semi-fiction (Haasan 2000, Scene 19: 74).[14] The ambivalent feelings expressed by Mythili and Saket Ram over Gandhi's book thus do not carry the same libidinal component as that of Savarkar's book, as the latter provides the compensatory vision for the chasm introduced by the former. Once again, such ambiguities or contradictions abound only to assert Saket Ram's certainty of what counts as redeeming history and what does not count as such.

In short, all these textual manoeuvres sufficiently indicate that the film is not merely acknowledging the 'public will ... to kill the father' (Vasudevan 2002: 2925). Nor is it eventually surrendering 'the excesses of militant masculinity as a futile excursion' (Gopalan 2002: 191), as that would imply the return of the protagonist to his earlier feminised position, without his divine imaginary partner providing him the shield against castration. On the contrary, the central agenda of the film is to construct a hypermasculine Hindu subjectivity, and to provide that cultural psychosis a megalomaniacal coherence by forging a homoerotic relationship by fusing two divine authorities. Notwithstanding the cracks that reveal themselves as a compromised position of masculine virility exactly in the place where they are ironed out by such a mighty libidinal fusion, what is more disconcerting is the virulent certainty that informs this narcissistic mission.

VI

It is intriguing that in the history of Tamil cinema, *Hey Ram* is the first major attempt ever to broach the subject of Partition and its traumatic overtones. The only exception to this is *Andhaman Kaidhi* (1952) that makes a brief reference to Partition, at the beginning of its narrative. In this film, Chidambaram Pillai, Kamakshi Ammal, and their son Natarajan and daughter Leela flee the riot-torn city of Karachi to arrive in Tiruchirappalli expecting help from relatives and fellow Hindus, only to be ironically exploited by them and cheated out of their remaining possessions (Govindan 2001: 123–24).

The fact that no Tamil film other than *Hey Ram* has aspired to provide a centrality to the issue of Partition over the past seven decades in itself apparently constitutes a puzzle. However, the fact that even during the unbearably terrifying moment of Partition there were no widespread communal backlashes in the region provides the required explanation for this conspicuous and prolonged absence in the region's cinematic oeuvre. The agony of Partition, in other words, did not carry the same degree of weight and intensity in Tamil Nadu as it did in Bengal and Punjab. It may not be preposterous then to underline the obvious geographical fact that Partition, as the most excruciating historical experience, did not transpire in the region. Nevertheless, considering the engagement of Tamil Nadu in the Independence struggle, and on which there is quite a corpus of films, this does not necessarily implicate it as a remote region where such horrendous occurrences lack any significance whatsoever. Being just the opposite, it registers the fact that Tamil Nadu is one of the few places that enjoyed considerable communal concord during those times, which lent the indispensable balance to its composite and hybrid communities, despite the dreadfulness of the events that tore them apart elsewhere on the subcontinent. We cannot conclude on that basis, however, that communal antagonisms were entirely absent in Tamil Nadu during the colonial period. For various reasons, these tensions did not take the kind of ugly turn they took in Bengal or Punjab, although some Muslim families did migrate to Pakistan.[15]

No doubt Hindu–Muslim relations increasingly worsened in the period 1930–36. Yet, communal conflicts and riots which occurred during this time did not reach the kind of proportions they did in North India, for in these disturbances that occurred intermittently over a period of six years, only three lives were lost. Extensive damage to property was, however, reported (More 1997: 102–03). Principally, a great deal of ethnic similarities between various communities, specifically the use of a common language, popular religious syncretism and its associated practices that makes a visit or pilgrimage obligatory to many Tamil Hindus to Islamic or Christian shrines, and the impact of the Dravidian movement, its longstanding relationship with the Muslim community and the vanguard role played by Tamil Muslims in the Madras Presidency Muslim League, resulted in a great deal of give and take (ibid.: 109–20). So much so that even the miniscule Urdu-speaking minority of aristocratic Deccani Muslims, who predominantly live in Chennai, although ethnically trace their roots to Hyderabad and Persian lineage, are well integrated into the region. In the 1940s, despite the acceleration towards Partition, things did not get out of hand as they did in Bengal or Punjab because if on the one hand Periyar had close correspondence with Jinnah, firmly supporting the idea of Pakistan, then on the other Rajagopalachari was the first major Congress leader to accept the demand for Pakistan as a separate Muslim State before 'any other Congress leader could even think about it' and despite the stiff opposition of the All-India Congress Committee (AICC) (ibid.: 185–87), earning him the high esteem of the local Muslim community.

It is owing to such understanding and mutual respect that the Direct Action Day, unlike in Calcutta and Bihar, passed off as a peaceful day of several meetings and processions in Chennai and rest of Tamil Nadu (ibid.: 199). Moreover, knowing very well that Pakistan was brought about as much by the support of south Indian Muslims as that of northern Muslims, but recognising that eventually Tamil Muslims cannot belong to it as a territorial entity, the president of the Madras Presidency Muslim League, Muhammed Ismail, popularly known as Quaid-e-Millat, leader of the community, declared:

> Mussalmans of Hindustan must realise that the new Indian flag is no longer a party flag as it has been accepted as the national flag of the Indian Union with the consent of all the parties in the Constituent Assembly. It is therefore only right that we Muslims living in the Union should henceforth regard it as our flag and respect it. We are not joining the Independence Day celebrations in any spirit of compulsion but as free citizens of a free Indian Union. (Moore 1997: 204)

It does not follow, however, that Hindu militancy was entirely absent during colonial times in Tamil Nadu. Legendary names like Vanchinathan, Subramanya Shiva and Subramania Bharathi provide ample evidence for its presence. Spearheaded as it was mainly by upper-caste Tamils, its influence, however, did not become widespread owing to two reasons. The Non-Brahmin Movement created a rupture between upper-caste elites and subaltern participation in the Congress-led Independence struggle was greater because of figures like Kamaraj.

Things began to change, no doubt, in the 1990s with the increasing presence of Hindu Munnani (Hindu Front) and its unholy activities, culminating as they did in the bloody riots of Coimbatore (29 November to 1 December 1997), followed by the Al-Umma retaliatory blasts (14–16 February 1998). A clear repetition of the pattern that was first established at Bombay in December 1992 and January 1993.

Consequently, in addressing the associated anxieties of this contemporary antagonism in Tamil Nadu[16] and elsewhere, *Hey Ram* finds a convenient ground to invoke the trauma of Partition riots. The objective is to primarily negate the causes of present conflict by way of a detour through a past trauma, so that the responsibility for both the Partition bloodletting and contemporary communal riots is located 'evidentially' in a singular agency. Collective memory being as well known for its amnesia as individual memory is, the Great Calcutta Riots of 1946, provided the way they evolved there on Direct Action Day, offer a sure-fire opportunity for a narrative strategy of this kind to coherently rest the entire blame on Muslims as the initiators of all violence in every corner of the subcontinent, and with the same stroke implicate Gandhi as the principal supporter of such violence and bloodshed. In the process, a series of highly significant historical events are absolutely silenced—the designs of colonialism, specifically its first partition of Bengal along communal lines; the importance of the Muslim question, raised on the threshold of self-rule; the hysteria whipped up by the Hindu press; the administrative haste with which the Partition of the subcontinent and the transfer of power was implemented; the contradictions thrown up by the predominantly Sikh–Muslim Partition riots in Punjab as against events in Bengal; the extensive efforts taken by Gandhi amidst all this mayhem and bloodshed; and last but not the least, the kind of balance that existed in Tamil Nadu despite all the tensions.[17] Specifically, the film evades the peaceful response to Direct Action Day in Tamil Nadu, and in its place creates a mythical contemporary scenario, as if come every 6 December, the city of Chennai is besieged by some inevitable Hindu–Muslim riot. All such elisions and fabrications are further smoothened out by an imagined past in which the nation is mapped as belonging unquestionably to the *self* as against the demonised *other*, who is figured as a natural-born killer and an alien aggressor. The closure of the gaps and discontinuities between a colonial past and a postcolonial present, or the North and the South, are thereby not effected, before the film extracts maximum pay-off by way of its most telling cultural narcissism that inextricably anchors it in the Hindu national imaginary.

The question arises as to what exactly is the nature of the central trauma addressed by the film. I hope that the foregoing analysis would have clearly suggested that it has nothing to do about engaging in the necessary mourning work for the painful losses incurred during Partition or contemporary Hindu–Muslim riots or, for that matter, the disturbing assassination of Gandhi—and has everything to do with an aggressive recovery of a narcissistic hypermasculine Hindu authority legitimising a Brahminical vanguard. That even after a century of challenge, initiated by the Non-Brahmin Movement in the region, the fact that this historical loss of Brahminical authority is still not mourned but relentlessly reclaimed, and with an increasingly loud voice, finding a fresh lease of life in the highly problematic popularity generated by the discourse of the Sangh Parivar, is something that is inadvertently revealed by the mechanisms of the film itself. With the compulsion to repeat thus dominating the present scenario, the possibilities of a new beginning are forever receding.

Notes

[1] Such a moment of silence occurs in Kurosawa's *Rhapsody in August* (1991) when two old women, who have lost their husbands in the atomic explosion in Nagasaki, meet each other. In what is a sustained long take, they do not utter a single word.

[2] Some old city-names have been used in this chapter in the historical context in which they are mentioned.

[3] At the time when these two readings were published, as I was simultaneously working on my previous draft of this essay, which was published in *MICA Review*, I did not have the time to clarify my differences with the claims made by Ravi Vasudevan and Lalitha Gopalan in their respective essays on *Hey Ram*. In this revised version, I hope that I have been able to do some justice to the same.

[4] It should be emphasised, however, that Kamal Haasan, the director and star of the film, has not openly identified himself with Hindutva. In fact, at one time he directly associated himself with the Dravidar Kazhagam, founded by Periyar.

[5] It is not necessary that the symbolic father must be present in some way in every film. Often, it could be an impersonal agency like the law, community or other things, which can take its place. Sometimes a figure mistaken for an obscene father may later emerge as the symbolic father. See Sharpe (2002) for a lucid introduction to the *name of the father* and the role it plays in films.

[6] All parenthetical references to the scenes in the film are drawn from the screenplay of the film (Haasan 2000), published after the release of the film.

[7] Daniel Paul Schreber makes a similar paradoxical compromise with his god. It is with that his delusion reaches its culminating point. See Freud (2001: 18–29) and Lacan (1997: 351).

[8] See 'The Hysteric's Question I and II' (Lacan 1997: 161–82).

[9] For instance, the film *Terminator* (1984) narrates the impossible fantasy of a subject witnessing his own birth. See Penley (1989: 121–40).

[10] Renunciation as a real ethical value, according to psychoanalysis, entails the renunciation of all forms of narcissistic gratifications. This is something Saket Ram or the film cannot envisage, as such a possibility is excluded by the very terms set by the narrative. See Zizek (1992: 167–73)

[11] For instance, Saket Ram flings the axe of 700 years of Muslim rule on Amjad Khan who, as if he is confessing before a Stalinist trial, says apologetically, 'I was not born then' (Haasan 2000, Scene 65: 163). The onus of proving one's secular credentials, thus, always rests with the other. This point was brought out by Pandian during one of my discussions with him on secularism.

[12] For a more elaborate discussion on the fetishism of the cinematic image, see Metz (1986: 244–80).

[13] For a detailed description of the concept of masquerade in relation to the representation of women in cinema and its implications for the female spectator, see Doane (1991: 17–43).

[14] There are a number of other problematic disavowals in the film, but they cannot be explored here because of reasons of space and time.

[15] For instance, S. M. Basha, an Urdu-speaking Muslim, the president of the Madras Presidency Muslim League, 1941–45, migrated to Pakistan after Partition (More 1997: 246).

[16] In contrast to the representation of the past, the entire present in the film is restricted to one singular day, 6 December 1999, depicting it as if there are periodical riots every year in Chennai on this day. This is a blatant distortion. Only recently, that is, around 6 December 2002, a nation-wide hysteria was generated by making bogeymen out of Muslim fundamentalists, as witnessed by the various security checks at public spaces like railway stations, airports, bus stands and check-posts.

[17] For a historical account of the various causes that contributed to the communal riots in Bengal, see Das (1991), and for the events that preceded and followed Partition, see Khosla (1989).

References

Borderick, Mick (ed.). 1996. *Hibakusha Cinema: Hiroshima, Nagasaki and the Nuclear Image in the Japanese Film*. London: Kegan Paul International.

Chakravarthy, Venkatesh. 2003. 'Encountering the Traumatic: *Hey Ram* and its Cultural Narcissism'. *MICA Communications Review* 1(1): 52–73. Mudra Institute of Communications, Ahmedabad,

Das, Suranjan. 1991. *Communal Riots in Bengal (1905–1947)*. Delhi: Oxford University Press.

Doane, Mary Ann. 1991. *Femmes Fatales: Feminism, Film Theory, Psychoanalysis*. New York: Routledge.

Freud, Sigmund. 1991a. *On Metapsychology: The Theory of Psychoanalysis*, Volume 11. London: Penguin Books.

—— 1991b. *On Sexuality*, Volume 7. London: Penguin Books.

—— 2001. *The Standard Edition of Complete Psychological Works of Sigmund Freud, Volume 12 (1911–1913): The Case of Schreber, Papers on Technique and Other Works*, trans. James Strachey, Anna Freud, Alix Strachey and Alan Tyson. London: Vintage Books, Hogarth Press and Institute of Psychoanalysis.

Gopalan, Lalitha. 2002. 'Digital Imaginings in Indian Popular Films'. In *Cinema of Interruptions: Action Genres in Contemporary Indian Cinema*, 187–96. London: BFI Publishing.

Govindan, Mu. Ka. 2001. *Tamil Thiraipadangalil Jathi Madha Bedhangal* (Representation of Caste and Religious Differences in the Tamil Cinema). Chennai: Kumaran Publishers.

Haasan, Kamal. 2000. *Raaj Kamal's* Hey Ram: *An Experiment with Truth* (A Screenplay). Chennai: Bama Pathipagam.

Khosla, G. D. 1989. *Stern Reckoning*. Bombay: Oxford University Press.

Lacan, Jacques. 1977. *Four Fundamental Concepts of Psychoanalysis*, ed. Jacques-Allain Miller, trans. Alan Sheridan. London: Hogarth Press.

—— 1997. *The Psychoses (1955–1956): The Seminar of Jacques Lacan*, Book 3. New York: W. W. Norton & Company.

Metz, Christian. 1986. *Imaginary Signifier (Excerpts) in Narrative, Apparatus, Ideology: A Film Theory Reader*, ed. Philip Rosen. New York: Columbia University Press.

More, J. B. P. 1997. *The Political Evolution of Muslims in Tamilnadu and Madras: 1930–1947*. Chennai: Orient Longman.

Penley, Constance. 1989. *The Future of an Illusion: Film, Feminism and Psychoanalysis*. Great Britain: Routledge.

Prasad, Madhav. 1998. *Ideology of the Hindi Film: A Historical Construction*. Delhi: Oxford University Press.

Sharpe, Matthew. 2002. 'What is the Name of the Father?: An Officer and a Gentleman?'. *Cinetext: Film and Philosophy*, June. Available at http://cinetext.philo.at/magazine/msharpe/matthew_sharpe-what_is_the_name_of_the_father.html (accessed 19 October 2002).

Venkatachalapathy, A. R. 1994. *Bharathiyin Karuthu Padangal: India (1906–1910)*. Chennai: Narmatha Pathipakam.

Vasudevan, Ravi. 2002. 'Another History Rises to the Surface: '*Hey Ram*'—Melodrama in the Age of Digital Simulation'. *Economic and Political Weekly* 37(28), 13 July: 2917–25.

Zizek, Slavoj. 1992. *Enjoy Your Symptom!: Jacque Lacan in Hollywood and Out*. New York and London: Routledge.

____ 1993. *Tarrying with the Negative: Kant, Hegel and the Critique of Ideology*. Durham: Duke University Press.

13. Political Surplus in Retrospect

On the Decline of Cinematic Sovereignties

M. Madhava Prasad

The historic era of sovereign stars spanning five decades and three south Indian states has just gone into terminal decline. The stars are still there but the people who crown them kings are either no longer flocking to the coronation or are being turned away at the gates. A recent newspaper headline bears witness to this: 'Where have all the diehard film fans of Andhra Pradesh gone?' (*The Hindu* 2015). Even more recently, Rajinikanth fans created a ruckus at a theatre when they felt themselves cheated out of the privilege of watching the first day, first show. Enjoying the privileges of fandom and imposing upon their heroes political and moral obligations, these bands of followers had ruled the theatres on release day. But lately their stock has fallen and the virtual worlds they sustained have come crumbling down. In *Cine-politics: Film Stars and Political Existence in South India* (2014), I characterised this as a shift from political to economic surplus. In this chapter, I will expand upon that statement to argue that what we have witnessed here is nothing short of a restaging of the historic transition from the supremacy of political power to the reign of the economy. I will discuss the late careers of the last generation of stars with cine-political potential (Rajinikanth, Chiranjeevi, etc.) to capture the drama of the erosion of political privilege by a rampaging capitalist economy. For the demobilised fans, the protective shadow of the sovereign lost forever, the only option left is a fetishistic veneration shorn of the old sense of privilege.

The occasion of the release of Rajinikanth's latest film, *Kabali* (2016), directed by Pa. Ranjith, has once again highlighted the sorry plight of the once-privileged community of Rajini fans. A YouTube video provides proof.[1] The fans were robbed of their longstanding privilege of being the star's first spectators—concretely realised by being in the audience of the 'first day, first show'—by a peculiar circumstance: While typically a film is released on a Friday and the first show happens sometime in the morning, this time, special shows were organised at 1 a.m. and 4 a.m. during the night, for which tickets were priced in the thousands and sold through the internet. Fans reacted angrily to what they perceived as a trick played on them by the theatre management. In the video, one fan claims that none of those who went into the theatre were Rajini fans 'and we are all very disappointed'. Another angry fan directly questions the star, addressing him as *Thalaiva* (chief). 'Should we poor people not see your film, *Thalaiva*', he asks. 'What wrong have we committed? We are the ones who were there from the beginning, not these IT people.' 'People who don't even know *Thalaiva* are coming to watch.' 'They conned us.' 'Are the IT guys going to come and do (the work that fans do)?' And so on. In a gesture of protest, some of them took away the banners which they had brought along to display at the theatre.

With this, the stripping of all the privileges the superstar's fans, which began 10 years ago with *Sivaji* (2007), directed by S. Shankar, may now be said to be complete. Rajinikanth's superstardom has transcended the conditions which nurtured it and has become the property of the world. Two transitions can be noted here: On the one hand, there has been a massive increase in what, from the 'original' Rajini fan's perspective, can only be termed vicarious fandom. Like Duke Orsino in Shakespeare's *Twelfth Night*, who was in love with the idea of love, which made him incapable of loving in truth, it would seem that for the old Rajini fan, the new Rajini fan is an intruder, someone who is not a fan *per se*, but a fan of fandom, a consumer of it. But their anger and resentment at this turn of events will be drowned out by the loud and exuberant scenes of the new fans' celebrations spread out across the world which suffuse the media. Can they reconcile themselves to this diminished status and continue to worship the star as before? Or will these developments, making it impossible to experience the same feeling of exclusive privilege, cure them once and for all of that old passion? We are not about to answer these questions. But it is beyond doubt that there has been a sea change in the very nature of the fandom that Rajinikanth now enjoys.

Not just an expansion in numbers, but a qualitative change in the very character of fan discourse. This is the first of the two transitions involved here.

The second transition is not specific to Rajinikanth, but concerns the passing of that phase of star–fan relations which, beginning with MGR in the 1950s, has over a half century played a significant role in the political life of not only Tamil Nadu but also Andhra Pradesh and Karnataka. This transition is not a fading or disappearance of that moment, but a transformation into something new. This is what I characterised in *Cine-politics* as the mutation of political surplus into economic surplus. It is observable in many fields of human activity that when an old order passes, the material remains of it acquire a new value in the order that takes its place. Thus, the grand and imposing architecture of the British Empire now serves the accommodation needs of a republican State, imparting to the latter at least some of the aura of imperial power. Likewise, and especially in the case of Rajinikanth, we can see that the body of the star now yields spectacular profits by virtue of its accumulated scarcity value built up over time.

In the rest of the chapter, I will outline the history of the half century of reign of film stars as sovereigns, introduce and explain the difference between political and economic surplus, and in conclusion reflect upon the significance for contemporary culture of the transition.

'Cine-politics' as I define it in the volume of that title is primarily a concept intended to capture the singularity of a political phenomenon that the southern states of India named earlier have witnessed beginning in the 1950s, and which we have observed in its terminal decline in recent years. The defining element in the concept is a particular type of star–fan relationship, which differs from the more commonly prevalent forms in that it metamorphoses into a political formation, albeit virtual but capable of and known to have produced real political effects. The first and to date the only book-length study of these effects is Pandian's *The Image Trap* (Pandian 2015). Pandian's focus is on what he termed 'a modern day political myth', the story of MGR's rise to political power, his image as 'a patron saint of the poor' and, above all, the sordid truths concealed behind the mythical haze of corruption, profiteering and violent suppression of dissent. One of the first efforts to interpret Indian sociocultural reality with the Gramscian conceptual tools such as cultural hegemony and common sense, *The Image Trap* was an exemplary work of transdisciplinary scholarship. Pandian's aim was to elaborate through a detailing of the discourse of MGR's films—the song lyrics, the dialogue, the visual symbols—how the star discourse permeates common sense and thereby succeeds in winning popular adulation. Other scholars who have studied the MGR phenomenon include K. Sivathamby, Robert Hardgrave, Jr, and Duncan Forrester, all social scientists.

My own foray into this area of investigation was in the context of the spread of the cine-political discourse beyond the borders of Tamil Nadu into Andhra Pradesh and Karnataka. In 1982, N. T. Rama Rao (NTR), having launched the Telugu Desam Party, won a spectacular victory over the Congress and became chief minister. It was also in the same year that Rajkumar entered the so-called Gokak agitation for primacy to Kannada in administration and education, and turned it into a state-wide uprising. It seemed to me that the repetition of an event such as this required shifting the focus so that it was examined in a historical frame as a political event to be explained within the context of Indian political history, rather than within a synchronic frame where the power of the message or the receptivity of the masses alone served as the explanatory factor.

My conclusion in that work (Prasad 2014) was that the cine-political event is best understood as occurring in a situation where a majority of the population had been deprived of political existence. To exist is to appear in a world, to exist politically is to have 'the intensity of the appearance of a being in the world' (Meillassoux 2011: 8), in this case, the political world. Historically, it is sovereignty that has been the manifest form of political existence. In democracies, sovereignty is no longer embodied in the body of the king, but is supposed to be distributed among the people themselves who become sovereign subjects. In reality, however, given the vastness of the Indian political formation and the multiple axes of difference which divide the population—caste, religion, region, language, history, literacy—the assumption of sovereignty is not an available option for the greater majority. Democracy came through the seemingly benevolent action of politicians and civil servants, an empty form which merely encircled the population but did not substantially transform it. As Ambedkar (1994) memorably described it, in the republic that was inaugurated on 26 January 1950, social inequality, which meant the in-built inequalities of pre-republican society, remained intact even as an abstract political equality was introduced. This meant that there was no ideological bridge between the political process and the social substance, no hegemony. In such a context, the prevailing ideas of political power—monarchic, imperial, charismatic—remained intact and continued to operate within the new political infrastructure. This is not to say that it did so at the level of the political structure as a whole, that is, at the level of Indian national political life, but at those levels where people were previously ensconced in a variety of sovereign orders. The republic was an inert enclosure. It is in such a context that scholars have noted the political scene in India as dominated by a multitude of fragmentary sovereignties, in which the place of the sovereign can be occupied by big men, religious leaders, nationalities, caste groups, etc. (Hansen 2005). Thus, for most people, political existence (as we translate sovereignty) derives from participation in one of these groupings rather than from the political order established by the Constitution. Such a reality constitutes a living indictment of the emptiness of the political gesture with which the dominant classes try to legitimise their rule.

In cine-politics, we encounter three newly invented sovereign formations, each of them centered on a film star. These, like the fragmented sovereignties mentioned earlier, function as alternatives to the proclaimed political order. The elevation to kingly status that this has involved has not necessarily been predicated upon factors which have featured predominantly in the explanations usually offered. Thus, the films do not always include pro-poor messages and are, on the contrary, often quite routine melodramas in which aristocratic or landowning families recover their possessions after they have been deceitfully taken from them by villainous relatives. Family reunions are almost invariably accompanied by recovery of lost property and the justice rendered is in conformity with a social order marked by traditional hierarchies. The mythological films do not constitute the decisive genre for the formation of the cine-political equation either, an argument frequently made in relation to NTR, implying further that these films work on the spectator by inducing a belief in the godly character of the artist himself. The cine-political event is an expressly *contemporary* occurrence, and it is through his modern roles, and modern clothes and appearance, that he is able to trigger the entry into a virtual world of monarchic make-believe. However, it is also a fact that not everybody who has donned such roles has been able to command such subaltern allegiance, and here we see that the industry has ascribed to the first male stars of this type fairly stable genre associations, which are all-important. Thus, in all the three industries—Tamil, Telugu and Kannada—we see the rise of two male stars, each with a distinct set of assigned meanings. In the Kannada industry, this division of labour and meaning proves somewhat difficult to sustain due to a variety of reasons, including the relatively small size of the market. But the attempt was made there too. As a result, we have the star duos of MGR and Sivaji Ganesan in the Tamil industry, NTR and A. Nageswara Rao (ANR) in the Telugu industry, and Rajkumar and Kalyan Kumar in the Kannada industry. For all of them, the social is the defining genre, but it is only the first named in each of these pairs that rises to the virtual political position.

The difference between the two is best captured by describing their positions in terms of the relation to the spectator, or the nature of the spectatorial identification with the roles they played and their star personae. The first named in each pair may be seen as triggering *symbolic* identification and the second *imaginary* identification, or, to use a different terminology, political and cultural identification. This is very well substantiated by the industry discourse itself as reflected in the film journalism of the time. Thus, the star personae of ANR and Sivaji Ganesan, as well as Kalyan Kumar during his brief occupation of this position in Kannada, were focused on their acting abilities, which were further defined as the skill of authentic cultural portrayal. From these, the associations multiply: women's roles and women-related issues are given prominence in their films, they are romantic, which means that they are shown in companionate relationships where emotional bonds and conflicts are foregrounded, and so on. The social space depicted is most often a middle-class familial space. Their films are less likely to have fights at the end or if they do, these tend to be brief and not too spectacular. Their films emphasise narrative development as opposed to action and spectacle, and are often based on well-known novels (many of ANR's films were based on the stories of the Bengali writer, Sarat Chandra Chattopadhyay). Many of the same melodramatic elements are to be found in the films of the action heroes as well. Formally they are nevertheless quite distinct. A crucial difference is that while the middle-class or culturally authentic heroes have definite social roles or positions in the narratives, such as unmarried youth headed towards romantic fulfilment or a married man engaged in resolving domestic discord, the action hero, though also usually an unmarried youth, quite often appears to bear an additional burden: that of the head of the family. This is sometimes because of the absence of the father, but it could even be because a father or sometimes an elder brother, who is present as the legitimate head of the family, is unable to withstand the forces of evil attacking the family from outside, due to their innate goodness.

The hero figure in these films is thus a composite figure whose identity is not easily traceable to any extra-filmic social reality. It is only in the history of film genres that we can find elements which have gone into its composition. He is a 'romantic hero' like the middle-class hero in so far as he, too, along one narrative trajectory, falls in love with a girl and will be united with her at the end. But unlike the latter, he also has a mission which is extra-familial. As this type of film evolves under the pressure of the industry's need for constant innovation and the entry of new stars, this extra familial domain will take on strong political overtones and often explicitly bring in the modern political world of MLAs, Members of Parliament (MPs) and chief ministers. By virtue of this doubling of roles, the hero's romantic relationship lacks the mutuality of feeling of the middle-class hero's relationship with his love interest. Instead, the relationship is often one-sided and in many instances it appears as if the head of the family, rather than the unmarried youth, is romancing the girl, leading to scenes of paternalistic chiding and an attitude of indulgently putting up with the girl's advances.

This composite figure and the particular variant of the social genre in which he figures, when examined in light of the history of film genres in India, proves to have been put together by bringing into the social, in its middle-class form, elements of the folk action adventure genre. The hero of that genre, which, unlike the mythological, figures prominently in the early careers of all the three stars—MGR, NTR and Rajkumar—has this quality which we have just seen as distinguishing these stars' version of the social. He too has a mission on whose success depends the survival of the kingdom in which he resides. We could construe that the virtual kingdom of the star–fan relation is constituted when the shadow cast by the kingdom, that is invariably the setting of the folk action adventure film, falls on the present. There the genre setting of an earlier age allowed for the kingdom to be spoken of as such. Here that genre and its elements, as well as the spectators who patronised it, find themselves in a new space where everything looks different, and instead of a kingdom, a society, a place ruled by nobody as it were, has engulfed them. The anxiety caused by the overwhelming sense of being demobilised and left to one's own devices is relieved by adopting as one's king a figure who offers himself for such a function from the cinema screen.

It is not the elaboration of some social scientific law of political supplementation that we are engaged in here. Rather, our main theoretical move has been to approach the problem as a historical one, a singular event whose explanation must be sought in a complex tangle of elements. Considered primarily as a demonstration of the power of communication, this event begs the question as to why such power did not produce similar results in other parts of the country. The same problem arises in relation to the 'gullibility thesis' adopted by the film critic Chidananda Dasgupta (1991), who avers that Indians (by which is meant those Indians who have not been remade by modernity and education) are unable to distinguish image from reality. This then is proposed as an explanation for the mythological's ability to fool people into thinking that NTR is endowed with divine powers, or for MGR's films to convince them that he can defeat a tiger in hand-to-hand combat. While the gullibility of the illiterate masses to the tricks played upon them by various forces, living or shadowy, cannot be denied, it still leaves us wondering why the consequences of such a deception are felt in the political rather than the religious field. In addition, the same objection still applies: Why only here and not elsewhere?

A historical event may be said to occur when, as a result of a unique combination of factors coming together, a new situation results that is not predictable by reference to any of the properties of the factors concerned. Thus, in the situation we are looking at, my own examination brought forth the following elements as participating in the production of this supplement to reality.

First, it is clear that without the existence of a film industry and spread of the film-viewing habit among the population, this could not have happened. We learn from film historians such as Theodore Baskaran (1981) that the southern region had, by the 1950s, the highest density of cinema theatres in the subcontinent. By the late 1940s, production facilities had begun to converge upon the city of Madras (now Chennai) with several studios and strong independent production houses basing themselves in that city. Before this, production of films in south Indian languages happened on a small scale all over the South and in the facilities in major production centres like Calcutta (Kolkata) and Bombay (Mumbai).[2] Madras now became the pre-eminent centre for the production of films in all the south Indian languages and would, in time, also enter into its own unique brand of Hindi films.

Second, the 1950s were the decade in which on the political scene, a victory of sorts was won by the nationalities against the self-serving repressive instincts of the ruling elite. Instead of welcoming the existence of nationalities, nurturing and employing them as means to effective democratisation, the ruling national elite, whose interests had before then begun to sharply diverge from the interests of the republic, resorted to repressive tactics accompanied by a hollow rhetoric to oppose the demand for the reorganisation of the interior into linguistically homogeneous states. Public sentiment prevailed in the end, but the manner in which the demand was granted meant that ever since, a Centre–state tug-of-war, at points overlapping with and contributing to class antagonisms, has been a constant feature of political life in the republic. Since the formation of linguistic states was against the wishes of the ruling elite at the Centre, prospects for a properly federal cooperative state design became ever more remote. For our purposes, the main point to be noted is that the creation of new nationality-based states prompted changes in the production strategies of the studios and independent production houses in Madras, giving rise to star systems, which are the third factor in the production of the cine-political event.

The story of south Indian film stars is tied up with the history of popular theatre, which was a major entertainment industry throughout the first half of the twentieth century. To begin with, many of the actors in the film industry, male and female, came from the theatre. In the early days of the talkies, the reliance on the popular theatre companies was near total. In the silent era, Indian cinema had developed a film language of some sophistication, including a brisk pace of narration achieved by cinematic means, as evidenced by extant silent films like *Diler Jigar* (1931) and *Ghulami nu Patan* (1931) [see the entries on these films in Rajadhyaksha and Willemen (1999)]. With the advent of the talkies, cinema came to rely on the theatre to an overwhelming extent which effectively robbed it of its discursive autonomy. Unlike actors in the silent era who were spared the bother of speaking, the talkies called for actors trained in dialogue delivery. Such performers were available only in the theatre. Another thing the cinema needed which the theatre had in abundance was precisely the dialogue to be spoken, in the form of popular plays which had been performed widely and were well-received by audiences. The camera's relative inertia in this period is thus the result of a dependence on theatre, which tilted the balance of resources in the latter's favour and left its mark on the nature of the films produced. The earliest stars of the talkie era were thus mostly stage actors, many of whom had enjoyed star status in the theatre which they brought in as additional value to the film. In the early talkie era, the most important stars on stage and screen were women. Male stars came a little later. As an example, one can look at the career of Chittoor Nagaiah, who was a successful stage actor and aspired to be a screen star. Nagaiah's aspirations were fuelled by the influence of Hollywood but they could not be fulfilled due to the peculiar conditions under which he entered the industry, which was still heteronomous to the popular stage. Although films enjoyed success among audiences, their status as extensions of stage productions remained. Stardom was not yet exclusively film stardom, it was more likely to be stage stardom rendered grander by the screen image. Thus, the first truly *film* stars were those promoted by the Madras studios in the 1950s. These too had come from the theatre: from the 'boys' companies' and other theatre troupes. They too would continue for some time to be defined by their theatre origins. But studio publicity campaigns (more systematic and aided by film magazines printed in colour) combined with the new importance acquired by the social genre to give them star personae that were recognisably modelled on the Hollywood stars of the time (this is, of course, true only for the male stars): rolling brylcreemed hair, brightly lit smiling faces, suits and ties. With the linguistic reorganisation of states, the industry began to consciously incorporate an address to the citizens of these newly constituted polities. Male stars in particular now began to acquire a primary linguistic identification and very soon, the top male stars would find themselves obliged to act exclusively in their own language films. The division of labour between two male stars described earlier thus came to be repeated across these language-specific industries.

Fourth, the linguistic nationalities had previously found their elaboration in literature and intellectual discourse, and it was for the first time in the cinema hall that the unlettered members of these nationalities were interpellated by the address to them incorporated in the wake of the reorganisation of states.

A fifth factor may also be briefly noted: With the rise of the talkies, we see a shift away from the dominance of female stars in the industry and women-centred narratives on screen towards more hero-centric narratives and the overwhelming importance of male stars. A patriarchal ideology begins to drive the narrative. In a way it might be that the very introduction of speech might have contributed to this reformation, since speech brings the symbolic dimension into the reckoning and begins to influence the production of visuals.

The genre-mixing that resulted in the action hero–centered version of the social is another factor already discussed earlier. In this new variant, as we have seen, the hero of the folk action adventure film is imported into the social.

Even the enumeration of all these factors does not automatically explain the emergence of a virtual kingdom. The mechanics of the causal process remain obscure but on the whole, the enumerated elements allow us to posit the production of alternative virtual sovereignties, enabling political existence in the new and unfamiliar context of a republic which, given the contradictions noted by Ambedkar (1994), was in no position to guarantee such existence.

It is this unique intersection of factors that led to the formation of these virtual kingdoms in the three southern states of Tamil Nadu, Andhra Pradesh and Karnataka. To reiterate an important point elaborated in *Cine-politics* at greater length, what we are describing as the political supplement or surplus here is not to be equated to the formation of a political party or ascent to the seat of the chief minister of the state. In short, this is not an argument about the importation of star charisma into the political process in order to win votes. If that were indeed the defining mode in cine-politics, then the Kannada star Rajkumar would not fit the bill. But who can deny that Rajkumar was the ruler of a shadow kingdom more or less coextensive with the state of Karnataka? Thus, entry into electoral politics is a post–cine political event rather than the realisation of cine-politics. Electoral politics tends rather to weaken the cine-political bond as the figures concerned struggle to find their feet in a terrain they are unused to and in the process often end up displaying their true colours.

The cine-political phenomenon seemed to enter a new phase with the rise of new stars to what seemed a comparable status of political power. Notably Rajinikanth in the Tamil film industry and Chiranjeevi in Telugu seemed to have walked into the positions vacated by MGR and NTR, respectively. It is in their careers that we can observe the conversion of the political surplus into economic surplus, and the beginning of the end of cine-politics.

A surplus means something extra. As film stars, MGR, NTR and Rajkumar were, of course, earning money for the roles they played and given their popularity, they would have accumulated large amounts of it. But what they acquired through the fan relation is something else and this is what I call here the political surplus. There is money involved to be sure, but it is the power and authority that is bestowed on the star by fans that defines their persona and constrains their actions. Like pre-capitalist wealth, it is meant to be displayed, to be spent and lavished upon others in ceremonies that further enhance the power of the giver. As opposed to this, capitalist profits, as much as wages, tend to be private income. In theory, after work, the worker and the employer could end up in the same bar. Now we all know that these big stars had personae that were controlled by the fans. There were certain things that could not be done. But there is one other constraint that only gets revealed retrospectively, in the time of decline of cine-politics. The star should not seem to be doing it for the sake of the income. Here a very crucial difference between types of payment needs to be noted. To earn rent is one thing, but to work for a wage is quite another. What distinguished the sovereign star was the illusion that he was earning rent rather than selling his labour power. It was an illusion essential to the maintenance of the virtual political order.

Chiranjeevi broke this illusion by appearing in beverage and hair oil commercials. Once a monarch stoops to commercial transactions of this kind, there is no looking back. The spell is broken, even though both parties (star and fan) will try desperately to hold on to the illusion as long as possible. The Nigerain writer Wole Soyinka tells a story somewhere of a tribe whose identity was crucially tied up with a nugget of gold ore, which served as the tribe's deity. In a time of great economic hardship, the tribe faced a choice: maintain the tribe's unity by preserving the deity even at the risk of starvation deaths or risk the dissolution of the tribe by selling the gold and using the returns to survive. While the circumstances are very different and the deities' market value was not about to accrue to the fans, the separation of the political from the economic is common to both these narratives. The neoliberal era has been characterised as precisely the triumph of economic forces over political formations. And it was with the advent of global capitalism in the wake of the reforms of 1991 that the processes that would spell the end of cine-politics were introduced.

But it is not a case of something ceasing to exist, simply disappearing as its time passes, and ceding ground to new things. Rather, and especially in the case of Rajinikanth, what we see is the successful reinvestment of the Rajini assets in the production of new goods. (As a parallel, we might think of the woodwork and other materials from a demolished bungalow being reused in a new building.) Chiranjeevi earned himself some money by appearing in ads. Rajini, on the other hand, did not compromise himself, but others did the job while he remained as if unaffected. These others include the director, Shankar, and the star's family. It was the task of these people to convert Rajini from a fount of political authority into a cashable asset. As far as they were concerned, the time had come to kill the golden goose. The conversion was effected in a series of films beginning with *Sivaji*. By the time the latest, Ranjith's *Kabali*, hit the screens, the deed was done. The transmutation was complete.

Beginning with *Sivaji*, Rajini films and the fan-following spread across the world, began to be regularly covered by national television channels in the run up to the films' release. This was part of a new development called media tie-ups. The Japanese craze for Rajini films gave this process a boost but what the film publicity machine, working with the national media, was both revealing and producing at the same time was a second layer of vicarious fandom, which was essential for the process of expropriation that ensued, leaving the old Rajini fan feeling cheated. This is a process of reflexive commodification or a commodification of fetishes, which is one of the modalities of capitalist growth in an unevenly developed country like India.

In conclusion, I should perhaps clarify that in tracking this process of the dissolution of the cine-political bond and the rise of a new expanded field of vicarious fandom, it is not my intention to lament this passing, or to portray the old fan as a victim of injustice. On the contrary it is quite possible, even observable, that by releasing all that congealed value from the fan apparatus, it has become possible to mix it into other signifying projects, such as the one Ranjith has undertaken where he overwrites an otherwise apolitical narrative with the signifiers of Dalit identity, a strategy which seems to have gone down well with audiences. Perhaps it was only through the market route opened up by Shankar, in other words, the market as that concrete universal that melts all that is solid, that the Dalit could lay claim to the Rajini mystique and make it speak to them.

Notes

[1] See https://www.youtube.com/watch?v=l0CcWFh84EA (accessed 27 July 2016). I thank M. Parthasarathi for bringing this video to my notice.

[2] Some old city-names have been used in this chapter in the historical context in which they are mentioned.

References

'Where Have All the Diehard Film Fans of Andhra Pradesh Gone?' 2015. *The Hindu*, 27 November.

Ambedkar, B. R. 1994. 'Speech in the Constituent Assembly on November 4 1948'. In *Writing and Speeches*, Volume 13, ed. Vasant Moon, 61. New Delhi: Dr Ambedkar Foundation.

Baskaran, S. T. 1981. *The Message Bearers: The Nationalist Politics and the Entertainment Media in South India, 1880–1945*. Chennai: Cre-A.

Dasgupta, Chidananda. 1991. *The Painted Face: Studies in India's Popular Cinemas*. New Delhi: Roli Books.

Forrester, Duncan. 1976. 'Factions and Filmstars: Tamil Nadu Politics since 1971'. *Asian Survey* 16(3): 283–96.

Hansen, T. B. 2005. 'Sovereigns beyond the State: On Legality and Public Authority in India'. In *Religion, Violence and Political Mobilisation in South Asia*, ed. Ravinder Kaur, 109–44. Delhi: Sage.

Hardgrave, Jr, Robert. 1979. 'When Stars Displace the Gods: The Folk Culture of Cinema in Tamil Nadu.' In *Essays in the Political Sociology of South India*, 92–122. New Delhi: Manohar Publications.

Meillassoux, Q. 2011. 'History and Event in Alain Badiou'. *Parrhesia* 12: 1–11.

Pandian, M. S. S. 2015. *The Image Trap: M. G. Ramachandran in Film and Politics*. Delhi: Sage Publishing India.

Prasad, M. M. 2014. *Cine-politics: Film Stars and Political Existence in South India*. Delhi: Orient BlackSwan.

Rajadhyaksha, A., and P. Willemen. 1999. *Encyclopedia of Indian Cinema*, 2nd edition. Delhi: Routledge.

Sivathamby, Karthigesu. 1981. *The Tamil Film as Medium of Political Communication*. Chennai: New Century Bookhouse.

Notes on the Editors and Contributors

S. Anandhi is Professor, Madras Institute of Development Studies, Chennai.

M. Arivalagan is Assistant Professor, PG Department of Folklore, St Xavier's College, Palayamkottai.

Venkatesh Chakravarthy is Dean, Ramanaidu Film School, Ramana Naidu Studios, Hyderabad.

J. Jeyaranjan is Director, Institute of Development Alternatives, Chennai, and Visiting Professor, Council for Social Development, Hyderabad.

Sundar Kaali teaches Tamil language and literature, and media studies at Gandhigram Rural Institute (deemed to be university), Gandhigram.

A. Kalaiyarasan is Assistant Professor, Madras Institute of Development Studies, Chennai.

Karthick Ram Manoharan is Assistant Professor of Political Science, Centre for Studies in Social Sciences, Calcutta.

Ajit Menon is Professor, Madras Institute of Development Studies, Chennai.

M. S. S. Pandian was Professor of Modern History, Jawaharlal Nehru University, New Delhi.

Arun Kumar Patnaik is Professor, Department of Political Science, University of Hyderabad.

M. Madhava Prasad is Professor, Department of Cultural Studies, English and Foreign Languages University, Hyderabad.

A. Srivathsan is Academic Director, Centre for Environmental Planning and Technological University, Ahmedabad.

V. Ravi Vaithees is Senior Scholar and former Associate Professor of Modern South Asian and World History, University of Manitoba, Winnipeg, Canada.

M. Vijayabaskar is Professor, Madras Institute of Development Studies, Chennai.